The publisher gratefully acknowledges the generous support of the General Endowment Fund of the University of California Press Foundation.

1995

ALSO BY W. JOSEPH CAMPBELL

Getting It Wrong: Ten of the Greatest Misreported Stories in American Journalism

The Year That Defined American Journalism: 1897 and the Clash of Paradigms

Yellow Journalism: Puncturing the Myths, Defining the Legacies

The Spanish-American War: American Wars and the Media in Primary Documents

The Emergent Independent Press in Benin and Côte d'Ivoire: From Voice of the State to Advocate of Democracy

1995

The Year the Future Began

W. Joseph Campbell

UNIVERSITY OF CALIFORNIA PRESS

University of California Press, one of the most distinguished university presses in the United States, enriches
lives around the world by advancing scholarship in the
humanities, social sciences, and natural sciences. Its
activities are supported by the UC Press Foundation and
by philanthropic contributions from individuals and
institutions. For more information, visit www.ucpress.edu.

University of California Press
Oakland, California

Library of Congress Cataloging-in-Publication Data

Campbell, W. Joseph.
    1995 : the year the future began / W. Joseph
Campbell.
        pages   cm
    Includes bibliographical references and index.
    ISBN 978-0-520-27399-3 (cloth : alk. paper) —
    ISBN 978-0-520-95971-2 (e-book)
    1. United States—Politics and government—
1993–2001.   2. United States—Social conditions—
20th century.   3. Nineteen ninety-five, A.D.   I. Title.
    E885.C36   2015
    973.92—dc23   2014010239

Manufactured in the United States of America

24 23 22 21 20 19 18 17 16 15
10 9 8 7 6 5 4 3 2 1

In keeping with a commitment to support environmen-
tally responsible and sustainable printing practices, UC
Press has printed this book on Natures Natural, a fiber
that contains 30% post-consumer waste and meets the
minimum requirements of ANSI/NISO Z39.48–1992
(R 1997) (Permanence of Paper).

To Ann-Marie

Contents

Illustrations

a pivotal year, arguing that the emergence of the Internet into main-stream American life, the terrorist bombing at Oklahoma City, the months-long double-murder trial of O. J. Simpson, the accords reached at Dayton, and the incipient Clinton-Lewinsky sex-and-lies scandal all rendered 1995 a moment of surpassing exceptionality. This work turns a fresh lens on each of those cases and examines how each of them has projected lasting significance. Each was a watershed moment of a water-shed year.

It is important and appropriate to describe what this work is not: It is not a diary, not an almanac, not an exhaustive catalog or chronicle of the year. It does not seek to return to the fads of the time or revisit devel-opments in sport and popular culture of 1995. It makes no glib or expan-sive claims that 1995 was a year that changed everything.[3] It is mindful of the hazards of thematic overreach, of claiming too much significance for a moment in time. It is tempting, for example, to identify 1995 as the starting point in Barack Obama's rise to the presidency; it was, after all, the year when his memoir, *Dreams from My Father,* was published—to little immediate critical notice.[4] To make such a claim would be mis-taken; a far more compelling case can be made for the following year, when Obama won election to the Illinois state senate, beginning a run that culminated in 2009 with his inauguration as president.

Historians of the recent past are known to agonize about a dearth of relevant and accessible archival material.[5] Such a limitation did not impede or impair this study. It did not emerge as a serious constraint in researching 1995. This work taps a rich variety of sources, including exhibits in the Justice Department's antitrust case that was set in motion by the "browser war" between Microsoft Corporation and Netscape Communications; oral histories and archival holdings of the Oklahoma City National Memorial and Museum; documents and memoranda related to Bosnia and the Dayton peace talks in a collection of post–Cold War materials at the National Security Archive in Washington, D.C.; supplemental materials submitted by the Office of the Indepen-dent Counsel in its referral to Congress that identified prospective grounds for impeaching President Clinton; and archival collections and subject files of the Newseum, the museum of news in Washington, D.C. The extensive and unmatched collections of U.S. newspapers on micro-film at the Library of Congress were vital to this study; newspaper con-tent of 1995 offered a sense of the moment and a sense of verisimilitude. That content also points up flaws and shortcomings that were apparent in the news coverage of nearly every decisive turn in 1995.

I conducted interviews with several figures associated with the watershed moments of 1995, and I paid visits to venues important to the year. These included the site of the federal building in Oklahoma City, destroyed in an unprecedented spasm of domestic terror; the ninth-floor courtroom of the Los Angeles criminal justice center, the theater of Simpson's trial; and the sprawling Wright-Patterson Air Force Base near Dayton, where the Bosnia peace accords were reached.

This work has been written with an eye toward revealing anecdotes and personal narratives that help capture the vigor, spirit, suspicions, and novelty of 1995. It opens with an eclectic introduction to the year and its improbable moments. The rise of the Internet and the World Wide Web is treated in Chapter 1. The narrative proceeds chronologically from there. Chapter 2 considers the Oklahoma City bombing and the subsequent deployment of security-oriented restrictions in American life. Chapter 3 takes up the Simpson trial and identifies as its most important lasting contribution the introduction of forensic DNA evidence into the public consciousness. Chapter 4 examines the making of the Dayton accords, the success of which initiated a period of muscular American diplomacy, undergirded by resurgent "American Exceptionalism." Chapter 5 revisits the partial shutdowns of the federal government, which created the conditions in which Clinton and Lewinsky began their dalliance at the White House, a liaison that led to the extraordinary spectacle of a president's impeachment.

So, critical readers may ask, what should we take away from this examination of 1995? What flows from a recognition of the year's exceptionality? The best and most candid response is that the year and its watershed moments live on—that the present, as we know it, began to take shape during those consequential twelve months. The separate watersheds of 1995, when pulled together and examined with the detachment granted by the passing of twenty years, reveal a time of remarkable intensity and of enduring consequence.

W. Joseph Campbell
Kensington, Maryland

Acknowledgments

This examination of 1995 might have remained unwritten were it not for the encouragement and enthusiasm of Reed Malcolm, senior acquisition editor at the University of California Press. From the time in 2010 when I first spoke with him about such a project, Reed very much liked the idea. His suggestions were invaluable, and his patience and advice helped keep the project focused and streamlined.

Reed's colleagues at the press likewise offered vital support, especially so Stacy Eisenstark, whose good humor and ready laugh were always welcome. Dore Brown, an outstanding project editor, kept production on track, and Julia Zafferano, whom the press hired to copyedit the manuscript, did some terrific work.

My colleagues at American University—including Phyllis Peres, Jeff Rutenbeck, Kathryn Montgomery, Larry Kirkman, John Watson, Frank Fitzmaurice, and Donna Femenella—were generous in their support and encouragement. Alyah Khan was outstanding as a graduate research assistant on this project. Other graduate assistants—including Stephanie Foul, Odna Nb, Erin Powell, and Jeremiah Patterson—made important research contributions over the years as well. I am indebted to Ruxandra Giura for her help and expertise, especially on the photographs and tables that appear in this book.

The recollections of Peter Arenella, Ward Cunningham, Sue Hale, Jeff Hall, Shel Kaphan, Donald Kerrick, Michel Mayor, and Mike McCurry enriched the book. A good deal of research on this project was conducted at the Library of Congress, where Georgia Higley, Jeff Flannery, and their colleagues were unfailingly generous with their assistance. I am grateful to Paul Sparrow, Cathy Trost, and Rick Mastroiani for allowing me access to 1995-related archival material at the Newseum, the museum of news in Washington, D.C.

Mary Curry was most helpful in identifying and making available relevant holdings of the National Security Archive in Washington. Helen Stiefmiller and Pam Bell showed me much courtesy during visits to the archives of the Oklahoma City National Memorial and Museum. John W. McCance was generous with his time in showing me around the Wright-Patterson Air Force Base outside of Dayton.

My very good friend, Hugh D. Pace, was an unstinting source of encouragement, and his daughter, Alexis Pace, was most welcoming during a research trip I made to Los Angeles. My thanks to Keith Sanders, executive director of Kappa Tau Alpha, for the research grant that supported the Los Angeles trip.

Media historians Michael Sweeney and Dale Cressman deserve special mention for their thoughtful comments on an earlier version of the manuscript. Fred Blevens also offered helpful suggestions at an important stage of the project. Don Ross, Karen Davison, and Jessica Ling offered important editing suggestions on the manuscript. The book, moreover, draws upon and benefitted from the work and observations of other authors, including Peter Beinart, Derek Chollet, John F. Harris, Dan Herbeck, Lou Michel, Andrew Morton, Robert H. Reid, and Jeffrey Toobin.

Special thanks go to my wife, Ann-Marie C. Regan, for her patience and interest; never did she seem to tire of hearing about 1995.

Introduction to an Improbable Year

Nineteen ninety-five was the inaugural year of the twenty-first century, a clear starting point for contemporary life.

It was "the year of the Internet," when the World Wide Web entered mainstream consciousness, when now-familiar mainstays of the digital world such as Amazon.com, eBay, Craigslist, and Match.com established their presence online. It was, proclaimed an exuberant newspaper columnist at the time, "the year the Web started changing lives."[1]

Nineteen ninety-five was marked by a deepening national preoccupation with terrorism. The massive bombing in Oklahoma City killed 168 people, the deadliest act of domestic terror in U.S. history. Within weeks of the bombing, a portion of Pennsylvania Avenue—the "Main Street" of America—was closed to vehicular traffic near the White House, signaling the rise of security-related restrictions intended to thwart the terrorist threat—restrictions that have since become more common, more intrusive, more stringent, and perhaps even more accepted.

Nineteen ninety-five was the year of the sensational and absorbing "Trial of the Century," when O. J. Simpson, the popular former football star, answered to charges that he had slashed to death his former wife and her friend. The trial stretched across much of the year, not unlike an indelible stain, ending in Simpson's acquittal but not in the redemption of his public persona. Ironically, the trial's most tedious stretches produced its most lasting contribution: the Simpson case introduced into popular consciousness the decisive potential of forensic DNA evidence in criminal investigations and legal proceedings.

Nineteen ninety-five brought an unmistakable though belated assertion of muscular U.S. diplomacy, ending the vicious war in Bosnia, Europe's deadliest and most appalling conflict in forty years. Crafting a fragile peace in the Balkans gave rise to a sense of American hubris that was tragically misapplied not many years later, in the U.S.-led invasion of Iraq.

The year brought the first of several furtive sexual encounters between President Bill Clinton and a nominal White House intern twenty-seven years his junior, Monica Lewinsky. Their intermittent dalliance began in 1995 and eventually erupted in a lurid sex scandal that rocked the U.S. government and brought about the first-ever impeachment of an elected American president.

The emergence of the Internet, the deadliest act of homegrown terrorism on U.S. soil, the "Trial of the Century," the muscular diplomacy of the United States, and the origins of a sex scandal at the highest levels of American government were significant events in 1995, and each is explored as a chapter of this book. They were profound in their respective ways, and, taken together, they define a watershed year at the cusp of the millennium. Nineteen ninety-five in many ways effectively marked the close of the one century, and the start of another.

With the critical distance afforded by the passing of twenty years, the exceptionality of 1995 emerges quite clearly. It was not altogether obvious at the close of 1995, at least not to commentators in the media who engaged in no small amount of hand-wringing about the year. A writer for the *Boston Herald,* for example, suggested that history books "may well remember 1995 as one sorry year."[2] It was, after all, the year when Israel's prime minster, Yitzhak Rabin, was assassinated at a peace rally in Tel Aviv, in the Kings of Israel Square. It was the year when a troubled woman named Susan Smith was tried and convicted on charges of drowning her two little boys in 1994, of having strapped them in their seats before rolling her car into a lake in South Carolina. Smith at first blamed an unknown black man for having hijacked the car and making off with the boys inside. She recanted several days later and confessed that she had killed her sons.

In a summing up at year's end, the *Philadelphia Inquirer* recalled the massacre at Srebrenica in July 1995, when Bosnian Serb forces systematically killed 8,000 Muslim men and boys in what the United Nations had designated a safe area. "So base were the emotions, so dark the actions, that at times you had to wonder which century we were in," the newspaper declared. "Was it 1995 or 1395? A tribal war with overtones of genocide? We bring you Bosnia and the mass graves at Srebrenica. . . . At least there's one difference between now and 600 years ago. The killing's become more efficient."[3]

But not all leave-taking assessments of 1995 were so grim. *Reason* magazine observed that, at the end of 1995, Americans were living the good old days; they "never had it so good." Living standards, *Reason* argued, were higher than ever. Americans were healthier than ever. They had more leisure time than ever. "Americans will swear life is more hectic than it used to be, that there's not enough time anymore. What's crowding their lives, though, isn't necessarily more work or more chores. It is the relentless chasing after the myriad leisure opportunities of a society that has more free time and more money to spend."[4]

It is striking how a sense of the improbable so often flavored the year and characterized its watershed moments. Oklahoma City was an utterly improbable setting for an attack of domestic terrorism of unprecedented dimension. Dayton, Ohio, was an improbable venue for weeks of multiparty negotiations that concluded by ending the faraway war in Bosnia. The private study and secluded hallway off the Oval Office at the White House were the improbable hiding places for Clinton's dalliance with the twenty-two-year-old Lewinsky.

The improbable was a constant of the year. In February, a twenty-eight-year-old, Singapore-based futures trader named Nick Leeson brought down Barings PLC, Britain's oldest merchant bank, after a series of ill-considered and mostly unsupervised investments staked to the price fluctuations of the Japanese stock market. Leeson's bets went spectacularly wrong and cost Barings $1.38 billion, wiping out an aristocratic investment house that was 232 years old. The rogue trader spent four years in prison in Singapore and wrote a self-absorbed book in which he gloated that auditors "never dared ask me any basic questions, since they were afraid of looking stupid about not understanding futures and options."[5]

The most improbable prank of the year came in late October when Pierre Brassard, a twenty-nine-year-old radio show host in Montreal, impersonated Canada's prime minister, Jean Chrétien, and got through by telephone to Elizabeth, the queen of England. Speaking in French and English, they discussed the absurd topic of the monarch's plans for Halloween as well as the separatist referendum at the end of the month in Quebec, Canada's French-speaking province. Could her majesty, Brassard asked, make a televised statement urging Quebecers to vote against the referendum? "We deeply believe that should your majesty have the kindness to make a public intervention," said Brassard, "we think that your word could give back to the citizens of Quebec the pride of being members of a united country." Replied the queen, after briefly consulting an adviser: "Do you think you could give me a text of what you would like me to say? . . . I will probably be able to do something for you."[6] Their conversation was broadcast live on CKOI-FM and went on for seven minutes. Only after it ended did Buckingham Palace realize the queen had been duped.[7]

Nineteen ninety-five was a memorable time for the U.S. space program. NASA that year launched its 100th human mission, sending a crew of five Americans and two Russians into Earth orbit on June 27. They traveled aboard the space shuttle Atlantis, which docked two days later with the Russian space station, Mir, forming what at the time was "the biggest craft ever assembled in space."[8] When Atlantis returned to Earth on July 7, it brought home from Mir Dr. Norman E. Thagard, an astronaut-physician who had logged 115 days in space, then an American space-endurance record.[9] The year's most improbable moment in space flight had come about five weeks earlier, on a launch pad at Cape Canaveral. Woodpeckers in mating season punched no fewer than six dozen holes in the insulation protecting the external fuel tank of the shuttle Discovery. As the New York Times observed, the $2 billion spacecraft, "built to withstand the rigors of orbital flight, from blastoff to fiery re-entry," was driven back to its hangar "by a flock of birds with mating on their minds."[10] Discovery's flight was delayed by more than a month.

No celebrity sex scandal that year stirred as much comment and speculation as Hugh Grant's improbable assignation in Hollywood with the pseudonymous Divine Brown, a twenty-three-year-old prostitute. The floppy-haired British actor, star of the soon-to-be-released motion picture Nine Months, had been dating one of the world's most attractive models, Elizabeth Hurley, for eight years. On June 27 around 1:30 a.m., Grant was arrested in the streetwalker's company in his white BMW. "Vice officers observed a prostitute go up to Mr. Grant's window of his vehicle," the Los Angeles police reported, and "they observed them have a conversation, then the known prostitute got into Mr. Grant's vehicle and they drove a short distance and they were later observed to be engaged in an act of lewd conduct."[11] Grant was chas-

tened, but hardly shamed into seclusion. He went public with his contri-
tion, saying on Larry King's interview program on CNN that his conduct had been "disloyal and shabby and goatish."[12] When her agent
told her the news about Grant's dalliance, Hurley said she "felt like I'd
been shot."[13] Their relationship survived, for a few years. They split up
in 2000.[14]

"Firsts," alone, do not make a watershed year. But they can be contrib-
uting factors, and 1995 was distinguished by several notable firsts. For
the first time, the Dow Jones Industrial Average broke the barrier of
5,000 points. The Dow set sixty-nine record-high closings during the
year and, overall, was up by 33 percent. It was a remarkable run, the
Dow's best performance in twenty years. And it had been quite unfore-
seen by columnists and analysts at the outset of the year. John Crudele,
for example, wrote in the *San Francisco Chronicle* that 1995 "could be
the worst year for the stock market in a long time" and quoted an analyst as saying the Dow could plunge to 3,000 or 3,200 points. At year's
end, the Dow stood at 5,117.12.[15]

The first feature-length computer-animated film, Disney's imaginative *Toy Story,* was released at Thanksgiving in 1995—not long after
the prominent screenwriter William Goldman had pronounced the
year's first ten months the worst period for movies since sound.[16] *Toy
Story* told of a child's toys come to life and won approving reviews. The
New York Times said *Toy Story* was "a work of incredible cleverness in
the best two-tiered Disney tradition. Children will enjoy a new take on
the irresistible idea of toys coming to life. Adults will marvel at a witty
script and utterly brilliant anthropomorphism. And maybe no one will
even mind what is bound to be a mind-boggling marketing blitz."[17]

The year brought at long last the first, unequivocal proof that planets
orbit Sun-like stars beyond Earth's solar system. Extra-solar planets—or
exoplanets—had long been theorized, and confirmation that such
worlds exist represented an essential if tentative step in the long-odds
search for extra-solar intelligent life. The first confirmed exoplanet was
a blasted, gaseous world far larger than Jupiter that needs only 4.2 Earth
days to orbit its host star in Pegasus, the constellation of the winged
horse. It is an inhospitable, almost unimaginable world. The planet's
dayside—the side always facing the host star—has been estimated to be
400 times brighter than desert dunes on Earth on a midsummer's day.
Its nightside probably glows red.[18] The exoplanet is more than fifty light
years from Earth and was inelegantly christened "51 Pegasi b." It was

FIGURE 1. In October 1995, Swiss astronomer Michel Mayor announced the discovery of a planet orbiting a Sun-like star far beyond the Earth's solar system. Identifying the first "exoplanet" was a tentative step in the long-odds search for intelligent life elsewhere in the universe. (Photo credit: Ann-Marie C. Regan)

detected by two Swiss astronomers: Michel Mayor of the University of Geneva, and Didier Queloz, a twenty-eight-year-old doctoral student.

Mayor announced the discovery on October 6 at the Ninth Cambridge Workshop on Cool Stars, Stellar Systems, and the Sun meeting in Florence, Italy. About 300 conference-goers were in attendance as the cordial and low-key Mayor told of finding 51 Pegasi b. He and Queloz had used a technique called "radial velocity," in which a spectrograph measured slight, gravity-induced wobbling of the host star. His remarks were greeted by polite applause—and by no small measure of skepticism. The discovery of exoplanets had been reported many times since at least the nineteenth century.[19] All such reports had been proved wrong. What's more, a huge planet orbiting so near to its host posed an unambiguous challenge to the then-dominant theory of planetary formation.[20] A giant planet, it was thought, could not long survive the extraordinarily high temperatures and other effects of being so close to its star.[21] "Most people were skeptical," Queloz recalled. "The expectation was to find giant planets in long period orbit [that took years, as] in our solar system—we had challenged that paradigm."[22] Soon enough, however, other astronomers verified the discovery of 51 Pegasi b.[23]

Three months before the conference in Florence, Mayor and Queloz had confirmed the discovery to their satisfaction, in observations at the Observatoire de Haute Provence in France. Doing so, Mayor recalled, was akin to "a spiritual moment."[24] He, Queloz, and their families celebrated by opening a bottle of Clairette de Die, a sparkling white wine from the Rhone Valley.[25] Since then, the search for exoplanets has become a central imperative in what has been called "a new age of astronomy" that could rival "that of the 17th century, when Galileo first turned his telescope to the heavens."[26] Animating the quest is the belief that the universe may be home to many Earth-like exoplanets orbiting host stars at distances that would allow temperate conditions, liquid water, and perhaps even the emergence of intelligent life.[27] More than 1,700 exoplanets have been confirmed since the discovery of 51 Pegasi b, and, before it broke down in 2013, the planet-hunting Kepler space telescope had identified since 2009 more than 3,500 candidate-exoplanets.[28]

One of the year's pleasantly subversive books, a thin volume of short essays titled *Endangered Pleasures: In Defense of Naps, Bacon, Martinis, Profanity, and Other Indulgences,* posited that simple earthly pleasures were slipping into disfavor and even disrepute. The author, Barbara Holland, wrote that, in small and subtle ways, "joy has been leaking out of our lives. Almost without a struggle, we have let the New Puritans take over, spreading a layer of foreboding across the land until even ignorant small children rarely laugh anymore. Pain has become nobler than pleasure; work, however foolish or futile, nobler than play; and denying ourselves even the most harmless delights marks the suitably somber outlook on life."[29]

Holland's was an impressionistic thesis, and somewhat overstated. But undeniably, there was something to be said for celebrating what made the scolds and killjoys so sour. "Now in the nineties," she wrote, "we're left to wring joy from the absence of joy, from denial, from

FIGURE 2. Barbara Holland's *Endangered Pleasures* was a delightfully subversive book of 1995. In it, she argued that "joy has been leaking out of our lives. Almost without a struggle, we have let the New Puritans take over." (Photo credit: Mel Crown)

counting grams of fat, jogging, drinking only bottled water and eating only broccoli. The rest of the time we work."[30] Holland's wry and engaging musings on topics such as napping, profanity, wood fires, and the Sunday newspaper drew the admiring attention of Russell Baker, a humor columnist for the *New York Times* and one of the most wry and engaging observers of the national scene.

Baker wrote appreciatively of Holland's book, saying she "makes her case with a light touch and a refusal to speak solemnly of anyone, even those grimmest of gloom-spreaders, the smoke police" eager to crack down on cigarettes. "Appropriately for an author promoting pleasure in joyless times, Ms. Holland makes her case in a mere 175 pages," Baker observed. "Books that say their say without droning on at encyclopedia length are also one of our endangered pleasures."[31] Baker himself achieved a bit of lasting distinction in 1995. His commencement speech that year at Connecticut College in New London—titled "10 Ways to Avoid Mucking Up the World Any Worse Than It Already Is"—sometimes is ranked among the best of its genre.[32] Baker offered such sardonic guidance as: "The best advice I can give anybody about going out into the world is this: Don't do it. I have been out there. It is a mess." More seriously, and grimly, he touched on what he considered to be the angry national mood in 1995:

> I have never seen a time when there were so many Americans so angry or so mean-spirited or so sour about the country as there are today. Anger has become the national habit. You see it on the sullen faces of fashion models scowling out of magazines. It pours out of the radio. Washington television hams snarl and shout at each other on television. Ordinary people abuse politicians and their wives with shockingly coarse insults. Rudeness has become an acceptable way of announcing you are sick and tired of it all and are not going to take it anymore. . . . The question is: why? Why has anger become the common response to the inevitable ups and down[s] of nation[al] life? The question is baffling not just because the American habit even in the worst of times has traditionally been mindless optimism, but also because there is so little for Americans to be angry about nowadays. . . . So what explains the fury and dyspepsia? I suspect it's the famous American ignorance of history. People who know nothing of even the most recent past are easily gulled by slick operators who prosper by exploiting the ignorant. Among these rascals are our politicians. Politicians flourish by sowing discontent. They triumph by churning discontent into anger. Press, television and radio also have a big financial stake in keeping the [country] boiling mad.[33]

But it is difficult to look back now at 1995 and sense a deeply angry time. Not when the stock market routinely set record high closings. Not when *Friends* and *Seinfeld* were among the most popular primetime fare on network television. Not when the historical fantasy *Braveheart* won the Academy Award for best motion picture of 1995. Nineteen ninety-five was neither a frivolous nor a superficial time, but real anger in the land was to emerge later, in the impeachment of Bill Clinton in 1998, in the disputed election of George Bush in 2000, and in the controversies that followed the invasion of Iraq in 2003.

Nineteen ninety-five was not without controversy, of course, and some of the year's most heated disputes were attached to the Million Man March, a huge and peaceful assembly on the National Mall in Washington, D.C., on October 16. The march was the inspiration of Louis Farrakhan, leader of the Nation of Islam, who envisioned the rally as a "holy day of atonement and reconciliation,"[34]an opportunity for black men to "straighten their backs" and recommit themselves to their families and communities.[35]

But Farrakhan's toxic views and antisemitic rhetoric, as well as the exclusion of black women[36] from the event, threatened to overshadow the march and its objectives.[37] Neither the national NAACP nor the Urban League endorsed the march. For many participants, the dilemma was, as one journalist described it, "whether to march for a message they can believe in—unity—without marching to a drummer they may not follow."[38] (The *Washington Post* surveyed 1,047 participants and reported they generally were "younger, wealthier and better-educated than black Americans as a whole," were inclined to view Farrakhan favorably, and expected him to raise his profile on the national scene.)[39]

The twelve-hour rally itself was joyful, almost festive. Participants spoke of being awed by the turnout and sensed that they had joined a once-in-a-lifetime occurrence. "I can't begin to explain the beautiful sight I saw when I arrived at the Mall that morning," recalled André P. Tramble, an accountant from Ohio. "If critics expected the March to be chaotic and disruptive, their expectations were unfounded. I thought, if we could come together in this orderly way and establish some commonsense [principles] of unity, how easily we could solve half of our self-imposed problems."[40] Neil James Bullock, a mechanical engineer from Illinois, wrote afterward:

> I was stunned to see masses of Black men. As far as I could see, there was a sea of Black men. I had never seen so many people in one place at one time, and I imagined I never would see such a sight again. There we were: all shapes, sizes, colors, and ages; fathers with sons, uncles, and brothers. It was truly a family affair. . . . Fathers, sons, brothers, and uncles were all in Washington for one reason—atonement. The question was "atonement for what?" There were many things that one could say African American men need to atone for, not the least of which is the sin of disrespect. We have been disrespectful to our women, families, communities, and most of all to ourselves.[41]

The crowd was addressed by a stream of speakers that included Jesse Jackson, Rosa Parks, Stevie Wonder, and Maya Angelou. Farrakhan spoke for nearly two hours. His oratory at times seemed to wander; he ruminated at one point about the number nineteen, saying: "What is so deep about this number 19? Why are we standing on the Capitol steps today? That number 19—when you have a nine you have a womb that is pregnant. And when you have a one standing by the nine, it means that there's something secret that has to be unfolded."[42] He also pledged "to collect Democrats, Republicans and independents around an agenda that is in the best interest of our people. And then all of us can stand on that agenda and in 1996, whoever the standard bearer is for the Democratic, the Republican, or the independent party should one come into existence. They've got to speak to our agenda. We're no longer going to vote for somebody just because they're black. We tried that."[43]

It was a spectacular autumn day in the capital, and the turnout for the march was enormous. Just how large became the subject of bitter dispute. Drawing on aerial photographs and applying a multiplier of one person for every 3.6 square feet, the National Park Service estimated the march had attracted about 400,000 people.[44] Farrakhan was outraged: he insisted the crowd reached 1.5 million to 2 million people, and he alleged racism and "white supremacy." He threatened to sue the Park Service to force a revision of the crowd estimate.[45] Within a few days, a third estimate was offered by a team of researchers at Boston University's Center for Remote Sensing, who applied a multiplier of one person for every 1.8 square feet. They estimated the crowd size at more than 800,000.[46]

The controversy gradually faded, and Congress soon took the Park Service out of the crowd-counting business, a decision received with more relief than disappointment. "No matter what we said or did, no one ever felt we gave a fair estimate," said J.J. McLaughlin, the official charged with coordinating Park Service crowd estimates. "It got to the point where the numbers became the entire focus of the demonstration."[47]

The year brought a burst of contrived giddiness and worldwide extravagance that would be unthinkable today: that's because the hoopla was about the release of a computer operating system, Microsoft's Windows 95. Microsoft reportedly spent $300 million[48] to preface the launch with weeks of marketing hype.[49] So successful was it that, even among computer illiterates, Windows 95 became a topic of conversation.[50]

The company spent millions for rights to the Rolling Stones hit "Start Me Up," which became the anthem for the Windows 95 launch.[51] It bought out the print run of the venerable *Times* of London on August 24,

Windows 95 Launch Felt Around World

By Peter Sinton
Chronicle Senior Writer

The computer business looked more like show business yesterday as the long wait for Microsoft Corp.'s Windows 95 software program built to a crescendo.

Shoppers in New Zealand, where the program first went on sale because it was already past midnight last night, jammed stores to buy the new computer program.

INSIDE

■ At Microsoft headquarters, the industry pays homage
SEE BUSINESS,
PAGE D1

Computer users lined up in the street to rush store shelves as Microsoft orchestrated a first buyer's event at an Auckland, New Zealand, bookstore called Whitcoulls'.

Five TV crews watched as Jonathan Prentice, a 19-year-old student, made the purchase as it turned midnight there.

FIGURE 3. Microsoft's launch of its Windows 95 computer operating software in late August 1995 was preceded by weeks of hype and hoopla in the United States and abroad.

the day of the launch, and gave away the newspapers—fattened with advertising for Windows 95.[52] A huge banner, stretching some thirty stories and proclaiming "Microsoft Windows 95," was suspended from the landmark CN Tower in Toronto.[53] In New York, the Empire State Building was illuminated in three of Microsoft's four corporate colors—the first time a company's colors had so bathed the Manhattan skyscraper.[54]

Not since "the first landing on the moon—or, at any rate, since the last Super Bowl—has America been more aflutter," a U.S.-based correspondent for London's *Independent* newspaper wrote about the Windows 95 fuss, his tongue decidedly in cheek.[55] It was easy to lampoon the hype. After all, said the *New York Times* a few weeks before the launch, "It is not a lunar landing or the cure for disease. It is simply an improved version of a computer's operating system—like a more efficient transmission for a car."[56] Barely heard above the din was Apple Computer's rather cheeky counter-campaign, which pointed out that many features of Windows 95 were already available on Macintosh machines. "Been there, done that," Apple proclaimed in its publicity. Even so, Apple in 1995 commanded only about 8 percent of the computer market.[57]

The hoopla was as inescapable as Microsoft's objective was obvious— to establish Windows 95 as the industry standard and encourage users to move from the older Windows 3 platforms and promptly embrace the new operating system.[58] The big day finally came and, just after midnight on August 24 in Auckland, New Zealand, a nineteen-year-old student named Jonathan Prentice made the first purchase of Windows 95. As midnight approached in New York City, "a jostling scrum of technophiles" was reported outside a mid-Manhattan computer store, waiting to buy the software as it went on sale.[59] But it was not as if consumers were strung out in blocks-long lines to buy the product. At some computer stores that opened at midnight on August 24, employees had the place pretty much to themselves thirty minutes or so after Windows 95 went on sale.[60]

After the initial surge in late summer, sales of Windows 95 began to tail off. By December 1995, sales were about a third of what they had been in September. Many consumers, it turned out, chose not to buy and install the software themselves—an often-exasperating task—but waited to adopt it when it came bundled with their next computers.[61] Even so, the launch of Windows 95 easily qualified as "the splashiest, most frenzied, most expensive introduction of a computer product" up to that time, as a *New York Times* writer put it.[62] The manufactured extravagance was more than a little silly, but the product did turn out to be a memorable one. Nearly twenty years later, technology writer Walter Mossberg included Windows 95 as one of the dozen "most influential" technology products he had reviewed for the *Wall Street Journal* since the early 1990s.[63]

Some of the launch-related giddiness can be laid to consumers' embrace of the personal computer as a mainstay device in the workplace and at home.[64] By 1995, a majority of Americans were using computers at home, at work, or at school, the Times Mirror Center for the People & the Press reported. The organization figured that eighteen million American homes in 1995 had computers equipped with modems, an increase of 64 percent from 1994.[65] The popularity of the computer and the prevalence of modems helped ignite dramatic growth in Internet use in the years following 1995.

The hoopla over Windows 95 was also illustrative of the hyperbole afoot in 1995 about things digital. The hype spawned sweeping predictions, such as those by James K. Glassman, a syndicated columnist who wrote that computers "could displace schools, offices, newspapers, scheduled television and banks (though probably not dry cleaners). Government's regulatory functions could weaken, or vanish. . . . Even collecting taxes could become nearly impossible when all funds are transferred by electronic impulses that can be disguised."[66] Even more expansive was Nicholas Negroponte, founding director of MIT's Media Lab and a prominent tech guru in 1995. Negroponte argued that the real danger was to be found in not enough hype—in *understating* the importance of the emergent digital world. "I think the Internet is one of the rare, if not unique, instances where 'hype' is accompanied by understatement, not overstatement," he said[67] shortly before publication of his best-selling book, *Being Digital*. The book was a provocative clarion call, an assertion that a profound and far-reaching transformation was under way. "Like a force of nature," Negroponte wrote, "the digital age cannot be denied or stopped."[68]

His book, essentially a repurposing of columns written for *Wired* magazine, was not a flawless road map to the unfolding digital age; it was not a precision guide to what lay ahead. Negroponte, for example, had almost nothing to say about the Internet's World Wide Web. Some of the book's bold projections proved entertainingly wrong, or premature by years. Negroponte asserted that it was not at all far-fetched to expect "that twenty years from now you will be talking to a group of eight-inch-high holographic assistants walking across your desk," serving as "interface agents" with computers.[69] He suggested that by 2000 the unadventurous wristwatch would "migrate from a mere timepiece today to a mobile command-and-control center tomorrow. . . . An all-in-one, wrist-mounted TV, computer, and telephone is no longer the exclusive province of Dick Tracy, Batman, or Captain Kirk."[70]

In other predictions, *Being Digital* was impressively clairvoyant—spot on, or nearly so. Negroponte anticipated "a talking navigational system" for automobiles.[71] He discussed a "robot secretary that can fit in your pocket," something of a nod to the Siri speech-recognition function of the contemporary iPhone.[72] He rather seemed to foresee iPads, or Smartphones with bendable screens,[73] in ruminating about "an electronic newspaper" delivered to "a magical, paper-thin, flexible, waterproof, wireless, lightweight, bright display."[74] Video on demand, he wrote, would destroy the video-rental business. "I think videocassette rental stores will go out of business in less than ten years," a prediction not extravagantly far off.[75]

Negroponte notably anticipated a profound reshaping in the access to news, from one-way to interactive. Invoking "bits," the smallest components of digital information, he wrote: "Being digital will change the nature of mass media from a process of pushing bits at people to one of allowing people (or their computers) to pull at them. This is a radical change."[76] He was hardly alone in foreseeing the digital challenge to traditional mass media. In February 1995, *Editor & Publisher,* the newspaper industry's trade publication, had this to say in a special section devoted to "Interactive Newspapers": "The Internet may be a tough lesson that some newspapers won't survive. It is more than just another method of distribution. It represents an enormous opportunity in the field of communications that's neither easy to describe nor easy to grasp." The emergent online world, the article noted, "is truly the Wild West. Only this time there are a lot more Indians and they aren't about to give up the land. They are dictating to us what they want to see in our online offerings."[77]

Such warnings were largely unheeded. No industry in 1995 was as ill-prepared for the digital age, or more inclined to pooh-pooh the disruptive potential of the Internet and World Wide Web, than the news business. It suffered from what might be called "innovation blindness":[78] an inability, or a disinclination, to anticipate and understand the consequences of new media technology. Leading figures in American journalism took comfort in the comparatively small audiences for online news in 1995. Among them was Gene Roberts, the managing editor of the *New York Times* who, during the 1980s, had become a near-legend in American journalism for transforming the *Philadelphia Inquirer* into one of the country's finest daily newspapers. In remarks to the Overseas Press Club meeting in New York in January 1995, Roberts declared: "The number of people in any given community, in percentage terms, who are willing to get their journalism interactively is— blessedly, I say as a print person—very slim and likely to be for some time."[79] Roberts was right, but not for long. Just 4 percent of adult Americans went online for news at least once during the week in 1995.[80] But that was the starting point: within five years, more than 20 percent of adult Americans would turn regularly to the Internet for news.[81]

The Internet's challenge to traditional media was not wholly ignored or scoffed at in 1995. In April, representatives of eight major U.S. newspaper companies announced the formation of the New Century

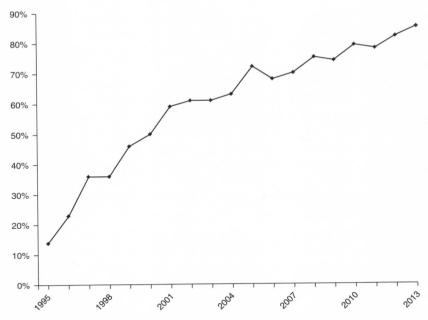

FIGURE 4. Internet adoption. Internet use has surged in America since 1995, when just 14 percent of adults were online. By 2013, that figure had reached 85 percent. (Source: Pew Research Center)

Network.[82] It was meant to be a robust, collaborative response to the challenges the Internet raised. As it turned out, New Century was emblematic of traditional news media's confusion about the digital challenge. "In the spring of 1995," the *New York Times* later observed, "a partnership of large newspaper companies formed the New Century Network to bring the country's dailies into the age of the Internet. Then they sat down to figure out what that meant."[83]

New Century's principal project was a Web-based news resource called NewsWorks, through which affiliated newspapers, large and small, would share content. But NewsWorks was seen as competitive with the online news ventures that member newspaper companies had set up on their own.[84] In March 1998, New Century was abruptly dissolved, an abject failure that has been mostly forgotten.[85]

Wildly popular among some mid-sized American newspapers in 1995 was a fad known as "public" or "civic" journalism.[86] It was a quasi-activist phenomenon in which newspapers presumed they could rouse a lethargic or indifferent public and serve as a stimulus and focal point for rejuvenating civic culture. The wisdom of "public" journalism was vigorously debated by news organizations,[87] but the disputes were largely beside the point. In a digital landscape, audiences could be both consumers and generators of news. They would not need news organizations to foster or promote civic engagement. Whatever its merits, "public" journalism suggested how far mainstream journalism had strayed from truly decisive questions in the field in 1995.

None of the missteps by American news organizations in 1995 was as humiliating as network television's capitulation to heavy-handed tactics of the tobacco industry. In August 1995, ABC News publicly apologized for reports broadcast on its primetime *Day One* news program in 1994 that tobacco companies Philip Morris and R. J. Reynolds routinely spiked cigarettes by injecting extra nicotine during their manufacturing. The companies sued for defamation; Philip Morris asked for $10 billion in damages, and R. J. Reynolds sought an unspecified amount.

To settle the case—which some analysts said the network stood a strong chance of winning—ABC agreed to the apology, which was read on its *World News Tonight* program and at halftime of an exhibition game on *Monday Night Football*.[88] Philip Morris celebrated its victory by placing full-page advertisements in the *New York Times*, the *Wall Street Journal*, and the *Washington Post*. "Apology accepted," the ads declared in large, bold type. The ads incorporated a facsimile of ABC's written apology, which read in part: "We now agree that we should not have reported that Philip Morris adds significant amounts of nicotine from outside sources. That was a mistake."[89]

Fears were that ABC's climb-down would exert a chilling effect on aggressive coverage of the tobacco industry[90]—fears that seemed to be confirmed when CBS canceled plans in November 1995 to broadcast an explosive interview in which Jeffrey S. Wigand, a former tobacco industry executive, sharply criticized the industry's practices. Wigand was the most senior tobacco industry executive to turn whistleblower. But the network's lawyers feared CBS could be sued for billions of dollars for inducing Wigand to break a confidentiality agreement that barred disclosure of internal information about his former employer.[91] No news organization had ever been found liable on such grounds. But the lawyers were adamant, and the interview with Wigand was pulled.

The interview was to have been shown on the newsmagazine program *60 Minutes*, which prided itself on its aggressive and challenging reporting. Mike Wallace, the star journalist of *60 Minutes* who had interviewed Wigand, said the ABC News settlement and apology had figured decisively in the CBS decision. "It has not chilled us as journalists, but it has chilled lawyers," Wallace said, adding, "It has chilled management."[92] Wigand, formerly the vice president for research and development at Brown & Williamson Tobacco Corporation, said in the interview that his former employer included in pipe tobacco an additive suspected of causing cancer in laboratory animals. Wigand also accused the chief executive of Brown & Williamson of lying to Congress about the addictive nature of cigarettes.[93]

Months later, after the *Wall Street Journal* published details of Wigand's deposition in a lawsuit in Mississippi, CBS finally put the suppressed interview on the air. By then, its impact had been blunted, and CBS was subjected to withering criticism for its timidity. "It is a sad day for the First Amendment," said Jane Kirtley, the executive director of the Reporters' Committee for Freedom of the Press, "when journalists back off from a truthful story that the public needs to be told because of fears that they might be sued over the way they got the information."[94]

But nothing in 1995 invited more media self-flagellation than coverage of the double-murder trial in Los Angeles of O.J. Simpson, the former professional football star and popular television pitchman. The trial was the year's biggest, most entrancing, yet most revolting ongoing event. Simpson stood accused of fatally stabbing his estranged wife, Nicole, and her friend, Ronald Goldman, in June 1994 outside her townhouse in the Brentwood section of Los Angeles. The trial's opening statements were delivered in late January 1995, and the proceedings stretched until early October, when Simpson was found not guilty on both counts.

Coverage of the Simpson trial was unrelenting, often inescapable, and occasionally downright bizarre—as when television talk-show host Larry King paid a visit in January 1995 to the chambers of Lance Ito, the presiding judge. A reporter for the *Philadelphia Inquirer* recalled King's visit this way:

> After receiving a private audience with the judge in chambers, King bounded into court like an overheated Labrador retriever, drooling over the famous lawyers and waving to the audience as if he were the grand marshal at a parade. . . . After yukking it up with the lawyers, he eagerly shook hands with the judge's staff, the court reporters and everyone else in sight. Only when he approached Simpson did King learn that in Superior Court, even celebrity has limits. As King extended his hand with a hearty "Hey, O.J.!" two surly sheriff's deputies stepped between them and firmly reminded the TV host that double-murder defendants aren't allowed to press the flesh. King smiled and shrugged sheepishly. Simpson smiled and shrugged back.

Then, seeing no one left to shake hands with, the famous man turned to leave. Unfortunately, he picked the wrong door, walking toward the holding cell where Simpson is held before court. Deputies turned him around, pointing to the exit, where King paused to wave again before departing. "So long, everybody," he said.[95]

Howard Rosenberg, a media critic for the *Los Angeles Times,* was not exaggerating much when he wrote in the trial's aftermath: "We in the media have met the circus, and we are it."[96]

Nor was humor columnist Dave Barry entirely kidding when he addressed the Simpson case in his year-end column, observing that the news media "were thrilled to have this great big, plump, juicy Thanksgiving turkey of a story, providing us with endless leftovers that we could whip up into new recipes to serve again and again, day after day, night after night. . . . Of course you, the public, snorked these tasty tabloid dishes right down and looked around for more. Not that you would admit this. No, you all spent most of 1995 whining to everybody within earshot how sick and tired you were of the O.J. coverage."[97]

At times, the coverage seemed to scramble the hierarchy of American news media. On separate occasions in December 1994, for example, the *New York Times* quoted unsourced pretrial reports that appeared in the supermarket tabloid *National Enquirer*. The *Times* was taken to task for doing so.[98] The tabloid press seemed most familiar and comfortable with the grim tawdriness of the Simpson saga, which was overlaid with wealth, celebrity, race, spousal abuse, courtroom posturing, and no small amount of bungling by police and prosecutors.

In the end, the case left little lasting influence on American jurisprudence. But it was, as James Willwerth of *Time* magazine put it, the "Godzilla of tabloid stories."[99] The *National Enquirer* assigned as many as twenty reporters to the story and sometimes offered up its most extravagant prose. For example, it said in describing the slaying of Nicole Simpson: "The night ended with the bubbly blonde beauty dead in a river of blood on her front doorstep—her throat slashed, her body bludgeoned, her face battered and bruised."[100] As the trial got under way, the *Columbia Journalism Review* observed that the biggest secret wasn't Simpson's guilt or innocence. The biggest secret was that "so many reporters were reading the *National Enquirer* religiously."[101]

When the trial ended on October 3, 1995, with announcement of the verdicts, many tens of thousands of Americans made sure to find a place in front of television sets or radio receivers—signaling how analog-oriented, how tethered to traditional media most Americans were in 1995.

But even then, that dependency was undergoing gradual but profound alteration. Live coverage of the Simpson verdicts would be one of the last major national events in which the Internet was only a modest source for the news. As the passage of twenty years has made clear, the most important media story of 1995 was not the Simpson trial but the emergence into the mainstream of the Internet and the browser-enabled World Wide Web.

The highly touted and much-anticipated "information superhighway"—expected to be a complex environment of high-speed interactive television, electronic mail, home shopping, and movies on demand—fell definitively by the wayside in 1995, overtaken and supplanted by the Internet and the Web. "Nowadays, no one mentions the you-know-what without referring to it as the 'so-called' Information Superhighway," the *San Francisco Examiner* noted at year's end. "The buzz has clearly shifted to the Internet."[102]

The Web in 1995 was primitive by contemporary standards, but its immense potential was becoming evident. As we shall see in Chapter 1, the Internet's exceptional vetting capacity—its ability to swiftly and effectively debunk half-baked claims and thinly sourced news reports—was dramatically displayed in 1995. Amorphous fears about Internet content likewise became prominent in 1995, giving rise to an ill-advised and ill-informed effort by Congress to inhibit speech online.

There also was a growing sense that the Web had much more to offer, and a three-day trade show in Boston called Internet World 95 provided a glimpse of what it soon might look like. The trade show took place in late October and attracted 32,000 visitors—nearly three times the turnout at a similar conference in 1994. It featured demonstrations of online audio news programming, live netcasts of sporting events, and long-distance telephone calls over the Internet.[103] "All the ways of using the Internet today are so rudimentary in terms of what they'll be like in a few years," said Alan Meckler, chief executive of the trade show's sponsoring company, MecklerMedia Corporation. Meckler said the trajectory of the Internet would be like moving "from a horse-drawn carriage to a supersonic jet."[104] It was a prescient observation, and in 1995 that trajectory brought the Internet into the mainstream.

1

The Year of the Internet

The novelty days of the World Wide Web tend to be recalled in sharply different ways. One way is to remember them wistfully, as an innocent time when browsing came into fashion, when the still-new Web offered serendipity, mystery, and the whiff of adventure. The prominent technology skeptic Evgeny Morozov gave expression to early-Web nostalgia in a lush essay a few years ago that lamented the passing of *cyberflânerie*, the pleasure of wandering leisurely online without knowing where one would go or what one might find. He wrote that those days of slowly loading Web pages and "the funky buzz of the modem" offered "their own weird poetics" and the promise of "opening new spaces for play and interpretation."[1]

Far more common than gauzy nostalgia is to look back at the early Web with bemusement and sarcasm, to liken the emergent online world of the mid-1990s to a primordial place, when the environment of the Web was mostly barren and boring, not a place to linger, not a place to do much at all. The "Jurassic Web," Farhad Manjoo called it, in an essay posted at Slate.com. What's "striking about the old Web," he wrote, "is how unsure everyone seemed to be about what the new medium was for."[2]

Fair enough. The Internet of 1995 was a place without Facebook, Twitter, or Wikipedia. Google was barely on the horizon: its founders, Sergey Brin and Larry Page, were graduate students who met in 1995 on the campus of Stanford University. Their mutual first reaction was that the other was pretty obnoxious.[3] The Google of the early Web was the Alta Vista search engine, which claimed to be able to access eight billion words on sixteen million websites.[4] Commercial online services such as America Online, CompuServe, and Prodigy were prospering then, offering an online experience that mostly was segregated, circumscribed, and walled-off to nonsubscribers. By digital reckoning, 1995 was a long time ago—a time before Smartphones, social media, and ubiquitous wireless connections. Even enthusiasts acknowledged that navigating the Internet in 1995 demanded as much patience as knowhow. Surfing the Web then was likened to "a journey to a rugged, exotic destination—the pleasures are exquisite, but you need some stamina."[5]

But to look back and smirk at the primitive character of the online experience, to snicker at the "Jurassic Web," is to miss the dynamism and to overlook the extraordinary developments that took place online in 1995. It was a time when the Internet and its World Wide Web showcase went, in the words of Vinton G. Cerf, one of the fathers of the Internet,[6] "from near-invisibility to near-ubiquity."[7] "World Wide Web" was the word of the year, the American Dialect Society declared.[8] Nineteen ninety-five was when the Internet and the World Wide Web moved from the obscure realm of technophiles and academic researchers to become a household word, the year when the Web went from vague and distant curiosity to a phenomenon that would change the way people work, shop, learn, communicate, and interact.

By the end of 1995, most Americans had at least *heard* about the Internet and vaguely understood that it was a worldwide network of interlinked computers.[9] Everyone seemed to be paying at least some attention to the Internet, and many people could recognize a Web address when they saw one. Although a consciousness about the Internet had taken hold, most people in 1995 had yet to go online. At midyear, the Internet Society estimated that at least twenty million people but not more than forty million people were Internet users.[10] More significantly, 1995 was the year of the emergence of notable entities and applications that shaped and helped define the online world. The year was a moment of innovation crucial to the character, content, and vitality of the World Wide Web.

Nineteen ninety-five saw the emergence of powerful if conflicting sentiments still associated with the Internet: a cocksure swagger encouraged by novelty; a promise of vast treasure to be found in the digital marketplace; and a spirit of collaboration and community that an online environment could uniquely promote. Those cross-cutting sentiments found expression in 1995 in the pretensions of Netscape, the California

This way to the INTERNET

Don't be intimidated by the hype. Here's an easy-to-understand introduction.

BY DAVID PLOTNIKOFF
Mercury News Staff Writer

FOR the most part, we're in the answer business. But just this once, before we ply our stock-in-trade, we have a question we'd like you to field: The Internet is (choose one) A) a piece of software that came with your new computer.

C) a new way to shop for cubic zirconia earrings without cable TV.
D) something I know I should look into but haven't had the time or energy to figure out just yet.
E) a network of many networks running on the TCP/IP protocol suite, primarily over leased trunk lines.
If you answered anything but

might want to go read something else, because this isn't meant for Net-savvy people such as yourself. (Still, even you might learn something.) This no-geekspeak, basic guide is mostly for those souls who are still sitting on the edge of the global information pool wondering whether to dive in, dip a cautious toe or go hide in the changing room until the

FIGURE 5. Most Americans had not yet gone online in 1995. But most of them had heard about the Internet, in part because of newspaper articles that offered introductions to the emergent digital world.

startup that made a breakthrough Web browser and, with its remarkable initial public offering of stock, catalyzed the dot.com boom of the second half of the 1990s. They found further expression in the quiet emergence of Amazon.com, which has become the Web's greatest commercial success story. And they found expression in the development of the unassuming wiki, the open-editing software that enables Web users to collaborate across distances. Netscape, Amazon, and the wiki, each in its way, testified to the Web's emergent dynamism in 1995; each will be discussed in some detail in this chapter.

To be sure, the digital innovations of 1995 went beyond Netscape, Amazon, and the wiki. Many mainstays of the online world date their emergence to that year. The predecessor to Craigslist.org began in 1995 as a free email listing for apartments, jobs, and the arts in San Francisco. Its founder, Craig Newmark, has called Craigslist "a happy accident"[11] that is "passionate about the mundane and the boring."[12] The online auction site eBay was launched in 1995 as AuctionWeb. Its founder, Pierre Omidyar, wrote the original code over Labor Day weekend while holed up at his home office in California.[13] Omidyar was then twenty-eight years old; he became a billionaire three years later when eBay went public.[14]

The online dating service Match.com got its start in 1995, and cyber-dating gained recognition as "more than just a passing whim."[15] The *New York Times* made its first, top-dipping forays into the digital landscape in October 1995, posting reports at http://www.nytimes.com /pope about the visit to the United States of Pope John Paul II. The forerunner of Salon.com, an early venture into online news, was launched in San Francisco in 1995 as a weekly arts and literature "e-zine." Yahoo! was incorporated in 1995, a little more than a year after the Web directory went online. Yahoo! was the work of Stanford graduate students Jerry Yang and David Filo, who first called their directory "David and Jerry's Guide to the World Wide Web."[16]

Progressive Networks that year introduced its RealAudio technology, bringing streaming sound and live broadcasts to the Web.[17] Sun Microsystems in 1995 unveiled Java, the programming language that helped awaken and animate the heretofore static world of the Web.[18] Brendan Eich, then a programmer for Netscape, developed JavaScript, a powerful but fairly easy-to-use scripting language popular among Web designers and developers.[19] The first version of Internet Explorer, Microsoft's anemic entry into the market of graphical Web browsers, became available in August 1995. In a few years, the successor versions of Explorer became the Web's dominant browser.

So what made 1995 so digitally fecund? Why were so many veins of innovation fruitfully tapped that year? A variety of factors converged to make the year so rich and exceptional. For one, the Web was still new but had moved beyond its infancy. Tim Berners-Lee, a British software engineer, had developed the Web's fundamental protocols by August 1991, and Mosaic, the first popular graphical Web browser, was available online less than two years later. Mosaic was a marvelous breakthrough; it was easy to install and easy to use, and it illuminated the Web for technophiles and early adopters. By 1995, moreover, computer use had crossed an important threshold: more than half of American adults were using computers at home, in school, or at work.[20] And many new computers then were shipped with modems installed, encouraging access to the online world.[21] Additionally, the growth of multifaceted, commercial online services such as America Online, CompuServe, and Prodigy signaled emergent popular interest in going online, however circumscribed the experience might be.[22] It was no major leap for subscribers to move directly to the Web and its promise of vast, unrestricted content.

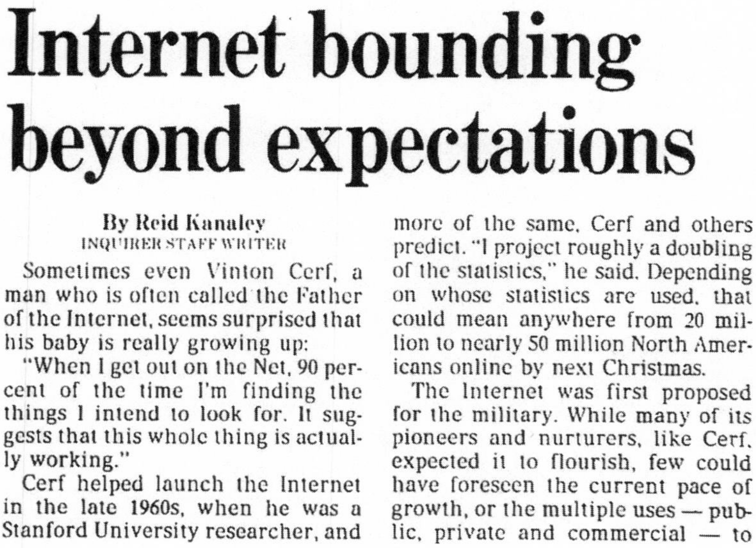

Internet bounding beyond expectations

By Reid Kanaley
INQUIRER STAFF WRITER

Sometimes even Vinton Cerf, a man who is often called the Father of the Internet, seems surprised that his baby is really growing up:

"When I get out on the Net, 90 percent of the time I'm finding the things I intend to look for. It suggests that this whole thing is actually working."

Cerf helped launch the Internet in the late 1960s, when he was a Stanford University researcher, and

more of the same, Cerf and others predict. "I project roughly a doubling of the statistics," he said. Depending on whose statistics are used, that could mean anywhere from 20 million to nearly 50 million North Americans online by next Christmas.

The Internet was first proposed for the military. While many of its pioneers and nurturers, like Cerf, expected it to flourish, few could have foreseen the current pace of growth, or the multiple uses — public, private and commercial — to

FIGURE 6. The Internet was the subject of much gee-whiz attention from the news media in 1995. At year's end, an article in the *Philadelphia Inquirer* called attention to the Internet's growing popularity.

The Web, moreover, came to be recognized as a barrier-lowering, micro-targeting platform that could facilitate connections otherwise difficult or impossible to achieve. To varying degrees, entities such as Amazon, Craigslist, eBay, and Match.com all seized on this capacity. They embraced the flexibility, versatility, and relative efficiency of the online world. Their founders recognized the Web's capacity to promote convenience and to foster, if loosely and temporally, a sense of connection among consumers across distances. The feedback option, notably promoted by Amazon, emerged as a confidence-building mechanism for online consumers.

The Internet in 1995 also became the topic of much gee-whiz attention from the news media—attention that had the effect of deepening curiosity about the Web and its potential. For sheer hyperbole, few characterizations exceeded *Newsweek*'s cover story at the end of 1995. It had been "the Year of the Internet," *Newsweek* declared, adding: "Remember when surfing was something you did outdoors, in a bathing suit? That was 1994. Now it's what you do on the Internet—the worldwide network of computers that in 1995 was embraced as the medium that will change the way we communicate, shop, publish and ... be damned."[23]

"You talk about revolution?" *Newsweek* went on. "For once, the shoe fits."[24]

The Internet hype of 1995 was met by no small amount of scoffing and eye-rolling. Net skeptics and detractors were not especially hard to find. Some of them suggested the Internet was but a transient fad, perhaps a latter-day Citizen's Band radio, the short-range communications device that was popular for a while in the 1970s before lapsing into obscurity.[25] Among the year's most prominent and often-quoted skeptics was Clifford Stoll, a forty-five-year-old astrophysicist with wild, thinning hair. Stoll had been online many years before 1995, when he brought out *Silicon Snake Oil: Second Thoughts on the Information Highway,* a scattershot and sometimes-crabby book that offered a head-on challenge to Internet euphoria. Twenty years on, *Silicon Snake Oil* remains entertaining—if mostly for its jaw-dropping collection of off-target projections. Here is a notable sampling:

> I don't believe that phone books, newspapers, magazines, or corner video stores will disappear as computer networks spread. Nor do I think that my telephone will merge with my computer, to become some sort of information appliance.[26]

> I suspect Big Brother won't have an easy time tracing us. . . . Our privacy will be protected, as it always has been, by simple obscurity and the high cost of uncovering information about us.[27]

> What will the electronic book look like? Some sort of miniature laptop computer, I'd guess. We'll download selections and page through them electronically. Try reading electronic books. They're awful.[28]

> Video-on-demand, that killer application of communications, will remain a dream.[29]

> It's easy to make fancy home pages on the World Wide Web. But jumping from one document to another baffles me even more than watching someone channel surf. I'm never certain of my location in a twisty maze of cross-references.[30]

> Why not send a fax? It's far more universal than e-mail—we not only find fax machines everywhere, but they can all speak to one another. . . . I find it easier [than e-mail] to just scribble a note on a plain piece of paper and send it over a fax. Or address an envelope, lick a stamp, and mail the letter.[31]

Stoll's predictions and observations can be scoffed at as naive and short-sighted. That is easy to do. They also can be recognized as a baseline for understanding what a robust place cyberspace was becoming

twenty years ago. Although Stoll clearly misjudged the Internet's dynamism and potential to produce innovations, it was not as if he were a
neo-Luddite. "I have a half-dozen computers in my home," he told an
interviewer in 1995. "I have no shortage of e-mail addresses."[32]

A preview of Stoll's book appeared in *Newsweek* in February 1995,
beneath the memorable headline "The Internet? Bah!"[33] More so than
his book, Stoll's commentary has achieved something approaching cult-
like status online. The essay is constantly to be rediscovered online,
gaining fresh life and circulation on platforms such as Twitter. Although
not especially prominently, Stoll has acknowledged the shortcomings of
his predictions in 1995. "Of my many mistakes, flubs, and howlers," he
wrote in a discussion forum on BoingBoing.net in 2010, "few have been
as public as my 1995 howler. Wrong? Yep." He added: "Now, whenever I think I know what's happening, I temper my thoughts: Might be
wrong, Cliff . . ."[34]

Nearly as stunning as Stoll's misguided prophesies was Bob Metcalfe's bizarre prediction that "the Internet will soon go spectacularly
supernova and in 1996 catastrophically collapse," leaving behind "only
World Wide Web ghost pages."[35] Metcalfe was the multimillionaire
inventor of Ethernet technology and founder of 3Com Corporation. He
also was publisher of *InfoWorld,* where his "supernova" prediction
appeared in December 1995. In his column, Metcalfe wrote that a
number of factors would bring about the Internet's spectacular collapse, including security breaches that would send many Internet sites
to the safety of firewalls and intranets.[36] In a follow-up commentary,
Metcalfe upped the stakes by promising to eat his Internet-collapse column should the "supernova" prediction prove wrong.[37]

It proved wrong, of course, and in what *Wired* magazine described as
"highly theatrical public penance,"[38] Metcalfe made good on his pledge
to eat his column. He took the stage in April 1997 at an international
World Wide Web conference in Santa Clara, California, and acknowledged that the Internet "supernova" had not occurred. Metcalfe put to a
voice vote the question of his eating the column; the response was overwhelming. "Eat, baby, eat," conference-goers shouted. Metcalfe then
wheeled onto the stage a large cake decorated to look like his misguided
InfoWorld column. He proposed to eat a large slice of the cake instead—
a suggestion greeted by much booing. Metcalfe relented. He ripped his
wrong-headed column from *InfoWorld,* tore it into shreds, and sprin-
kled the remains into an electric blender containing a bit of water. The
blender whirred, producing a milky, pulpy substance. To cheers from

the audience, Metcalfe ladled the goop into a bowl and slurped it down.[39] It was, he later boasted, his "greatest publicity stunt of all time."[40] Before taking the stage at Santa Clara, Metcalfe had assured himself that the *InfoWorld* ink was not toxic.[41]

More common than expansive and spectacularly wrong predictions was the tentativeness that attached to the emergent online world of 1995, a tentativeness that nowadays seems quaint and droll. This was evident in phrases devised by journalists to describe the Web and explain its novelty. The phrases were not wrong necessarily, but they clearly were cautious and uncertain, as if the journalists were grabbing in the dark. After all, the vernacular for talking about the online world was still evolving in 1995.[42] As the year began, the *New York Times* described the Web as "a section of the Internet overflowing with sights and sounds."[43] Not long afterward, a *Times* writer referred to the Web as "an electronic amalgam of the public library, the suburban shopping mall and the Congressional Record."[44] In February 1995, a wire service report called the Web "a string of data bases available through the global maze of computer networks known as the Internet."[45]

Near the end of the year, the *New York Times* declared the Web had become "a full-fledged media star, hailed and hyped, part technology and part fashion accessory."[46] About that time, a report in the *Philadelphia Inquirer* about the "fascination with the World Wide Web" described it as "an electronic publishing service for pictures, sound and video, as well as text."[47] Earlier in the year, the *Inquirer* had introduced the Web to its readers by asking: "What do O.J. Simpson, the Louvre, an Australian guy called Wigs, prostitution, the Franklin Institute and a coffeepot in England have in common? Maybe nothing, except that they are all on the Web—the World Wide Web—a multimedia digital universe probably appearing on a computer screen near you."[48] And *Newsweek*'s effervescent year-end cover story hailing 1995 as "the year of the Internet" described the Web as "an awesome construct where the publishing efforts of thousands of people are interlinked into a massive seething monument to human expression, enabling everything from shopping for a new car to keeping track of Madonna's biological clock."[49]

Although the Web was hardly a "massive seething monument" in 1995, it was sufficiently prominent to stir fears about what it would become and what content it would carry. In April 1995, the National Science Foundation ended its management of the Internet's U.S. backbone, handing responsibility to three commercial carriers—Sprint,

Ameritech, and Pacific Bell.[50] The changeover was scarcely noted by users, but it provoked vague fears that the online world was destined to become a corporatized domain, where dissent would be muted and unwelcome.

The *Nation* magazine gave voice to such worries in an article by Andrew L. Shapiro. "Speech in cyberspace," he warned, "will not be free if we allow big business to control every square inch of the Net. The public needs a place of its own." Shapiro suggested the Internet could become a "cyberia," with "no spaces dedicated to public discourse. No virtual sidewalks or park, no heated debate or demonstrators catching your attention, no street-corner activist trying to get you to read one of her leaflets. In fact, you can shape your route so that you interact only with people of your choosing and with information tailored to your desires."[51] Shapiro's fears about "cyberia" were not entirely off-target; it is of course not difficult to shape online visits so as to interact exclusively with views and arguments of one's choosing. Even so, the Internet has hardly turned into a bleak, corporatized landscape, empty of dispute. Web logs—popularly known as blogs—and social media platforms offer viewpoint diversity in teeming profusion.

A fear more prominent and widely shared in 1995 was that the Internet was becoming awash in pornography and that smut was readily accessible to children. These fears were stoked into a media firestorm in June 1995 when *Time* magazine came out with a cover story about "cyberporn." On the cover was an illustration of a pasty youth at a computer, his eyes bulging and his mouth agape in the apparent shock of confronting images of some unmentionable sex act. Inside the magazine, an illustration depicted a naked man in suggestive embrace with a computer.

The centerpiece of the *Time* story was described as "an exhaustive study of online porn" conducted by a "research team at Carnegie Mellon University" that drew on "elaborate computer records of online activity" and measured "for the first time what people actually download, rather than what they say they want to see." The "Carnegie Mellon researchers discovered . . . an awful lot of porn online," the cover story said—specifically that 83.5 percent of images stored at online Usenet newsgroups "were pornographic."[52] The ABC News program *Nightline* drew on the study in devoting an episode to pornography on the Internet. "It's the kind of smut many of the porn stores won't even carry," the *Nightline* host, Ted Koppel, declared in introducing the show. "Now, it's the kind of material you and your kids can see with just the click of a button."[53]

Such characterizations lent an unmistakable impression that much of the Internet abounded in filth. *Time*'s "cyberporn" report implicitly impugned the value of going online: why do so if the place were a virtual cesspool? But soon enough, the online world struck back in what was an early and impressive demonstration of the Internet's capacity to debunk and deflate, to act as a potent vetting mechanism. In the days and weeks following publication of the "cyberporn" story, the corrective power of the Internet was on display in a blizzard of condemnation and commentary posted at online discussion forums.[54] The online commercial magazine *HotWired* memorably took on the "cyberporn" story in a report titled "Journoporn."[55]

Together, the online critiques made clear that *Time*'s cover story was exceedingly alarmist, a messy blend of exaggeration, thin research, and dubious analysis. What *Time* called the "Carnegie Mellon study" was really the work of Marty Rimm, a thirty-year-old undergraduate student in Carnegie Mellon's electrical and computer engineering program. Although Rimm's study was published in the *Georgetown Law Review*, it had been subjected to no rigorous peer-review by experts without a stake in the research. Critics pointed to the study's ambiguous data and methodological shortcomings.[56] They noted that Rimm's study generalized from a narrow data set. Moreover, the research was based largely on data extracted from private online bulletin boards that sold pornographic content to adults using credit cards, which meant they were not readily accessible by children.[57] It was as if Rimm had surveyed adult bookstores in Times Square and then generalized about what was sold in Barnes & Noble stores, said Mike Godwin, general counsel at the Electronic Frontier Foundation, and an implacable critic of Rimm's research.[58]

Confronted with a storm of critiques and complaints, *Time* backpedaled from its "cyberporn" cover story—"at a trot if not a gallop," media critics Jeff Cohen and Norman Solomon wrote.[59] *Time* conceded that serious questions had been raised about the study's methodology and how its data were gathered. A follow-up *Time* article cited management professors at Vanderbilt University who had read Rimm's study and found the statistics "misleading or meaningless." They said, according to *Time*, "that pornographic files represent less than one-half of 1 percent of all messages posted on the Internet."[60]

Fears about cyberporn were hardly extinguished by *Time*'s acknowledgment of error. Debate about pornography online, and how to keep it from children, was percolating in Congress. In February 1995, J. James Exon, a gravelly voiced Democratic senator from Nebraska, introduced the Communications Decency Act, declaring the measure an urgently needed bulwark against smut online.[61] "I want," Exon said, "to keep the information superhighway from resembling a red light district."[62] The Communications Decency Act was attached to a broader telecommunications-reform bill, which won the Senate's overwhelming approval in mid-June 1995.

To help ensure that the Senate would wrap the Communications Decency Act into the telecommunications bill, Exon compiled a "blue book" of raunchy and explicit images that had been downloaded from the Internet. These graphic images were placed in a thin binder that Exon showed to perhaps a dozen fellow senators. Exon said he doubted whether his colleagues fully understood "the depths of depravity that's available" online. "They think it's just pictures of naked women."[63] Interestingly, Exon, who was seventy-three years old and had announced his retirement from the Senate before taking on cyberporn, was only faintly familiar with the medium he was seeking to regulate. Exon claimed no extensive, first-hand experience with the digital world. In mid-1995, Exon's office on Capitol Hill had neither email address nor Internet connection.[64] The images in Exon's "blue book" binder had been downloaded by a friend.[65]

The Communications Decency Act moved forward despite reservations about its constitutionality and despite the imaginative opposition of online activists. On December 12, 1995, they organized an "Internet Day of Protest," during which more than 10,000 people placed telephone calls and sent email and fax messages to members of Congress, objecting to the measure as little more than heavy-handed censorship.[66] Nevertheless, the telecommunications bill was approved by Congress on February 1, 1996, and President Bill Clinton signed it into law a week later,[67] in a ceremony at the landmark Main Reading Room of the Library of Congress.

Clinton declared the telecommunications measure "truly revolutionary legislation that will bring the future to our doorstep."[68] But he said nothing specifically about the Communications Decency Act, which in its final form forbade the display or transmission of "indecent" or "patently offensive" online material to minors and provided for prison sentences of up to two years and fines of as much as $250,000. As Clinton signed the legislation, hundreds of websites—including those of some members of Congress, radio stations, and the City of Houston—began going dark, to protest the assault on free speech online.[69] In Philadelphia that day, a coalition of civil liberties groups sought a federal restraining order against imposition of the Communications Decency Act.

In June 1996, a panel of three federal judges in Philadelphia unanimously ruled the act an unconstitutional violation of the First Amendment and barred its enforcement.[70] That ruling was affirmed a year later, when the U.S. Supreme Court struck down key provisions of the decency act. Justice John Paul Stevens wrote in the high court's decision that "in the absence of evidence to the contrary, we presume that governmental regulation of the content of speech is more likely to interfere with the free exchange of ideas than to encourage it. The interest in encouraging freedom of expression in a democratic society outweighs any theoretical but unproven benefit of censorship."[71] It was a major victory for free speech online; it was the day, said the *Washington Post,* when the First Amendment went digital.[72]

James Exon and his allies thought of the Internet as a cesspool oozing smut. Far more enticing and motivating was to think of the Internet as a place of vast and untapped potential, where riches were waiting to be made. In 1995, no entity better represented the panache and wealth-making potential associated with the Internet than Netscape Communications Corporation, a startup in California's Silicon Valley that made a terrific digital product: a graphical Web browser called Netscape Navigator. The first version of Navigator had been shipped in December 1994, just eight months after the company's incorporation. Netscape sold the browser for $39 to commercial users but allowed them to evaluate the product for free, and the company gave the browser away to academics and nonprofit users. Navigator took off quickly, surpassing more humble rivals and winning a commanding share of the emerging browser market.

Netscape was an immediate success, if not in turning a profit then in attracting the goodwill of millions of new Web users. It was an immensely interesting company; its leading figures were said to be right out of central casting.[73] Netscape's chairman was James H. Clark, a founder of Silicon Graphics who was looking for the next big thing. He seeded Netscape with $5 million[74] and infused the company with a certain ardor. "Jim had the Jedi mind trick, the ability to convince you of pretty much anything," said Lou Montulli, one of Netscape's first programmers. "And he really filled our heads up with the idea that we can go and we can change the world—and we're going to make a [lot] of money doing it."[75] Clark recruited James Barksdale, a Mississippi native, from McCaw Cellular to become Netscape's chief executive.

FIGURE 7. Marc Andreessen, the voluble cofounder of Netscape Communications, was hailed by *Newsweek* magazine in 1995 as "the über-super-wunder whiz kid of cyberspace." He was just twenty-four. (Photo credit: Louie Psihoyos/Corbis)

Barksdale was modest and gentlemanly; he was "as mellow as shoofly pie," one technology writer said.[76]

Netscape's defining and most colorful figure was its cofounder, Marc Andreessen, a programmer with an agile mind who talked fast, persuasively, and seemingly nonstop. He was a big guy, standing 6-feet-4, and full of amusing quirks and habits. Andreessen turned twenty-four years old in 1995; he was less than two years out of college and had not shed all the trappings and eccentricities of undergraduate life. He worked late and got up late. His taste in clothes, it was said, ran to "frat-party ready."[77] Barksdale once observed that Andreessen ate hamburgers "like a horse, both in quantity and mannerisms."[78] His technique for interviewing prospective employees hewed to the eccentric. Todd

Rulon-Miller, Netscape's vice president of sales, recalled meeting with Andreessen in 1994 to discuss the job. "When I interviewed with him, he was on a workstation staring intently into the screen. I don't think he looked at me," Rulon-Miller said. "I sat in a chair next to him. He was playing Doom," a then-popular shooter-video game. "And I didn't even know what Doom was."[79]

Andreessen seemed an unlikely character to be identified as "the über-super-wunder whiz kid of cyberspace," as *Newsweek* called him at the end of 1995.[80] Andreessen had grown up in New Lisbon, an information-poor town in rural Wisconsin, where, Andreessen said, "we had the three TV networks, maybe two radio stations, no cable TV. We still had a long-distance party line in our neighborhood, so you could listen to all your neighbors' phone calls. We had a very small public library, and the nearest bookstore was an hour away. So I came from an environment where I was starved for information, starved for connection."[81]

He enrolled at the University of Illinois at Urbana-Champaign and studied computer science, after a fashion. "I was in a degree program," Andreessen said in an interview in 1995, "but it wasn't highly structured. I just tried to keep up. I basically never studied. I attended classes, but that's about it."[82] Andreessen found part-time work at the university's National Center for Supercomputing Applications. There, he and a few fellow programmers developed Mosaic, the predecessor-browser to Netscape Navigator. Mosaic was launched in 1993 and quickly won followers for granting relatively easy, point-and-click access to the previously hard-to-access World Wide Web.[83] In December 1993, Andreessen graduated from the University of Illinois and headed for California.[84] His team of programmers stayed behind in Champaign—for a while.

Andreessen met Clark in early 1994, and they soon decided to set up a company that would outdo Mosaic. Andreessen and Clark recruited several of Andreessen's former undergraduate colleagues at the National Center for Supercomputing Applications and brought them to California as core programmers at Mosaic Communications Corporation, the predecessor to Netscape Communications. Andreessen and his team set to work to develop a better browser. They called it Mosaic Netscape. Officials at the University of Illinois soon learned what was up, cried foul, and threatened to sue, claiming an infringement of its intellectual property. Clark and Andreessen insisted that not a line of the Mosaic code appeared in the new browser. The university was not mollified and insisted that Mosaic Communications change its name and pay a hefty royalty.[85]

Eventually, and quite reluctantly, Clark and Andreessen changed the name: Mosaic Communications became Netscape Communications; the browser was renamed Netscape Navigator. But they balked at the demand for royalties. In the end, Netscape paid the university about $3 million to settle the dispute, which embittered Andreessen. "They basically tried to shut us down," he later told Rick Tetzeli of *Fortune* magazine. "They started a campaign in the press to make us look like thieves."[86] In doing so, Andreessen said, the university forfeited millions of dollars in his prospective donations.[87]

Netscape was quite capable of impressive innovation. Pre-release "beta" versions of its Navigator 2.0 browser came out in October and December 1995 and were hailed as something of a technological feat. Navigator 2.0 was faster and more powerful than its predecessor, which had claimed about 70 percent of the browser market.[88] Among other advances, Navigator 2.0 incorporated plug-in architecture, allowing programmers to develop applications on the browser. Netscape 2.0 also supported the Java applets that made Web-browsing a more lively and animated experience.

In the summer and fall of 1995, Netscape was on a roll. They were the best of times for the swaggering startup. The company's workforce had grown to 500 employees, a five-fold increase since the beginning of the year. Revenues were climbing, topping $40 million in the year's fourth quarter, which was almost double sales in the previous three-month period. (Netscape's sales came mostly from corporate licensing of its high-profile browser and from a diverse line of Internet servers and server software.) During those heady weeks, Netscape was touted as "the Microsoft of the Internet"[89] and seemed to delight in poking at the software giant and its chairman, Bill Gates. "From a scientific point of view, none of us really respected Microsoft," Lou Montulli recalled years later. "There was definitely a sense of: they've put out of business three or four major companies, and they did it simply by copying what they did and outpricing or outmanuevering them in the market."[90]

Gates had been slow to recognize the potential of the Internet and the Web. He mistakenly thought the Internet was just a precursor to some sort of elaborate, multidimensional information superhighway. He said as much in his 1995 book, *The Road Ahead*.[91] But as Netscape's browser demonstrated, the Web was becoming *the* information superhighway. And the browser's potential as a platform for software applications represented an undeniable threat to Microsoft's Windows operating system. Andreessen—who sometimes during the mid–1990s was called the "next Bill Gates"[92]—supposedly boasted that Netscape would reduce Windows to a mundane set of poorly debugged device drivers.[93] The insult meant that Microsoft's operating systems, installed on millions of computers, risked becoming superfluous in a robust, Web-based environment. Clark, for his part, likened Microsoft to the "Death Star" of the evil empire in *Star Wars* movies.[94]

The insults were not overlooked at Microsoft's sprawling campus headquarters in Redmond, Washington. Hadi Partovi, the group manager for Microsoft's browser, Internet Explorer, printed out the most provocative comments by Netscape executives and placed them in the hallway of the offices of the Internet Explorer team.[95] Gates himself had cited Netscape in a lengthy memorandum in May 1995 to his executive staff and direct reports. Gates titled the document "The Internet Tidal Wave," and it signaled a definitive though belated embrace of the technology. "A new competitor 'born' on the Internet is Netscape," Gates wrote. "Their browser is dominant, with 70% usage share, allowing them to determine which network extensions will catch on. . . . They have attracted a number of public network operators to use their platform to offer information and directory services. We have to match and beat their offerings."[96]

The smoldering hostility between the companies turned acute on June 21, 1995, at a four-hour meeting at Netscape's headquarters. In the run-up to the meeting, Netscape and Microsoft had tentatively explored a strategic relationship. But according to detailed notes that Andreessen took at the meeting in June, Microsoft's representatives came on strong and proposed that the companies carve up the browser market—with Netscape Navigator confined to the older, less lucrative versions of Windows.[97] Andreessen, who could be disarmingly candid, likened the conduct of Microsoft's team to "a visit by Don Corleone" of *The Godfather* films. "I expected to find a bloody computer monitor in my bed the next day."[98] Microsoft disputed Andreessen's account, saying its representatives had made no attempt to intimidate Netscape.[99]

In any case, the meeting ended without agreement, and Netscape moved forward with plans for its most audacious act of all: a public offering of its shares. Netscape was not quite sixteen months old and had not come close to turning a profit. Typically, as the *New York Times* observed, companies were expected to "show a pattern of profitability over two or more quarters before an underwriter would try to

take them public, but the Internet, as with some other promising tech-
nologies, is apparently different."[100]

Netscape had been contemplating an IPO—initial public offering of
its shares—for several months. "I wanted us to go public because I
thought it'd be good for us from a PR standpoint," recalled Clark, the
chairman, "and I did go into this thing to make money, so I was looking
for a reward as well."[101] The IPO, underwritten by Morgan Stanley and
Hambrecht & Quist, included five million shares of Netscape, priced at
$28 per share. The shares went up for sale August 9 on the Nasdaq
exchange. But for nearly two hours that morning, an order imbalance
kept them from being traded. Finally, the stock opened—at $71 per
share. It climbed as high as $74.75 a share before settling at day's end
to $58.25.[102]

It was a smashing debut by any measure—"the best opening day for
a stock in Wall Street history for an issue of its size," the *New York
Times* said.[103] The IPO demonstrated that the Web could be a place to
make fortunes fast. Clark's stake in Netscape was worth more than half
a billion dollars; Andreessen's was worth more than $58 million. The
Wall Street Journal observed that it had taken General Dynamics forty-
three years to become a corporation worth $2.7 billion in the stock
market. It had taken Netscape "about a minute."[104] The IPO, as Robert
H. Reid wrote in *Architects of the Web,* "put the Internet indelibly on
the map with millions of people who hadn't been there yet."[105]

Fifteen days after Netscape's IPO, Microsoft unveiled its much-anticipated Windows 95 operating system, which coincided with the release
of Internet Explorer 1.0, Microsoft's Web browser. Explorer 1.0 was a
meager product[106] that, ironically, was based on a licensed version of
the Mosaic code that Andreessen had developed at Illinois.[107] Then, on
December 7, 1995, came Microsoft's "Pearl Harbor Day" announcement and the unequivocal emergence of a mortal threat to Netscape:
Gates spelled out for journalists and industry analysts a comprehensive
strategy to insert and expand Microsoft's presence online. Gates
declared that Microsoft was "hard-core about the Internet."[108] Among
other moves, Microsoft's browser would be improved, made faster, and
offered online for free.[109]

The "browser war"—the blood feud between Netscape and
Microsoft—was under way. Gates, according to an internal memorandum, acknowledged that Netscape was "quite an impressive competitor."[110] Barksdale, Netscape's chief executive, said the looming browser
war promised "to be a dogfight. But we think we have God on our

side."[111] Markets, though, tended to think otherwise. Two days before Gates's "Pearl Harbor Day" announcement, Netscape's per-share price had touched $171. It would never again reach that high. Netscape mania had crested as markets sensed the unfolding browser war could become a lopsided fight that Microsoft would win.

Even so, Netscape entered the browser war with a huge advantage in market share. Its dominance unnerved Microsoft. "Netscape is already entrenched in our markets all over the world," a senior Microsoft executive, Brad Chase, wrote in a confidential internal memorandum in April 1996. "The situation today is *scary*," Chase stated. "We have not taken the lead over Netscape in any market yet."[112] But in time, that equation would change dramatically. As Gates had promised, the Microsoft browser was improved. Internet Explorer 3.0, introduced in 1996, was seen as at least the technological equal to Netscape's latest version, Navigator 3.0.[113]

What's more, computer users, especially new users, had little incentive to download and install Navigator on the Windows platform: Internet Explorer was already there, and technically it was just as good. Moreover, Microsoft had muscled its way into the commercial online market, and the largest service providers—including America Online, CompuServe, and AT&T Worldnet—replaced Netscape Navigator with Internet Explorer as their preferred browsing software.[114] According to an America Online internal email, Gates asked an AOL executive in January 1996, "How much do we need to pay you to screw Netscape?" by designating Internet Explorer as AOL's featured browser. "This is your lucky day," Gates was quoted as saying.[115]

In the months that followed, Netscape Navigator steadily lost market share to Internet Explorer. At Netscape's encouragement, the Justice Department began investigating Microsoft's tactics on anticompetitive grounds. But the government's inquiry would come much too late to rescue Netscape. The company lost $88 million in the fourth quarter of 1997, and its shares shed more than 20 percent of their value, sliding to less than $20.[116] By August 1998, Internet Explorer eclipsed Navigator as the most popular Web browser. The "writing was on the wall," said Brendan Eich, the Netscape software engineer who developed Javascript. "Microsoft was driving their monster truck after us and they were about to pin us to the wall."[117]

Netscape's celebrated run as the flamboyant startup of Silicon Valley reached a bitter end in November 1998, when Barksdale announced the company's acquisition by America Online in a stock deal valued at $4.2

billion.[118] It was the first major merger of Internet companies,[119] and it reduced the once-cocksure Netscape to a forlorn and mostly forgotten outpost of AOL. (In a final indignity years after the "browser war," Microsoft in 2012 acquired from AOL the patents underlying the Netscape browser.)[120]

For a time, Andreessen stayed with the merged entity, as chief technology officer at America Online. He bought a house near AOL headquarters in suburban Virginia as if to underscore his commitment. But a few months later, he returned to California. Many of Netscape's 2,200 employees also left after the merger; the clash of cultures between buttoned-up AOL and freewheeling but humbled Netscape was too pronounced.

Microsoft and the "browser war" were the major but not the exclusive reasons for Netscape's inglorious descent. Netscape never converted its many browser users into paying customers.[121] It never quite knew what to do with its much-visited home page, which, somewhat belatedly, it turned into a Web portal called Netcenter.[122] The Netscape saga—from spectacular rise to near-hegemony to decline and humiliating absorption by AOL—spanned fewer than five years. In its run, Netscape helped define "Internet time," an idiom of the late 1990s that meant everything moved more swiftly online. The compressed arc of Netscape's meteoric trajectory was itself emblematic of Internet time.

More significantly, the rise of Netscape and the popularity of its browser signaled the centrality of the Web in the digital age. Novelist Charles Yu described it this way: "I entered college in 1993 and graduated in 1997. Halfway through, the Internet became a thing. Netscape said: 'Here you go, here's a door to a brand-new place in the existence of the universe. We just started letting people in. Go ahead, it's fun. It'll keep getting bigger for the rest of your life.'"[123] Like no other single event of the early digital age, Netscape's IPO in 1995 brought the Web into popular consciousness. "If the World Wide Web had not yet gotten the public's full attention," Tim Berners-Lee said, the Netscape IPO "put it on center stage."[124]

It can be forgotten how innovative Netscape really was. It developed JavaScript. It was quick to embrace the Java programming language. It introduced the Secure Sockets Layer protocol, which enabled encrypted transactions to be completed online.[125] Netscape's early browsers were marvels for their time. "Every time you go to a Web page," technology writer Walter Mossberg wrote in late 2013, "you are seeing the legacy of Netscape in action."[126] But more than that, Netscape epitomized the swagger and flamboyance of the early Web and its exuberant promise of wealth swiftly made. Amazon.com in 1995 represented great promise of a less spectacular sort—that the Web could be a reliable, efficient, and customer-friendly source of commerce. Amazon demonstrated this potential by selling a decidedly analog product with a centuries-old past: the book.

Amazon's online bookstore opened on July 16, 1995, and not many people took notice.[127] Such obscurity seems in hindsight a bit astonishing, given how embedded Amazon has become in American life and culture. In the years after 1995, Amazon demonstrated that the Web could be an opportune venue for retailing and, in doing so, dramatically altered the businesses of selling books, music, and video. It became the Walmart of the digital world, and much more. With its line of Kindle devices, Amazon has made electronic books popular and readable. It has become a leader in Web technology services, and it rents space on its formidable computer infrastructure to startups and established businesses[128] as well as government agencies such as the CIA. It is in the same-day grocery-delivery business in a few cities. The company's founder—a geeky guy with large brown eyes and a bellowing, full-body laugh—began the company figuring it had a 70 percent chance of failing. Within a few years, he had a net worth of several billion dollars and was being proclaimed the "Internet's ultimate cult figure."[129] He is a rare 1990s technology-entrepreneur—a founder/chief executive—who still runs the company he started. He's Jeff Bezos, a driven and complex figure of many interests, a man of deep intelligence and a sometimes-savage temper.

The saga of Amazon.com began in 1994 when Bezos, in his telling, saw great opportunity in the Internet's astonishingly swift growth. He quit a well-paying job at the D. E. Shaw investment management firm in New York City and, with his wife, MacKenzie, headed west for Puget Sound in Washington state. Over the next several months, Bezos made a couple of key hires, raised startup money from family and friends, and incorporated the company.

Bezos has cultivated a founding myth that Amazon began inauspiciously, in a poorly heated, unprepossessing garage in Bellevue, Washington. The company's press releases in its early years seldom neglected to mention the humble birth.[130] Bezos has said he purposely looked for a house to rent in suburban Seattle that came with a garage—"in part because we wanted some of that garage-startup legitimacy" that attaches to companies such as Apple and Hewlett Packard. "It wasn't . . . full legitimacy because the garage was enclosed" and had been con-

FIGURE 8. Few people noticed when Jeff Bezos launched Amazon.com on the Internet in mid-July 1995. The company was quick to recognize the power, versatility, and novelty of the Web—and demonstrated how it could be a secure place for commerce. (Photo credit: Brian Velenchenko/Corbis)

verted into a sort of work room, Bezos conceded.[131] But "it wasn't insulated," he said, and "it was very cold, and that gave us some legitimacy."[132] That Amazon got its start humbly, in a suburban garage, has become the stuff of Internet legend; even nowadays, when it matters very little, references to Amazon's undistinguished origins often appear in news reports about Bezos or the company.[133]

By July 1995, when Amazon began selling books online, Bezos had moved the fledgling company from Bellevue to an industrial neighborhood in Seattle and office space above a Color Tile store.[134] Launching Amazon when he did turned out to be impeccable timing: had Amazon .com gone live a year earlier, Robert Spector wrote in his book, *Amazon*

.com: Get Big Fast, "there barely would have been enough personal computers connected to the Internet to keep the company afloat; a year later and the competition would have had an insurmountable lead."[135]

Bezos, who turned thirty-one in 1995, has said he figured it would take years and years for book-buyers to grow accustomed to making purchases online. It was neither instinctive nor intuitive in 1995 to go online and buy a book. Or anything. A report by the Times Mirror Center for the People & the Press in October 1995 said that just 1 percent of all Americans had made a recent purchase online. But the Times Mirror study also noted that "even small percentages can translate into millions of people."[136]

Bezos later acknowledged that he had not anticipated the importance of those online shoppers, the early adopters who typically have a fairly high tolerance for risk and uncertainty.[137] "The thing we had over-looked, at that time, was everybody on the Internet, 100 percent of the population, was what demographers called 'early adopters,'" Bezos said. "These are the first people to use cell phones. The first people to use computers. They're the first people to do everything. And so these guys were very facile at learning new habits, and they adopted very quickly" to buying books at Amazon.com.[138]

The company's first employee, Shel Kaphan, said that it was soon after its launch when Amazon began "getting some traction" online.[139] "It was an exciting time," said Kaphan, who developed the technology that made the Amazon site interactive and responsive to individual users. In the company's early days, he "was often the only person in the office on the weekends and [I remember] just getting phone calls from all over the country, people excited to find the site and wanting to know about us." It was novel in 1995 to be "doing commerce on the Web," Kaphan said, and that "caught people's imagination in a lot of ways. They were excited about it."[140]

In the week after its launch, Amazon logged $12,000 in orders, and $14,000 the week after that.[141] The novelty of online commerce was such that the company's computer terminals were programmed to ring when an order came through. At first, the ringing was entertaining and reaffirming. Bezos recalled that the computers would ring and "you would jump up and go over and look and see what it was. But then it started to be annoying." After a couple of weeks, Amazon's sales had reached a point where the ringing had become a frequent and irritating distraction. So the computers were programmed to silence the sound.[142]

Amazon was extraordinarily cost-conscious in its early days, and a strain of frugality still characterizes the company, despite its riches. Its desks, for example, were repurposed from doors and four-by-fours. Bezos built the first door-desks himself. Later, he arranged for a Seattle carpentry company to produce them for $130 apiece: $70 for materials, $60 for labor.[143] They are large and functional work surfaces, and not all that ugly.

For a while after Amazon opened for business in 1995, Bezos and the first employees packed books for shipping—on hands and knees, on the cement floor of a small distribution center he had rented. "And we did this for like two weeks and it was back-breaking work and our knees would be raw," Bezos recalled. "I said, 'We've got to do something about this. . . . We've got to get knee pads.'" One of the employees looked at Bezos as if he were from Mars and asked, "Well, what about packing tables?" Bezos said he "thought it was the most brilliant idea I had ever heard in my life. And so we did that, which radically improved things."[144] Bezos also said he would sometimes trundle the packages of books to a post office late at night.[145]

Sales in 1995 topped half a million dollars, but Amazon that year lost a little more than $300,000,[146] the first of many years in which the company did not turn an annual profit. Its focus has been not on earnings but on spending nearly every dollar it brought in, to establish an unrivaled presence online. To "get big fast" was Amazon's central objective.[147] And it did: in 1997, the year of its IPO, Amazon.com reported revenues of $147.8 million, an increase of 838 percent from the year before.[148]

From the start, Amazon sought to promote a sense of the outsize. Its website declared the company "Earth's largest bookstore" and said it offered one million titles. The assertions were more than slight exaggerations.[149] Amazon carried little inventory, preferring to order books from wholesalers after customers had placed their orders.[150] "We didn't have a million books," Kaphan recalled, "but we had a million titles in the sense that we could *order* them. We might find out that the publishers might take several months to get them to us. But in most cases, it would be a matter of weeks and we were always trying to make accurate promises about how long it was going to take to get something" in the early days.[151]

The Amazon.com of today was unimaginable twenty years ago. The company has become a giant of the Internet, the world's largest online retailer—"the everything store," as Brad Stone described Amazon in his book about the company and Bezos.[152] The buildings of its headquarters complex are clustered on the edge of Seattle's downtown. Amazon's annual revenues were nearly $75 billion in 2013, most of it from sales of electronics and other merchandise. It has more than 115,000 full-time and part-time employees. The company's first employee, Kaphan, has said that at the company's creation no one had any idea how big Amazon could be if it did succeed. "We had modest ideas about what was possible at the beginning," he said.[153] Not only did Bezos expect a far more modest company, he did not intend to call it Amazon.

The company was incorporated in 1994 as Cadabra Inc., a name taken from the magician's incantation, "Abracadabra." But Bezos soon realized that "Cadabra" sounded too much like "cadaver." So it was dropped.[154] He eventually settled on Amazon. The name, he told an audience a few years later, "has absolutely nothing to do with single-breasted female warriors" of mythology. Rather, he said, it was meant to encourage the association of "Earth's biggest river, [with] Earth's biggest bookstore."[155] For a while, Bezos had thought of calling the company "Relentless," to suggest unstinting attention to customer service. But Kaphan helped scotch that name. It was a "horrible" prospective choice, he said. "And I let that be known, and that's one of the reasons it didn't happen." Kaphan said that "both Jeff and his wife looked pretty crestfallen when I objected to 'Relentless.' And I think maybe that was one reason when he proposed 'Amazon,' he did it in such a way" that made it clear he was not going to entertain "any objections to it."[156]

Relentless attention to customer service has been a mantra of Amazon since its early days. In 1999, Bezos said at a program in Washington, D.C., that Amazon's vision "is to be the world's most customer-centric store," a place where "people can come to find and discover anything they might want to buy online."[157] But the obsession on being customer-centric has exacted a toll on Amazon employees. A few months before Bezos's talk in Washington, a former employee described in an article in an alternative newspaper in Seattle the sweatshop-like conditions of Amazon's customer-service department. Richard Howard said he had been a $10-an-hour customer service representative at Amazon.com for a few weeks before being dismissed for failing to fit in and meet the company's performance expectations. Howard's account, titled "How I 'Escaped' from Amazon.cult," described a humorless and inflexible operation that emphasized speedy response while discouraging imaginative interaction or engagement with customers.[158] He wrote:

> As a Customer Service rep, the half of your daily shift not spent on the telephone is consumed by grinding out responses to customer e-mail inquiries.

These can range from requests for help in finding a particular out-of-print title to suggestions that the company shove a particular policy up its corporate ass. One of the first surprises you encounter on the job is that you almost never respond to these queries from scratch. Instead you learn to troll the Blurb Index—a roster of pat responses, or "blurbs"—designed to address practically every conceivable scenario a customer might present. If a genuinely new situation arises more than once, there will probably be a blurb written for it. As my trainer explained, the use of blurbs saves Customer Service reps time and helps impose a consistent voice (in terms of both tone and policy matters) on official interactions with customers. Naturally, we were encouraged to tailor the blurb to fit the specific situation in question, as well as to disguise the more obvious signs of blurbosity. But to respond to the questioner as a person rather than simply a customer, to insert a genuinely personal—much less quirky, off-beat, or engagingly eccentric—tone into the transaction was deemed to be crossing the line and was emphatically discouraged.[159]

Howard also observed that "for all the well-intentioned idealism around Amazon, a sense of humor was in strikingly short supply there; people were too busy taking themselves and their corporate mission oh-so-seriously. Adding to this tone of quasi-religiosity was the unspoken taboo against any speech or expression (including gallows humor) that betrayed your lack of commitment to the long-term success of the enterprise; if you weren't prepared to stoically endure the present purgatory of low wages, long hours, and sweatshop working conditions for a shot at a blissful future of profitability and soaring stock prices, then you were best advised to head back out into the world of cynics and naysayers where you belonged."[160]

Amazon was the occasional subject of other barbed reporting in the late 1990s. Slate.com called the company "Amazon.con" in 1997, disputing its claim to be "Earth's biggest bookstore" and asserting Amazon's deliveries were no speedier than its rivals'.[161] *Barron's* described the company as "Amazon.bomb" in 1999, as the dot.com boom was fading. "Increasingly," the *Barron's* report said, "Amazon's strategy is looking like the dim-bulb businessman who loses money on every sale but tries to make it up by making more sales."[162] But such reports have tended to be anomalous over the years. More often, the company and its founder have been the subjects of glowing media coverage, a tendency that can be traced to 1996 and an admiring front-page article published in the *Wall Street Journal* just ten months after the company opened for business.[163]

The article gave Bezos and the company unprecedented attention, helped boost sales, and represented the ironic effect of old media spurring the rise of a new media entity.[164] The *Journal*'s article described Amazon as "a singular case in which the frequently hyped Web is actually changing consumers' lives."[165] Extravagant praise has been not uncommon for Bezos, even though it has long been known he can be a harsh and intimidating boss, given to what Stone called "melodramatic temper tantrums that some Amazon employees called, privately, nutters. A colleague failing to meet Bezos's exacting standards would predictably set off a nutter."[166]

Bezos seldom grants interviews, and when he does, it is usually to tout new products, such as additions to Amazon's line of Kindle readers, or to reveal that Amazon has been developing plans to deploy unmanned drones in delivering small packages to some parts of the United States.[167] Otherwise, Bezos makes himself remote from the news media—although he surprised nearly everyone in the media business by buying the *Washington Post* in 2013 for $250 million.[168] "Extending the big buzz-off to the press and the public is a tradition that Jeff Bezos has restored to the commonweal," Jack Shafer, a leading U.S. media critic, wrote shortly after the sale was announced. "The company's disdain for the press seems to know no limits." The no-comment brushoff, Shafer wrote, has become "the default response by Bezos and the company."[169]

Bezos's standoffishness has made the glowing media coverage all the more remarkable. And there has been plenty of fawning over Jeff Bezos. In declaring him its "person of the year" in 1999, *Time* magazine declared: "Every time a seismic shift takes place in our economy, there are people who feel the vibrations long before the rest of us do, vibrations so strong they demand action—action that can seem rash, even stupid. . . . Thomas Watson Jr., overwhelmed by his sense that computers would be everywhere even when they were nowhere, bet his father's office-machine company on it: IBM. Jeffrey Preston Bezos had that same experience when he first peered into the maze of connected computers called the World Wide Web and realized that the future of retailing was glowing back at him."[170] Bezos, said *Time*, "has done more than construct an online mall. He's helped build the foundation of our future."[171]

Wired magazine has said "Bezos may well be the premier technologist in America, a figure who casts as big a shadow as legends like Bill Gates and the late Steve Jobs."[172] In 2012, *Fortune* magazine named Bezos its "businessperson of the year," saying he was "the cerebral founder and chief executive of a $100 billion empire built on books."[173]

Built on books, certainly. But, more accurately, Amazon was built on a reality that began to come into focus in 1995—that the Internet, however chaotic it seemed, could be harnessed, could be made reasonably reliable and efficient for consumer transactions. Amazon was the first online pioneer to exploit the Web's merchandizing potential, to demonstrate that the commercial Web could be welcoming, dependable, and secure. Such virtues were attractive and reassuring to the mainstream populations who in 1995 were just beginning to find their way to the Web.[174]

Bezos and his company responded deftly to the newness of the Web and its versatility and power. In upending the book industry so unequivocally, Amazon demonstrated the Internet's remarkable capacity to innovate and disrupt. Amazon has been a seminal disrupter of the digital age, establishing and developing an expansive presence online that no rival has come close to matching.

Before Amazon.com opened its online store, before Netscape's eye-opening IPO, the first wiki went live and in doing so affirmed that the Internet could be a space for creative collaboration and collective knowledge-sharing. The development of the "wiki"—that is, server-based software allowing users to create, revise, update, expand, and delete Web content using only a browser and a text-entry form[175]—was an early signal that the Web could be more than an environment where, in the words of Berners-Lee, "a few published and most browsed."[176]

The wiki's best-known and most elaborate application is Wikipedia, the popular online encyclopedia read, written, and edited by thousands of people. The wiki's first use was more mundane: it was to enable computer programmers to write about and refine their techniques. The wiki's inventor was Ward Cunningham, a genial technologist and software programmer in Oregon who has called the wiki "a new way to write."[177] On March 25, 1995, Cunningham placed his technology on the Web. At first, though, it lacked a name.

"I started using it and I could tell that it was important," Cunningham recalled. "I had enough of a feel that I knew it was going to work. . . . I knew it needed a name, it needed a good name."[178] He said he thought of calling it "Quick Web," because the software allowed for rapid revisions. Cunningham chose "WikiWikiWeb" instead. He knew from his honeymoon in Hawaii that "wiki" meant "quick" in Hawaiian and that sometimes Hawaiian words were doubled for emphasis. The shuttles running between terminals at the Honolulu International

Airport were called "Wiki Wiki" buses. Cunningham figured that "WikiWikiWeb," though a bit odd, was more fun to say than "Quick Web." The alliteration of "WikiWikiWeb" was appealing, too, Cunningham said, and it evoked "World Wide Web," as well.[179] In time, "WikiWikiWeb" was shortened to "wiki."

Cunningham said he never tried to patent the wiki; he certainly made no fortune from his invention. He showed the then-new technology to a handful of friends and colleagues, one of whom told Cunningham: "I hope you patented this thing. It is amazing." While he saw the importance of the invention, Cunningham said he "also knew that I wasn't going to get any money from a patent unless I went out and sold it. I thought, 'Well, what's the chance of [my] selling this?' About zero." He also said: "I mean, if I wanted to sell rights to use my patent, if I got a patent, I'd have to go to an executive and tell him that I had invented a technology that would allow anybody in the world to write all over [his company's] Web site. And I thought, 'Nobody's going to pay to have somebody abuse their Web site.' So the only thing I could do is develop a community and accomplish something. So I devoted myself to putting it to work for my community" of computer-programmers, he said. Cunningham did concede to a fleeting sense of regret not long after developing the wiki. "I said, 'Gosh, could I have thought about it longer to figure out a way [to monetize it]? And I thought, 'Well, I am using it as a calling card. I'm presenting myself as the person who organized this, as the person who wrote this software, the person who made this happen.' . . . I realized that I didn't have any other option. There was no way somebody was going to pay me for it."[180]

Wiki technology spoke to the Internet's altruistic and selfless side, to virtues of cooperation, community, and collegiality. It helped ensure that the Internet would be something more than a place for retail. The wiki, Cunningham once said, can be thought of as "shopping mall—not."[181] The Internet "actually makes a pretty good shopping mall," he said. "But I wanted to . . . make it a creative space, not just a shopping space: a place where you could do work as well as spend money."[182]

In a real sense, then, the wiki was an affirmation of the Internet's fundamental ethos of promoting collaboration among users across distances and in a decentralized way.[183] In a way, it was an elaboration of a defining objective of Berners-Lee, the Web's inventor. "My vision," Berners-Lee has written, "was a system in which sharing what you knew or thought should be as easy as learning what someone else knew."[184] The writing and editing components of early Web browsers tended to be ignored or minimized by developers.[185] Without a hypertext editor in the browser, "people would not have the tools to really use the Web as an intimate collaborative medium," Berners-Lee observed.[186] With the wiki, Cunningham effectively confronted that shortcoming. The "editable part" of the Web "got left behind," Cunningham has said. "I figured out a way around that omission" in developing the wiki.[187]

Of course, flaws in wiki use can be striking. Collaboration online can turn ugly. Spamming, abuse, digital vandalism, and pitched battles over obscure arguments and interpretations all can be drawbacks to open-source wikis.[188] Few public experiments in wiki use proved more embarrassing, and short-lived, than the test-run of the wiki-editorial—or "wikitorial"—in 2005 at the *Los Angeles Times*. Seeking to enliven its opinion pages, the newspaper encouraged readers to go online to revise and alter an editorial about the Iraq War. It described its experiment as part of a "constantly evolving collaboration among readers in a communal search for truth."[189] What the *Times* got was chaos. Soon after the wikitorial went live, profanity and pornographic images defaced the site. Within two days, editors were forced to end the experiment.[190] Two months after that, Michael Kinsley, editorial and opinion editor for the *Times* and the wikitorial's principal advocate, was dismissed. He told his staff the publisher "actively wants me gone."[191]

But even open-source wikis are not entirely at the mercy of vicious online trolls. As Robert Niles, then editor of *Online Journalism Review*, pointed out, the *Los Angeles Times*'s wiki software could have been configured to reject images users tried to submit; a "dirty-word filter would have blocked most of the obscene language." And, Niles wrote, "a reasonably competent computer programmer could have found a way to force wikitorial contributors through the Times' website registration process, which would have given the paper a better way to identify, and thus deter, would-be vandals."[192]

A wiki's community of users can be effective in identifying and expunging offensive or superfluous content. Wikipedia relies in part on such collaborative oversight. In fact, Wikipedia's founder, Jimmy Wales, was caught in 2005 making repeated edits to his Wikipedia biography. Among other things, the changes downplayed the contributions of Wikipedia's cofounder, Larry Sanger, who in 2002 cut ties with the site. *Wired* magazine reported that edit logs showed that Wales had changed his Wikipedia biography eighteen times, "deleting phrases describing . . . Sanger as a co-founder of the site." After the deletions were exposed, Wales said contritely: "I wish I hadn't done it. It's in poor taste. . . . People have a lot of information about themselves but staying objective is difficult."[193]

Wikipedia, which was launched in 2001, has only conceptual ties to Ward Cunningham. He recalled receiving a query one day from Wales, who said the wiki seemed "pretty interesting for you guys. Do you think it would work to write an encyclopedia?" Cunningham replied, saying, "Yes, it would work. But when you were done, you would have to call it a wiki."[194]

If the rise of the wiki demonstrated the Web's potential as a collaborative and intellectual environment, the hours after the bombing of the federal office building in Oklahoma City in April 1995 provided a glimpse of the Web's potential for the rapid dissemination of news about major events. The attack in Oklahoma City signaled that the Internet was destined to be a medium of mass communication. By contemporary standards, the online coverage of the Oklahoma City bombing was halting and pedestrian. Emergent online news sites scrambled to report about the attack, which killed 168 people, devastated Oklahoma City, and stunned the country. The online operation at *USA Today* was just in its third day when the bombing occurred on April 19, 1995. The *USA Today* site was updated within ten minutes of the first wire service report about the attack. Within an hour, screen-grabs of television images were posted online. Not long after that, the site had uploaded a package of articles, photos, and graphic illustrations.[195]

Soon after the bombing, the site Internet Oklahoma had put up a Web page offering news reports, lists of survivors, and telephone numbers for hospitals in Oklahoma City. Jon Katz, then a columnist for *Wired,* noted the Internet Oklahoma response and wrote, presciently: "Inevitably, as the number of online users grow, online news will converge with a massive story, and digital news will become part of the media mainstream."[196]

Going online, though, was a maybe-someday prospect for many news organizations in 1995. Soon after the bombing, the *Daily Oklahoman* newspaper in Oklahoma City found its way to an online presence in a most unintended and unlikely manner. Late on the night of the bombing, Sue Hale, the newspaper's assistant managing editor, took a call from a young man from Internet Oklahoma named Matt Williams.[197] "I would like to put your photos and your stories up on the Internet," Williams told her. As Hale recalled, the *Daily Oklahoman* had been looking into establishing an Internet presence, but covering the bombing was such a demanding priority that going online was a remote concern.

"Have you any idea what I'm going through right now?" Hale asked her caller.[198] "I won't have time to send you stories. I don't have time to get photos for you."

"You don't have to do that," he said. "All you have to do is . . . after the last edition tonight . . . just put the stories on a disk and leave them downstairs at the guard's desk. And any photos you just happen to have laying [sic] around, put 'em down there and I'll build you a Web site" featuring the newspaper's stories and photos.

Hale consulted her boss, Ed Kelly, the newspaper's managing editor. "Do you even want to mess with this?" she asked.

She said Kelly replied: "Well, it would certainly get the story out to the world. A lot more people could see if it we did that."

"OK," Hale said. "We'll do it."

That night, Williams stopped at the newspaper's front desk and retrieved the material Hale had left for him. From a floppy disk, he uploaded *Daily Oklahoman* news reports. From prepress proofs known as "color keys," which editors used to adjust the color quality of newspaper pages, Williams scanned and uploaded photographs. The process and the product may have been crude, but, as Hale said, the newspaper "had an Internet site without having an Internet site." When the *Daily Oklahoman* established a full-fledged Internet presence in 1996, Hale was named the site's general manager. Her first hire was Matt Williams.

2

Terror in the Heartland, and a Wary America

Nineteen ninety-five is never very distant in Oklahoma City. Reminders of the year are not everywhere apparent in the small city steeped in civility and modesty, nor are they openly worn. But not far from the surface, 1995—especially April 19, 1995—is close, inescapably close.

On that day, the heart of Oklahoma City was ground zero for the deadliest attack of mass terror in twentieth-century America. The attack came at 9:02 that morning, moments after Timothy J. McVeigh, an embittered Army veteran of the Gulf War, eased a twenty-foot Ryder rental truck into a sidewalk cutout at the north side of the Alfred P. Murrah Federal Building. McVeigh parked the truck, got out, locked it, and walked away without looking back. In the truck's cargo hold, two fuses burned toward a payload of thirteen 55-gallon drums containing 7,000 pounds of ammonium nitrate and nitromethane racing fuel.[1] McVeigh had prepared the huge bomb the day before, with help from a former Army buddy and his principal accomplice, Terry J. Nichols. In the cargo hold, they arranged the drums roughly in the shape of a backward "J" to enhance the bomb's destructive power.[2]

McVeigh, who was twenty-six years old, thought that by bombing the Murrah Building he would teach the federal government a grievous lesson for what he considered a series of abuses—in particular, the fiery assault exactly two years before at the compound of the Branch Davidian cult in Waco, Texas. Nearly eighty people were killed there in 1993 after federal law-enforcement agents closed in on the compound to end a fifty-one-day standoff.[3] The Murrah Building housed offices of several federal agencies, including one of McVeigh's principal targets: the Bureau of Alcohol, Tobacco, and Firearms.

At 9:02 a.m. on April 19, the Murrah Building was filling with federal employees and visitors doing routine business at government offices. With no warning, the truck bomb exploded in a terrifying roar that was heard for miles. At first, the detonation was mistaken for a plane crash or a natural gas explosion or an earthquake. The blast's intensity ripped a gaping hole in the north-facing facade of the nine-story building and violently collapsed all the floors. Scenes of horror and destruction radiated outward from the devastated structure. Buildings across downtown Oklahoma City shuddered and shifted on their foundations. Structures near the explosion were knocked down or badly damaged. The blast's concussion swept the streets nearby, overturning cars, sending debris and plate-glass shards flying everywhere.

The toll in human lives was staggering and unprecedented for an act of domestic terror in the United States. Inside the stricken building, 163 people were killed, including federal agents, Secret Service personnel, and armed forces recruiters. Five other people were killed nearby. More than 680 people were injured, many of them severely. The fatal victims ranged in age from three months to seventy-three years. They included nineteen children—fifteen of whom were at the America's Kids day-care center on the Murrah Building's second floor, the windows of which allowed a view of Northwest Fifth Street and the sidewalk cut-out where McVeigh had parked the truck bomb.

Among the dead were Terry Rees Chumard, 41, a collector of Teddy bears, and Lakesha R. Levy, 21, an airman 1st class who had gone to the Murrah Building that morning to obtain a new Social Security card.[4] Donald Fritzler, 64, and his wife, Mary Anne, 57, also died in the blast. It was the day after their thirty-fifth wedding anniversary.[5] John K. Van Ess III, 67, was another fatal victim. He was to have retired at the end of 1995 from his job at the Department of Housing and Urban Development.[6]

Jaci Rae Coyne was one of the youngest victims. She was fourteen months old and loved the song about the Itsy Bitsy Spider, which her mother sang to her from the day she was born. "She would run across the room whenever she heard it. But she couldn't quite get her fingers to make the spider," her father, Scott Coyne, told the local *Daily Oklahoman* newspaper.[7] Baylee Almon, whose first birthday was April 18, 1995, was fatally injured in the attack. On April 19, around 8:15 a.m.,

FIGURE 9. A truck bomb tore away the north face of the Alfred P. Murrah Federal Building in Oklahoma City on the morning of April 19, 1995, just as its offices were filling with government workers and visitors. The blast killed 168 people and destroyed or damaged some 300 other buildings. (Photo credit: FEMA)

Baylee's mother had dropped her off at the America's Kids day care at the Murrah Building and headed to work. Baylee did not want to stay, her mother, Aren Almon-Kok, would recall.[8]

Twenty years on, the bombing's staggering irrationality and sense of loss it caused are still keenly sensed in Oklahoma City. The city's grief has eased but has never abated. That this is so is confirmed every year on the morning of April 19, when the bombing is remembered in a solemn ceremony etched in sorrow. The remembrance ceremony takes place at or near the site of the Murrah Building. At 9:02 a.m., the moment in 1995 when McVeigh's bomb went off with such destructive force, the remembrance service in Oklahoma City falls silent for 168 seconds—one second for each of the bombing's fatal victims. The silence is heavy and lasts nearly three minutes. It seems twice as long, at least. Later, during the memorial service, survivors and family members, many of them with tears in their eyes and in voices that catch and choke, read the 168 names, one by one.

The attack in Oklahoma City was the most brazen and spectacular act of terrorism in a year remarkable for the frequency with which terrorism intruded. Four days after the bombing, the elusive Unabomber struck for what would be the final time in an intermittent, seventeen–year letter-bombing spree. The month before the bombing in Oklahoma City, members of a Japanese cult attacked the Tokyo subway system with Sarin gas, killing twelve people and sickening more than 5,000 others. In early October 1995, the blind sheik Omar Abdel Rahman and nine other militant Muslims were convicted in federal court in New York City of plotting terror attacks and assassinations across the city. Rahman was sentenced to life in prison. In addition, a secret U.S. National Intelligence Estimate warned presciently in 1995 that Islamist terrorism posed a coldblooded threat to the country.[9]

The bombing in Oklahoma City was so deadly, horrific, and unsettling that it stood out among the episodes of terrorism in 1995. It projected consequences long afterward, notably in the rise of preemptive security measures that would become ever tighter, more conspicuous, and more commonplace. The broad and lasting effects of the Oklahoma City bombing lie not in awakening Americans to the deadly threat of domestic terrorism, nor in exposing vulnerabilities of American life. The epiphany was not of that sort. Rather, as this chapter will discuss, the bombing in Oklahoma City signaled the rise of a more guarded, more suspicious, more security-inclined America, and of what can be called "a national psychology of fear."[10]

As dimensions of the bombing became clear, the question "Why Oklahoma City?" was asked everywhere. It was such an unassuming city—a place, the *Daily Oklahoman* newspaper said the day after the attack, "where terrorists don't venture. . . . Car bombs don't kill children here."[11] As the newspaper's reporting suggested, it seemed so improbable that Oklahoma City would be the theater of such carnage and terror, the target of such a vicious and irrational attack. Amid the chaos that morning, individuals were thrust unwittingly and unexpectedly into the vortex created by the bombing. Their actions and split-second decisions were to shape and define how the attack on the Murrah Building would be remembered for years afterward.

It is almost impossible to think about the bombing and not conjure the image of the Oklahoma City fireman delicately cradling the battered body of a lifeless little girl. The photograph captured like no other image the senselessness of the attack. It did so in ways that words could not. The image was taken by an amateur photographer and was the result of a near-miss turn of fate.

On the morning of April 19, 1995, Chuck Porter, a twenty-five-year-old loan specialist, was at work in a high-rise about two and a half blocks from the Murrah Building. At 9:02 a.m., the building shook violently, knocking objects from desks and people to the floor. Through the windows, Porter could see a rising cloud of smoke and debris: the signature of a controlled demolition of a nearby building, Porter thought to himself. That might be worthy of a few photographs for his portfolio. With that in mind, Porter took an elevator headed for the lobby. He was going to go to his car to retrieve his camera. But en route, Porter thought again. "I don't really want to go over there for that," not for a building demolition, he told himself. He got on an elevator, going up. It had climbed three floors and Porter reconsidered again: he would go and take those photographs after all.[12]

From the car he retrieved his camera, a Canon A2E, and headed on foot toward the smoke, now thick and billowing. Glass shards were on the streets and the sidewalks. "Holy cow," Porter said to himself, "what is this?" He began taking photographs. The corner of Robinson Avenue and Northwest Fifth Street offered Porter a view of the Murrah Building. Its facade was nearly gone, as if some gigantic, diabolic force had come down and scooped it away. "That's not a demolition," Porter thought to himself.

Porter moved down the street, taking pictures as he went. He saw bloodied people who were staggering or lying on the sidewalk. He

FIGURE 10. The iconic image of the Oklahoma City bombing was of a firefighter cradling the battered body of a little girl. The image was taken by an amateur photographer and won a Pulitzer Prize. (Photo credit: ©Charles Porter IV/ZUMA Press/Corbis)

passed a man with a bloodied shirt pulled up to his head. He came upon a cluster of people tending to an injured woman. From the corner of his eye, Porter saw a police officer across the street, clutching a bundle. He was running. Porter traced the officer's movement with his camera and snapped a photograph as he handed the bundle, the battered body of a little girl, to a fireman. A split second later, Porter took the photograph of the fireman gazing at the infant cradled in his arms. The little girl was Baylee Almon, and, at the moment of Porter's photograph, she was dead or dying of her injuries. Holding her was Chris Fields, a captain in the Oklahoma City fire department. Porter knew none of that at the time. As if on autopilot, he moved on, circling the shattered building twice, taking forty-eight frames in all before returning to his office. He was not aware that he had taken what would become the defining image of the Oklahoma City bombing.[13]

Office workers in downtown Oklahoma City were sent home around 10 that morning, and Porter took his film to the one-hour photo-processing service at a Wal-Mart store. His photos were ready within thirty minutes. Porter flipped through them, mostly to see if they were in focus. They were. He called a friend at the University of Central Oklahoma, his alma mater, and offered to show him the photos.

"You don't need to waste your time with me," he told Porter. "You need to go and get those to somebody who might want to see them."

"Who?" Porter asked.

"I don't know," his friend said. "Associated Press, somebody."

"Who is the Associated Press?" Porter asked.

"They're probably in the phone book," his friend replied.

Porter consulted a telephone directory, found the address for the Associated Press bureau in Oklahoma City, and drove there. He found the place a madhouse, given the demands of covering the bombing. Porter was granted a few moments to show the photographs to Lindel Hutson, the bureau chief, and David Longstreath, a staff photographer.

"What could this kid have that we don't have?" Hutson thought. He nearly sent Porter on his way. Instead, Hutson said: "Yeah, well, let's take a look." He flipped through five or six photos before one caught his attention. It was of the police officer handing the little girl's body to the fireman. "I was pretty much stunned by that one," Hutson recalled. And by the next one, too. It was of the fireman, cradling the little girl.[14]

Hutson turned to Longstreath. "We're gonna have to have these," he said.[15]

"Do you mind if we use them?" Hutson asked. Porter said he did not, and handed Hutson the negatives. Hutson told Porter to take a seat and fill out some paperwork, giving his name and address and contact information. "We'll be right back with you," he said.

The photos were soon sent on the Associated Press wire to its newspaper clients; magazine and television clients were excluded.

Hutson returned and asked Porter, "OK, so now what do you want for these?"

"What are you talking about?" Porter replied.

"We will pay you for one-time use," Hutson said, "whatever you want."

Porter was surprised. "I have no idea," he told Hutson. "I have no clue. I've never done this. I don't know what you are talking about."

"But I'll tell you what," Porter said. "You have my name. You have my address. You send me a check, whatever you think is fair. Whatever you think is right and fair, you send me a check, and that will be good enough for me."

"OK," said Hutson. "Good enough."

With that, Porter went home. He thought his photos might appear the next day in the *Daily Oklahoman.* Porter had little understanding about the workings of the Associated Press. Within the hour, he learned much more about the wire service and its worldwide reach.

The phone rang at Porter's apartment. At the other end was a woman with a striking British accent who asked Porter if he had taken the photographs of the little girl and the fireman.

"Sure, yeah," he replied. "I did. How did you get my name?"

"Well, I got it from the Associated Press," the caller said. "Can you tell me about the fireman and about the baby?"

"I don't know anything about them," Porter replied. "I have no clue. How did you get my name?"

"Do you know what the AP wire is?" she asked.

Porter said he did not. Not really.

"Let me ask you one question then," she said. "Tell me how you will feel knowing that the photographs that you took are going to be on the cover of every newspaper worldwide tomorrow?"

"You're kidding," Porter told her.

"No, I'm not," she said, adding: "Mark my words, Mr. Porter. Any newspaper you pick up tomorrow will have your photographs" in them.

She was quite right. Porter's photographs appeared in newspapers around the world. The images were stunning, and they moved even veteran journalists to tears. The national editor at the *Philadelphia Inquirer*, Ashley Halsey, went into the parking lot after the newspaper had gone to press that night, and wept. "I have never done that before," he said later. "It touched me very deeply, because I have a child that same age."[16]

The little girl's identity was not widely known until the next day. That morning, Aren Almon-Kok picked up the *Daily Oklahoman* and saw on the front page, below the newspaper's fold, a compact version of Porter's photograph. She said she immediately recognized the little girl in the photo as her daughter, Baylee. "I knew that it was her," she said. "I don't know why."[17]

By the time Porter had taken his memorable photos, Timothy McVeigh was out of Oklahoma City, driving north toward Kansas, undetected and unimpeded. After leaving the Ryder truck parked in front of the Murrah Building, McVeigh had worked his way north and east on foot, zig-zagging through alleys and parking lots. He entered a long alley, about a block and a half from the truck, when he heard the roar. McVeigh was wearing earplugs and the buildings on either side of the alley offered some protection from the blast. Even so, the explosion's roar was deafening. McVeigh could see buildings wobble from the concussion. Shards from shattered plate glass windows rained down around him. McVeigh told his biographers that he kept walking, never looking back to assess the devastation his bomb had wreaked on Oklahoma City.[18]

McVeigh soon reached the parking area where, three days before, he had left his getaway car—a massive and exceedingly ugly 1977 Mercury Grand Marquis. It was a yellow sedan twenty feet long, with a primer spot prominent on one quarter panel.[19] The Mercury was so hulking that a previous owner had referred to it as the "party barge"—meaning that the car could be driven to a party and not be damaged were it to strike every tree on the way home.[20] McVeigh slipped into the Mercury to make his escape from Oklahoma City. The engine failed to turn over. He tried again and again, and finally the car started. By 9:10 a.m., he was on his way out of town, traveling north on Interstate 35.[21]

The Mercury was not bearing a rear license plate—intentionally so, McVeigh told his biographers, Lou Michel and Dan Herbeck. He "wasn't exactly eager to get caught," they wrote, but "there was a part of him that was curious to see how things would play out if he did."[22] The missing plate was an obvious invitation to police to stop his car.

About eighty miles north of Oklahoma City, McVeigh was pulled over by Charles J. Hanger, a veteran Oklahoma highway patrolman known for his unbending, by-the-book approach to police work. "He'd arrest his own mother for a traffic violation," a friend of his would tell a reporter for the *New York Times*.[23]

Hanger had little reason to believe that pulling over the Mercury would become anything more than a routine traffic stop. He flipped on the emergency lights of his cruiser, and the driver of the Mercury pulled over. Hanger opened the door of his cruiser and stood behind it, to give himself some cover should the traffic stop turn violent. "Step out," he shouted to the driver. The door to the Mercury swung open and the driver turned away from the steering wheel and sat on the edge of the front seat.

What is he doing? Hanger wondered.[24]

McVeigh, according to his biographers, was weighing options. Holstered beneath his windbreaker was a Glock semiautomatic pistol. McVeigh considered drawing the handgun and shooting the trooper on the side of the highway. Had Hanger been a federal agent, McVeigh would probably have opened fire, the biographers wrote. "But McVeigh had a grudging respect for local and state cops and sheriffs, and their right to do their jobs. . . . He would not draw his gun on this officer of the law."[25]

Hanger shouted again, "Driver, step out of the car." With this, McVeigh slid out of the car and walked toward Hanger, who stepped around his open car door. They met between the two cars. "The reason I have stopped you is because you don't have a tag on your car," Hanger said. McVeigh cast a glance at the rear bumper, where the license plate should have been. "I knew I did not have a tag," he told Hanger. "I just recently purchased this and I haven't had time . . . to purchase a tag."

Odd, Hanger thought: Why would he look at the bumper if he knew he had no license plate?

The driver had no bill of sale and no proof of insurance. As wretched as it was, Hanger was beginning to think the Mercury might have been stolen.

"Well, do you have a driver's license?" Hanger asked.

McVeigh said yes, and he reached for the billfold in a back pocket of his jeans. As he turned, the windbreaker tightened across his chest and Hanger could make out a bulge near McVeigh's left arm.

McVeigh gave Hanger the driver's license, which the trooper tucked into his gun belt. "Now," he said, "I want you to take both hands and

I want you to slowly unzip your jacket, and I want you to slowly pull it back so I can look under it."

As McVeigh unzipped the windbreaker, he looked at Hanger and said, "I have a weapon."

With that, Hanger grabbed the jacket bulge and spun McVeigh around. The trooper pulled his handgun and held it to the back of McVeigh's head. "Raise your hands," he ordered, "and walk to the trunk of your car."

McVeigh told the trooper as they walked, "My weapon is loaded." Hanger nudged his handgun to the back of McVeigh's head. "So is mine."

He spread McVeigh on the trunk and pulled back his windbreaker. McVeigh was carrying his Glock in what Hanger recognized as a suicide holster—the barrel pointed upward, toward the armpit. Hanger realized why McVeigh had told him the gun was loaded: he feared it would discharge accidentally while Hanger gripped it tightly.

Hanger tossed the Glock to the shoulder of the highway. He did the same for a sheathed knife McVeigh had clipped to his belt. McVeigh was handcuffed and seated in the cruiser. Hanger retrieved the weapons and unloaded the Glock. In the chamber was a Black Talon, a bullet known as a cop-killer.[26]

The trooper did not associate McVeigh with the bombing in Oklahoma City and might have let him go with a ticket, if not for the concealed handgun. Hanger drove the handcuffed McVeigh to Perry, Oklahoma, seat of Noble County, and booked him on the concealed weapon charge and on three other misdemeanors.

McVeigh spent two days in jail in Perry. Normally, he would have been arraigned on the day after his arrest. But the local judge, Dan G. Allen, had cleared his docket that day for a divorce case. And the day after that, Allen's son missed a bus to a band excursion in Stillwater, Oklahoma. So the judge had to drive the boy to the outing, which meant Allen was late arriving that morning, again delaying McVeigh's arraignment.[27]

By then, federal authorities had tracked McVeigh to the jail in Perry. Key to their doing so was the rear axle of the Ryder truck in which McVeigh had packed the bomb. The explosion blew apart the truck, sending the axle skyward, spinning like a boomerang.[28] It landed some 200 yards away, striking a small red Ford before clanging into the street. Etched on the axle was the truck's identification number, which authorities traced to Ryder headquarters in Florida. They quickly learned that the bomb truck had been rented at Elliott's Body Shop in Junction City, Kansas, to a "Robert Kling," one of McVeigh's several aliases. The body shop owner and two employees described "Kling" to FBI agents and, from their descriptions, a composite sketch was prepared. It looked much like McVeigh.

That's what the owner of the Dreamland Hotel in Junction City told investigators when they visited her. McVeigh had stayed at the Dreamland four nights, registering in his own name and giving an address in Decker, Michigan. Agents ran McVeigh's name through the National Crime Information Center database—and learned that Hanger had done the same two days before.[29]

That McVeigh was still in jail on April 21 was a stroke of good fortune. Divine intervention, Hanger later would say. The judge was about to convene McVeigh's arraignment, which promised to be a routine hearing for a first-time offender. That meant McVeigh was about twenty minutes from being set free on bail when federal authorities called, asking that a hold be placed on him.[30] Word spread quickly that a suspect in the bombing had been tracked down and was in custody in Perry. Some 300 people soon gathered outside the Noble County jail, waiting for federal agents and police to lead McVeigh from the building and into a waiting van. He was wearing an orange jumpsuit and was manacled at the hands and feet. His pinched features, military-style haircut, and the hint of fear that played across his face gave McVeigh an odd resemblance to a possum. He seemed to be surveying the buildings nearby for snipers. Shouts rose from the crowd: "Murderer!" "Killer!"[31]

The first public glimpse of McVeigh in custody was disconcerting: the bombing suspect was a white American, not a foreigner.[32] He clearly was not of Middle Eastern descent. For the two days after the attack, the prevailing presumption had been that Middle Eastern terrorists blew up the Murrah Building. The U.S. news media rode that angle hard, and they were wrong, a telling example of how news reports in the first hours and days after a disaster can be terribly misleading. It is a vulnerability the news media seldom seem to anticipate, or to learn from.[33]

Rumor and extravagant conjecture had swirled in Oklahoma City in the bombing's wake. Stephen Sloan of the University of Oklahoma, a terrorism expert who lived just blocks from the Murrah Building, was thrust into sudden prominence. He recalled being approached that day by an African-American journalist who said she heard the attack had been committed by "a black Muslim group." Sloan also said he took a call from a West Coast radio station inquiring whether it was possible the CIA was involved in the bombing.[34]

But suspicions fell most decidedly on Middle East terrorism, as speculation congealed with rumor into what seemed to be a plausible and urgent narrative.[35] Sloan, himself, went on CNN that night to say: "I think there's a real possibility that it was a Middle Eastern group" that attacked the Murrah Building.[36] Connie Chung, who was in her final weeks as a CBS News anchor,[37] declared at the outset of a special report from Oklahoma City that night: "This is the deadliest terror attack on U.S. soil ever. A U.S. government source has told CBS News that it has Middle East terrorism written all over it."[38] On ABC News, the network's national security correspondent, John McWethy, reported that "if you talk to intelligence sources and to law enforcement officials, they all say . . . that this particular bombing probably has roots in the Middle East."[39] On CNN earlier in the day, news anchor Frank Sesno said: "We have been told that a number of extremist Islamic groups have been traced to the Oklahoma area, and while there is no specific link yet [to the bombing], I've been told that they are among those who are being looked at very, very closely."[40]

The news media leaned heavily that day on familiar points of reference—on roughly similar cases of spectacular terrorism that had targeted the United States or American interests abroad. Among them were the terrorist attack that had killed six people at the World Trade Center in February 1993 and the truck bombing at the Marine Corps barracks in Lebanon in October 1983. The devastated Murrah Building bore visual similarities to the facade of the U.S. embassy in Beirut after it was bombed in April 1983. Beirut was an angle not lost on journalists. A *Wall Street Journal* story likened the attack in Oklahoma City to a "Beirut-style car bombing."[41] The *Daily Oklahoman* said the glass and debris littering the city's streets brought to mind "Bosnia or Beirut, not Oklahoma City."[42]

The suspected Middle Eastern connection was not a matter of invention by journalists.[43] Their sources bore no small measure of blame. Notable in this respect were the FBI officials who put out word on the day of the bombing that they were looking for three suspects, at least one of whom was believed to be of "Middle Eastern descent."[44] A *USA Today* report said that was the "only hard lead" to emerge on the day of the bombing.[45] The Oklahoma Highway Patrol issued an all-points bulletin for the trio, which was thought to have escaped the city in a brown pickup truck with tinted windows.[46] Charles Hanger, the trooper who arrested McVeigh, was sent to Interstate 35 to watch for suspects in the pickup truck. Hanger said he spent "a considerable amount of time" out there, but saw no pickup truck that matched the description he had been given.[47]

Later, CNN aired the names of three men of Middle Eastern descent who had been detained for questioning. Their names were flashed on the screen beneath the logo: "Bombing in Oklahoma City."[48] It turned out they were wanted for questioning in an immigration matter unrelated to the bombing.

The most stupefying, Kafkaesque encounter with fate on the day of the bombing was that of Ibrahim Abdullah Hassan Ahmad, a Jordanian-American. On the morning of the bombing, Ahmad had set out from Oklahoma City to travel by way of Chicago and Rome to Jordan, where he planned to visit his ailing grandfather and other relatives. Ahmad, who had lived in Oklahoma City for thirteen years, said he was unaware of the bombing until he reached Chicago, where customs agents confronted and detained him. FBI agents questioned him at length about his American citizenship, his religious practices, and his acquaintances with Muslims in Oklahoma City. His luggage, which went on to Rome, stirred suspicions, too: in it, he had packed electronic devices such as a telephone-fax machine and a video-cassette recorder, items that typically are expensive in Jordan. His luggage also contained wires and tools, which also raised suspicions. Eventually, Ahmad was permitted to resume his trip. Before leaving Chicago, he said, authorities at the airport apologized to him for his inconvenience.[49] Ahmad had missed his flight to Rome, so he was routed through Heathrow airport in London.

At Heathrow, Ahmad was detained again, strip-searched, and questioned for four to five hours. "I was treated like a dog," Ahmad said.[50] He was marched in handcuffs through the airport and put aboard a flight to Washington, D.C. His flight was met at Dulles International Airport outside Washington by federal agents who whisked him away in a van with darkened windows. He was read Miranda rights, and he "really freaked out," he later said. "I thought 'this is it, they are going to frame me for the Oklahoma City bombing.'"[51] Word soon leaked that Ahmad was being questioned by authorities. Back in Oklahoma City, trash was dumped on his front yard, he said, and insults were shouted at his family, who took refuge with friends. Ahmad was set free on April 21, 1995, the day federal authorities took McVeigh into custody.

The arrest of McVeigh and reports that he nursed grudges against the federal government opened a fresh vein of speculation in the news media. Suspicions about a Middle East connection were supplanted by speculation about a conspiracy of far-right-wing militia mistrustful of the federal government. A *New York Times* report said as much, four days after the bombing: "Federal investigators said they believed there was a broader plot behind the bombing and were searching for evidence of a conspiracy hatched by several self-styled militiamen who oppose gun laws, income taxes and other forms of government control."[52] The *Times* returned to that theme a few days later, in a news report that declared:

> Whoever blew up the Federal building in Oklahoma City used tactics that are strikingly similar to those urged by far-right advocates of "leaderless resistance" against the Government, according to civil liberties experts who keep track of militant groups. The idea was developed by two former leaders of the Ku Klux Klan and has been promoted by some of the self-styled citizen militias that have sprung up across the county. "Leaderless resistance" refers to the need to keep the planning of terrorist attacks confined to individuals or very small groups to prevent infiltration by the police.[53]

The militia connection was at best tenuous. Although McVeigh harbored extreme, antigovernment views, he never was conclusively linked to antigovernment militias. He certainly was neither a leader of, nor an activist in, such extremist groups.[54] McVeigh insisted that he, alone, had rented the truck in which he built the bomb; that he, alone, had driven the truck to the Murrah Building; and that he, alone, knew when the attack would be carried out. His accomplices were Nichols and, less centrally, Michael Fortier, another Army buddy who lived in Arizona and who knew generally about McVeigh's plans.

Nichols and Fortier were supporting cast, McVeigh insisted, and federal agents found both of them quickly. The belief that the conspiracy was small and amateurish rested on more than McVeigh's word: investigators had pieced together what amounted to a diary of the bomb plot, in the form of records of telephone calls that McVeigh and Nichols had placed in developing their plans.[55] They placed the calls using a debit card obtained using false names. And the nearly 700 calls they charged to the debit card revealed no compelling evidence of conspirators other than McVeigh, Nichols, and Fortier.[56]

But suspicions of a wider and more ominous conspiracy have never fallen away.[57] They endure in part because of the desperate search after the bombing for a suspected accomplice who, the authorities eventually concluded, was a mirage. The suspected accomplice was neither Terry Nichols nor Michael Fortier. He was known as John Doe No. 2, and he owed his existence to a succession of three artists' sketches drawn for the FBI in the days after the bombing. The first sketch was drawn April 20, 1995, based on recollections of the owner, the clerk, and the mechanic at Elliott's Body Shop in Junction City, where McVeigh had rented the truck. He did so under the alias "Robert Kling." Their descriptions of "Kling" were turned into a sketch of John Doe No. 1, which resembled McVeigh. "Kling," they told investigators, was accompanied by a man who had lurked in the background. The body shop mechanic, Tom Kessinger, said he had the best look at John Doe No. 2 and recalled him as a beefy guy with dark hair and a tattoo showing on one arm.

The sketch of John Doe No. 1 helped authorities determine that "Kling" was McVeigh and led them to the Noble County jail. The release of the sketch of John Doe No. 2 brought an avalanche of tips—and to the arrests of at least a dozen men—including a fugitive in Arizona, an Army deserter in California, a drifter in Missouri,[58] and an Australian tourist who was held at gunpoint in Canada.[59] None of them was the elusive suspect, and the manhunt came up empty.

As it turned out, the FBI's sketchwork was inexact and misleading. As Peter Carlson of the *Washington Post* later reported, Kessinger, the mechanic, never saw John Doe No. 2 from the front. Yet the sketch the FBI produced was a front view. Kessinger remembered John Doe No. 2 wearing a baseball cap; the FBI sketch showed him hatless.[60] A second sketch was produced, this one showing a cap atop John Doe No. 2. Not long afterward, authorities released a third sketch of John Doe No. 2, this one showing him in profile. But by then the first sketches of John Doe No. 2—showing him glowering and face-on—had been burned into the public's consciousness.[61]

The third sketch showed John Doe No. 2 in a cap emblazoned with a vivid flame-like or zig-zag design, not unlike the logo of the Carolina Panthers, a new team in the National Football League. Todd Bunting, a twenty-three-year-old Army private stationed at Fort Riley, Kansas, had such a hat. And he had been at Elliott's Body Shop almost exactly twenty-four hours after McVeigh was there.[62] Bunting went there with a friend, Army Sergeant Michael Hertig, who rented a Ryder truck for a move to Georgia. Bunting and Hertig were off-duty and wearing civilian clothes. Bunting had a tattoo on his arm, and he wore his Carolina Panthers cap.

The FBI found and questioned Bunting and Hertig, and theorized that Kessinger, the mechanic, had confused McVeigh's visit with that of Bunting and Hertig a day later, a phenomenon known as "unconscious transference."[63] Kessinger ultimately acknowledged as much after being shown photographs of Bunting wearing the Carolina Panthers cap and clothing he wore that day. John Doe No. 2, the FBI concluded, was Todd Bunting—and Bunting had nothing to do with the Oklahoma City bombing.[64] The FBI's theory explained away McVeigh's purported sidekick when he rented the truck. But it by no means did away with John Doe No. 2.[65] His specter surfaced conspicuously at Terry Nichols's trial in federal court in late 1997.

Nichols was tried separately from McVeigh, who was convicted by a federal jury and later sentenced to death. At trial, one of Nichols's lawyers, Ron Woods, claimed that authorities had nabbed the wrong suspect, that the shadowy John Doe No. 2 was McVeigh's real accomplice.[66] Prosecutors dismissed the John Doe No. 2 defense strategy as a red herring. But Nichols's lawyers sowed enough doubt at the trial to win something of a split verdict from the jury: he was convicted of conspiring with McVeigh and of eight counts of involuntary manslaughter, but he was acquitted of more serious charges of using a weapon of mass destruction. Nichols was sentenced to life imprisonment.[67]

The unending speculation about John Doe No. 2—and the notion that unpunished conspirators were still at large—led in 1997 to the empanelling of a grand jury in Oklahoma City. The grand jury took testimony over eighteen months and, in the end, endorsed the FBI theory that John Doe No. 2 was Todd Bunting and that Bunting had no connection to McVeigh or the Murrah Building bombing. In its report, the grand jury went to lengths to underscore just how improbable John Doe No. 2 was, and how erratic and uneven the witness descriptions of him really were. The grand jury said twenty-six witnesses testified that they had seen someone resembling the phantom suspect—but the witness accounts differed dramatically. Based on those accounts, the grand jury said, John Doe No. 2 ranged in height from 5-feet-3 to 6-feet-3. He weighed anywhere from 140 pounds to 210 pounds. He was slim, stocky, skinny, or muscular in build. He was white. Or Hispanic. Or Middle Eastern. Or Asian. His complexion was white, or olive, or dark. His hair color was dark blond, or red, or brown, or black. He wore a crew cut. Or his hair was two inches long. Or he wore his hair shoulder-length. He had a moustache. Or no facial hair.[68] The sightings of the presumptive John Doe No. 2 varied that much.

Despite the contrary evidence, the grand jury gave the phantom John Doe No. 2 something of a lifeline. It said it was unable to "put closure to the question of the existence of John Doe II."[69] Even so, it is puzzling how McVeigh's putative accomplice could have been so visible in the days *before* the bombing but afterward concealed himself so thoroughly as to remain at large since 1995. In that contradiction lies evidence that John Doe No. 2 never existed.

McVeigh's disavowal of John Doe No. 2 cannot be dismissed, either. In a letter to the *Houston Chronicle* in 2001, a few weeks before he was put to death by lethal injection, McVeigh wrote that there was no John Doe No. 2. His letter was written in response to the newspaper's inquiry about a claim by McVeigh's court-appointed former lawyer, Stephen Jones, that McVeigh had inflated his role in the Oklahoma City bombing. "Jones has been thoroughly discredited, so I'm not going to break a sweat refuting his outlandish claims point-by-point," McVeigh wrote, adding, "Does anyone honestly believe that if there was a John Doe 2 (there is not) that Stephen Jones would still be alive?"[70]

McVeigh and Jones were at odds throughout McVeigh's trial in federal court in 1997, and afterward they fell out completely. A key element in the dispute was Jones's opinion that McVeigh was a cog in a much wider conspiracy to attack the Murrah Building. McVeigh routinely told his lawyers that he had been the mastermind of and the prime mover behind the bombing. "There was no big conspiracy. It was mostly me," McVeigh was quoted by his biographers as saying. "The few friends who helped me were acting under duress, and none of them had any control over when I was going to blow up the Murrah Building."[71]

Jones, however, suggested that McVeigh was but a patsy[72] who lacked the training and technical know-how to build the device that blew up the Murrah Building.[73] In his book about the case, Jones spun an extravagant if unpersuasive theory that the Oklahoma City bombing was the work of a vast and elusive international conspiracy. "The real story of the bombing . . . is complex, shadowy, and sinister," Jones wrote. "It stretches weblike, from America's heartland to the nation's capital, the Far East, Europe, and the Middle East, and much of it remains a mystery."[74] Jones hinted—but offered no compelling proof—that Terry Nichols had met in the Philippines with Ramzi Ahmed Yousef, who organized the attack in 1993 on the World Trade Center. If Yousef "had used the Philippines as a base, and Terry Nichols had made numerous visits there, who knew who might have been recruited? Or whom might have recruited whom?" Jones wrote.[75] He added that, if Nichols had "gone to the Philippines to be instructed by Ramzi and his band in the art and techniques of blowing up a nine-story building— then mightn't he have learned another part of Ramzi Yousef's modus operandi? That it's always most prudent to leave someone else holding the bag?"[76]

Much of Jones's book was like that: provocative in raising questions but failing to answer them with compelling evidence. He speculated profusely and invoked the likes of Yousef and even Osama bin Laden to imply that a vast international plot loomed behind the Oklahoma City bombing.[77] But it was mostly disjointed conjecture—vaguely suggestive but unpersuasive. A "rhetorical game," as one reviewer wrote.[78]

The passage of time, moreover, imposes stern tests on theories of vast, far-flung conspiracies like the one Jones proposed. Such plots, given their complexity, are exceedingly difficult to keep intact for extended periods.[79] Mistakes and missteps are inevitable; conspirators can fall prone to disputes and rivalries. Incentives to explode the conspiracy from within can be many. The prominence of the criminal act— the bombing in Oklahoma City was, and remains, the worst act of domestic terror in U.S. history—attracts ceaseless interest and attention, adding to pressures on the conspirators. As time passes, a vast, far-flung plot becomes increasingly difficult to sustain and conceal. The case of Watergate, America's greatest political scandal, is instructive in this regard: the cover-up of the crimes of Watergate began unraveling within months of the break-in at offices of the Democratic National Committee in June 1972. Twenty men associated with Richard Nixon's presidency or his reelection campaign eventually went to prison for crimes such as perjury, obstruction of justice, and conspiracy.

Indeed, the absence of plausible evidence of widespread conspiracy argues powerfully against the notion of a vast international plot in the Oklahoma City bombing. As Vincent Bugliosi noted in his monumental debunking of conspiracy theories in the assassination of President John F. Kennedy:

> Perhaps the most powerful single piece of evidence that there was no conspiracy in the murder of President Kennedy is simply the fact that after all these years there is *no credible evidence*, direct or circumstantial, that any of the persons or groups suspected by conspiracy theorists (e.g., organized crime, CIA, KGB, FBI, military-industrial complex, Castro, LBJ, etc.) or anyone else conspired with Oswald to kill Kennedy. And when there is *no evidence* of something, although not conclusive, this itself is very, very persuasive evidence that the alleged "something" does not exist. Particularly here where the search for the "something" (conspiracy) has been the greatest and most comprehensive search for anything in American, perhaps world, history.[80]

Similar factors apply to the Oklahoma City bombing: A vast plot probably never existed. McVeigh, most likely, was truthful in telling his biographers that he initiated, developed, and pulled off the attack on the Murrah Building. Had there been a wider conspiracy, McVeigh's accomplices, Nichols and Fortier, would have had incentives to bargain for reduced prison sentences by offering up the identity of other conspirators. They never did.[81]

McVeigh was the remorseless ringleader. Nichols was his primary accomplice. Fortier knew about the plot but did nothing to thwart it. That was the likely extent of a ragtag conspiracy that brought about the Murrah Building's destruction. But for many Americans, it was just too ragtag, too improbable to embrace. The gravity of the attack in Oklahoma City—not unlike the assassination of President Kennedy—seemed to cry for a plot more substantial and a conspiracy more elaborate and sophisticated than misfit Army buddies angry at the federal government.

Public opinion polling conducted in the years following the bombing indicated that large majorities of Americans suspected the conspiracy went beyond McVeigh, Nichols, and Fortier. A survey conducted in 1997 for *Time* magazine and CNN reported that 77 percent of respondents in a nationwide survey thought other conspirators in the Oklahoma City bombing had yet to be arrested.[82] A Gallup poll conducted in 2000 on the fifth anniversary of the attack on the Murrah Building found that 64 percent of respondents thought others were responsible for the bombing.[83] Another Gallup poll, conducted just before McVeigh was executed in June 2001, reported that 65 percent of Americans thought McVeigh had not disclosed the names of everyone who assisted him in the bombing.[84]

Running down rabbit holes in pursuit of the likes of the chimerical John Doe No. 2 or of shadowy, international conspirators[85] serves to obscure the broader significance of the Oklahoma City bombing—that the attack represented a turning point in domestic security and security precautions for Americans. The attack did not usher in a period when bombings became "a brutal commonplace of American life," as the *New York Times* had speculated.[86] Nor did it bring a sudden awakening for Americans to the harsh realities of terrorism at home. The World Trade Center bombing in 1993 had accomplished that. Rather, the Oklahoma City bombing helped to mold and put in place a hypercautious, security-first mindset that encouraged the imposition of restrictions intended to thwart the prospect of terrorist attack, a prospect that often seemed vague, amorphous, or abstract. These restrictions became tighter and more obsessive over the years, especially after terrorists flew

FIGURE 11. A lasting consequence of the Oklahoma City bombing was the imposition of security restrictions intended to thwart prospective terrorist attacks. The far-reaching nature of the response was lampooned by Herb Block, editorial cartoonist at the *Washington Post*. (Photo credit: A 1995 Herblock Cartoon; ©The Herb Block Foundation)

hijacked aircraft into the World Trade Center in New York and the Pentagon outside Washington, D.C., on September 11, 2001.

The security-minded restrictions introduced following the Oklahoma City bombing were not without strong popular support. Trading a measure of civil liberties for enhanced security was a deal most Americans seemed inclined to make in 1995. A national survey conducted by the *Los Angeles Times* shortly after the Oklahoma City bombing found that 58 percent of Americans would be willing to give up some civil liberties if necessary to curb terrorism; 20 percent were opposed, and 17 percent said it would depend on other circumstances.[87] At the same time, though, Americans doubted whether law enforcement officials, even given enhanced tools to combat terrorism, would be able to prevent terrorist attacks in the United States.[88]

Striking evidence of the preemptive, security-first mindset came in Washington, D.C., a month after the Murrah Building's bombing. Before dawn on May 20, 1995, authorities set up concrete barriers to detour vehicular traffic from two blocks of Pennsylvania Avenue nearest the White House. The closure was ordered unilaterally, without public debate and without prior notice. It was justified under the Treasury Department's broad mandate to protect the president and his family. Although the closure had been privately under consideration for weeks, it became inevitable following the bombing in Oklahoma City. "It was really just a question of whether [Pennsylvania Avenue] was going to close before we had an explosion," the Secret Service director, Eljay B. Bowron, said, "or after we had an explosion."[89]

The move was prudent and practical, insisted President Bill Clinton, who likened the closure to installing metal detectors at airport terminals. Think of it, he said, as "a responsible security step necessary to preserve our freedom, not part of a long-term restriction on our freedom."[90] But the effect was to make the White House seem more fortresslike, and the president seem even more remote, even more deeply ensconced within a security cocoon.[91] The two-block closure was "a concession to terrorism that should not be made permanent," the *Washington Post* railed in an editorial, deploring what it called the conversion of "America's Main Street" to little more than a sidewalk. "Two world wars did not close Pennsylvania Avenue," the *Post* declared. "Neither did the Civil War or past attempts on presidents' lives. . . . The avenue stayed open despite a British invasion, and despite street riots in the 1960s. But now, because of the devastation in Oklahoma City, the history of Pennsylvania Avenue may be erased by bulldozers."[92]

The closure stirred extravagant rhetoric in Washington. Eleanor Holmes Norton, the district's nonvoting delegate to the House of Representatives, said the closure had left downtown Washington "dysfunctional and disfigured." Pennsylvania Avenue, Holmes Norton added, "is not a park. It is the major downtown east-west artery in the nation's capital."[93] And in a commentary written for the *Washington Post*, Rod Grams, a Republican senator from Minnesota, urged Clinton to reopen Pennsylvania Avenue to traffic. "We must not allow fear to claim the victory," Grams declared. "Dismantle the barricades, Mr. President, and may the souls of the patriots who founded this nation in freedom's name take pity on us if we don't."[94]

It wasn't to be. The *Post* from time to time renewed its call to reopen the avenue while deploring the unsightly clutter of concrete planters and Jersey barriers. But after the terrorist attacks of September 11, 2001, the issue lost momentum. Pennsylvania Avenue in front of the White House has since been landscaped to remove the Jersey barriers, but the portion of "America's Main Street" nearest the White House remains off-limits to vehicular traffic and is patrolled by police on motorcycles, on bicycles, and in vans. Twenty years later, that portion of Pennsylvania Avenue wears the obvious look of a closed-off street masquerading as a pedestrian mall.

The case of Pennsylvania Avenue signaled not only an embryonic security-first mindset but the emergence of the capital as a bunker: several streets near the Capitol also were closed to vehicular traffic in the summer of 1995. Concrete planters and Jersey barriers went up near other government buildings that were presumed to be potential targets of terrorists. An architecture of defensiveness became plainly visible in the capital, and its trappings—the barriers and the steel gates—have lent a shabby look to the avenues in the heart of Washington. Witold Rybcznski, a professor of urbanism at the University of Pennsylvania, has observed wryly: "We used to mock an earlier generation that peppered the U.S. capital with [statues of] Civil War generals on horseback; now I wonder what future generations will make of our architectural legacy of crash-resistant walls and blast-proof glass."[95]

It was the Oklahoma City bombing, the *Washington Post* observed years later, "that ended the capital's life as an open city. Suddenly, driving into a garage involved guards wielding mirrors to inspect car bottoms. Jersey barriers undid the designs of landscapers and architects. An architecture of fear came into vogue. . . . Defenders of the American tradition of openness cried out against the capital as bunker, but their arguments were usually trumped by the security officers' simple retort: 'Are you ready to risk lives?'"[96] The urgency of preemptive security easily trumped the aesthetic appeal.[97]

The effects of the Oklahoma City bombing went far beyond aesthetics in the capital. The attack revived antiterrorism legislation that had been stalled in Congress. And while it took more than a year, Congress passed, and Clinton signed, the Antiterrorism and Effective Death Penalty Act of 1996. The measure allocated about $1 billion to be spent over four years on counterterrorism initiatives, enhanced criminal penalties for terrorist acts, banned fund-raising in support of terrorist organizations, required manufacturers of plastic explosives to include microscopic markers called "taggants" to make them easier to track, and restricted habeas corpus appeals by federal and state death-row inmates.[98]

The measure also permitted U.S. officials to deport noncitizens suspected of terrorism or supporting terrorism—and to do so while sharing little more than a summary of classified evidence against them. Civil libertarians deplored that component of the bill. "For the first time in 200 years, secret evidence will be allowed in a U.S. court," David Cole, a Georgetown University law professor, said at the time. "It is impossible to challenge or refute evidence you cannot see."[99] That aspect of the law was of such dubious constitutionality that it has never been invoked.

Cole and James X. Dempsey offered a withering critique of the 1996 antiterrorism law in their book, *Terrorism and the Constitution,* saying the measure represented "some of the worst assaults on civil liberties in decades."[100] Cole and Dempsey pointed out that the law could be used to punish people "not for crimes that they commit or abet, but for supporting wholly lawful acts of disfavored groups." Had such a measure been on the books during the 1980s, they noted, "it would have been a crime to give money to the African National Congress, during Nelson Mandela's speaking tours here, because the State Department routinely listed the ANC as a 'terrorist group.'"[101] The antiterrorism law also "revived the practice of denying visas to foreigners based on mere membership in undesirable groups" as designated by the State Department.[102]

Clinton, however, praised the legislation as representing "tough new tools to stop terrorists before they strike." In fact, he wanted a tougher and more expansive measure than what Congress passed: he had sought broader wiretapping authority for law enforcement agents, greater access to telephone, hotel, and other records in cases of suspected terrorism, and expanded use of taggants in explosives made from black powder.[103] Although such provisions had been stripped from the bill he signed, Clinton had begun to prepare the ground for sterner and more expansive measures to combat terrorism—measures of the sort that were embedded in the controversial USA Patriot Act, enacted in the aftermath of the attacks of September 11, 2001.

Clinton signed the Antiterrorism and Effective Death Penalty Act on April 24, 1996, at a ceremony on the South Lawn of the White House. In attendance that day were survivors and family members of victims of the Murrah Building attack. A few of them wiped away tears as the president signed the measure into law. "While this is a good day for America," Clinton said, "you can't really say it is a happy day."[104]

Oklahoma City has not languished since 1995. Far from it. In recent years, it has ranked highly on comparative assessments of the country's "most affordable" cities or its "most recession-proof" places.[105] A key to Oklahoma City's renewal and vitality lies in decisions taken in the early 1990s to impose a one-cent sales tax to raise funds for building projects for the city's commercial districts and neighborhoods. The tax revenues helped build a minor league baseball stadium, a library, a museum, schools, and a canal that is a centerpiece of the Bricktown entertainment district, a short walk from the high-rise buildings downtown.[106] "Anyone visiting our downtown in the early 1990s," the *Daily Oklahoman* noted a few years ago, "would find it unrecognizable to the one they see today."[107]

The renaissance is striking and even a bit surprising, considering how the bombing so shocked and devastated the city. Its bold response to the attack lent a measure of confidence and quiet self-assuredness. Oklahoma City undeniably is a hospitable place where visitors can quickly develop affinity for the city and its people. That feeling is borne not from pity for what happened in 1995 but rather from the ready congeniality of a city that is not full of itself. The site of the bombing has been impressively remade since 1995. The hulking, bombed-out shell of the Murrah Building was brought down four weeks after the attack, in a controlled demolition watched by hundreds of spectators and broadcast live on CNN. The demolition took all of eight seconds. Afterward, many spectators wept quietly and stared at the smoking ruins.[108]

Since then, the site has been transformed into an outdoor memorial—a soothing, well-manicured place that seems almost pastoral, an anomaly in a city. It is hard to believe that the park-like memorial was ground

FIGURE 12. The site of the Oklahoma City bombing has been transformed into a contemplative, open-air memorial dotted with 168 glass, bronze, and stone chairs—one for each person who died in the attack. The empty chairs face a shallow reflecting pool and stand as mute testimony to irrecoverable loss. (Photo by author)

zero for an attack of deadly terror. Standing as sentinels at either end of the outdoor memorial are bronze "Gates of Times," one marked 9:01 and the other 9:03, designating the minute before the bombing and the minute after. A long, shallow reflecting pool shimmers in the midst of the memorial, delineating where Northwest Fifth Street used to pass in front of the Murrah Building. On the plaza above the reflecting pool stands an old American elm tree that was so buffeted by flames and debris on the day of the bombing that it was thought to have been killed. But in the spring after the attack, it sent out buds and then leaves. The elm soon came to be known as the Survivor Tree. It is a talisman, a battered but living symbol of the city's resilience. A likeness of the Survivor Tree has become the emblem of the nearby Oklahoma City National Memorial and Museum.

The site of the bombing is commemorated by what is called the Field of Empty Chairs. There, 168 glass, bronze, and stone chairs—one for each person who died in the attack—are arrayed in rows that roughly correspond to the floors of the Murrah Building. The empty chairs project a solemn and dignified ambiance, offering mute testimony to absence and irrecoverable loss. The outdoor memorial is a contemplative place, especially so at night when the base of each chair is softly illuminated.

For all its ingenuity and quiet appeal, the outdoor memorial is somehow anodyne. There are few obvious or specific references to the havoc and horror of the attack. There are no reminders about the perpetrators or their names. There is nothing obvious that tells visitors where McVeigh parked and locked the Ryder truck, fuses burning into the cargo hold. There is nothing explicit about the perfidy of the man who in his delusions dealt so much death and destruction at this site in 1995. The central figure in the 1995 bombing is neither demonized nor condemned—just improbably absent and ignored.

3

O.J., DNA, and the
"Trial of the Century"

Nineteen ninety-five produced two flashbulb events in America—
moments so powerful and memorable that for years afterward people
remembered where they were, and what they were doing, when they
heard about them.[1] One was the bombing of the federal building in
Oklahoma City. The other came on October 3, 1995, when verdicts
were announced in the O.J. Simpson double-murder trial in Los Angeles, proceedings that had become so protracted and at times so graphic
and repellant that they had spread like a stain across the year.

A jury of nine African Americans, two whites, and one Latino had,
on October 2, 1995, decided the fate of Simpson, a popular black football star turned movie actor and rental car pitchman who was accused
of the gruesome fatal stabbings of his former wife, Nicole Brown Simpson, and her friend, Ronald Goldman, both of whom were white. The
presiding judge, Lance A. Ito, deferred unsealing and reading the verdicts until the following day at 10 a.m., Pacific time. As that hour
approached on October 3, almost everything in America went on hold,
in an astonishing national vigil.[2]

To be in a position of not knowing the outcome was intolerable. So
almost everyone, it seemed, found a place near a television set or a radio
receiver to get the news of the verdicts,[3] which were to be announced
live from the ninth-floor courtroom in downtown Los Angeles where
the trial had played out since January 1995.

Nothing that day could compete with the announcement of the Simpson verdicts. Beaches near Los Angeles seemed almost deserted, even though the weather was pleasantly summerlike.[4] In San Francisco, truck drivers pulled to the side of highways to concentrate attention on their radios.[5] At international airports in Atlanta and Chicago, airline passengers refused to board flights and gathered around television monitors in waiting lounges.[6] The trading pits of the Chicago Board of Trade fell uncustomarily silent.[7] Boston was reported to be "strangely still" at the hour of Simpson's reckoning; business of all kind seemed to grind to a halt.[8]

At the White House, President Bill Clinton made his way to a secretary's office to listen to the outcome; he worked a crossword puzzle rather than watch the television screen.[9] Elsewhere in Washington, events were canceled or postponed so as not to compete with the Simpson verdicts. The State Department's midday briefing was delayed.[10] Senator Joseph Lieberman of Connecticut rescheduled a news conference. "Not only would you not be here," Lieberman told reporters, "but I wouldn't be here, either."[11]

Electric consumption climbed as television sets were clicked on across the country. Long-distance telephone calls dropped off. The communal-like anticipation on that October day was remarkable: no news event in recent American history—save, perhaps, the first lunar landing in July 1969—was anticipated by such vast audiences and characterized so thoroughly by uncertainty.[12] It was a moment of drama both unpredictable and absorbing, and shown live on television. The audiences awaiting the verdicts that day were more than merely curious: they felt invested somehow in the fate of an African American sports star and celebrity who long ago had transcended race, who once told the *New York Times:* "My biggest accomplishment is that people look at me like a man first, not a black man."[13]

The national vigil was an extraordinary close to a trial that had transfixed the country. It was a televised saga around which much seemed to revolve in 1995.[14] The trial, it seemed, was always on, always up for discussion, and inevitably smothered in hyperbole: it was called, and not without some justification, "The Trial of the Century," an epithet invoked both in irony and in all seriousness.[15] There were other outsize and extravagant characterizations, too. The trial was likened to "a modern day Greek tragedy"[16] and to "a great trash novel come to life."[17] It was described as "a lens through which we saw ourselves."[18] It was "the year's most ignoble spectacle,"[19] freighted with searing allegations of domestic violence, police corruption, lawyerly excess, and overt racism.[20] It was "the *Othello* of the Twentieth Century,"[21] the "Super Bowl of murder trials."[22] It was, wrote David Shaw of the *Los Angeles Times,* "a Bayeux tapestry of contemporary American culture."[23]

It was hardly surprising, then, that nearly everyone in America stopped what they were doing on October 3, 1995, when time came for the reading of the verdicts. The Simpson case had embraced those rare and salient features that make for an exceptionally high-profile trial: The defendant was well-known and well-liked, at least before the trial. The crimes were appalling and the victims were especially vulnerable; they had had little chance to defend themselves from their killer. Hot-button social issues, such as domestic abuse, police misconduct, and race relations, crowded into the case.[24]

No less important was multimillion dollar wealth, which enabled Simpson to recruit a high-powered legal team that went toe-to-toe with prosecutors for months, and usually got the better of them. The trial was notable, too, for the prominence it gave to an emergent evidentiary methodology, forensic DNA analysis. The Simpson trial was hardly the first in which complex genetic evidence figured prominently, but it was the first widely followed, high-profile criminal trial in the United States in which evidence about DNA—deoxyribonucleic acid, the complex and distinctive genetic material found in blood, hair, saliva, semen, skin tissue, and elsewhere—was a crucial component. At the Simpson trial, DNA testing was on display as never before.[25] As will be discussed in this chapter, the trial's most important and lasting contributions centered around DNA: the Simpson trial helped to settle disputes about the value and validity of DNA evidence and anticipated popular interest in the potency of DNA testing.

Precise data are elusive, but perhaps 100 million people or more were watching on television in the United States as the clerk in Ito's courtroom began to read the verdicts, the culmination of a trial that took more than eight months to complete, far longer than had been reasonably expected. It had produced more than 850 exhibits, heard from more than 120 witnesses, and generated a court transcript that exceeded 50,000 pages.[26] Yet the jurors reached their verdicts after deliberating less than four hours—far fewer than almost anyone had anticipated.[27] And now, on October 3, Simpson was told to stand and face the jurors. His lawyers, unbidden, stood, too. Simpson was well turned-out, but he looked slightly befuddled as the clerk read the first verdict, to the charge that he had killed Nicole Simpson: not guilty. He sighed deeply and

SPORTS FINAL San Francisco Chronicle

NORTHERN CALIFORNIA'S LARGEST NEWSPAPER

| •••••• | WEDNESDAY, OCTOBER 4, 1995 | 415-777-1111 50 CENTS |

'I will pursue as my primary goal in life the killer or killers who slaughtered Nicole and Mr. Goldman'
— O.J. SIMPSON

O.J. SET FREE

As whole world looks on, he is found not guilty

FIGURE 13. Americans held their collective breath on October 3, 1995, as they awaited the verdicts in O.J. Simpson's double-murder trial in Los Angeles. News of Simpson's acquittal made headlines around the world.

smiled slightly. To the second charge, that he had killed Goldman: not guilty.

The crimes that gave rise to the "Trial of the Century" were committed on the night of June 12, 1994, in the well-to-do west Los Angeles neighborhood of Brentwood, outside the townhouse of Nicole Brown Simpson where she awaited Ronald Goldman. He was a waiter, delivering to Nicole Simpson the prescription eyeglasses that had been retrieved outside of Mezzaluna, a small, trendy restaurant in Brentwood. She had dined there that night with family members, including her mother, who misplaced the eyeglasses that Goldman was returning.

The attacker nearly beheaded Nicole Simpson and stabbed Goldman repeatedly in the face, chest, and thigh. The victims' battered bodies were found in pools of congealing blood in the small front yard of the townhouse. A trail of bloody footprints and blood droplets led from the murder scene to an alley behind the townhouse. In bedrooms inside, the two young children Nicole had with O.J. Simpson slept through the savage attack.

Late that night, O.J. Simpson left his mansion in Brentwood and traveled by stretch limousine to Los Angeles International Airport to board a flight to Chicago. He had a promotional engagement the following day. Los Angeles police reached him by telephone at his hotel room in Chicago and told him about the slaying of his former wife.[28] He promptly returned to Los Angeles, was questioned by police, and was released. As the investigation proceeded that week, evidence increasingly pointed to Simpson's culpability; his lawyer, Robert Shapiro, agreed that Simpson would surrender on June 17, 1994. When the appointed hour came, however, Simpson had slipped away, and authorities declared him a fugitive, a "wanted murder suspect."[29]

Simpson was spotted hours later, a passenger in a white Ford Bronco driven by a friend and former football teammate, Al Cowlings. A phalanx of police cars followed the Bronco at low speeds across Southern California freeways, a pursuit that went on for sixty miles and was followed by millions of people watching on television. Simpson sat in the back seat during the chase, at times holding a handgun to his head.[30]

The surreal drama ended on the cobblestone driveway of Simpson's estate in Brentwood. Simpson remained in the Bronco for about an hour before stepping out with a framed family photograph in hand. He went inside his mansion for a few minutes, then surrendered and was taken by a motorcade of police cars to jail in downtown Los Angeles.[31]

The Simpson case was nothing if not *sui generis*, an anomaly built on anomaly—"a distorted example of American justice, in the same way the Playboy Mansion is a distorted sample of American housing," wrote David Dow, a journalist who covered the trial.[32] Susan Caba, another journalist, said "watching the Simpson trial and using it to draw conclusions about trials in general is like reading *War and Peace* and saying, 'Gee, this must be what all novels are like.'"[33]

Most murder cases do not go to trial. Those that do usually are concluded quickly; few of them drag on for months and months. Most defendants are poor and plead guilty; they cannot afford the high-priced legal talent that Simpson assembled in his defense, lawyers who cost him millions of dollars in fees. It was a high-powered team that included Shapiro and Johnnie L. Cochran, Jr., a black lawyer well known in Los Angeles for representing victims of police brutality. It included luminaries such as F. Lee Bailey, a trial lawyer who won fame in the "Boston Strangler" case in the 1960s; Alan M. Dershowitz, an appellate expert at Harvard Law School; and Barry Scheck and Peter Neufeld, authorities on forensic DNA evidence. It was a "Dream Team" of legal talent, journalists declared, a characterization more hyperbolic than precise.[34]

The prosecution—led by Deputy District Attorneys Marcia Clark and Christopher Darden—proved little match for the "Dream Team." By the close of the trial, Clark and Darden were exhausted and clearly overwhelmed by the defense lawyers, who had kept them off-balance and had effectively and shrewdly turned the trial into an indictment of the conduct, practices, procedures, and personnel of the Los Angeles police.

The Los Angeles Police Department was certainly a source of controversy and racial tension in the early 1990s. The brutal police beating in 1991 of Rodney King, a black motorist, was captured on videotape and shown around the world. Four police officers accused of assault and excessive force in the King beating were acquitted in 1992, setting off riots in Los Angeles that left more than fifty people dead. In the O.J. Simpson case, as well, police conduct was questionable from the outset. In the hours after the slayings of Nicole Simpson and Goldman, detectives scaled a wall and entered Simpson's compound without a warrant. They testified that a spot of blood on Simpson's white SUV parked outside prompted fears that there were other victims of the grisly attack. While inside the compound, a veteran detective named Mark Fuhrman found a blood-stained leather glove, the mate to the blood-stained glove that had been found near Goldman's body.

Beyond problematic policework, the prosecutors faced formidable challenges in making a case against Simpson. The killer's knife was never found. No witnesses to the slaying ever came forward. Simpson's statement to the police contained a few ambiguous hints of culpability[35] but was no confession. No murder weapon, no witnesses, no guilty plea: all were major impediments to proving Simpson was the murderer. But the prosecution did have considerable DNA evidence, in blood stains and blood droplets retrieved from the crime scene, from inside Simpson's SUV, and from the driveway at his mansion. Prosecutors theorized that Simpson cut a finger on his left hand during the attacks, and blood from the wound was left at the crime scene. Moreover, Simpson could offer no good explanation or alibi for his whereabouts during the time when the slayings took place.

Motive for the killings, the prosecutors argued, was Simpson's obsession with his former wife, whom he had stalked, beaten, and threatened on several occasions during their marriage and after their divorce in 1992. Simpson had been convicted of spousal abuse in 1989. He was, the prosecutors asserted, "a batterer, a wife-beater, an abuser, a controller."[36] They theorized that Simpson went uninvited and unannounced to Nicole Simpson's townhouse after 10 p.m. on June 12, 1994, and surprised her as she stepped outside to greet Goldman when he arrived with the eyeglasses. Simpson, prosecutors argued, stabbed her repeatedly and slit her throat after overwhelming Goldman, who also was stabbed repeatedly. Simpson fled, the prosecutors said, and returned home where the limousine was waiting to take him to the airport and the flight to Chicago.

Defense lawyers maintained that Simpson was a well-liked celebrity wrongly accused and framed by corrupt and racist police officers. Defense lawyers tracked down audiotapes made in 1986 that revealed Fuhrman to be racist and a perjurer. Fuhrman, the detective who had found the blood-stained leather glove at Simpson's estate, was heard on the audiotapes boasting about planting evidence and abusing suspects in other criminal cases. In excerpts of the tapes played for the jury, Fuhrman was heard uttering the racial slur "nigger." In testimony early in the trial, Fuhrman had denied using racial epithets. He was a rogue cop and a godsend to the "Dream Team."

Simpson never took the stand at his trial.[37] Even so—in a striking anomaly of an anomalous case—Simpson at trial was never very far from center stage, certainly not at key moments in the proceedings. He was a dominant presence in the courtroom, projecting "undeniable star quality," as one frequent observer said.[38] Simpson's words, actions, and lifestyle commanded frequent attention during the trial, sometimes spontaneously, sometimes in scripted ways. Rarely did Simpson recede into unimportance as the trial wore on in Ito's crowded and cluttered courtroom.

Simpson wanted center stage from the outset. Through his lawyers, he sought Ito's permission to address the jury in late January 1995, during opening statements at the trial. Simpson also proposed showing jurors evidence of scars, injuries, and physical limitations, to suggest he was incapable of committing the vicious attacks of which he was accused.[39] Although his request to speak to jurors was rejected, Simpson was permitted to roll up his pants leg to show them scars left by surgeries to his left knee.

A few days after that, a slapped-together book under Simpson's name came out and shot to the top of the best-seller lists, passing works such as Pope John Paul II's question-and-answer book, *Crossing the Threshold of Hope.* Simpson's book, *I Want to Tell You: My Response to Your Letters, Your Messages, Your Questions,* was a largely unrevealing, self-serving response to some of the 300,000 letters he had received since his arrest. *I Want to Tell You* was based on tape-recorded interviews with Simpson while in jail and contained his pledge, never redeemed, to give testimony at the trial. "Let me get in front of the jury," Simpson stated. "Let everybody say what they're going to say, then I'll get up there and say my piece—and let them judge."[40]

The book was a commercial success, selling more than 650,000 copies[41] and providing funds for Simpson's legal defense. It was most striking in its narcissism and raging self-pity. "The first week I was in jail," Simpson wrote, "I thought about Jesus being crucified."[42] He also wrote: "I felt there were three homicides. Some unknown killers murdered Nicole and Ronald Goldman; now the press was murdering me."[43] And: "My biggest concern is what all of this has done to me inside. I never really felt hatred before. But now I have, for the first time in my life. This bothers me."[44]

Simpson's tape-recorded voice filled Ito's courtroom early in the prosecution's presentation of evidence. The recording was of an emergency call Nicole Simpson placed in October 1993. In it, she pleaded with a 911 operator to send help. O.J. Simpson was at her back door, cursing and bellowing with rage. He pummeled the door, trying to get in. "He's O.J. Simpson," Nicole Simpson was heard to say. "I think you know his record. He's . . . going nuts."[45] The tape ran for fourteen uncomfortable minutes, filled with the sounds of Simpson's wild tirade. His words were mostly indistinguishable. As the tape played, Simpson muttered a stream of commentary to his lawyers. They seemed only to half-listen to him.[46]

In mid-February 1995, Simpson's walled estate on North Rockingham Avenue in Brentwood was center stage for a court-approved field trip by the jurors—an outing in a fourteen-vehicle caravan that also took them to the scene of the slayings. For Simpson, it was his first visit home since his arrest eight months before. He spent most of the time on the lawn outside his Tudor-style mansion, chatting with deputy sheriffs, his guards. At one point, Simpson ogled an alternate juror wearing tight jeans and long blonde hair. "Oh, man, look at her in those pants," he was heard to say. "I want to get at her. . . . Look at her in those jeans!"[47]

The trial's dramatic turning point found Simpson again at center stage. This came in mid-June 1995 when Darden, one of the prosecutors, asked Simpson to face the jury box and try on the blood-stained brown leather gloves that the killer was believed to have worn in attacking Nicole Simpson and Goldman. One glove had been found at the murder scene; its mate was found by Fuhrman, the police detective, outside Simpson's mansion.[48]

Facing the jury box, Simpson appeared to struggle mightily in pulling the leather gloves over the latex gloves he was required to wear to avoid

FIGURE 14. O.J. Simpson took center stage at a turning point of his double-murder trial. Prosecutors asked him to try on leather gloves believed to have been worn by the killer of Simpson's former wife and her friend. The gloves did not fit. (Photo credit: Reuters/Corbis)

contamination. Simpson grimaced repeatedly and in a voice loud enough for jurors to hear, said: "Too tight."[49] The gloves did seem small for Simpson's hands. But they likely had shrunk in the testing that they had been through. Still, the ill-advised demonstration had allowed Simpson to testify in effect, without having to face cross-examination.[50] It was widely recognized as a pivotal moment in the trial,[51] and it opened rifts within the prosecution team.[52] The bungled demonstration inspired a rallying cry for defense lawyers—an idiom familiar twenty years later. In closing remarks at the trial, Johnnie Cochran recalled the glove demonstration and told jurors: "[R]emember these words; if it doesn't fit, you must acquit."[53]

Simpson found another way to testify without facing cross-examination in the trial's closing days. In formally agreeing to waive his right to testify, Simpson stood and told the judge while the jury was absent that he "did not, could not and would not have committed this crime" and added before Ito cut him off: "I want this trial over."[54] Simpson's statement had an air of spontaneity, but he had rehearsed it with his lawyers.[55] The prosecution saw it for what it was—a dodgy move that allowed Simpson to insist on his innocence without testifying under oath. His statement was sure to reach sequestered jurors, through twice-weekly visits with their families. Marcia Clark, the lead prosecutor, was infuriated. She dared Simpson to take the stand "and we'll have a discussion."[56] Simpson did not respond and did not take the stand. He did not have to.

Simpson was at center stage in the trial's final act, the reading of the verdicts on October 3. He may have learned the night before that he was going to be acquitted. Jeffrey Toobin, author of a detailed book about the case, wrote that sheriff's deputies guarding the sequestered jury told deputies guarding Simpson that "O.J. was going to walk." They passed word to the defendant. It was, Toobin wrote, "the last leak in the case."[57]

When the second "not guilty" verdict was read in Ito's courtroom, Simpson looked at the jurors and mouthed "thank you." Cochran, standing behind him, clasped Simpson's shoulders and rested his cheek on Simpson's back in a gesture as much of relief as of celebration.[58] The prosecutors seemed dumbstruck. In the gallery, Goldman's sister Kim wailed in shock and disbelief. Minutes later, as the jurors filed from the courtroom, one of them turned and thrust his left fist in the air in a "black power" salute to Simpson.[59]

Similarly stark and contrasting reactions greeted the verdicts elsewhere in the country. Television footage showed African Americans celebrating Simpson's acquittal with hugs, cheers, and fist pumps—reactions that black novelist Dennis Williams likened to a jubilant "end zone dance" in a football game.[60] Such images often were juxtaposed with shots of white Americans reacting slack-jawed to the verdicts, in shock and dismay.[61] The disparate reactions were vivid and seemed to confirm what pollsters had detected throughout the trial: black and white Americans interpreted the evidence against Simpson quite differently. The clashing reactions to the verdicts also were interpreted as illuminating a yawning, race-based divide—as evidence of a lamentable state of race relations in America. The disparate reactions to the verdicts prompted much anguished commentary that America's racial divide was more profound than had been understood.[62] The stunning images "of blacks cheering while whites muttered or choked back tears when the verdict was announced chillingly captured the widening separation of interests that increasingly defines American life in the 1990s," columnist Ronald

Brownstein wrote in the *Los Angeles Times*.[63] An article in the *San Francisco Chronicle* said: "Contrast the black students from Howard University in Washington shown cheering the verdict with the stone-faced disbelief of white UCLA students and you have a snapshot of U.S. race relations in 1995."[64]

Richard Cohen, a columnist for the *Washington Post,* wrote grimly the day after the verdicts: "We are two nations—one black, one white. Yesterday, one celebrated Simpson's acquittal, the other did not."[65] The verdicts may have set race relations back thirty years, said David Horowitz, president of the Center for the Study of Popular Culture, a conservative think tank in Los Angeles.[66] The British newsweekly the *Economist* declared that the verdicts made clear "what so many Americans—and so many of their friends abroad—had not wanted to believe. Thirty-odd years after the civil-rights revolution, America is two countries, not one. And they are growing apart, not together."[67]

Such interpretations have been strikingly resilient. At the tenth anniversary of Simpson's acquittal, Toobin, who had covered the case for the *New Yorker* and wrote *The Run of His Life: The People versus O.J. Simpson,* said in an interview with the PBS *Frontline* program that "the only reason we will care about this case 10 years after, 20 years after, is what it told us about race in this country."[68]

But the lasting effects of the Simpson trial on race relations in the United States proved to be far less dramatic and more nuanced than they seemed in October 1995. Although it is undeniable that whites and blacks largely held conflicting opinions about Simpson's guilt, the verdicts certainly did not set back race relations by thirty years. The outcome of the Simpson case dented but did not reverse the trajectory of gradually improving relations among blacks and whites in America.

It is clear that perceptions of race relations in the United States suffered markedly in the trial's immediate aftermath. This is evident in two Gallup polls conducted in October 1995. In both surveys, respondents were asked whether they thought "relations between blacks and whites will always be a problem for the United States" or whether "a solution will eventually be worked out." Fifty-four percent of respondents to the survey taken October 5–7 in the trial's immediate aftermath said they thought race relations always would be a problem. When the question was asked again in a poll October 19–22 after the reactions to the verdicts had solidified, and just after the Million Man March in Washington, D.C., nearly 70 percent of respondents said they thought race relations always would be a problem.

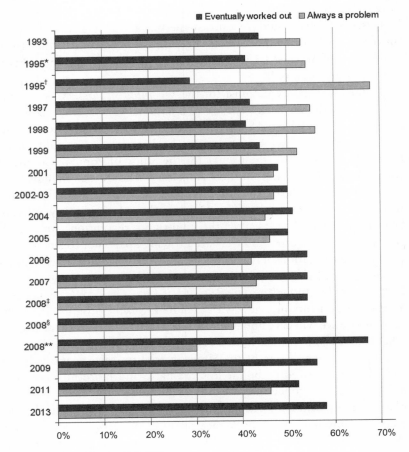

■ Eventually worked out ☐ Always a problem

1993
1995*
1995†
1997
1998
1999
2001
2002-03
2004
2005
2006
2007
2008‡
2008§
2008**
2009
2011
2013

0% 10% 20% 30% 40% 50% 60% 70%

*Survey conducted October 5–7, 1995
†Survey conducted October 19–22, 1995
‡Survey conducted May 1–3, 2008
§Survey conducted June 5–July 6, 2008
**Survey conducted November 5, 2008

FIGURE 15. Views about race. Americans' perceptions of relations between blacks and whites became more negative after verdicts were reached in the O.J. Simpson trial. But perceptions have become more positive in the years since then. Shown here are the results of survey questions asked over the years about whether race relations will "always be a problem" in the United States or whether "a solution will be eventually worked out." (Source: Gallup Organization)

That result would be a low point in Gallup's polling on that question. By early 1997, 55 percent of respondents said black-white relations in America would always be a problem. By spring 2001, the percentage of respondents saying relations would always be problematic had slipped to 47 percent. A poll conducted in June 2007 found that view was supported by 43 percent of respondents. In early November 2008, just after Barack Obama became the first African American elected to the U.S. presidency, only 30 percent of respondents said race relations would always be a problem. In Gallup's reading in August 2013, that response was 40 percent. Fifty-eight percent said "a solution will eventually be worked out."[69] Although fluctuations intrude in the polling data, the overall trajectory since 1995 is that perceptions of race relations have been improving.[70]

Other national data have suggested a deepening racial tolerance in the years after the Simpson verdicts. Notably, Americans' approval of interracial marriage has climbed markedly since the mid-1990s. In 1994, 48 percent of respondents told Gallup they supported marriage between blacks and whites; 37 percent said they disapproved. Ten years later, 75 percent of respondents said they approved of marriages between blacks and whites. By 2013, 87 percent said they approved. The deepening levels of approval, Gallup said, follow "the trend toward increasing racial tolerance on other measures such as voting for a black president and an increasing belief in progress and equality for blacks in the U.S. more generally."[71]

Moreover, Gallup reported in 2013 that 72 percent of white Americans felt relations between blacks and whites were "very good" or "somewhat good," sentiments shared by 66 percent of blacks. About 30 percent of all Americans said racial relations were "somewhat bad" or "very bad."[72] Black and white Americans differed sharply, however, in perceptions about the country's criminal justice system. Twenty-five percent of white respondents and 68 percent of black respondents said in 2013 they believed the justice system was "biased against black people."[73] Those perceptions were strikingly little changed from twenty years before. In 1993, 33 percent of white respondents and 68 percent of black respondents told Gallup they believed the justice system was "biased against black people."[74] Such clashing perceptions about equality of justice in America provide a revealing framework for interpreting and understanding the disparate reactions to the Simpson verdicts in 1995.

Even so, the anomalous character of the Simpson trial made it a weak case from which to generalize about a topic as thorny, complex,

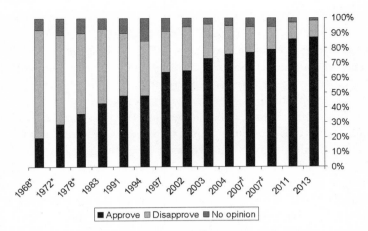

■ Approve ▨ Disapprove ■ No opinion

*From 1968 to 1978, the question was worded: "Do you approve or disapprove of marriage between whites and nonwhites?" After 1978, it was worded: "Do you approve or disapprove of marriage between blacks and whites?"
†Survey conducted June 4–24
‡Survey conducted September 7–8

FIGURE 16. Views of interracial marriage. Americans' approval of marriages between blacks and whites has climbed steadily since the mid-1990s and now approaches 90 percent. Only 48 percent of respondents said they approved in 1994. (Source: Gallup Organization)

and multidimensional as race relations in the United States. A single, uncharacteristic case that centered around a single, wealthy defendant who before his trial was little invested in issues and controversies of race simply could not have transmitted a widely applicable message about the state of race relations in America. And to argue that the Simpson case did offer a singularly revealing assessment about race in America in the mid-1990s is to ignore other dynamics of the time—in particular, the popular appeal of Colin Powell, the black former chairman of the Joint Chiefs of Staff and a hero of the 1990–91 Gulf War with Iraq. In 1995, Powell emerged as a strong prospective Republican candidate for president.

Powell was described as the "most popular American of any color."[75] There was much talk at the time about "Powell-mania,"[76] and news reports said popular esteem for the general had reached papal-like dimensions. He was characterized as "America's unsullied presidential candidate, a natural healer in a divisive era, a blank slate on which Americans can write their dreams."[77]

Powell's popularity was buoyed by a nationwide tour to promote his memoir, *My American Journey,* which came out in September 1995 to mostly admiring reviews.[78] The memoir debuted atop the *New York Times* best-seller list on October 1, 1995,[79] just as the Simpson trial was reaching its denouement. Powell's tour was closely scripted but still attracted large and diverse crowds of admirers—"black and white, old and young, affluent and unemployed," the *Times* reported.[80] Some of Powell's well-wishers waited hours in long lines for a chance to say a few words to the general and have him sign a copy of his book.[81]

The clashing narratives presented by Powell-mania and the Simpson verdicts were not entirely overlooked in the early autumn of 1995. Ellen Goodman, a nationally syndicated columnist, called attention to the contrasting cases shortly after Simpson's acquittal. "These two men," she wrote, "have nothing in common except their skin color and our attention. But these are names and stories that we attach to a tough ongoing dialogue about race. The country that looks at this verdict is deeply divided, an apartheid of perceptions, an America of separate realities. But the same country that looks to Powell is not blinded by color. It's united by overarching values and indeed longs for the reconciliation he personifies. The point is that both possibilities coexist in this best-of-times, worst-of-times moment in race relations."[82]

Goodman did not address the question, but she might have: How did one square the popularity of Colin Powell with the view that the Simpson verdicts had exposed deep racial divisions in America? An obvious answer was that the Simpson case was not all-revealing about race in America in 1995, that it was a misleading anomaly or an imprecise metaphor. (Another answer was that Powell and Powell-mania were antidotes, or perhaps palliatives, to the divisiveness of the Simpson trial. At the very least, as Carl Rowan, a nationally syndicated black columnist, observed at year's end, "1995 wasn't all downhill, racially speaking.")[83]

Powell's prospects seemed promising, were he to make a run for the presidency. A poll taken in October 1995 placed him ahead of all likely Republican candidates in New Hampshire, home to the first presidential primary election in 1996. Among Republicans nationally, Powell led Senator Bob Dole, by then an announced candidate for president, by 34 percent to 29 percent, according to a *New York Times*–CBS poll. He also topped Dole and President Clinton in a nationwide survey measuring such elements of leadership as integrity, vision, and values.[84] "The mania for Powell," Clinton's biographer recalled years later, "was driving Clinton to distraction."[85]

Powell, though, was ever-cautious and invariably hedged when asked about seeking the presidency in 1996. "If I ever do decide to enter politics," he wrote in his book, "it will not be because of high popularity ratings in the polls. . . . And I would certainly not run simply because I saw myself as the 'Great Black Hope,' providing a role model for African Americans or a symbol to whites of racism overcome. I would enter only because I had a vision for this country."[86] Finally, in early November 1995, Powell announced he would not seek public office in 1996, saying that a run for the presidency was "a calling that I do not yet hear."[87]

Judge Ito's decision to announce the verdicts at a specific hour[88] helps explain why the verdicts became a flashbulb moment of 1995. Designating a precise time for the announcement gave the lawyers and family members ample time to reach the courtroom in downtown Los Angeles. Designating a time also allowed anticipation to swell and ensured that the trial's final act would be closely followed and widely watched. It further guaranteed that *reactions* to the verdicts would be scrutinized as well.

The contrasting images of jubilation and despair that greeted the verdicts arguably were manifestations of pent-up anticipation, an upshot of a timed announcement. Scenes of jubilation among blacks and disillusionment among whites undoubtedly would have been far fewer had the verdicts been announced on the day the jury reached its decisions. Had the verdicts been announced promptly on October 2, there would have been little time for disparate reactions to congeal or crystallize in a communal, highly visible manner. The black-white reactions would not have been so striking or prominent. Without the timed announcement, the contrasting reactions to Simpson's guilt or innocence would not have burst so dramatically into view as they did on October 3.

The images of joyous blacks and dumbfounded whites in some ways masked a more subtle reality: the reactions suggested, said Peter Arenella, a UCLA law professor and a widely quoted observer of the trial, that racial solidarity was more pronounced than it was.[89] "I think it's an exaggeration to say all African Americans were happy with the verdict or all whites were upset with the verdict," Arenella said on the tenth anniversary of the trial.[90] Not all whites felt that Simpson had cheated justice. Many whites believed the prosecution failed to present a persuasive, airtight case that overcame reasonable doubt. Simpson may well have killed his former wife and her friend, but the prosecution had not overcome the deficiencies that defense lawyers so frequently identified, especially in the sloppy collection, handling, and processing of DNA evidence.[91]

Arenella said the elation among African Americans did not necessarily mean they believed Simpson innocent. Nor were all blacks cheering acquittal, Arenella said, adding that some of them believed Simpson guilty but were pleased that a racially mixed jury had expressed its distrust of police authority and did not embrace police misconduct.[92] At least some of the cheering on October 3, 1995, was for the reprimand the jury had so sharply delivered to the Los Angeles police.

Arenella's nuanced interpretation finds some support in a close reading of news accounts about the verdicts. The *New York Times,* for example, noted in a report published the day after the verdicts that "there were more than a few black people who said yesterday that they thought Mr. Simpson was guilty, and a larger number of whites said they believed there was a reasonable doubt" in the case.[93] "I think he's guilty. I suspect a lot of black folks think that he's guilty—know he's guilty," Syrie Fried told a reporter for the *Philadelphia Inquirer.* Fried, a former public defender who is African American, was further quoted as saying: "I always thought there would be a conviction in this case. But I could understand why a jury would acquit" Simpson.[94]

The jurors, notably, were adamant that race and racial issues were not decisive to their thinking or to the verdicts they reached. Doubt shaped their verdicts, they said, not race. Indeed, some jurors bristled at suggestions that race had to have been the defining factor. "We didn't even get to that issue," said one of the jurors, Brenda Moran.[95] Simpson, she said, "was not guilty. It was not proven. I didn't have enough evidence to convince me he was guilty."[96] Moran also invoked the prosecution's ill-advised request to Simpson during the trial to try on the leather gloves. "In plain English, the gloves didn't fit," she said.[97]

Interestingly, reactions were quite subdued—and without prominent black-white division—when verdicts were announced at Simpson's civil trial in Los Angeles in 1997. He was found responsible for the deaths of his former wife and Goldman, and ordered to pay their estates a total of $33.5 million. The civil verdicts were announced February 4, 1997, a few hours after they were reached. News of the verdicts that evening overshadowed Clinton's State of the Union address, but they produced nothing akin to the vivid and disparate reactions to Simpson's acquittal in 1995.[98] "This time," said a *New York Times* article, "almost no one erupted in ecstatic cheers or gasped in stunned dismay. This time, almost no one seemed surprised."[99]

Nor was there an outcry—or even much public interest at all—when Simpson was convicted at a criminal trial in Las Vegas in 2008 on twelve charges of armed robbery and kidnapping—a verdict returned, coincidentally, thirteen years to the day of his acquittal in Ito's courtroom. Simpson was sentenced to prison for a maximum of thirty-three years and incarcerated at Lovelock Correctional Center near Reno. The absence of protests and the few demonstrations of support in Simpson's favor were striking. "In 1995," a writer for the *New York Times* observed, "Simpson was a *cause célèbre* for many blacks who viewed him as suffering a raw deal from a racist judicial system. This time, not a single black activist in Las Vegas picketed, protested or even commented on the case."[100] Few people cared much about Simpson's fate.

To evaluate the Simpson verdicts of 1995 principally through a lens of race relations is to discount what perhaps was the most decisive factor in the case: Simpson's multimillion dollar wealth, which allowed his cadre of lawyers to even out the adversarial relationship with the state. Simpson's wealth allowed him to put on a defense the likes of which few murder defendants could ever hope to mount. The aggressive, confrontational strategy his lawyers developed may not have been lofty or inspired. But it was devastatingly effective. Without Simpson's wealth, that strategy would have remained theoretical.[101] "What this verdict tells you," Arenella said after the verdicts were returned, "is that the quality of justice depends on how much money you spend to hire the best lawyers, and how much you can match the power of the state by sewing up the best experts to fight."[102]

Simpson, too, was aware that his wealth was a decisive factor. "If I didn't have some money, I would have no chance at all," he stated in his 1995 book, *I Want to Tell You*. "I wouldn't be able to afford all these people" on his legal team.[103] The American public also recognized the decisiveness of wealth. A Gallup poll reported that 73 percent of Americans thought Simpson would have been found guilty had he not been rich; only 19 percent thought he would have been acquitted.[104] "Poor people's justice is different from what O.J. Simpson" experienced in 1995, Abbe Smith, then deputy director of Harvard University's Criminal Justice Institute, said as the trial closed. "I think people in this country have always thought that rich people get a different quality of justice in this country than poor people."[105]

Poor people's justice would never have mustered the challenge to forensic DNA evidence that Simpson's lawyers mounted so successfully. The DNA evidence pointed overwhelmingly to his guilt, but what

Simpson's legal team presented in court was a kind of road map for challenging such evidence. To be sure, the presentation of DNA evidence at the trial was grueling, tedious, and often snooze-inducing. Dramatic it usually was not. The intricacies and arcana of DNA typing were not readily grasped by the jury or the public.

But in what was another anomaly of an anomalous case, those tedious hours were to bear the most lasting significance. The trial's lasting importance was not in what it may have suggested about race relations in late-twentieth-century America, nor in the insights it may have offered about the effects of wealth in criminal justice. The "Trial of the Century" exerted little lasting impact on American jurisprudence and legal doctrine.[106] Instead, the trial's most significant contributions were to forensic DNA analysis, to introduce the promise and benefits of genetic evidence to mainstream American culture. Through the Simpson case, the American public gained a measure of familiarity with forensic DNA testing that was to deepen in the years after 1995.

The trial marked a delineation in the recognition of forensic DNA testing as decisive in criminal trials, and Simpson's acquittal encouraged a push for improved procedures in collecting, storing, processing, and analyzing DNA evidence. "We've come a long way since O.J.," Laurie Levenson, a Loyola Law School professor who helped analyze the trial for ABC News, said in 2002. "We've become accustomed to DNA evidence and it's not as controversial anymore. It's become one of the most valuable pieces of evidence you can have."[107]

It came as little surprise that the trial would bring unprecedented scrutiny to forensic DNA evidence. The scrutiny had been widely anticipated. "In the Simpson trial," a *Wall Street Journal* report stated in early January 1995, "DNA testing will be subjected to the most intense public scrutiny ever focused on a forensic procedure."[108] Similarly, an article in the *New York Times* speculated that the trial would become "something of a landmark for forensic science."[109]

Odd as it may seem these days, DNA evidence in the years before the Simpson trial was intensely debated and the subject of no small controversy. Disputes flared in the late 1980s and continued into the 1990s in what were called the "DNA Wars." At issue principally was whether DNA tests were sufficiently sensitive to distinguish among people sharing similar DNA patterns; also at issue was which scientific communities had the appropriate expertise to assess the validity of DNA testing.[110]

In late October 1994, as the start of the Simpson trial drew nearer, two leading protagonists in the "DNA Wars" jointly called a truce, declaring in an article in the journal *Nature* that there is "no remaining problem that should prevent the full use of DNA evidence in any court." The protagonists, Eric S. Lander, a molecular biologist at the Massachusetts Institute of Technology,[111] and Bruce Budowle, a forensic scientist at the FBI, declared that DNA typing "is soundly rooted in molecular biology" and that the DNA Wars should be declared over.[112] Their article opened with a reference to the coming Simpson trial, saying the proceedings would likely offer "the most detailed course in molecular genetics ever taught to the U.S. people."[113]

Significantly, Simpson's lawyers neither challenged nor attacked the *science* of forensic DNA analysis. They accepted it. Instead, they went after the sloppy and imprecise ways in which the Los Angeles police had gathered, stored, and processed the DNA evidence in the Simpson case. That they did not challenge the science lent tacit confirmation to the Lander–Budowle thesis that the DNA Wars had ended, that the time had come "to recognize that forensic DNA typing has become a mature field."[114]

The defense strategy thus signaled a high-profile affirmation of the relevance of DNA evidence in criminal trials. As Barry Scheck later observed, Simpson's lawyers "never attacked the validity of DNA technology, because it's a valid technology, it's a revolutionary technology."[115] But in pointing to the lapses in gathering DNA evidence, the Simpson defense team demonstrated that evidence collection had not caught up to the science. As Scheck noted in an interview several years after the trial, "They were using nineteenth-century evidence collection techniques for twenty-first century technology, which had more than the potential, but the reality, of producing contaminated results."[116]

During cross-examination at the trial, Scheck extracted acknowledgments by Los Angeles police criminalists that they had mishandled or overlooked DNA evidence at the crime scene. They had placed DNA evidence inside plastic bags, where it was prone to degradation. DNA samples were placed in a police evidence van that lacked air-conditioning. Crucial blood evidence was collected at the gate near Nicole Simpson's townhouse three weeks after the killings. A portion of a reference sample of O.J. Simpson's blood was spilled at the police laboratory where DNA evidence samples were tested.[117] The prosecution's most damning evidence against Simspon became its bane.

The missteps and the evidence-gathering irregularities allowed Simpson's lawyers not only to impugn and neutralize the prosecution's best evidence; it allowed them to claim that the evidence had been tampered with in a brazen attempt to frame the defendant. Such claims seemed far-fetched and were unsubstantiated by direct evidence, but they were not altogether implausible, given the extent of police bungling. In any case, the DNA evidence collected in the Simpson case was too suspect and unreliable to support a conviction; guilty verdicts became all the more improbable.

The work of Simpson's defense team offered lessons for forensic laboratories around the world about the sorts of practices to avoid.[118] An upshot, then, of the Simpson trial was to encourage improvements in the methodology of collecting DNA evidence. A brochure was produced for law enforcement officers describing the techniques for proper collection and handling of DNA evidence.[119] Scheck has claimed that the defense strategy to attack the collection, processing, and testing of the DNA samples in the Simpson case "actually changed forensic science in a very profound way," as it underscored "that if you're going to get anything out of DNA testing you have to collect the evidence correctly, you have to make sure that the labs are handling it correctly, so that you don't screw up these results." The trial made clear, Scheck said, that proper techniques of "collection and handling of this evidence [are] essential to getting reliable results."[120]

The trial's focus on DNA anticipated and perhaps stimulated broad popular interest in DNA and its seemingly wondrous capabilities. Prime-time television series such as *CSI: Crime Scene Investigation* and its spinoffs draw on techniques of DNA collection and testing and have elevated the work to a dramatic and decisive level. Such portrayals of criminalists and detectives have been criticized for simplifying and minimizing the intricacies of forensic analysis,[121] but the shows are undeniably popular.[122] The CSI team invariably solves the baffling and horrific crime within the program's hour-long time slot. "People had an idea about what forensic science was, although they were a little confused at the O.J. trial," Anthony Zuicker, the creative and executive producer of *CSI: Crime Scene Investigation,* has said. "We found a way to make it sexy and educational and fun. And people now know what DNA and blood splatter are."[123]

The challenges Simpson's lawyers posed to forensic evidence collection in the 1995 case clearly inspired a *CSI* episode that aired in October 2002, on the seventh anniversary of Simpson's acquittal. The show, titled "The Accused Is Entitled," was about a shaggy-haired young movie star named Tom Haviland, played by actor Chad Michael Murray, who was accused of fatally stabbing two fans in a sexual encounter in his hotel suite. Haviland hired a high-profile lawyer and a veteran criminalist who turned up flaws and deficiencies in the CSI team's evidence-gathering procedures and in effect put the team on trial. "They're beating our heads in," one team member complained after enduring a grilling in court. "Judge is going to dismiss; you can feel it." The drama was quite over the top, but the parallels to the Simpson case were frequent, amusing, and impossible to miss.

Unlike the outcomes that typify *CSI* programs, forensic DNA evidence implicated Simpson but failed to convict him. By the end of the trial, Simpson's acquittal was predictable—or should have been—given how effectively his lawyers had shredded the prosecution's case and had injected serious doubts about the integrity of the DNA evidence. Considering the impugned quality of the evidence, the jury reached verdicts that were supportable, certainly, and probably inevitable.

Simpson's acquittal brought no exoneration, however. His conviction, such as it was, was left to the court of public opinion and to a controversial effect, abetted by television coverage, known as the "13th juror."[124] The television camera in Ito's courtroom allowed millions of Americans to follow the Simpson proceedings and enabled them to form judgments that were sharper and more insightful than if they had been restricted only to news reports about the trial.

Television was assailed in the Simpson case for many sins—prolonging the trial and encouraging lawyers and witnesses to grandstand and play to the camera, among them.[125] Critics also say that televised trials offer a mistaken sense of presence, that the camera is a very poor substitute for being in the courtroom.[126] However imperfectly, the camera's unblinking eye helped to establish the public as a 13th juror, decisive in the court of public opinion. The popular verdict, which has proven unshakeable over the years, was that Simpson killed his former wife and Goldman. No plausible suspect other than O.J. Simpson has emerged, and the not-guilty verdicts of October 1995 could not contradict that conclusion. Simpson became a pariah despite his acquittal. He would never recover the popular esteem he enjoyed before the trial.[127]

Within an hour of the reading of the verdicts, Simpson was on his way home, riding in a white van and pursued by news helicopters in a vague replay of the low-speed highway pursuit that preceded his arrest in June 1994, 473 days earlier. Simpson spent the evening at his mansion, where friends and family gathered to drink champagne and celebrate the verdicts. "It was all on television," *Vanity Fair* writer Dominick Dunne noted. "Women in pink pantsuits waved champagne toasts to the media. Everyone hugged. . . . Jubilation reigned."[128] Earlier, at an impromptu news conference in Ito's courtroom, Simpson's son by his first marriage had taken the floor to read a statement for his father. In it, O. J. Simpson pledged to "pursue as my primary goal in life the killer or killers who slaughtered Nicole and Mr. Goldman. They are out there somewhere."[129] It was a gratuitous and narcissistic vow that insulted the angry and grieving families of the victims. It was a vow that Simpson has never kept.

Interestingly, the landmarks closely associated with the Simpson case—the places in Brentwood mentioned so often during the trial—were scrubbed of their former identities, as if to purge their associations with the "Trial of the Century." People in Brentwood do not much like talking about the case, said Jeff Hall, editor of the local *Brentwood News*. Simpson, he said, used to be well liked in Brentwood. He was approachable and friendly, and relished the attention he received. Nowadays, Hall said, Simpson's name and memory are reviled in Brentwood, where his guilt in the murders is widely assumed.[130]

After the civil trial verdicts in 1997, Simpson left Brentwood for southern Florida, where he could better protect his assets and remaining wealth. His Tudor-style mansion on North Rockingham Avenue in Brentwood was sold to a savings bank at auction. It fetched $2.6 million, enough to satisfy the mortgage payments on which Simpson had defaulted,[131] and afterward it was sold to an investment banker for nearly $4 million.[132] The new owner razed the place in 1998 and put up a Mediterranean-style mansion, only glimpses of which can be seen behind hedges and high walls.

Nicole Simpson's townhouse on South Bundy Drive in Brentwood was sold for less than $600,000 in 1996, and the new owner landscaped the front entrance with a riot of Southern California vegetation to shield from passersby what once had been a bloody crime scene. Only a small, hand-lettered sign gives away the townhouse street number, which also has been changed since the slayings. The cozy Mezzaluna restaurant on San Vicente Boulevard, where Nicole Simpson ate her last meal and where Goldman waited tables, was closed and its contents auctioned off in 1997. A coffee and tea café has since opened in its place. Downtown, Ito's courtroom was closed to trials a few years ago in a round of budget cuts. But to step into the courtroom is to be returned to a setting that looks much as it did to television viewers in 1995: dingy, with blue and dark brown competing as the dominant colors. Still in place in 2013 was Ito's nameplate at the bench. Hanging on the back wall of the courtroom was a framed cover of *Newsweek* magazine that showed Ito presiding at the Simpson trial and looking glum. His chin rested on the palm of his hand. "What a mess," the headline said of the trial.

In some ways, the Simpson case seems as if it has never really ended, at least not for some of the principals. A few years ago, for example, Christopher Darden revisited the trial's greatest blunder—the demonstration in June 1995 when he asked Simpson to try on the blood-stained leather gloves. In remarks at a panel discussion in 2012 in New York, Darden said Cochran, the lead defense attorney, may have tampered with the lining of the gloves so that they would not fit Simpson's hands. Cochran had died of a brain tumor seven years earlier. Dershowitz, another Simpson defense lawyer, shot back at Darden, saying: "Having made the greatest legal blunder of the 20th century, he's trying to blame it on the dead man."[133]

More jarring and bizarre was Simpson's coy pseudo-confession in a ghost-written book titled *If I Did It*, which was set to be published in 2006. In it, Simpson described how, hypothetically, he would have killed Nicole Simpson and Ronald Goldman. The book's publication was to be accompanied by a two-part interview on Fox television. But an uproar about those arrangements forced the project's cancellation. Goldman's family subsequently won a decision in federal bankruptcy court to gain publication rights to the book, which was released under a slightly revised title: *If I Did It: Confessions of the Killer.*

4

Peace at Dayton
and the "Hubris Bubble"

Within an hour on a snowy November morning near Dayton, Ohio, a sure failure in diplomacy[1] swung improbably to breakthrough success. At almost the last moment possible in an extraordinary negotiation that had lasted three weeks and had careened from despair to optimism and back again, a deal came together to end Europe's deadliest and most vicious war since the time of the Nazis. The agreement at Dayton brought a fragile and uneasy peace to faraway Bosnia and Herzegovina, the theater of nearly four years of grim savagery and, until November 1995, serial diplomatic failure. The deal was brokered by the United States but salvaged, incongruously, at the eleventh hour by a pudgy, cold-eyed despot who had been most responsible for years of turmoil and bloodletting in the Balkans.

The talks were a fascinating collision of ego, power, veiled threats, arcane cartography, arm-twisting, and nights with little sleep. Seldom was the diplomacy of the late twentieth century so fraught or consequential. To revisit the Dayton talks is to reexamine an exceptional moment in American statecraft and to recall an episode that helped make 1995 a watershed year.

The negotiations at Dayton uniquely brought together the leaders of the warring parties in Bosnia—three men who were well-acquainted but could not stand one another. They met at the Wright-Patterson Air Force Base, a sprawling place that projected constant and unsubtle reminders of American military might. The talks were animated by a colorful American official who spoke loudly, assertively, and often to great effect. Dayton was his prized accomplishment.

The negotiations not only brought an end—an all-too-belated end, critics said—to the war in Bosnia; they revived a spirit of "American Exceptionalism" and launched the United States on a trajectory of increasingly forceful interventions abroad. Diplomatic success at Dayton gave rise to an interlude of American muscularity, both diplomatically and militarily—a willingness to take the lead, a willingness to use force in the pursuit of diplomatic objectives, and a willingness to sidestep or ignore the United Nations.

Revitalized "American Exceptionalism"—a malleable sentiment that has coursed deep in American culture and holds that the United States is a singularly virtuous force in a dangerous and troubled world—was accompanied by a growing sense of hubris, a "hubris bubble" that expanded as success begot ambition,[2] leading ultimately to anguish in Iraq in the aftermath of the invasion that toppled Saddam Hussein in 2003. Diplomatic success at Dayton brought the rhetoric of "American Exceptionalism" back in a full-throated way. President Bill Clinton gave it voice at the White House that November day, in announcing that agreement had been reached at Dayton. "The central fact for us as Americans is this," Clinton said. "Our leadership made this peace agreement possible and helped to bring an end to the senseless slaughter of so many innocent people. . . . Now American leadership, together with our allies, is needed to make this peace real and enduring."[3]

The war in Bosnia was the longest and most vicious in a series of conflicts touched off by the post–Cold War disintegration of Yugoslavia. Of the six constituent republics of the socialist Yugoslav Federation, Bosnia was the most ethnically diverse. It was a sort of Yugoslavia in miniature.[4] None of Bosnia's ethnicities—Croat, Muslim, and Serb—constituted a majority.

As Yugoslavia's republics began peeling away in 1991—first Slovenia, then Croatia, then Macedonia—Bosnia's Muslim government found itself in the unwelcome position of either remaining in a Serb-dominated rump Yugoslavia or leaving and facing the wrath of Bosnian Serbs who wanted no part of secession.[5] Following a referendum in late February 1992, Bosnia's parliament declared the country's independence, and the Bosnian Serbs responded with armed force, sweeping across 70 percent of Bosnian territory and 30 percent of Croatia in the first weeks of the war. The Serbs laid siege to Sarajevo, Bosnia's capital and site of the Winter Olympic games of 1984; they drove hundreds of thousands of Muslims and Croats from their homes and forced many more into concentration camps in a brutal campaign of "ethnic cleansing."[6] On the eve of 1995, an interagency U.S. intelligence report found that "sustained campaigns of ethnic cleansing by Bosnian Serbs since 1992 have resulted in the deaths of tens of thousands of non-Serbs, the displacement of hundreds of thousands more, and the radical recasting of Bosnia's demographic makeup."[7]

The Muslim-led Bosnian government had also faced assault by Bosnian Croats, who received arms and ammunition from Croatia and, in 1993, launched their own land grab in southern Bosnia.[8] The leaders of Serbia and Croatia dreamed for a time of carving up Bosnia, establishing an ethnically pure "Greater Serbia" and an ethnically pure "Greater Croatia" while leaving the Bosnian government with little more than landlocked enclaves around Sarajevo.[9]

Few Americans were familiar or conversant with the mind-numbing intricacies of the Balkans, and they mostly turned away from the region's conflicts and horrors. Nearly 80 percent of Americans responding in a nationwide survey in January 1993 gave the wrong answer, or said they did not know, which ethnic group had conquered most of Bosnia and had encircled Sarajevo. Just one respondent in five in that survey correctly identified the Serbs.[10] Polls also showed that Americans mostly were clueless as to how the war in Bosnia began, and few of them saw any vital U.S. interests at stake in the Balkans.[11] Surveys also indicated that Americans felt no moral obligation to intervene to end the fighting there.[12]

It was a fratricidal war utterly without redeeming figures. Of all the perfidious characters who were prominent in 1995, few were as profoundly offensive as Ratko Mladić, Slobodan Milošević, or Franjo Tuđman. Their very names seemed to ooze hostility. Mladić was the burly and swaggering commander of the Bosnian Serb military who once told his gunners on the heights above Sarajevo: "Shell them till they're on the edge of madness."[13] Twenty years later, Mladić is on trial at The Hague, answering charges of war crimes in Bosnia. Milošević promoted an ultranationalist vision of "Greater Serbia" and was principally responsible for fomenting the turmoil in the Balkans. Milošević—called by his biographers "the Saddam Hussein of Europe"[14]—died in a prison cell in 2006 while on trial at The Hague for war crimes. But, as we will see, it was Milošević's intervention that rescued the Dayton talks at their final hour.

Tuđman was the nationalist Croatian president who loved wearing ice cream–colored military uniforms festooned with gold brocade,[15] despised the Muslims of Bosnia, and dreamed of uniting ethnic Croats in a "Greater Croatia" under his leadership.[16] Tuđman died in 1999 before he could be indicted for war crimes.[17] Alija Izetbegović, the beleaguered Muslim president of Bosnia, once likened Milošević and Tuđman to leukemia and a brain tumor.[18] And Izetbegović, Milošević, and Tuđman were leaders of the respective Bosnian, Serb, and Croat delegations to Dayton.

A rare occasion when Americans did turn sustained attention to Bosnia came in June 1995, when Scott F. O'Grady, a U.S. Air Force pilot, was shot down over western Bosnia on a routine surveillance mission under NATO auspices.[19] It was unclear at first whether O'Grady had survived the destruction of his F-16 fighter jet, blasted from the sky by a Serb surface-to-air missile.[20] Intercepted radio transmissions, however, soon indicated that the Serbs had found O'Grady's parachute and were looking for the downed pilot. O'Grady likened himself to a "scared little bunny rabbit," saying: "Most of the time, my face was in the dirt, just praying that no one would see me."[21]

For nearly six days, O'Grady eluded his Serb would-be captors, sleeping little, drinking rainwater, and eating plants and insects after his rations ran out. A transmission from his radio, in his call sign "Basher 52," was picked up early on June 8, 1995. A massive rescue mission soon was set in motion from the USS *Kearsarge,* an amphibious assault ship in the Adriatic Sea. Forty warplanes and support aircraft, including Navy Super Stallions assault helicopters with Marines aboard, were sent to find O'Grady. As the aircraft approached, O'Grady set off an emergency flare, and its yellow smoke guided the Super Stallions to a clearing he had selected. He darted from a hiding place with pistol in hand and fear in his eyes.[22] "I'm ready to get the hell out of here," O'Grady shouted as he was pulled aboard one of the helicopters.[23] They were on the ground only a few minutes.

O'Grady was on the *Kearsarge* within two hours, receiving treatment for minor injuries and dehydration. Word of his rescue soon reached Washington, where it was almost one o'clock in the morning on June 8. Clinton and his national security adviser, Anthony Lake, broke out cigars to celebrate the news.[24] Mindful of a ban on smoking in federal buildings, Clinton and Lake lit up out of doors, on the Truman balcony at the White House.[25] Later, Clinton placed a call to O'Grady, telling the rescued pilot, "The country was on pins and needles, but you knew what you were doing. The whole country is elated."[26]

Clinton, though, was criticized by Democrats and Republicans alike for failing to retaliate against the Serbs for downing a U.S. warplane.[27]

It was another example, critics said, of the administration's dithering, incoherence, and fecklessness. Disarray did indeed seem to define Clinton's foreign policy, on Bosnia especially. Back-pedaling, humiliating setback, and inaction had characterized his administration's response to major challenges abroad. It was even said that the "commander in chief who avoided the Vietnam draft couldn't even manage a snappy military salute."[28] Clinton's foreign policy record in the first years after his election was uninspired.

Intervention in Somalia had resulted in trauma. A humanitarian and peacekeeping mission in Somalia, begun during the closing days of the administration of President George H.W. Bush, was ruined by a bloody ambush in October 1993 in the capital, Mogadishu. Eighteen U.S. servicemen were killed in the firefight while trying to capture the lieutenants of a Somali strongman and clan leader, Mohamed Farah Aideed. The humiliating disaster at Mogadishu, in which the body of a slain U.S. Army Ranger was dragged through the streets, prompted Clinton to announce the withdrawal of U.S. forces. Six months later, the Clinton administration stood by, declining to intervene as extremist Hutus rampaged in Rwanda, massacring hundreds of thousands of their countrymen. Those episodes—especially the debacle in Somalia—had powerful restraining effects on the administration's Bosnia policy,[29] the cornerstone of which was to avoid the deployment of U.S. forces.[30]

In office, Clinton retreated from promises made on the campaign trail to address the miseries of Bosnia by lifting an arms embargo against Bosnian Muslims and launch airstrikes against Bosnian Serb positions—moves that might have ended the war in 1993.[31] Instead, Clinton deferred to the Europeans,[32] allowing them to take the lead in attempting to resolve a European conflict. But the Europeans foundered in Bosnia in the face of horrors not seen on the continent since World War II.

O'Grady's rescue brought a rare moment of cheer from Bosnia, an occasion when Serb forces had been outfoxed and plainly embarrassed.[33] But what finally swept away the tentativeness and hesitation of the Clinton administration's policy on Bosnia was not O'Grady's deliverance but the worst massacre in Europe in fifty years.[34] In July 1995, Bosnian Serb forces under Mladić's command entered the U.N.-declared "safe area" at Srebrenica, a Muslim enclave in mountainous eastern Bosnia. The Serbs disarmed the hapless and meagerly equipped Dutch peacekeepers[35] and launched a cold-blooded orgy of violence. Cruelly, Mladić and his men handed out chocolates to Muslim children, telling them they had nothing to fear. "You'll be taken to a safe place," Mladić assured them.[36]

The Serbs separated Muslim men and boys from women and girls. Over the next several days, more than 8,000 men and boys were killed by execution or ambush.[37] Many of them were bound and blindfolded, then shot in the back of the head, their bodies dumped in mass graves. Muslim women and girls were raped. Mothers took desperate measures to keep their daughters from being targeted for sexual assault, dirtying their faces and making them wear peasant clothing so they would appear unattractive.[38] Word of the atrocities soon slipped out of Srebrenica, and NATO responded with a few ineffective airstrikes.[39] Otherwise, the outside world did little to stop the attacks.[40]

The massacre at Srebrenica was the single worst atrocity of an evil war,[41] and it stirred fierce criticism in the United States about Clinton's policy of nonintervention. A firestorm arose from the right and the left. William Safire, a conservative columnist for the *New York Times*, wrote that Clinton would be "remembered in history as a man who feared, flinched and failed," whose diffidence in the face of "Nazi-style ethnic cleansing" in Bosnia had "turned a superpower into a subpower."[42] Anthony Lewis, who wrote for the *New York Times* from the left, said the fall of Srebrenica pointed up "the vacuum of leadership in the White House." Clinton, he wrote, "does not want any change in the world's response to the Serbs, for a simple reason. Change is likely to mean American ground forces, and Mr. Clinton fears that would be politically damaging to him."[43]

Clinton soon recognized, though, that deference and nonintervention in Bosnia were beginning to harm him, politically.[44] The fall of Srebrenica and of another U.N. safe area at Žepa in late July 1995 were catalysts for a more assertive American policy[45] in which the United States would take the lead in seeking to end the war in Bosnia, coupling diplomacy with the genuine threat of military force. The policy began to take shape in late summer 1995 and would eventually culminate in the remarkable negotiation at Dayton.

Meanwhile, the military equation in Bosnia had slowly begun to shift away from Serb forces. An offensive in early August 1995 by the Croatian army reclaimed the Krajina region, which had been seized by the Serbs early in the war. The Croat offensive uprooted more than 150,000 ethnic Serbs from the Krajina in another spasm of "ethnic cleansing" in which homes were burned and civilians were fired on.[46] The United States privately endorsed the offensive because it shifted the dynamics on the ground and made a negotiated settlement somewhat more promising.[47] For the first time since the war began, Serb forces were in retreat and appeared vulnerable.

Their vulnerability deepened in August. NATO had warned the Serbs against attacking remaining U.N. safe areas in Bosnia, including Sarajevo. They faced intensive air strikes if they did. Late in the month, Serb forces besieging Sarajevo lobbed five mortar shells into the city, one of which killed thirty-seven people in an open-air market. Within days, U.S. warplanes under NATO authority responded with an aerial bombing campaign on Serb military barracks, ammunition depots, air-defense sites, and communications towers in what was the alliance's most extensive military action since its founding after World War II.[48] In mid-September, the battered Serb forces pulled back their heavy artillery, lifting the siege of Sarajevo after forty-one months. In that time, more than 11,000 people had been killed in Sarajevo, and much of the city had been turned to rubble.

Also in August, Clinton designated Richard Holbrooke, the assistant secretary of state for European and Canadian affairs, as lead negotiator on the U.S. initiative to end the war. The choice of Holbrooke was more than a little controversial. Holbrooke was fifty-four years old and an outsize, colorful, and complex character. He was by turns charming, abrasive, theatrical, and explosive—and seldom disinclined to offer his opinions. It was said that "hubris" and Holbrooke were inseparable.[49]

Not even his superiors quite knew how he worked or how to control him.[50] "I'm not always sure what you are doing, or why," Secretary of State Warren Christopher told Holbrooke as the talks in Dayton unfolded, "but you always seem to have a reason, and it seems to work, so I'm quite content to go along with your instincts."[51] Holbrooke was given alternately to cajoling, improvisation, and swings of emotion—all of which were on display amid the intensity and uncertainties of the talks at Dayton.[52]

Holbrooke advocated a muscular kind of diplomacy and recognized the importance of military force in the pursuit of diplomatic objectives. "He was comfortable with American power, Vietnam notwithstanding," Roger Cohen of the *New York Times* wrote shortly after Holbrooke's death in December 2010. "The Balkan bullies, Slobodan Milosevic chief among them, shrank before U.S. military brass; Holbrooke, adept at theater, knew that. . . . He knew how to close and how closing depended on a balance of forces."[53]

Holbrooke brought to Dayton the searing recent experience of losing three members of his negotiating team in a roadway accident outside Sarajevo. The mishap happened August 19 as American negotiators traveled a winding, mud-slick road on Mount Igman above Sarajevo,

FIGURE 17. Richard C. Holbrooke, a colorful assistant secretary of state, led the U.S. negotiating team at Dayton, Ohio. Holbrooke could be, by turns, abrasive, charming, melodramatic, and explosive. Those tendencies were all in evidence during the three weeks of talks, which frequently teetered on failure. (Photo credit: Charlie Parshley)

where they were headed for a meeting with Izetbegović, the Bosnian president. Holbrooke was on the same mountain road, in a Humvee ahead of the armored personnel carrier in which Robert C. Frasure, an assistant secretary of state, and the two other Americans were riding. The personnel carrier slipped off the narrow road, rolled over several times, caught fire, and exploded. Along with Frasure, Joseph J. Kruzel, a deputy assistant secretary of defense, and Colonel S. Nelson Drew of the Air Force were fatally injured.

They were on Mount Igman because the Bosnian Serbs besieging Sarajevo would not guarantee their safety had they flown into the city's airport.[54] Their deaths were a bitter and shattering blow that interrupted the emergent U.S. diplomatic initiative on Bosnia but did not derail it. Indeed, after funerals in Washington for Frasure, Kruzel, and Drew, Holbrooke and his team returned to the Balkans in a frenetic burst of shuttle-style diplomacy in late summer and early autumn. Later, during the negotiations in November, Holbrooke said publicly that he sensed that Frasure, Kruzel, and Drew were "with us here in Dayton at all times."[55]

Holbrooke was at Dayton for the duration of the talks. Christopher was there for the start, for the end game, and twice in between. Holbrooke and Christopher, then seventy years old, made for an odd yet surprisingly complementary team. The secretary of state was an earnest lawyer-diplomat: a bit stuffy, unfailingly courteous, and rarely confrontational. He was an earnest, if mediocre, secretary of state,[56] most in his element while negotiating. In contrast to Holbrooke's urgent manner and tousled appearance, Christopher was restrained and buttoned-up.[57] At Dayton, Christopher "played soft cop to tough cop Richard Holbrooke," as Britain's *Economist* magazine observed.[58] Christopher's senior rank within the Clinton administration lent gravitas that impressed the Balkan leaders.[59]

Dayton was an intriguing if odd choice as the site of the talks. The old factory town was preparing in late 1995 to commemorate its bicentennial. In its 200 years, Dayton had been something of a crucible for invention and innovation. Orville and Wilbur Wright designed their aircraft on the city's West Side. The cash register was invented in Dayton; so were the pop-top beverage can, the wooden folding stepladder, and the soft-rubber ice cube tray.[60] As the Bosnian peace talks began in their city, civic boosters claimed that Dayton had produced more patents per capita than any place in the United States.[61] To think of Dayton as a dull city where nothing much ever happened was to be more than slightly mistaken.

Its selection as the venue[62] for the talks had nothing to do with its culture of innovation. Dayton was halfway around the world from the Balkans and light years from the ethnic violence there, but it was just an hour's flight from Washington, D.C., allowing Christopher and other senior U.S. officials reasonably quick access to the talks. "We wanted a place that was far enough away from Washington" so ranking U.S. officials weren't always present, recalled Donald L. Kerrick, a retired Army general who was the National Security Council's representative on Holbrooke's negotiating team. "But we wanted a place close enough [to Washington] so that we could get them there if we needed them."[63]

The Wright-Patterson base sprawls over 8,200 acres. Its runways can accommodate jets of any size. The base employed 23,000 people, had a payroll greater than Bosnia's output,[64] and fairly bristled with reminders of U.S. firepower and military readiness—reminders not lost on the Balkan leaders.[65] It was a perfect place to conduct a high-stakes negotiation; it ensured seclusion and near-impregnable security. The news media could be kept at a distance, well beyond the high fence of the base, so a news blackout was easy to maintain.

Inside the Wright-Patterson perimeter was the Hope Hotel and Conference Center, named for actor and comedian Bob Hope. About 100 yards away was a cluster of low brick buildings known as the Visiting Officers' Quarters. Four buildings were grouped around a parking lot, and a fifth building stood nearby. These were turned into the similar-but-separate accommodations for the negotiating teams, housing the delegations from Bosnia, Serbia, and Croatia as well as the U.S. team and representatives from Europe and Russia. The rooms of the Visiting Officers' Quarters had been remodeled and repainted in the second half of October, and they were virtually identical, down to the lampshades.[66] They offered modest comforts and nothing lavish. In style, furnishings, and amenities, the Visiting Officers' Quarters were more Motel 6 than the Ritz.[67]

The people of Dayton were engaged by the improbable presence of a major international event in their town.[68] They styled their town as the "temporary center of international peace,"[69] placed peace candles in their windows, and mostly shrugged off Milošević's half-joking complaint that he did not want to be cooped up in Dayton like a priest.[70] They had only glimpses, though, of what Holbrooke was later to call "an all-or-nothing, high-risk negotiation."[71]

The talks opened November 1, 1995, in a brief, tightly choreographed ceremony at the B-29 Super Fortress conference room at the Hope Hotel and Conference Center. "It was a historic gathering," wrote Roger Cohen, a *New York Times* correspondent who had covered years of bloodletting in the Balkans. "The walls were off-pink. The plants looked miserable. The furniture was modest. The gray carpet did not quite conceal a stain or two. Versailles it was not."[72] Elegance was absent and awkwardness prevailed. The three Balkan presidents—Izetbegović, Milošević, and Tuđman—entered the conference room, one by one, each escorted by a senior U.S. diplomat serving in his country.[73] Only after encouragement from Christopher did the three leaders stand and perfunctorily shake hands for the cameras. They were not permitted by their American hosts to make remarks or speak to the scores of journalists crowding the conference room. And they made little eye contact with one another. They knew each other well, and mutual contempt was open and ran deep. To Kerrick, one of the American negotiators, the Balkan presidents were not unlike members of a Mafia family—they shared some interests but also pursued dissimilar goals and objectives.[74]

In his remarks, Christopher outlined the hoped-for outcomes of the talks: Bosnia was to remain a single state, "with an internationally recognized border and with a single international personality"; an agreement would have to address the history and significance of Bosnia's largest city, Sarajevo; human rights throughout the region must be respected and rights-abusers must be punished; and the dispute over the Serb-held region of Croatia's Eastern Slavonia must be resolved.[75] The goals were ambitious and the format of the talks—effectively sequestering leaders and top officials of three sovereign states far from their home countries—was without immediate precedent. The nearest approximation was the Camp David talks in 1978 that produced a peace agreement between Egypt and Israel.[76] But the talks at Dayton were more complex by many measures—in the number of participants, certainly, and in the depth of grievances and hatreds represented there. In the internecine warfare in Bosnia, as Richard Sale noted in his book about Clinton's foreign policy, "Serbs had attacked and fought Croats, Croats had attacked and fought Muslims and vice versa, then both the latter had joined together to fight against Bosnian Serbs."[77]

Given all the peculiarities, the Dayton talks were *sui generis.* Holbrooke called it "the Big Bang approach" to negotiating: "lock everyone up until they reach agreement."[78] These days, the "Big Bang approach" probably would be unsustainable for very long; enveloping negotiations in "radio silence"[79]—as the Americans insisted on at Dayton[80]—would be quickly undermined by video and text options that are routinely available on Smartphones and other mobile devices. In the digital century, Dayton would be impossible to duplicate, at least logistically.

In convening the talks, the Americans turned to fairly bleak rhetoric. "If we fail," Christopher said, "the war will resume and future generations will surely hold us accountable for the consequences that would follow. The lights . . . in Sarajevo would once again be extinguished, death and starvation would once again spread across the Balkans, across perhaps the entire region, threatening the region and perhaps Europe itself. To the three presidents, I say to you that it's within your power to chart a better course for the future of the people of the former Yugoslavia."[81]

The invariably reserved Christopher seemed rather out of character as he invoked a grim prospect of world war should the talks fail. "If the war in the Balkans is reignited," he said, "it could spark a wider conflict like those that drew American soldiers to Europe in huge numbers twice this century. If the conflict continues, and certainly if it spreads, it would jeopardize our efforts to promote peace and stability in Europe. It would threaten the viability of NATO, which has been the bedrock of European security for 50 years. If the conflict continues, so would the worst atrocities that Europe has seen since World War II."[82] No small measure of pessimism lurked behind the stern rhetoric. "I don't think anybody really thought we would succeed," Kerrick recalled.[83] There was ample reason for such gloom. No fewer than four international peace initiatives had failed in the years before Dayton. Bosnia seemed to defy diplomatic resolution.

Even so, a good deal of provisional understanding had been reached in the weeks before the Dayton talks began, as Holbrooke and his negotiating team shuttled through the Balkans. It was understood in principle that Bosnia would remain a single state with two self-governing entities—a federation of Muslims and Croats, and a republic of ethnic Serbs, called Republika Srpska. Fifty-one percent of Bosnia's land mass would be federation territory; forty-nine percent would be held by ethnic Serbs, a division that roughly reflected the confrontation lines at the time of the ceasefire in October 1995. It was further understood that a peace agreement would be policed by 60,000 NATO-led peacekeepers, including 20,000 U.S. troops—a controversial provision that polls indicated most Americans opposed.

Nonetheless, many issues awaited resolution at Dayton, including how Sarajevo would be governed, how suspected war criminals would be dealt with, what authority the peacekeeping force would have, and how the proposed Muslim-Croat Federation would function. The major impediment was in determining boundary lines for the 51/49 territorial split within Bosnia between the federation and the Serb republic.[84] U.S. delegates on the first night of the talks distributed draft copies of what they called the "Framework Agreement," along with several annexes.[85] It was clear soon enough that the negotiations would be a hard slog. The pace of the talks was languid, and the first week at Dayton brought no notable movement on the toughest issues.[86] "All going well, just unclear where all is going," Kerrick wrote in a memorandum to Anthony Lake, Clinton's national security adviser, at the close of the first week of talks.[87]

The following day, U.S. negotiators convened what essentially was a plenary on territorial issues and the governance of Sarajevo. It was a six-hour waste of time.[88] "Despite hours of heated, yet civil exchanges, absolutely nothing was agreed," Kerrick wrote afterward. "Astonishingly, at one moment [the] parties would be glaring across [the] table, screaming, while minutes later they could be seen smiling and joking together over refreshments."[89] Never again did the U.S. team call such a meeting. Instead, the Americans pursued the negotiations mostly by shuttling among the respective Balkan delegations.[90]

The first days at Dayton were embroidered by a notably surreal moment and by a major distraction. The surreal moment came during a dinner for all delegates that the Americans threw at the Air Force Museum at Wright-Patterson—a cavernous venue that Holbrooke called "the greatest military air museum in the world."[91] An Air Force band played Glenn Miller music as delegates dined in the shadows of a huge B-29 heavy bomber, several Stealth F-117 fighters, and, "appropriately to some, a Tomahawk cruise missile that seemed pointed right at Milošević's table," Derek Chollet wrote in his account of the Dayton talks.[92] Kerrick recalled during the dinner that he looked up at the cruise missile and pointed it out to Milošević. "I said, 'Mr. President . . . we have a lot of those.'"[93]

The distraction was created by the Bosnian Serbs' jailing of David Rohde, a reporter for the *Christian Science Monitor*. Rohde, who was twenty-eight years old, had rented a red Citroën automobile in Vienna and driven to Bosnia, seeking to investigate the killing ground at Srebrenica, from where he had reported a few months earlier. He was arrested and accused of being a spy.[94] Holbrooke, who later observed that Rohde showed "more courage than wisdom" in going to Srebrenica without papers or permission,[95] insisted on the journalist's release, telling Milošević that no agreement was possible at Dayton until Rohde was set free.[96] "We are pressing this hard," Holbrooke wrote in a memorandum at the close of the first week of talks.[97]

Despite the news blackout, journalism had intruded at Dayton.[98] With Holbrooke at Dayton was his wife, the writer Kati Marton, who was chair of the Committee to Protect Journalists, an advocacy organization based in New York. She, too, pressured Milošević for Rohde's release.[99]

The Serbs finally gave in, and on November 8, ten days after he was arrested, Rohde was taken to Belgrade and turned over to officials at the U.S. embassy. For years afterward, Holbrooke ribbed Rohde for having complicated the Dayton talks.[100] Which he had.[101]

More powerful rhythms were at work at Dayton. After ten days, a kind of high-tide, low-tide pattern emerged in the talks. Kerrick mentioned this in a memorandum to Anthony Lake. He wrote that the parties were "enjoying each other's company, but [the] more they see of each other [the] more they seem to be willing to chuck it all and return to war." Every twelve hours, Kerrick added, seemed to bring a sense of certain failure, "only to find real chances for success at the next high tide."[102] Progress had been made on a number of issues, including the structure of the Muslim-Croat Federation and a timetable for the Croats to regain Eastern Slavonia. But the most contentious issues, including political control of Sarajevo and the boundaries of the 51/49 territorial split, remained unsettled.

A modest opening on Sarajevo developed during a lunch at the Wright-Patterson officers' club; Chollet called it "napkin diplomacy." At one end of the club's wood-paneled dining room, Holbrooke took lunch with Milošević. At a table at the other end of the room was Haris Silajdžić, the Bosnian prime minister. Holbrooke at one point walked to Silajdžić's table to say hello and fell into discussion about establishing a land corridor from Sarajevo through Bosnian Serb territory to Goražde, a Muslim enclave in eastern Bosnia. Silajdžić outlined some options on napkins, which Holbrooke took across the room and handed to Milošević. After a number of similar trips back and forth, Holbrooke brought Silajdžić to his table, to include Milošević in the discussion. Milošević suggested that Bosnian Muslims deserved to govern Sarajevo, considering how they had withstood Bosnian Serb shelling for more than three years. Nothing was settled, but "napkin diplomacy" signaled the start of a serious negotiation about territorial questions.[103]

That night, Holbrooke renewed the discussions about the corridor, seating Milošević in front of a classified, three-dimensional simulation apparatus called "PowerScene." The device cost some $400,000 and had been used a couple of months before to select targets during the NATO-led bombing of Serb positions in Bosnia.[104] PowerScene was a joystick-driven imaging device that offered high-resolution views of Bosnia's topography. It was installed in the American delegation's quarters, in what came to be called the "Nintendo Room." Milošević was enthralled. The PowerScene images of Bosnia's landscape showed unmistakably that a land corridor two miles wide from Sarajevo to Goražde, as Milošević had proposed, would be untenable. After a few hours of PowerScene-driven overflights, as well as discussions lubricated by Scotch, Milošević agreed to a land corridor five miles wide.[105] "We have found our road," he said, draining his glass.[106] Inevitably, perhaps, the corridor was informally called "Scotch Road."

The "Scotch Road" deal represented movement, but a comprehensive agreement was still elusive, and the Americans set a deadline of midnight Sunday, November 19. They said they would close the negotiations, one way or the other, at that time.[107] Forcing the delegations to confront a deadline, the Americans figured, could have the salutary effect of concentrating attention, which tended to stray at Dayton. "These people had fought one another for a long time," Holbrooke later noted, "and were ready to sit in Dayton for a long time and just argue."[108]

As the talks had gone on, contrasts among the respective delegations became sharper. Tuđman, the Croat leader, had secured concessions on Eastern Slavonia, his major objective at Dayton. After that, he was mostly aloof. The Bosnian delegation headed by Izetbegović was plagued by internal tensions and disputes, and seemed ambivalent about reaching a deal.[109] The American negotiators grew increasingly frustrated with the Bosnian officials, whom they privately referred to as Izzy, Silly, and Mo[110]—for Izetbegović, Silajdžić, and Muhamed Sacirbey, the foreign minister. The Bosnians rarely acted in concert, and differences among them were too often apparent. They "continue to amaze us all with their desire to torpedo one another—and possibly even peace," Kerrick wrote as the talks ground on.[111]

The cold-eyed Milošević was the Balkan leader most eager for a deal. He knew that the ruinous international economic sanctions imposed on Serbia would be lifted only if the Dayton negotiations produced a peace agreement. That reality—and a related if unrealistic yearning to rehabilitate his reputation[112]—guided Milošević's conduct at Dayton. "I think he had a grander vision for Serbia that he knew he couldn't [achieve] without a peace agreement," said Kerrick. "He really wanted, I think, to walk the streets of New York and be seen as a guy who brought peace to Yugoslavia."[113] Milošević of course neither won nor deserved such respect. He was indicted in 1999 for crimes against humanity, turned from power in 2000, arrested in Belgrade in 2001, and sent to trial at The Hague.

At Dayton, though, the Americans found him to be engaging, accessible, flexible, and savvy. He effectively sidelined the Bosnian Serb representatives and treated them with contempt. They lurked at the fringes of the talks, suspicious of what was going on but kept in the dark, and mostly ignored.[114] In the decisive moments at Dayton, it was Milošević who made the concessions.

On the eighteenth day of the talks, Milošević unexpectedly capitulated and conceded control of Sarajevo to the Muslim-Croat Federation. He rejected a partitioned city or a federalized solution, à la Washington, D.C. "Izetbegovic has earned Sarajevo by not abandoning it," Milošević told the Americans. "He's one tough guy. It's his."[115] It was a major and surprising concession. Taking Sarajevo had been a major objective of the Bosnian Serbs since the war began, and now, astoundingly, Milošević was giving it away. He subsequently agreed to give up the Serb-controlled suburbs of Sarajevo as well.[116]

Ironically, the concessions on Sarajevo and on the land corridor to Goražde had complicated the task of establishing the 51/49 territorial split. Milošević's concessions on Sarajevo and the Goražde corridor had altered the ratio to 55/45. To achieve the 51/49 split, the Muslims and Croats would have to cede territory to the Bosnian Serbs.[117] The prospect was not an agreeable one.

Matters looked bleak indeed as the midnight deadline approached on November 19, and Holbrooke asked for a look at the so-called "failure statement" that the Americans had prepared as a contingency and would release should the talks break down. Holbrooke looked it over and found it too tepid. It is not "final" enough, he said, tossing the statement into the air. As the pages fluttered down in the Americans' conference room, the chief U.S. negotiator began dictating a blunt and more downbeat statement to the State Department speechwriter, Tom Malinowski. This remarkable, late-night scene was recounted by Chollet in *The Road to the Dayton Accords:*

> Standing over a computer, a visibly tired and agitated (and some thought crazed) Holbrooke dictated the language to Malinowski while the other Americans looked on in astonishment. His redraft reflected the frustration of the moment. "To put it simply," his statement concluded, "we gave it our best shot. By their failure to agree, the parties have made it very clear that further U.S. efforts to negotiate a settlement would be fruitless. Accordingly, today marks the end of this initiative . . . the special role we have played in recent months is over. The leaders here today must live with the consequences of their failure."[118]

The high-tide, low-tide dynamic that Kerrick had noted a few days earlier soon reasserted itself. As Holbrooke reworked the draft failure statement, Milošević and Silajdžić were meeting to discuss ways of achieving the 51/49 territorial split. They landed on an idea of ceding an egg-shaped swath of thinly populated, mountainous territory in western Bosnia to the Serbs. It would be enough to reach the 51/49 division. They went to the American conference room to describe their handiwork. It was about 4 a.m. and, suddenly, resolution of the major obstacle of the negotiation seemed at hand. Christopher, who had returned to Dayton for the end of the talks, took a bottle of California white chardonnay wine from his private reserve and opened it to toast the apparent breakthrough.[119]

Izetbegović was summoned, and the Bosnian president arrived wearing a coat over his nightshirt. He seemed cool to the tentative deal. The Croat foreign minister, Mate Granić, also was awakened and called to the conference room. He immediately asked to see the map showing the territorial division that Milošević and Silajdžić were proposing. Granić scanned it and exploded. "Impossible, impossible," he shouted. "Zero point zero zero percent chance my president [Tuđman] will accept this!"[120] Silajdžić had proposed to give away land that the Croat military had won in the summer offensive, and Croat officials would have none of that. Izetbegović spoke up, saying he would side with his nominal Croat allies and oppose the compromise that Silajdžić, his country's prime minister, had developed with Milošević. Silajdžić glared at Izetbegović and stormed from the conference room, shouting, "I can't take this anymore."[121] The deal had lasted all of thirty-seven minutes.

The Americans' midnight deadline had long since passed, and Holbrooke and Christopher agreed to give the talks one more day. Progress had been made on many other issues, and they asked Clinton to weigh in on the 51/49 conundrum. The president telephoned Tuđman, encouraging him to cede the territory needed to reach the 51/49 split. Tuđman was willing, but the Bosnians also would have to give up some territory for a deal to be struck. The Bosnians seemed reluctant. Finally, late on November 20, Christopher presented Izetbegović with an ultimatum: accept the revisions for the 51/49 split as well as the other agreements reached at Dayton, or the talks would be over. Raising his voice as he seldom did, Christopher told Izetbegović that almost everything the Bosnians had sought had been achieved in the talks.[122] He gave Izetbegović an hour to decide.

Shortly before midnight, Izetbegović sent word that the Bosnians would yield enough territory to the Serbs to close the deal—provided that Brčko, a strategic town in northeast Bosnia, be included in the

Muslim-Croat Federation.[123] This was a new and thoroughly unwelcome eleventh-hour demand. The town stood astride a narrow corridor that connected the western and eastern segments of the Serb republic in Bosnia. Brčko's fate, as far as the Americans were concerned, had already been decided: the Serbs were to have it.[124] The demand for Brčko, Christopher thought, was at last the deal-breaker: he suspected Milošević would never accept Izetbegović's demand and further suspected the Bosnians wanted "to avoid coming to grips with the end game" at Dayton.[125] In other words, they were not opposed to the talks ending in collapse.

In the early hours of November 21, Christopher went to bed thinking the talks were on the brink of failure.[126] The failure statement—revised and toned down from Holbrooke's draft of twenty-four hours earlier—was distributed to the Bosnians, Croats, and Serbs.[127] Milošević was incredulous, telling the American representatives who delivered the statement: "You're the United States. You can't let the Bosnians push you around this way. Just tell them what to do."[128] No, they told him, it is up to you to bring the others around.[129]

Not long after sunrise on the snowy morning of November 21, Milošević went to see Tuđman, suggesting the Serbs and Croats sign a peace agreement at Dayton while allowing the Bosnians to sign later. Such a tactic, Milošević figured, would exert great pressure on Izetbegović and the Bosnian team. Milošević went to the U.S. quarters to present the idea. He arrived just as Holbrooke had convened what was to be the delegation's close-out meeting. He and Christopher broke away from the meeting to speak privately with Milošević. An agreement without endorsement of all parties was impossible, they told him. If a three-way deal agreement could not be concluded, the talks would be shut down.[130] In any case, Christopher said, a two-sided deal would not be legally binding.[131]

Milošević had a final card to play: he proposed sending the question of Brčko's sovereignty to international arbitration. Once again, Milošević had yielded. In doing so, he cleared away the last obstacle to a deal. Holbrooke and Christopher took the arbitration proposal to Tuđman, who backed it, saying, "Get peace. Get peace now! Make Izetbegovic agree."[132] The Americans went to the Bosnians' quarters, outlined Milošević's offer, and demanded an immediate answer. After a lengthy pause, Izetbegović spoke, saying it was not a just peace "but my people need peace." Which meant he had at last agreed.[133] Fearing that the Bosnians might again raise fresh demands, Holbrooke whispered to

Christopher, "Let's get out of here fast."[134] They called Clinton with the news of a deal, and shortly before noon on November 21, the president stepped into the Rose Garden to announce the agreement. "American Exceptionalism" infused his remarks, especially those devoted to the deployment of 20,000 American troops as part of the international peacekeeping force to go to Bosnia. Clinton declared:

> Now that the parties to the war have made a serious commitment to peace, we must help them to make it work. All the parties have asked for a strong international force to supervise the separation of forces and to give them confidence that each side will live up to their agreements. Only NATO can do that job. And the United States as NATO's leader must play an essential role in this mission. Without us, the hard-won peace would be lost, the war would resume, the slaughter of innocents would begin again, and the conflict that already has claimed so many people could spread like poison throughout the entire region. We are at a decisive moment. The parties have chosen peace. America must choose peace as well.[135]

The Dayton accords—known formally as the "General Framework Agreement for Peace in Bosnia and Herzegovina"—covered 165 pages and included 12 annexes and 102 maps. It was comprehensive, or nearly so, embracing the 51/49 territorial split between the Muslim-Croat Federation and Republika Srpska.[136] It also affirmed Bosnia's international borders, set forth a constitution for the country, and specified that people displaced by the war could return to their homes. It established a central bank and single currency, and it obliged the parties to abide by the International Criminal Tribunal for the former Yugoslavia, which had been established at The Hague in 1993. The agreement would be enforced by an Implementation Force (or IFOR), consisting of 60,000 NATO-led troops, one-third of whom would be American.

The three Balkan leaders initialed the accords on the afternoon of November 21 in the B-29 Super Fortress conference room where the talks had begun so awkwardly three weeks before. Clinton thought of traveling to Dayton to attend the initialing ceremony, but Holbrooke dissuaded him, saying, "You don't want to be anywhere near these people today. They are wild and they don't deserve a presidential visit."[137]

The accords were signed in mid-December at Elysée Palace, the official residence in Paris of the French president. In a bit of Gallic pique, the French Foreign Ministry referred to the agreement as the Treaty of the Elysée and, according to Holbrooke, asked speakers at the signing ceremony "to omit any references to Dayton in their remarks."[138] As Holbrooke noted, the Dayton accords had shaken "the leadership elite

FIGURE 18. Three Balkan presidents initialed the Dayton peace accords on the afternoon of November 21, 1995, hours after the talks were rescued from collapse. The leaders were, seated from left, Slobodan Milošević of Serbia, Alija Izetbegović of Bosnia, and Franjo Tuđman of Croatia. (Photo credit: Brian Schlumbohm)

of post–Cold War Europe" and "some European officials were embarrassed that American involvement had been necessary" to bring the Bosnian conflict to a close.[139] Izetbegović, Milošević, and Tuđman played to form in Paris. "There were no tears of relief, no emotional scenes of reconciliation" from any of them, the *New York Times* reported. "They signed without saying a word, put the caps back on their fountain pens and shook hands perfunctorily."[140] The treaty, Izetbegović said, was akin to swallowing bitter medicine.[141]

The Dayton accords in many ways reflected the complexities, fragility, and contradictions that define the Balkans. The agreement was not without serious shortcomings; its flaws were unmistakable. It was, notably, inherently contradictory, containing elements that encouraged integration of Bosnia's ethnicities as well as elements that served to drive them apart. The fundamental tension lay in the fact that the accords established a weak central government and two semi-autonomous entities shaped by ethnicity. Both entities—the Muslim-Croat Federation and the Republika Srpska—were granted their own governing structure, parliament, police force, and state agencies. To critics, that looked a lot like partition beneath the fig leaf of a weak unitary government.[142] It hardly seemed to be a formula for developing a thriving, multiethnic state.

Moreover, the agreement rewarded Bosnian Serb aggression. Republika Srpska controlled just under half of the territory of Bosnia; before the war, the Serbs had controlled about a third of Bosnian territory. The Dayton accords also permitted the three once-warring parties in Bosnia to retain their respective armies.[143] One country, two entities, three armies: these, too, were hardly the ingredients of a sturdy peace. Ted Galen Carpenter, a foreign policy expert at the Cato Institute, a libertarian think tank in Washington, D.C., wrote that the "American-inspired peace plan is one of those convoluted enterprises that habitually enchant diplomats but have no connection to reality."[144] He further wrote that a Bosnia "with two political heads may be theoretically innovative, but it is utterly impractical."[145] In fact, the Bosnian state could be said to have three political heads: a three-person presidency that included two members from the Muslim-Croat Federation and one from the Serb republic. "American diplomacy kept Bosnia whole," said one critic, "by stitching it together like Frankenstein's monster."[146]

Nevertheless, the foremost priority of the Dayton negotiations had been to end the bloodshed in Bosnia, and in that central objective the talks were a success[147]—perhaps even "a remarkable achievement," as Stephen Sestanovich has written.[148] A war that claimed 100,000 lives has not flared again. A peace that seemed wobbly, even coerced, has held. That outcome can be attributed in measure to the presence of the NATO-led IFOR contingent in Bosnia. IFOR included 20,000 U.S. troops, and sending them to Bosnia represented for Americans the single most controversial element of the Dayton accords.

A clear majority of Americans opposed committing U.S. forces to Bosnia as part of the IFOR peacekeeping force.[149] The Pentagon was not enthusiastic about the troop deployment, either, fearing that Bosnia could turn into a bloody quagmire, akin to that of Vietnam.[150] "In their hearts," Holbrooke wrote, "American military leaders would have preferred not to send American forces to Bosnia."[151] Large numbers of body bags, Holbrooke later said, "had been prepared for the casualties that the Pentagon believed were certain to come" in Bosnia.[152]

In addressing the unease about troop commitments to Bosnia, Clinton turned again to "American Exceptionalism." He did not invoke the phrase, but his meaning was clear enough. In a televised address at the end of November, Clinton dismissed arguments that the United States had no vital interests in the Balkans and promised that the U.S. troop deployment would be "limited, focused, and under the command of an American general. In fulfilling this mission," the president said, "we will have the chance to help stop the killing of innocent civilians . . . and at the same time to bring stability to central Europe—a region of the world that is vital to our national interests. It is the right thing to do."[153] American leadership, he said, had "created a chance to secure the peace and stop the suffering" in Bosnia. "Securing peace in Bosnia will also help to build a free and stable Europe. Bosnia lies at the very heart of Europe, next door to many of its fragile new democracies and some of our closest allies."

If U.S. troops were not deployed to help keep the peace in Bosnia, Clinton said, then NATO "will not be there. The peace will collapse, the war will reignite, the slaughter of innocents will begin again. A conflict that already has claimed so many victims, could spread like poison throughout the region, eat away at Europe's stability and erode our partnership with our European allies. And America's commitment to leadership will be questioned, if we refuse to participate in implementing a peace agreement we brokered right here in the United States."[154] Clinton acknowledged that the United States "can't do everything" to keep peace in the world, "but we must do what we can. There are times and places where our leadership can mean the difference between peace and war and where we can defend our fundamental values as a people and serve our most basic strategic interests." There are, he said, "still times when America and America alone can and should make the difference for peace. The terrible war in Bosnia is such a case. Nowhere today is the need for American leadership more stark or more immediate than in Bosnia."[155]

Clinton closed by saying that the "people of Bosnia, our NATO allies and people all around the world are now looking to America for leadership. So let us lead. That is our responsibility as Americans."[156] It was not necessarily an electrifying speech, not a rousing statement of doctrine. Nor was it Kennedyesque in pledging that America would "pay any price, bear any burden, [or] meet any hardship." But the speech was striking for its unmistakable if tacit embrace of "American Exceptionalism" and for its assertion of muscularity in U.S. foreign policy. It signaled a renewed interventionist ethos for the United States as the "indispensable nation."[157] Clinton invoked that sentiment on other prominent occasions—in accepting the Democratic Party's nomination for a second term, for example,[158] and in celebrating his reelection to the presidency.[159] Madeleine Albright, who succeeded Christopher as secretary of state in Clinton's second term, was even more assertive in her rhetoric, declaring in 1998: "We are the indispensable nation. We stand tall. We see further into the future" than other countries.[160]

In some respects, to assert "American Exceptionalism" in 1995 was to assert the obvious: the United States was no longer confronted by a rival superpower; the collapse of the Soviet Union in 1991 had left a world in which the United States, alone, could project military might around the globe.[161] Still, the memories of the quagmire of Vietnam and of the more recent disaster in Somalia placed a significant brake on U.S. interventions. Vietnam and Somalia, as Holbrooke noted, still "hung like dark clouds over the Pentagon."[162] They created what he referred to as the "Vietmalia syndrome,"[163] a decided reluctance to commit U.S. forces to distant lands. U.S. casualties were a dread prospect, which served in 1995 to restrain American ambitions and interventions abroad.

U.S. forces began deploying to Bosnia at the end of 1995 as part of the IFOR contingent. The U.S. troop presence was supposed to last a year. As it turned out, the last U.S. troops did not leave Bosnia until 2004.[164] During that time, there was not one U.S. fatality in hostile action in Bosnia—a wholly unanticipated outcome.[165] The feared quagmire did not open in Bosnia, and that country was not again convulsed by war.

Still, IFOR was roundly criticized for having stood by in March 1996 as Bosnian Serb thugs evicted fellow Serbs from homes and apartments in Serb-populated suburbs and enclaves of Sarajevo before they were to come under the jurisdiction of the Muslim-Croat Federation. "We must not allow a single Serb to remain in the territories which fall under Muslim-Croat control," declared the head of the Bosnian Serb Resettlement Office.[166] The disaster, Holbrooke wrote, "could have been easily prevented if IFOR had taken action."[167]

An even greater failure was the reluctance of NATO forces to seek out and arrest suspected war criminals such as Mladić and Radovan Karadžić, Bosnian Serb leaders indicted in 1995 for war crimes in Bosnia. Mladić and Karadžić were "most vulnerable after Dayton," Holbrooke wrote in 2005, "but the opportunity [to arrest them] was essentially lost after the NATO commander in Bosnia, U.S. Admiral Leighton Smith, told Bosnian Serb television, 'I don't have the authority to arrest anybody.'" Smith's statement, according to Holbrooke, was "a deliberately incorrect reading of his authority" under the Dayton accords.[168] Mladić remained a fugitive until Serbian police caught up with him in 2011; Karadžić was at large until 2008, when he was captured in disguise in Belgrade, where he had worked as a doctor. Like Mladić, Karadžić is on trial at The Hague for war crimes.

Some analysts have argued that the Bosnian war was ended not so much by the imaginative and assertive U.S. diplomacy as by the sheer exhaustion of the warring parties. "The true lesson of Dayton is this," journalist Michael Goldfarb wrote in 2010. "When it comes to conflict resolution the United States is still the indispensable, international head cracker—but only when people are too tired to feel the pain."[169] The exhaustion thesis is appealing but untenable. Croat and Muslim forces were resurgent in the summer of 1995, reclaiming hundreds of square miles of territory that had been taken by Bosnian Serbs during the war's early days. Before the ceasefire took effect in October 1995, a joint Croat-Muslim offensive had threatened the Serb stronghold of Banja Luka.[170] An attack on the city never developed. But had it fallen, all of Serb-held western Bosnia was at risk. So Bosnia's warring parties were hardly played out by late summer 1995. Indeed, a persuasive case can be made that the pre-Dayton ceasefire halted the Croat-Muslim advances prematurely. Moreover, some of the war's most grievous atrocities— the massacre at Srebrenica, the deadly mortar attack on Sarajevo, and the "ethnic cleansing" of Serbs rousted by Croat forces from the Krajina—all occurred within a few weeks in the summer of 1995. Another year of war, wrote Carl Bildt, a former Swedish prime minister, probably would have been "even more brutal and horrific than the terrible year of 1995."[171]

Dayton is more accurately understood as the first major successful foreign policy initiative of Clinton's presidency.[172] After the fiasco in Somalia and the mortification of standing aside as genocide swept Rwanda, the Clinton administration finally found its bearings and a formula: robust if measured application of U.S. military force, especially air power, could be instrumental in ending conflict and in pursuing policy objectives.[173] Although Clinton certainly can be faulted for diffident and ineffective responses to attacks by Islamist extremists on U.S. interests abroad during the late 1990s, his foreign policy after Dayton was noticeably more aggressive. The Dayton accords led Clinton to realize, as Kerrick said, that the United States sometimes had to put its "power and prestige on line to do things."[174]

Success in ending the brutal war in Bosnia was bracing. It emboldened U.S. foreign policy,[175] helped shake off the "Vietmalia syndrome," rekindled "American Exceptionalism," and fired ambitions abroad. Bosnia was the first in a succession of ever-more ambitious military operations overseas.[176] As Richard Sale has observed, after the first years of his presidency, Clinton "was not in the least dainty about using force."[177] In December 1998, Clinton ordered an extensive four-day bombing of Iraq to punish Saddam's regime for failing to cooperate with U.N. inspectors investigating the country's suspected stocks of chemical and nuclear weapons.[178] Clinton at that time was about to be impeached on charges of lying under oath and obstructing justice, upshots of a sex scandal discussed in the next chapter. The timing of the bombing campaign stirred suspicions that the attacks were principally a diversion from Clinton's serious troubles at home.

Britain joined the attack on Iraq, a campaign that was undertaken without U.N. endorsement. The objective was to degrade Iraq's capacity to produce weapons of mass destruction and to weaken Saddam's grip on power.[179] Six weeks before the bombing, Clinton signed the "Iraq Liberation Act of 1998," which committed the United States to supporting efforts to remove Saddam and "promote the emergence of a democratic government" in Baghdad.[180]

Less than a year later, Clinton ordered the bombing of targets in Serbia to pressure Milošević to end the persecution of ethnic Albanians in the province of Kosovo. After more than ten weeks of NATO air strikes, Milošević gave in and withdrew Serbian troops from Kosovo, a first step toward the province's gaining political independence. The brief Kosovar War was won without U.S. casualties and fought without U.N. approval.[181] It was, in some ways, a preemptive war—a war "justified less by what Milošević had already done in Kosovo than by what Americans believed he would do there in the future, judging by his behavior" in Bosnia, Peter Beinart observed in *The Icarus Syndrome*, his discerning book about trends in U.S. foreign policy.[182] Moreover, Beinart wrote, the war in Kosovo "nudged open an intellectual door, a door George W. Bush would fling wide open four years later," in invoking preemption as a justification for the U.S.-led invasion of Iraq.[183]

Post-Dayton interventionism—and a willingness to deploy U.S. military power in pursuit of foreign policy objectives—lived on after the Clinton administration. As Derek Chollet and James Goldgeier have noted, "Clinton's policies and the George W. Bush administration's ideas about using military power to defend values [overlapped] more than many Americans have perceived, or partisans on both sides care to admit."[184] Both administrations were willing to apply that power without securing prior endorsement of the United Nations.

U.S. foreign policy was decidedly more activist after Dayton: it was embroidered by "American Exceptionalism" and accompanied by what Beinart has termed a "hubris bubble" that expanded as military success encouraged even more ambitious undertakings. "The more confident America's leaders became in the hammer of military force," Beinart wrote, "the more closely they looked for nails" in projecting force abroad.[185] Bush administration officials were hardly enamored of Clinton, but, "when it came to foreign policy," Beinart noted, "they stood on his shoulders."[186] The "hubris bubble" expanded with the swift destruction of the Taliban regime in Afghanistan after the devastating September 11, 2001, terrorist attacks on the United States. In 2003 came the U.S.-led invasion of Iraq. In his book about the Bush administration, *New York Times* reporter Peter Baker anonymously quoted an official in the administration as saying: "The only reason we went into Iraq . . . is we were looking for somebody's ass to kick. Afghanistan was too easy."[187]

The "hubris bubble" burst in the aftermath of the invasion of Iraq. After taking Baghdad and toppling Saddam's Baathist regime, the United States was thoroughly unprepared for the grinding insurgency that followed. The puncturing of the "hubris bubble" did not necessarily foreclose American ambitions abroad. But it led to a decided retrenchment. As if chastened, the United States in recent years has been far less inclined to apply force to diplomacy and far more content to lead from behind. Twenty years after Dayton, "muscular" is seldom invoked to describe U.S. diplomacy. The "American Exceptionalism" that embroidered the post-Dayton rhetoric of the Clinton administration has fallen decidedly out of fashion among policymakers—a subject of wincing discomfiture and scorn,[188] if seriously mentioned at all.[189]

Holbrooke left the State Department three months after the Dayton accords, saying he wanted to spend more time with his wife and family. He came to regret the decision, saying later that he realized "too late that I had left too early."[190] His departure removed a singular force for implementing the terms of the Dayton agreement. But he returned to the Clinton administration as special envoy to the Balkans and later became U.S. ambassador to the United Nations. He also served two mostly unhappy years in the administration of President Barack Obama as a special representative for Afghanistan and Pakistan,[191] a post he held at his death, after emergency surgery for a torn aorta in 2010.[192]

Dayton was Holbrooke's major achievement in public life; he relished the accomplishment and kept a dutiful watch on postwar Bosnia.[193] He also was known to overstate the significance of the agreement, asserting for example that, without the Dayton accords, al-Qaeda might have planned the terrorist attacks of September 2001 from a safe haven in Bosnia instead of Afghanistan.[194] That is a highly debatable, speculative, and in the end an unlikely thesis. The Dayton agreement did require the removal of some 3,000 Islamist fighters who entered Bosnia from Afghanistan, Iran, and Arab countries to join Muslim forces. These fighters constituted a battalion that was disbanded in 1996.[195]

It is highly improbable that al-Qaeda militants would have operated in Bosnia as freely as they had in Afghanistan before 9/11. Had the talks at Dayton failed and fighting resumed in Bosnia, Islamist extremists surely would have drawn the attention of Serb and Croat forces.[196] Moreover, Bosnia's Muslim leaders were moderate and had shown little affinity for radical Islam. They would have been less-than-eager hosts to an al-Qaeda affiliate in the Balkans.

5

Clinton Meets Lewinsky

Until the Dayton peace accords were reached, 1995 had been a mostly lackluster—even forgettable—year for Bill Clinton and his presidency. It was a low-tide kind of year.

Resurgent Republicans led by Newt Gingrich, the pugnacious speaker of the House of Representatives, had come to power in Washington at the start of 1995, following their sweeping victories in midterm elections the year before. Once in office, they pressed an ambitious agenda to trim federal spending, lower taxes, reduce government regulation, and balance the budget. Gingrich called it the "Contract with America."

By the spring, the tide of power and influence was flowing decidedly to the Republicans in Congress and away from Clinton. The one-sidedness was so stark that the president was moved to pleading his relevance in Washington. "The Constitution gives me relevance; the power of our ideas gives me relevance; the record we have built up over the last two years and the things we're trying to do give me relevance," Clinton declared at a primetime news conference on April 18, 1995. "The president is relevant here, especially an activist president."[1] It was hardly a stirring assertion of presidential authority. No troops, the *New York Times* wryly observed, would be inspired to march "to battle under a banner that reads, 'The President is relevant.'"[2]

The following day, the federal building in Oklahoma City was attacked, and the resolve Clinton demonstrated in response was impressive. He was praised for giving voice to the grief and anger that Americans were feeling and for vowing that "justice for these killers will be certain, swift and severe. We will find them. We will convict them. And we will seek the death penalty for them."[3] Within days, though, Clinton picked a needless fight with the voices of conservative talk radio, denouncing them for inflaming the public debate. He said the airwaves too often were used "to keep some people as paranoid as possible and the rest of us all torn up and upset with each other," and he urged Americans to speak out against "the purveyors of hatred and division."[4] His remarks carried special resonance in the wake of the Oklahoma City bombing. Clinton did not specifically mention the likes of Rush Limbaugh, but Limbaugh recognized himself as a target of the president's insinuations and said they threatened "a chilling effect on legitimate discussion."[5]

The controversy soon passed, but Clinton continued to be dogged by periodic gaffes and missteps, which lent a sense of unsteadiness and even clumsiness to his administration. Former senator Eugene McCarthy criticized Clinton for acting like "the governor of the United States."[6] The administration's dithering on what to do in Bosnia was mocked by Jacques Chirac, the French president, who declared in July 1995 that the position of leader of the free world had fallen "vacant."[7] In September, Clinton spoke informally with reporters aboard Air Force One about the "funk" he thought Americans were in, an off-hand but ill-advised comment that invited comparisons with the sense of "malaise" that came to be associated with the beleaguered administration of President Jimmy Carter in the late 1970s.[8] A few weeks later, at a fund-raising dinner in Texas, Clinton shocked fellow Democrats by seeming to repudiate a deficit-reduction package he had signed two years before, saying he had raised taxes "too much" in that deal.[9]

Even Clinton's friends and sympathizers in the news media wondered whether his presidency was adrift or out of its depth. A columnist for the *Washington Post* referred to "the terminally clumsy Clinton administration,"[10] and a veteran White House reporter, Helen Thomas of the wire service United Press International, ruminated about "Clinton's gaffe du jour."[11] In the same vein, E. J. Dionne of the *Washington Post* wrote that the president "makes life hardest on those who are for him."[12]

By late 1995, the prospect of a train wreck loomed in Washington—a sort of slow-motion collision that centered around a budget impasse between Clinton and the Congress, an impasse defined by the possibility of having to shut down the federal government.[13] The prospective train wreck threatened to become a reality by mid-November. At issue was whether the budget should be balanced in seven years, as Gingrich and the Republicans proposed, or in nine to ten years, as Clinton favored. Also in dispute was whether old people would pay more in Medicare premiums, which the Republicans supported but Clinton opposed. The president and the Republicans also were at odds on government spending for education and the environment.

Mike McCurry, the White House press secretary at the time, recalled "there was an utter lack of confidence at the White House that we would prevail in that showdown. There were long debates about who, at the end of the day, was going to bear the blame for [a government] shutdown: The president or . . . the Republican Congress? There was certainly no unanimous view that we [would] prevail against Gingrich and the Republicans."[14]

The train wreck—or what the *Washington Post* called the "Great Government Shutdown of '95"[15]—happened on November 14. The night before, Clinton had vetoed two spending measures that would have kept the government open, objecting to provisions that would raise Medicare premiums and trim spending on education and the environment. In Washington and across the country, about 800,000 federal employees deemed "non-essential" were sent home or told not to come to work. The government shutdown was partial but its effects were far-reaching. The Centers for Disease Control suspended disease surveillance.[16] Applications for U.S. passports and for visas to enter the United States piled up by the tens of thousands every day.[17] Ticket holders were turned away from the National Gallery of Art and the largest exhibition of the masterpieces of Johannes Vermeer since 1696.[18] The shutdown postponed the opening at the Ronald Reagan Presidential Library of an exhibit of watercolors by Britain's Prince Charles.[19] The country's 368 national parks, monuments, and recreation areas—including the Statue of Liberty, Independence Hall, Yosemite, and the National Zoo—all were closed.

"Only Washington Would Try to Close the Grand Canyon," a headline in the *Washington Post* declared.[20] And in that, Washington succeeded: an unusual calm replaced the noisy throngs of visitors at the Grand Canyon, a national park since 1919. Fife Symington, the governor of Arizona, showed up at the Grand Canyon with some fifty unarmed National Guardsmen, in what to some observers appeared to be an incipient state challenge to federal authority.[21] Symington's conduct later was described as his "best John Wayne" imitation.[22] That may have overstated matters, but the governor proposed calling on the guardsmen and state employees to keep at least a portion of the park open to tourists. He was rebuffed by officials of the Interior Department.[23]

The most jaw-dropping moment of the shutdown came on November 15, when Gingrich, ever voluble, told journalists at a breakfast meeting in Washington that he had toughened up the interim spending measure that Clinton vetoed in part because he felt the president had treated him badly. Clinton, Gingrich said, had ignored him aboard Air Force One during a trip to Israel to attend the state funeral of Yitzhak Rabin, the Israeli prime minister who was assassinated in Tel Aviv on November 4. Not only did Clinton pass up an opportunity to negotiate the budget impasse during the long flight home, Gingrich said, but he and Senate Majority Leader Bob Dole were made to leave the aircraft by the rear stairs after landing at Andrews Air Force base in Maryland.

"This is petty," Gingrich told the journalists, but "you land at Andrews and you've been on the plane for twenty-five hours [for the round trip to Israel] and nobody has talked to you and they ask you to get off the plane by the back ramp. . . . You just wonder, where is their sense of manners? Where is their sense of courtesy?" The perceived slights and rude treatment, Gingrich said, were "part of [the reason] why you ended up with us sending down a tougher" spending bill,[24] making Clinton's veto a certainty.

The speaker's rambling, almost stream-of-consciousness remarks qualified as the year's most astounding political gaffe[25] and invited a torrent of ridicule that helped tilt the shutdown battle in Clinton's favor—even perhaps rejuvenating his presidency.[26] Within hours of Gingrich's remarks, McCurry released a photograph of Clinton, Gingrich, and others at a conference table aboard Air Force One, during the trip to Israel. McCurry said he had done so "sort of mischievously," to lend an impression that "Clinton *did* talk to Gingrich on the plane, so what's Gingrich griping about?"[27]

The next morning's *New York Daily News* seized on Gingrich's peevishness in a memorably devastating caricature on its front page. The speaker was drawn as a chubby toddler in diapers, stamping his foot and howling. Above the sketch was a huge headline that declared: "CRY BABY. Newt's Tantrum: He closed down the government because Clinton made him sit at back of plane." The caricature was an immediate sensation. Democrats brought to the House floor a poster-size blow-up of the *Daily News* front page and made it their centerpiece as they ridiculed Gingrich. Congresswoman Patricia Schroeder of Colorado held up

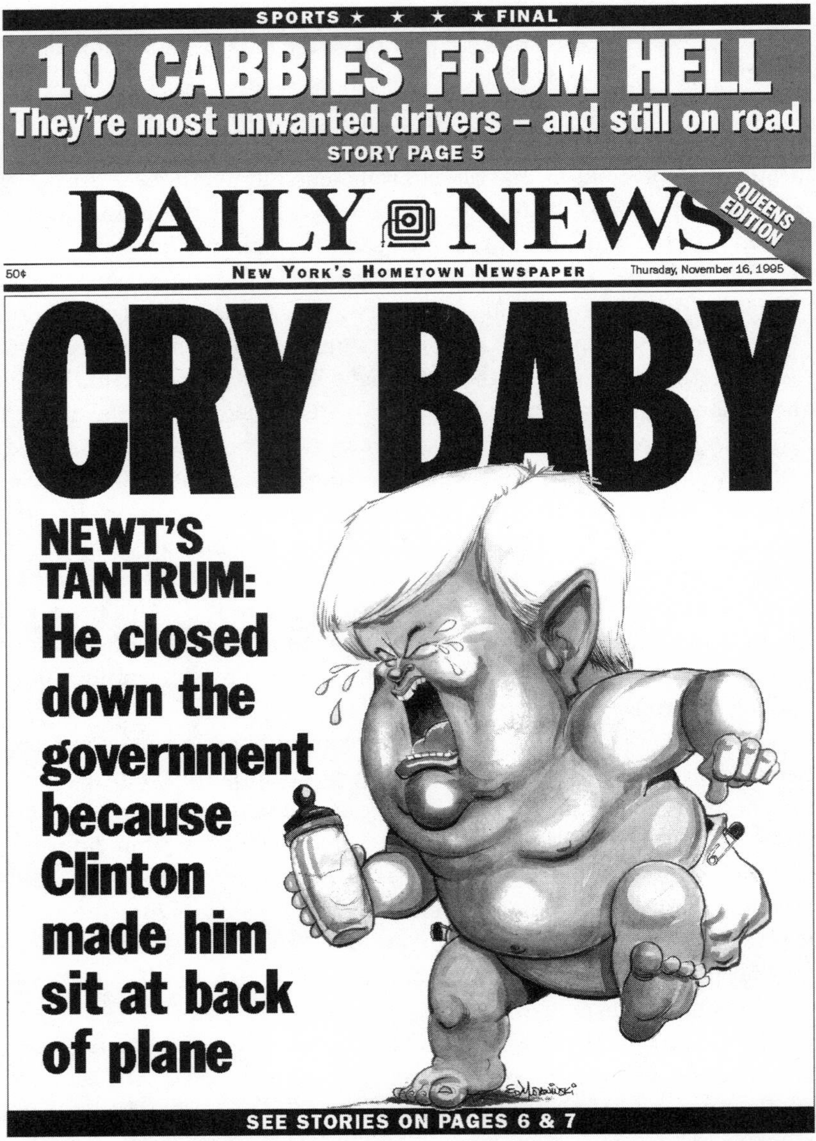

FIGURE 19. Newt Gingrich, speaker of the House of Representatives, committed the political gaffe of 1995 by complaining about his treatment aboard Air Force One and saying it contributed to the impasse that closed the federal government. The *New York Daily News* turned Gingrich's peevish outburst into a memorable, front-page caricature. (Photo credit: New York Daily News/Getty images)

a model of an Academy Award statuette and proclaimed that the speaker had "sewn up the category of best performance by a child actor this year."[28] The spectacle on the House floor turned into a bizarre farce when the Republican majority approved a measure ordering the blown-up front page removed from the chamber.[29]

The devastating send-up helped to cast Gingrich as the obnoxious poster boy of the federal budget crisis,[30] and it deepened the public's unease about the speaker and his blustering ways. Gingrich may have been a gifted political strategist, but he was a flawed leader who often came off as arrogant, petulant, and needlessly high-handed. But resolving the government shutdown took more than a stunning *faux pas,* of course. After five days, Clinton and congressional Republicans agreed to balance the federal budget by 2002, provided that entitlement programs like Medicare and Medicaid were protected. It was shaky compromise, but it led to reopening the government.[31] Gingrich once again turned to hyperbole, calling the compromise "one of the great achievements in the history of America."[32]

The partial government shutdown in November was preliminary to an even longer closure that began December 15, following the collapse of negotiations about how to calculate a balanced federal budget. The second shutdown lasted twenty-one days, until January 6, 1996. By then, the tactic of closing the government to force Clinton into an agreement on the budget had thoroughly backfired on Republicans.[33] Opinion polls showed that most Americans blamed them, not Clinton, for the shutdowns.[34] Gingrich's national favorability ratings dropped to 27 percent—rivaling those of President Richard Nixon at the depths of the Watergate scandal.[35] While *Time* magazine chose Gingrich its "man of the year" for 1995, the speaker never fully recovered from the blunder of forcing the government shut down.[36]

The government closure of November 1995 had even greater and more stunning consequences: it made possible an otherwise impossible liaison, one that would explode twenty-six months later in an extraordinary scandal of sex and lies, a scandal that dogged the president to his last full day in office. The scandal would humble Clinton, imperil his presidency, and deepen partisan cleavages to such an extent that they have never fully closed.

The shutdown had temporarily trimmed the number of full-time employees in the White House executive office to about 90 from 430.[37] Into that gap stepped a cadre of young interns who, given their unpaid status, suddenly found themselves working closely and quite unexpectedly with some of the most senior officials in the administration. Among them was Monica S. Lewinsky, who was six-and-a-half years older than Clinton's daughter.

Lewinsky began her White House internship in July 1995, two weeks before her twenty-second birthday and two months after she graduated with a degree in psychology from Lewis and Clark College, a small liberal arts college in Portland, Oregon. Until then, in writer Jeffrey Toobin's uncharitable assessment, Lewinsky had "spent most of her brief life obsessed with her weight. . . . Before she became obsessed with the president of the United States, her only other serious interest in life was dieting."[38] To land the internship, Lewinsky tapped a family connection—that of Walter Kaye, a retired insurance magnate and a generous contributor to the Democratic Party. Kaye was a friend of Lewinsky's mother and an acquaintance of Hillary Clinton. Kaye recommended Monica Lewinsky,[39] who was hired and assigned to the correspondence section in the office of the White House chief of staff, Leon Panetta.[40] The internship was to last six weeks.

Lewinsky worked out of the stately Old Executive Office Building next door to the White House. She saw the president a few times that summer, at events on the White House lawn to which interns were invited. They included a departure ceremony on August 9 at which Clinton shook hands with guests along a roped-off line. On that occasion, Lewinsky later told her biographer, Andrew Morton, the president spotted her and gave her an intense flirtatious look—or what she called "the full Bill Clinton." Lewinsky said: "When it was time to shake my hand, the [president's] smile disappeared, the rest of the crowd disappeared and we shared an intense sexual exchange. He undressed me with his eyes."[41]

The next day, the interns were invited to a Western-themed party on the South Lawn of the White House, an occasion to mark Clinton's forty-ninth birthday before he left on vacation in Wyoming. It was a casual and light-hearted event. Panetta and his top deputies showed up as cowboys on horseback. Vice President Al Gore arrived in a beat-up station wagon. George Stephanopoulos, Clinton's senior adviser, spent time playing in a sandbox.[42] The president wore a checked shirt and jeans. He kept looking and smiling at Lewinsky, who took a place in a line of well-wishers to shake Clinton's hand and wish him happy birthday. As she did, Lewinsky later recalled, Clinton "looked deep into my eyes and I was hooked." As the president moved on, Morton wrote, "his arm, casually but unnecessarily, brushed against her breast."[43] As the party was wrapping up, Lewinsky blew a kiss to the president. He laughed and tossed back his head, as if catching her air-smooch on his cheek.[44]

Lewinsky extended her internship, but her flirtation with Clinton lacked any chance of gaining intensity or intimacy. Then came the government shutdown. The closure allowed her "more access to the West Wing than she would have had, typically, as just a run-of-the-mill intern," McCurry noted.[45] Indeed, the shutdown produced extraordinary circumstances that gave rise to intimate sexual encounters that eventually tarred Clinton with the ignominy of impeachment.

By mid-November 1995, Lewinsky had secured a full-time, paid position in the correspondence section of the White House legislative affairs office. The paperwork authorizing her hiring had not been completed before the government was shut down. Nominally, therefore, she was still an intern and eligible to keep coming to work, despite the closure. Lewinsky was assigned to Panetta's West Wing office, answering telephone calls and running errands.[46] Just down the corridor was the Oval Office.

On November 15—the day Gingrich uttered his self-destructive complaints about his treatment aboard Air Force One—Clinton and Lewinsky had their first sexual encounter.[47] They had seen each other in passing that day, carrying on what Lewinsky called their "flirtation relationship."[48] At one point, as Clinton left Panetta's inner office, Lewinsky lifted the back of her jacket, showing him the straps of her thong underwear.[49] No one else noticed.[50] The *risqué* gesture "was over in an instant," Lewinsky's biographer wrote, and she "was rewarded with an appreciative look" as the president walked past.[51]

Later that evening, as she headed to a bathroom,[52] Lewinsky passed the office of George Stephanopoulos. Clinton was inside the office, alone, and beckoned her inside.[53] Their conversation was stilted at first. Clinton asked her where she had gone to college. Lewinsky blurted, "I have a crush on you."[54] That was his cue, she later said, "to proceed . . . in what he wanted and what he was feeling."[55] The president led her to his private office, behind the Oval Office. Lewinsky and Clinton spoke briefly, in her recollection, and "sort of acknowledged that there had been a chemistry" between them, that they were "attracted to each other." The president asked if he could kiss her. Without hesitating, she consented.[56] His kiss, Lewinsky told her biographer, was "soft, deep, romantic."[57]

She reckoned there was little chance of developing a relationship with Clinton. The president, she suspected, had a White House girlfriend who

FIGURE 20. If not for the partial shutdown of the federal government in November 1995, Bill Clinton and Monica Lewinsky would have lacked the opportunity to pursue a dalliance at the White House. Their intermittent affair lasted until March 1997—and led to Clinton's impeachment in December 1998. (Photo credit: Getty images)

had been furloughed during the government shutdown, and soon he would be back with her.[58] But before returning to her desk, Lewinsky gave Clinton a slip of paper on which she had written her name and telephone number.[59] Lewinsky was alone later that night in Panetta's office when the president came in. He invited her to meet him down the hall in a few minutes, in Stephanopoulos's office. She agreed. They met in the windowless hallway connecting Stephanopoulos's office to the Oval Office. "For all that Clinton may have wanted to pursue women during his presidency," Toobin noted, "his encounters with Lewinsky illustrated the logistical challenges. It took not only a determined partner, but one who didn't mind awkward and degrading circumstances. Monica Lewinsky fit the bill."[60]

She and the president kissed. She unbuttoned her jacket and his hands wandered, fondling her breasts and genitalia. Soon, a telephone call came for the president. He took it. While on the phone, the president kept his hand in Lewinsky's pants. She performed oral sex on him.[61] Ending the call, Clinton told her to stop. He said he needed to trust her before she brought him to a climax. The president also said, jokingly, that he "hadn't had that in a long time."[62]

The stealthy assignation at the White House that night was the upshot of happenstance, guile, and a measure of mutual desire. A canceled trip to Asia contributed to the improbable dalliance, too. Clinton had intended to travel in mid-November to Osaka, Japan, to attend a meeting of the Asia Pacific Economic Cooperation forum. Because of the government shutdown, Clinton stayed at the White House and sent Vice President Gore in his place.[63] Clinton would vaguely blame inner "demons" for his extramarital affair with Lewinsky. "During the government shutdowns," he wrote, "I was engaged in two titanic struggles: a public one with Congress over the future of our country, and a private one to hold the old demons at bay. I had won the public fight and lost the private one."[64]

He and Lewinsky took pains, of course, to conceal their flirtation and to keep their meetings covert.[65] Even so, others at the White House commented about what seemed to be an unlikely attraction. Barry J. Toiv, a senior adviser to Panetta, mentioned to Lewinsky that she seemed to be the recipient of a good deal of "face time" with the president.[66] On November 16, a fellow intern told Lewinsky, "I think the president has a crush on you." The comment, Lewinsky said, surprised and startled her.[67]

She and Clinton met next on November 17, after pizza was delivered late that night for the staff working in Panetta's office. Toiv accidentally bumped into Lewinsky, soiling her jacket with pizza toppings. She went down the hall to the restroom to wipe away the mess. Upon emerging, she saw Clinton nearby, standing in the doorway to the office of his personal secretary, Betty Currie. "You can come out this way," Clinton told her, and led Lewinsky through the Oval Office and into his private study. In the hallway or bathroom outside the study, they paused to chat and to kiss.[68] "I bet you don't even know my name," Lewinsky told him. Clinton replied: "What kind of name is Lewinsky, anyway?"[69]

After a while, Lewinsky said she had better go back to her desk. The president suggested that she bring him some slices of pizza. She did, returning in a few minutes. Currie opened the door and said, "Sir, the girl's here with the pizza." Clinton told Lewinsky to come in.[70] She and the president went to the area of Clinton's private study. There they kissed, and Clinton fondled Lewinsky's breasts. He unbuttoned his shirt and sucked in his stomach,[71] a reaction that struck Lewinsky as "very real and very human."[72] "You don't have to do that," she told him. "I like

your tummy."[73] Soon, Currie was at the door leading to the hallway, saying that the president had a telephone call. It was a congressman, and he
took the call. While on the phone, Lewinsky said, the president "unzipped
his pants and exposed himself."[74] She fellated him.[75]

Before their rendezvous ended, Clinton told her that he was "usually
around on weekends, no one else is around, and you can come and see
me."[76] Except for a brief meeting in early December, however, they
were not together for six weeks, until the afternoon of New Year's Eve.
Lewinsky by then was no longer an intern. She had begun her full-time
White House job in the legislative affairs office. That afternoon, Lewinsky was in the pantry of the president's private dining room, in conversation with Bayani Nelvis, a White House steward. She told him she
had just recently smoked her first cigar. Nelvis offered her one of the
president's cigars. At that moment, Clinton walked down the hallway
from the Oval Office and spotted Lewinsky. He sent Nelvis on an errand
to Panetta's office, and gave Lewinsky a cigar.[77]

Under the impression he had forgotten her name since their mid-
November encounters, Lewinsky told Clinton her name. He had called
her "Kiddo" when they had passed in the hallways.[78] The president said
he knew her name and had lost the slip of paper bearing her telephone
number. He said he had tried to find her number in the telephone directory but it was not listed. They soon moved to the study and kissed.
According to Lewinsky, the president "lifted my sweater and exposed
my breasts and was fondling them with his hands and with his mouth."[79]
She performed oral sex on him.[80] Afterward, Lewinsky said, Clinton
renewed his invitation that she visit him on weekends.[81] Later that day,
Clinton, his wife, and their daughter traveled to Hilton Head, South
Carolina, for a year-end retreat called Renaissance Weekend.[82] As the
New York Times reported, the Clintons marked the occasion with
1,000 friends; on New Year's Day 1996, he attended a "seminar on
personal growth and family values."[83]

Clinton and Lewinsky had seven other intimate encounters over the
next sixteen months, most of them in early 1996. Although Lewinsky
wanted to, they never had vaginal intercourse.[84] Usually, she fellated him
and he fondled her, sometimes bringing her to orgasm. Their furtive
encounters typically were in the president's private study near the Oval
Office, or in the hallway or bathroom nearby—secluded places that permitted them the greatest privacy. But being discovered was a constant
worry. On one occasion, Lewinsky noticed that the president was kissing
her with "his eyes wide open." She thought kissing that way "wasn't very

romantic" and expressed annoyance. "Well," Clinton told her, "I was just looking to see to make sure no one was out there."[85] Another tryst in 1996 was interrupted by Harold Ickes, a presidential aide, who arrived at the Oval Office for an appointment. "Mr. President?" Ickes called out. Clinton and Lewinsky were in the study off the Oval Office and looked at each other in surprise. The president rushed—"jetted," she said—into the Oval Office to meet Ickes. Lewinsky left by a back door.[86]

Sexual activity did not figure in every meeting between Lewinsky and the president. "We enjoyed talking to each other and being with each other," she recalled. "We were very affectionate. We would tell jokes. We would talk about our childhoods; talk about current events. I was always giving him my stupid ideas about what I thought should be done in the administration, or different views on things." Clinton, she said, "always made me smile when I was with him. It was a lot of—he was sunshine."[87]

Clinton broke off the relationship on President's Day in mid-February 1996,[88] only to renew it at the end of March 1996. Their final sexual encounter was on March 29, 1997. By then, Lewinsky had been moved to the Pentagon, where she was a confidential assistant to the assistant secretary of defense for public affairs. Her persistent efforts at the White House to get close to Clinton, and to ingratiate herself with senior officials, had become obvious and disquieting[89] and had prompted her transfer.

Evelyn Lieberman, the deputy White House chief of staff for operations, a formidable presence,[90] and a confidante of Hillary Clinton, saw to it that Lewinsky was moved out of the White House. Lieberman called Lewinsky a "clutch"—a hanger-on who was "always someplace she shouldn't be."[91] According to Lewinsky, Lieberman had encountered her in the West Wing of the White House in December 1995 and chided her, saying interns were not permitted near the Oval Office unescorted.[92] Lewinsky told her that she was not an intern but a full-time staff member. Lieberman replied: "They hired you?"—but then said she must have mistaken Lewinsky for someone else. Lewinsky took to calling her one of the White House "meanies."[93]

It was remarkable how much time the president devoted to Lewinsky, in person and on the phone. Lewinsky estimated that, in all, she and Clinton spoke by phone about fifty times, usually late at night and early in the morning.[94] During his campaign for reelection in 1996, Clinton sometimes called Lewinsky when his wife was not with him. In several calls that year, Clinton and Lewinsky engaged in steamy phone sex.[95]

Lewinsky was told of her transfer to the Pentagon in April 1996, and took the news badly. In tears, she offered to continue work without pay if she could stay at the White House job. No chance: Lewinsky said she was told that writing news releases at the Pentagon "was a sexier job" than her position at the White House.[96]

The Clinton-Lewinsky affair might never have been revealed—and never have become a vehicle for impeaching the president—were it not for a unanimous decision in 1997 by the U.S. Supreme Court. The justices agreed to allow a pending sexual harassment lawsuit against Clinton to move ahead while he was in office. The lawsuit had been filed in May 1994 by lawyers for Paula Corbin Jones, a former state clerical worker in Arkansas. She said that Clinton, while he was governor of Arkansas, arranged for a state trooper to bring her to meet him alone at a room in the Excelsior Hotel in Little Rock. During the encounter, Jones said, Clinton lowered his pants and asked for oral sex. She refused and left the room.

In ruling that a sitting president had no immunity from civil lawsuits, the Supreme Court said it believed the Jones case would scarcely be a distraction for Clinton. Writing for the court, Justice John Paul Stevens said it was "highly unlikely" the Jones case would "occupy any substantial amount" of the president's time.[97] So the case went ahead, and Jones's lawyers were permitted to subpoena and question under oath women with whom Clinton was suspected of having had extramarital affairs. Among them was Monica Lewinsky.

Her name was made known to Jones's lawyers by Linda Tripp, whom Lewinsky had befriended at the Pentagon. Tripp had been a secretary at the White House during the administration of President George H. W. Bush and stayed on for a while after Clinton's inauguration before taking a job at the Pentagon. Tripp loathed Clinton and had contemplated writing a tell-all book about chicanery at the White House. In conversations with Tripp, Lewinsky described her assignations with the president in some detail. Tripp eventually alerted Jones's lawyers to the Clinton-Lewinsky liaison. At a deposition in Washington on January 17, 1998, they asked the president about his dalliance with the former intern. The federal judge hearing the Jones case, Susan Webber Wright, presided in person at the six-hour session.[98] Clinton may have been taken aback by the detailed questions about his liaison with Lewinsky,[99] but he denied under oath having had a "sexual relationship" or a "sexual affair" with her. He also denied having been alone with Lewinsky.[100]

Tripp, meanwhile, also spoke with lawyers for Kenneth W. Starr, the independent counsel appointed in 1994 to investigate suspicions of misconduct by Clinton and his wife in the failed Whitewater real estate investment in Arkansas. The Clintons' business partners, James and Susan McDougal, were indicted in 1995 and convicted the following year of fraud and conspiracy charges in the far-reaching, many-tentacled Whitewater scandal. But the Clintons were never formally accused of wrongdoing. Not long after hearing from Tripp and receiving audiotapes that she secretly made of conversations with Lewinsky, Starr sought and was granted authority to expand his mandate to include suspected unlawful conduct stemming from Clinton's assignations with Lewinsky.[101]

Word soon leaked that Starr was investigating Clinton for perjury and obstruction of justice in an affair with a young former intern—news that electrified Washington as nothing had since the most dramatic revelations of the Watergate scandal in 1973 and 1974. Network television news anchors cut short assignments to Havana, where they had been covering the visit of Pope John Paul II, and returned to the United States.[102] ABC and CBS preempted primetime programming to broadcast reports about the Clinton-Lewinsky affair.[103] Matt Drudge of the online *Drudge Report*, which first reported word of Clinton's dalliance with an intern, went on NBC's *Today* show and said, "I go where the stink is."[104] The media frenzy, Clinton recalled, "was overwhelming."[105]

The president had had a reputation for womanizing, and suspicions of his extramarital liaisons had circulated in the West Wing of the White House.[106] But reports of Clinton's having had an affair with a former intern struck some White House officials as so improbable that it must be bogus. McCurry, the White House press secretary, recalled that, on the day the story broke, "I was told that this is about Clinton and Monica Lewinsky, and I said, 'You mean Monica—you mean the large intern?' And someone said yeah, and I remember just breaking out laughing. It was like, 'This is so wildly improbable that maybe finally we're going to be able to put the rumor-mongering to bed once and for all.'"[107]

Soon enough, though, "impeachment"[108] and "resignation" were in the air. Some commentators speculated that Clinton surely would quit if it were shown that he lied about his dalliance with Lewinsky. Sam Donaldson, a veteran White House reporter for ABC News, was among the pundits who said so. "If he's not telling the truth, I think his presidency is numbered in days," Donaldson declared on a Sunday talk show on January 25, 1998. "This isn't going to drag out. We're not going to be here three months from now talking about this. Mr. Clinton, if he's not telling the truth and the evidence shows that, will resign, perhaps this week."[109] On the same program, syndicated columnist George Will said Clinton's presidency "today is as dead—deader really—than Woodrow Wilson's was after he had a stroke" that incapacitated him in 1919.[110]

Clinton was not telling the truth, but he was not about to quit. He denied an affair with Lewinsky, most memorably in a defiant, finger-wagging declaration at the White House in late January 1998. "I want you to listen to me," the president said on that occasion. His face was reddened. It was clear he was seething. "I'm going to say this again: I did not have sexual relations with that woman, Miss Lewinsky. I never told anybody to lie, not a single time—never," he said. "These allegations are false. And I need to go back to work for the American people."[111] Later, he told senior White House advisers and officials essentially the same thing: the allegations were untrue, he never had a sexual relationship with Lewinsky. According to Sidney Blumenthal, an assistant to the president, Clinton said Lewinsky "came on to me and made a sexual demand on me."[112] Blumenthal also said that the president likened himself to a character in Arthur Koestler's novel *Darkness at Noon*—"somebody who is surrounded by an oppressive force that is creating a lie about me and I can't get the truth out."[113]

Clinton and his supporters were buoyed by opinion polls that indicated that most Americans had little appetite for impeaching the president or forcing his resignation[114]—at least not for the misconduct Starr was investigating. The polling data remained fairly consistent as Starr's investigation dragged on; months passed before his office reached an immunity agreement with Lewinsky in exchange for her testimony.[115] In the interim, Clinton's defenders mounted a fierce attack on the prosecutor and his investigation, characterizing him as a sex-obsessed Puritan and describing his inquiry as invasive and a needlessly partisan vendetta. Discrediting Starr was central to Clinton's strategy for surviving the scandal.[116] So was keeping the support of Democrats in Congress. While many of them were dismayed by the president's behavior, few of them wavered in their support for him.

Clinton was invited several times to testify to the grand jury that Starr had empanelled; he repeatedly declined. Finally, in July 1998, a subpoena was issued for the president's testimony. He agreed to appear before the grand jury provided the subpoena was withdrawn. It was, and on August 17, 1998, Clinton was questioned via closed-circuit television from the White House. Two weeks before then, he had given

Starr's investigators a DNA sample, which matched small semen stains on the blue dress Lewinsky had worn at their last sexual encounter, on March 29, 1997. Under oath, Clinton acknowledged having had an "inappropriate intimate" relationship with Lewinsky but insisted he had not committed perjury at his deposition in the Jones case seven months before. He said his statements then had been legally accurate.[117]

Hours after his grand jury testimony, Clinton went on national television and acknowledged in an angry, four-and-a-half-minute address that he had indeed had an "inappropriate relationship" with Lewinsky and that he had misled Americans about it.[118] The president's confession was belated, incomplete, and clearly unwilling—and it did nothing to deter the prosecutors. Three weeks later, Starr submitted an elaborately detailed, 445-page report, or referral, to Congress that identified eleven possible counts for impeaching the president. All of them arose from his dalliance with Lewinsky; none was related to Whitewater or its related scandals.[119] The prospective grounds for impeachment included five counts of lying under oath, four counts of obstructing justice, one count of witness-tampering, and one count of abusing constitutional authority.[120] The most serious allegations were that Clinton lied at his deposition in the Jones case, had lied before the grand jury, and had endeavored to conceal evidence of his dalliance with Lewinsky.

On December 19, 1998, the House of Representatives approved two counts of impeachment—that the president committed perjury in his grand jury testimony and obstructed justice by encouraging others to lie to conceal his affair with Lewinsky. The furtive and tawdry affair begun in 1995 had spun, unimaginably, into a national spectacle. Clinton thus became the first elected U.S. president ever to be impeached.[121] It was, John F. Harris wrote in the *Washington Post*, "an emblem he will wear through history. It was the one action that everyone who knows Clinton agreed will sting him."[122]

The Senate, as obliged by the Constitution, took up the impeachment charges at a trial that began January 7, 1999. By then, it was widely recognized that Clinton would never be convicted because the Senate lacked sixty-seven votes—the obligatory two-thirds majority—to remove the president on the impeachment charges. On February 13, 1999, the Senate voted to reject both counts against Clinton. Neither charge won even a majority vote.[123]

The extraordinary ordeal—which had its origins during the ill-conceived partial shutdown of the federal government and which took momentum from Clinton's willingness to engage the brazen overtures of an aggressive yet insecure young woman—left a stark and bitter legacy that can be detected even now, in the cleavages of an often-hostile political environment. Clinton's impeachment, R. W. Apple wrote in the *New York Times* the day after the House voted, "seemed to crystallize the long-term decline in political civility" in America.[124] That it did. The votes to impeach the president were largely along party lines: Republicans were mostly in favor, Democrats were mostly opposed. Those votes signaled a stark partisan divide that would deepen and intensify during the first fifteen years of the twenty-first century. Surveys have found that the Republican and Democratic parties have both become more ideologically unified and more homogeneous. Liberal Republicans and conservative Democrats became rarities—oxymorons, almost—a trend that has become most vivid in the House of Representatives[125] and in statehouses around the country.[126] Middle-ground positions are more often eschewed, and swing states in presidential elections have become fewer.[127] Republicans have come to be dominated by the party's conservative wing, while growing numbers of Democrats self-identify as liberals.[128]

Sharp and predictable partisan disagreement on a variety of matters came to characterize the country's riven political culture. Well into the twenty-first century, Republicans and Democrats were at odds, and often bitterly so, over the size and reach of the federal government, over national health care and other federal entitlements, over environmental policy, and over national security.[129] It would be a mistaken exaggeration, of course, to attribute political polarization exclusively to the storms provoked by the Clinton-Lewinsky scandal.[130] But the impeachment battles of 1998–99 contributed mightily. The centrist "third way" approach Clinton periodically espoused was badly damaged by the impeachment battle and did not long survive his presidency.[131] Clinton left office in January 2001, but the wounds opened by the scandal and his impeachment were not soon to close. They were aggravated by the disputed outcome of the presidential election in 2000, in which the Supreme Court declared Republican George W. Bush the winner over Vice President Gore. They were aggravated further by the long-running and inconclusive U.S.-led wars in Afghanistan and Iraq.

Clinton succeeded in beating back the impeachment charges, but his mendacity did not go unpunished. Two months after his acquittal by the Senate, the president was found in contempt of court by Susan Webber Wright, the federal judge who presided at his deposition in January 1998. In a scalding opinion, she wrote the "record demonstrates by clear and convincing evidence" that Clinton at the deposition gave "false, misleading and evasive answers that were designed to obstruct the judicial process." Simply stated, the judge wrote, "the President's deposition testimony regarding whether he had ever been alone with Ms. Lewinsky was intentionally false, and his statements regarding whether he had ever engaged in sexual relations with Ms. Lewinsky likewise were intentionally false."[132] Moreover, she wrote, "It appears the President is asserting that Ms. Lewinsky could be having sex with him while, at the same time, he was not having sex with her."[133]

The penalty the judge imposed was unprecedented: no court had held a sitting president in contempt. Wright also ordered the president to pay a $90,000 fine to cover legal fees and other expenses that Jones's lawyers had incurred as a result of the falsehoods he told under oath. In April 1998, Webber had dismissed the Jones lawsuit, saying the evidentiary record failed to reach the threshold of sexual harassment under federal law. Jones's lawyers appealed and, in November 1998, as the House was preparing to consider articles of impeachment, Clinton agreed to pay $850,000 to settle the Jones case out of court.

On the last full day of his presidency in 2001, Clinton acknowledged having given false testimony at his deposition and surrendered for five years his license to practice law in Arkansas, his home state.[134] He also agreed to pay a $25,000 fine to the Arkansas Bar Association.[135] Acknowledging false testimony and surrendering the law license were key elements of a deal struck with Robert W. Ray, who had succeeded Starr as independent counsel.[136] The agreement also removed the prospect of criminal prosecution after his presidency: Clinton out of office would not face indictment for misconduct arising from the sex-and-lies scandal. In his statement acknowledging false testimony—which was read aloud in the White House briefing room by his press secretary, Jake Siewert[137]—Clinton said: "I tried to walk a fine line between acting lawfully and testifying falsely, but I now recognize that I did not fully accomplish this goal and that certain of my responses to questions about Ms. Lewinsky were false."[138]

Although impeachment tainted his presidency and impaired his second term, Clinton survived the humiliating ordeal. The reasons he did so are several. Among them was that Clinton benefitted from the consistent good fortune of confronting foes who were inept or who lacked his political wiliness and instincts. In winning the presidency in 1992, Clinton had ousted an out-of-touch incumbent, George H.W. Bush. To win reelection in 1996, he handily defeated a hapless, seventy-three-year-old

Republican opponent, Bob Dole. During the government shutdowns of 1995, Clinton outmaneuvered Gingrich, a formidable but blunder-prone adversary, to reclaim political momentum in Washington. Kenneth Starr fit the pattern: he was another of Clinton's clumsy foes. Starr was earnest and gentlemanly but thoroughly unprepared for the fierce political combat unleashed by his investigation of the sex-and-lies scandal.

Starr's report to Congress identifying grounds for impeaching the president was arresting and disturbing in its graphic detail. Readers of the report, even at the remove of many years, are astonished by its intrusive content and graphic detail that, in places, seem gratuitous and intended principally to embarrass. Starr insisted that Clinton's falsehoods under oath made it necessary to present explicit detail. "If the President, in his grand jury appearance [in August 1998], had admitted the sexual activity recounted by Ms. Lewinsky and conceded that he had lied under oath in his civil deposition," Starr's report said, "these particular descriptions would be superfluous."[139]

Even so, the prosecutors' decision to freight the report with graphic detail was a serious misjudgment—and another reason why Clinton survived the scandal. As Richard A. Posner, a federal judge and frequent writer on legal matters, has pointed out, Starr "could have unmasked [Clinton's] lies simply by listing each of the ten sexual encounters by date, time, and place" and briefly describing what took place. "That would have been enough to show that the President had lied in denying that he had engaged in sexual relations with Lewinsky," Posner wrote. "There was no need to add that he stuck a cigar in her vagina and then put it in his mouth and said it tasted good."[140] Incorporating such details encouraged suspicions that Starr was bent on destroying the president.[141]

The explicit content backfired on Starr, undercutting the report's gravity and almost trivializing the allegations about the president's misconduct. The report was posted online two days after the House of Representatives received it, giving rise to what the *Washington Post* called "history's first simultaneous reading of smut."[142] Americans absorbed the report's salacious content, and cringed. But for the most part they did not turn against the president. Polling data consistently showed a majority of Americans felt Clinton's transgressions were not grounds for resignation or impeachment.[143] And a majority of Americans thought it inappropriate for Starr's report to have included so much explicit detail.[144]

If the case to unseat the president failed in part because of the misguided zeal of his opponents, it failed more significantly because Clinton's misconduct fell well short of a standard for impeachment effectively set by Nixon in the Watergate scandal.[145] Nixon was compelled to quit the presidency in August 1974 in the face of certain impeachment and conviction for authorizing a cover-up of the signal crime of Watergate—the burglary in June 1972 at the Washington headquarters of the Democratic National Committee. That Nixon committed crimes in Watergate was unequivocal: audiotape recordings he surreptitiously made of his conversations at the White House confirmed his misdeeds.[146] Clinton's falsehoods, evasions, and dishonest efforts to conceal his dalliance with Lewinsky scarcely rivaled the crimes of Watergate, a political scandal unique in the depths of wrongdoing it plumbed.[147] Clinton may have been a raffish, self-centered rogue who tortured the truth and recruited aides to do the same on his behalf. But he was no vindictive, score-settling crook oozing paranoia, as Nixon was.[148]

Also critical in Clinton's surviving the sex-and-lies scandal was America's robust economy of the late 1990s. The long run-up of the stock market, begun in 1995, had Americans feeling prosperous. It was said they cared far more about the Dow Jones than Paula Jones.[149] Robust, low-inflation economic growth that had dropped unemployment rates to less than 5 percent in 1999 contributed to a willingness to excuse Clinton's misconduct.

Also important in understanding why Clinton survived and served out his term was the immediate precedent for career-ending sex scandals in Washington—a case far uglier, more sordid, and more clearly embroidered with evidence-tampering and influence-peddling. That case centered around Bob Packwood, a Republican senator from Oregon who, in September 1995, announced his resignation to bring an end to a three-year inquiry into reports of his sexual misconduct.

Packwood was a twenty-seven-year incumbent who had gained a well-deserved reputation as an expert on tax policy. He also had a reputation as something of a lecherous figure who periodically took sexual advantage of women dependent on him for their jobs.[150] That reputation was confirmed in early September 1995 with the release of a report—179 pages long and supported by ten volumes of evidence—in which the Senate Ethics Committee documented Packwood's misconduct. The offenses were such that the committee unanimously called for his expulsion.

The report etched a devastating portrait of Packwood, accusing him of attempting "to obstruct and impede" the committee's inquiry "by withholding, altering and destroying relevant evidence" including portions of his audiotaped diary in which he discussed his sexual overtures and conquests. The senator also pressured lobbyists to pay consulting fees or retainers to his estranged wife as a way to reduce his financial obligations to her, the ethics committee found. The report identified eighteen separate encounters that took place from 1969 to 1990 in which Packwood had made "unwanted and unwelcome sexual advances" on women. It represented, the committee said, "a pattern of abuse of his position of power and authority."[151] Packwood's targets, the ethics committee said, "were effectively powerless to protest in the face of his position as a United States Senator."[152] His behavior was more grotesque, offensive, and unbidden than Clinton's in his relationship with Lewinsky.

Packwood was no Lothario. The senator's advances were graceless and "consisted chiefly of dropping sudden, surprise French kisses on women, usually after forcefully seizing them by their arms or wrists," as the *New York Times* described them. "The women, most of them members of Packwood's staff, lobbyists and campaign volunteers, [denied] sending any signals of romantic interest. . . . He didn't flirt suavely or invite women for candle-lit dinners. No, he swooped down out of the blue, usually embracing a woman under the fluorescent lights of an inner office. According to many accounts, his groping was wooden and his open-mouthed kisses oddly passionless."[153]

The committee's bipartisan demand for his expulsion left Packwood with few options. He insisted he would not resign but abruptly changed his mind and, on September 7, 1995, delivered a farewell speech from the floor of the Senate. His valedictory was mawkish, disjointed, and at times excruciating. Tears came to Packwood's eyes as he recalled successes, failures, and frustrations of his years in the Senate. He spoke of "the dishonor that has befallen me in the last three years."[154] By way of departure, he declared: "I leave this institution not with malice, but with love."[155] He was the first U.S. senator to quit involuntarily in thirteen years. Had he not resigned, Packwood likely would have been the first U.S. senator expelled since Southerners were kicked out during the Civil War.

When Packwood finished speaking, several of his close friends in the Senate—Mark O. Hatfield, John McCain, Alan K. Simpson, and Daniel Patrick Moynihan among them—took the floor, one by one, to lament Packwood's resignation and to say how they would miss his presence. There was, the *Washington Post* reported, "little talk . . . about the allegations that brought him down, no puffed-chest pronouncements of good riddance."[156]

Also rising to pay tribute to Packwood that afternoon was Senator Dianne Feinstein of California. She had been an early voice calling for his resignation.[157] Feinstein prefaced her remarks by saying she did not know Packwood well. Nonetheless, she said, "it is the sign of a wise man, and even a giant man, who stands and does what has to be done, and goes on to fight another day."[158] Surprised and moved by the charity of her remarks, Packwood crossed the floor, took Feinstein's hand, and wept.[159]

Unlike Clinton, Packwood managed no Houdini-like escape from serious trouble, but the disgraced former senator was soon to recover a measure of status in Washington. Like many erstwhile members of Congress, Packwood turned to lobbying after leaving the Senate. In early 1998, *Washingtonian* magazine declared him one of the capital's fifty top lobbyists. "Despite his well-publicized troubles," the magazine said, "Packwood remains a formidable intellect and an insightful analyst of the legislative landscape. Few know the tax code like Packwood."[160]

Conclusion

The Long Reach of 1995

Nineteen ninety-five closed the way it began—on a Sunday, with the farewell appearance of a popular newspaper comic.

The delightfully bizarre *Far Side,* a single-panel cartoon drawn by the low-profile artist Gary Larson, entered retirement on January 1, 1995, ending a fifteen-year parade of oddities and lighthearted grotesqueries that included talking bears, cows driving cars, and dinosaurs facing extinction from smoking cigarettes. It was half-seriously suggested that Larson decided to give up *The Far Side* because it had become more and more "difficult to out-weird the rest of the newspaper."[1] In an interview before ending the strip, Larson said his "humor is sometimes on the dark side, or whatever you want to call it. But I don't think that's altogether unhealthy."[2] Not at all: *The Far Side* was inspired in its quirky weirdness. Its final installment was a takeoff on the closing scene of *The Wizard of Oz* and depicted Larson waking up in bed at home, after an extended visit to a strange place populated by cavemen, monsters, and nerdy little kids.

The year closed with publication of the last original *Calvin and Hobbes,* drawn by Bill Watterson, who also was famously publicity-shy. "My interests have shifted," Watterson told his syndicate in giving up the strip after a ten-year run, "and I believe I've done what I can do within the constraints of daily deadlines and small panels."[3] The retirement of *Calvin and Hobbes* marked the passing of a "national cultural treasure," one critic said[4] about the consistently imaginative strip that featured the antics of a mischievous six-year-old named Calvin and his stuffed-tiger straight man, Hobbes. In the exclusive company of Calvin, Hobbes became a lithe, wise-cracking tiger, six feet tall.[5] In the valedictory strip on December 31, 1995, the boy and his tiger set off into a brilliant landscape of newly fallen snow. "It's a magical world, Hobbes, ol' buddy," Calvin exclaimed, launching a toboggan down a snowy hill. "Let's go exploring."

There was something eccentric and droll about a year bracketed by the leave-taking of immensely popular comics. Their departures were coincidental, just happening to fall on the first and last days of 1995. Even so, they respectively anticipated and confirmed 1995 as a year of notable watersheds. It was, as we have seen, a decisive year, the time when the Internet entered the mainstream of American life; when terrorism reached deep into the American heartland with devastating effect; when the "Trial of the Century" enthralled and repelled the country and brought forensic DNA to the popular consciousness; when diplomatic success at Dayton gave rise to a period of American muscularity in foreign affairs; and when the president and an unpaid White House intern began a furtive and intermittent dalliance that would shake the American government and lead to the extraordinary spectacle of impeachment.

Given that it was a year of milestones, it is not surprising that 1995 extends a long reach: it is a year that matters still. The major events and leading actors of 1995 return to the public eye from time to time to command attention and commentary. Even the reclusive Bill Watterson was the subject of a documentary a couple of years ago, a paean to his still-admired and much-missed *Calvin and Hobbes*.[6] Nineteen ninety-five lives on in many ways: as context, as a curiosity, and as a point of reference. And sometimes as a combination of all three.

There was much reminiscing about 1995 when, for example, Republicans in Congress forced a partial shutdown of the federal government in October 2013. They sought to strip away or delay federal funding for the Affordable Care Act national health plan (often known as Obamacare), but failed utterly. The shutdown lasted sixteen days and in some ways seemed like a strange replay of the government closures of 1995. Dan Zak noted as much in the *Washington Post* in a snarky look back at 1995 that included nods to *Tommy Boy,* a little-remembered film that starred Chris Farley and David Spade:

> During the last government shutdown, some of us were 12 years old and wearing out our VHS tape of "Tommy Boy," that comic masterpiece about

responsibility, duty and friendship. The disapproving public might think the 113th United States Congress is full of both Tommy Callahans (entitled oafs) and Richard Haydens (sniveling bean counters), but this is no time to discuss how "Tommy Boy" is an allegory for our legislature. Instead, after a week of thinking shutdown thoughts, the heart of the matter is how culture changes faster than politics, and how the time between this shutdown and the last shutdown is somehow both an eon (when measured in how we live) and a blip (when measured in how we govern).[7]

The government shutdown of 2013 also brought published reminders that President Bill Clinton and White House intern Monica Lewinsky began their furtive liaison during the closure of November 1995. "It was during that enforced idleness," the *Independent* newspaper in London pointed out, "that the President began his fateful dalliance with Monica Lewinsky."[8]

The former intern is now in her early forties and still compels fascination, which not infrequently brings her back into the news. An example of this phenomenon came in early 2014, when it was reported that at the height of her husband's sex scandal Hillary Clinton privately referred to Lewinsky as a "narcissistic loony toon." She so confided to Diane Blair, a close friend who recorded the "loony toon" comment in a memorandum on September 9, 1998. Blair died in 2000, and her papers were donated to the University of Arkansas where she had taught political science. The memorandum of 1998 and other contents of the archive were publicized in early 2014 by a conservative website, the *Washington Free Beacon*.[9] In the memorandum, Blair addressed the Clinton-Lewinsky scandal and recounted her conversation with Hillary Clinton, to whom she referred as HRC. She indirectly quoted Hillary Clinton as saying the president's dalliance with Lewinsky "was a lapse" but that "to his credit, he tried to break it off, tried to pull away, tried to manage someone who was clearly a 'narcissistic loony toon'; but it was beyond control. And, HRC insists, no matter what people say, it was gross inappropriate behavior but it was consensual (was not a power relationship) and was not sex in the real meaning of the word."[10]

As if in response, Lewinsky broke a prolonged silence in 2014, in an essay of more than 4,000 words published by *Vanity Fair*. Lewinsky wrote that she "deeply regret[s] what happened between me and President Clinton. . . . At the time—at least from my point of view—it was an authentic connection, with emotional intimacy, frequent visits, plans made, phone calls and gifts exchanged. In my early 20s, I was too young to understand the real-life consequences, and too young to see that I would be sacrificed for political expediency. . . . I would give anything to rewind the tape."[11]

Lewinsky said she bristled in reading of Hillary Clinton's harsh characterization of her as a "narcissistic loony toon." It was, Lewinsky wrote, "the latest twist on Me as Archetype." Yes, she added, "I get it. Hillary Clinton wanted it on record that she was lashing out at her husband's mistress. She may have faulted her husband for being inappropriate, but I find her impulse to blame the Woman . . . troubling. And all too familiar: with every marital indiscretion that finds its way into the public sphere—many of which involve male politicians—it always seems like the woman conveniently takes the fall."[12]

Lewinsky's essay underscored anew the odd, even scandalous pull that she exerts on the American consciousness[13]—a fascination of which she is quite aware. "Every day someone mentions me in a tweet or a blog post, and not altogether kindly," she wrote. "Every day, it seems, my name shows up in an op-ed column or a press clip or two—mentioned in passing in articles on subjects as disparate as millennials, [the television series] *Scandal,* and French president François Hollande's love life."[14] That such fascination endures is testimony to a deep and lingering suspicion that there remains more to know about why Bill Clinton took the risks he did, trysting with an intern who, when it began in 1995, was barely twenty-two years old.

O. J. Simpson is another figure prominent in 1995 who tugs from time to time at the collective conscious. He can still make news, even from behind bars at the Lovelock Correctional Center in northern Nevada, where he is serving a sentence of up to thirty-three years for kidnapping and armed robbery. In early 2013, Simpson was reported to have thrown a Super Bowl party in his cell, where he had installed a television. "If you have the money, you can buy a TV at the inmate store and put it in your cell," Norman Pardo, a friend of Simpson was quoted as saying, adding, "He's like the Godfather of the prison now."[15]

Simpson was back in court, in Las Vegas, for several days in 2013, seeking retrial on the criminal charges that sent him to jail. At times during the hearings, Simpson seemed confused, tentative, and weary. He looked very much unlike a Godfather. He was by then sixty-five years old and was much heavier than in 1995 when he cut such a sharp figure at the "Trial of the Century."[16] The proceedings in Las Vegas inevitably brought comparisons to the trial in 1995, some of which were edged with disdain. "This was no 'trial of the century,'" the *Los Angeles Times* reported from Las Vegas.[17] "The bland courtroom narrative held none of the theatrics and high drama of Simpson's mid-1990s murder trial for the deaths of ex-wife Nicole Brown Simpson and her friend Ronald Goldman. Missing this time were the public frenzy, the 'Free O.J.' signs and legal dream team" who won Simpson's acquittal in 1995. "On this day," the *Times* said, "there would be no rock star treatment for Simpson, who spent the lunch hour eating a simple jail bag lunch of a sandwich, piece of fruit and drink." Simpson's plea for a new trial was a long shot; he claimed he had been represented by incompetent counsel in 2008, when he was tried on the kidnapping and armed robbery charges. Almost predictably, Simpson's request was turned down.[18]

But the "Trial of the Century" in 1995 remains a standard against which other sensational murder cases are measured and invariably found wanting. No murder trial in the United States since 1995 has matched the Simpson saga for mania, duration, infamy, and unrelenting media attention. The six-week trial of Casey Anthony in 2011 perhaps came closest. Anthony was a single mother accused of killing her two-year-old daughter, Caylee, and hiding her remains; Anthony did not report her daughter missing for thirty-one days. But no forensic evidence tied her to the girl's death, and jurors acquitted her of murder after deliberating eleven hours. The not-guilty verdict provoked outrage, disbelief, and crude comparisons to Simpson's acquittal. "O.J. Simpson is alive and free and living in the body of a 25-year-old sociopath named Casey Anthony," the *New York Post* declared.[19]

The Anthony trial's outcome returned Marcia Clark briefly to the limelight. Clark, who was the lead prosecutor at Simpson's trial in 1995, declared that Anthony's acquittal was "far more shocking" than the not-guilty verdicts in the Simpson case. "Why? Because Casey Anthony was no celebrity," Clark wrote. "She never wowed the nation with her athletic prowess, shilled in countless car commercials, or entertained in film comedies. There were no racial issues" of the kind that shaped the Simpson case. "And while there was significant media coverage before the [Anthony] trial," Clark stated, "it didn't come close to the storm that permeated the Simpson case. . . . Because of those factors, many predicted from the very start in the Simpson case—in fact, long before we even began to pick a jury—that it would be impossible to secure a conviction. There was no such foreshadowing" in the trial of Casey Anthony.[20]

The verdict prompted Alan M. Dershowitz of Harvard Law School, a high-profile lawyer who was on Simpson's legal "Dream Team," to point out, as if lecturing, that "a criminal trial is not a search for truth.

Scientists search for truth. Philosophers search for morality. A criminal trial searches for only one result: proof beyond a reasonable doubt," he wrote in a commentary for the *Wall Street Journal*. The evidence presented at the Anthony trial—as in the Simpson case in 1995—had left reasonable doubt in the minds of the jurors. "In real life," Dershowitz wrote, ". . . many murders remain unsolved, and even some that are 'solved' to the satisfaction of the police and prosecutors lack sufficient evidence to result in a conviction,"[21] a decisive feature of both trials.

Simpson was a professional football star. But he is hardly thought of as much of a hero these days: he lost such status long ago, a casualty of his trial in 1995. He has instead become the occasional subject of ridicule and derisive humor. His lingering notoriety and his plea for a new trial inspired a Top Ten list in 2013 on the CBS *Late Show with David Letterman*. "Top Ten O.J. Simpson Excuses," the list was called. Among its entries were these jibes: "Remember, I'm innocent until proven not guilty and then found liable in civil court," and "Give me a break, I'm a widower."[22]

Easily one of the most perfidious actors of 1995 was Timothy McVeigh, the mass murderer of Oklahoma City. He was executed by lethal injection in 2001 at the federal penitentiary in Terre Haute, Indiana. McVeigh was unrepentant to the end, clinging to the delusion that bombing the federal building in Oklahoma City was a deed necessary to punish a wayward government.[23] Ten years later, McVeigh's attack was a source of perverse and indirect inspiration to Anders Behring Breivik, a Norwegian anti-Islamic extremist who killed seventy-seven people in a methodical, lone-wolf bombing-and-shooting rampage. As in Oklahoma City, the attacks in downtown Oslo and soon afterward at an island summer camp were at first wrongly believed to have been the acts of Islamic terrorists.[24] At his trial in 2012, Breivik said that in planning the attacks he had conducted research on the powerful truck bomb McVeigh had set off in Oklahoma City.[25] Breivik was sentenced to twenty-one years in prison; Norway imposes no death penalty.

Few events darkened the canvas of 1995 like the atrocity at Srebrenica. In July 1995, Bosnian Serb forces entered the U.N.-designated "safe area" around the town and rounded up and executed more than 8,000 Muslim men and boys in the worst single outrage of the long and brutal war in Bosnia. The massacre's mercilessness and scale stirred the United States, belatedly, to confront the horrors of Bosnia. The aftermath of Srebrenica brought diplomatic moves, backed by air strikes on Serb positions, that cleared the way for peace talks at Dayton, where the war was brought to a close after nearly four years.

"Srebrenica" lives on as a point of reference, a grim reminder of the hazards of inaction in the face of barbarity. "Srebrenica" has found resonance and relevance in the prolonged civil war in Syria, especially after the slayings of more than 100 people, most of them women and children, near the town of Houla in 2012. "Syria's Srebrenica," the *Wall Street Journal* declared.[26] "Houla: Shadows of Srebrenica" was the headline in the *Washington Post*.[27]

But Houla gave rise to no international intervention in Syria, its similarities to Bosnia notwithstanding. The parallels are striking: the ruthlessness, random shelling, sectarian violence, gruesome imagery, and feeble international response have all made Syria seem much like a grim replay of the Bosnian war. Moreover, the diplomatic démarche that ended the war in Bosnia has been studied for insights that might be applied to Syria, where a despotic regime—backed by Russia and Iran—is pitted against the splintered forces of loosely allied rebels.[28]

Despite surface similarities, Syria is no Bosnia. The differences are profound, and even a ghastly "Srebrenica moment" is unlikely to force NATO to intervene, as it did in Bosnia in 1995. The images of Syria's horror have had strikingly little effect on Western public opinion even though, as one observer has noted, they "evoke the horror of the Holocaust. They are a call to action."[29] It may be that the images from Syria—including those of children killed in nerve gas attacks in 2013—are unbearable, or that they demand more potent responses than their audiences can muster.[30]

No matter how disturbing the imagery, Americans have demonstrated little appetite for another military intervention in the Middle East, not after the agony of the Iraq War and the bursting of the post-Dayton "hubris bubble." Perhaps the most decisive difference between Bosnia and Syria is that Russia is far less accommodating nowadays than it was in 1995, when it was reeling from the breakup of the Soviet Union four years before. The autocratic Vladimir Putin is intent on returning Russia to an international power, and crucial to his ambitions is blocking U.S. initiatives in Syria and elsewhere. So the civil war in Syria may grind on as a conflict of attrition, producing more horrors and bloodshed. But Syria is not likely to have its Dayton.

In the twenty years since entering the American mainstream, the Internet extended its reach deep into the economic, political, social, and cultural facets of contemporary life—so much so that it has come to be taken almost for granted. Occasionally, though, there are echoes of Bob

Metcalfe's famously wrong prediction in late 1995 that the Internet was headed for a catastrophic collapse.[31] For example, *Network World* published a column a few years ago by Johna Till Johnson, an engineer and technologist. The column appeared beneath the headline "Is the Internet Doomed to Fail?" It suggested that demand for Internet access would soon exceed capacity. Johnson acknowledged that predicting the Internet's pending failure seemed "crazy . . . in this era of Facebook, Twitter and a 'digital millennial' generation that's grown up never not knowing the Internet. But there are worrying signs that the Internet's architecture may not be able to scale effectively much longer. . . . Demand for access bandwidth is growing exponentially, while provider investment is growing linearly. The lines cross—demand exceeds capacity—sometime around 2012."[32] The year came and went, and the Internet lives on.

Probably no one has defined the era of the Internet as consistently and singularly as Marc Andreessen, an inventor of the Mosaic browser and cofounder of Netscape whom a *Newsweek* report in 1995 declared to be "the über-super-wunder whiz kid of cyberspace."[33] Andreessen is only in his forties, but he has become a kind of *éminence grise* in Silicon Valley—an *éminence grise* who shaves his head. He is respected more than ever. *Wired* magazine said in 2012 that no one in the preceding twenty years had "done more than Marc Andreessen to change the way we communicate."[34]

Andreessen these days heads a venture capital firm, Andreessen-Horowitz, that has backed such winners as Facebook, Twitter, Skype, Groupon, and Pinterest. Andreessen also is much sought-after for his predictions and assessments, which tend to be sweeping and colorful. He still marvels at the still-unfolding digital world. In a commentary in the *Wall Street Journal* a few years ago, he declared that "software is eating the world"[35]—which meant that the Internet will continue to deploy its disruptive effects on industry after industry.[36] And in 2014, Andreessen observed: "We're just now starting to live in the world where everybody has a supercomputer in their pocket and everybody's connected. And so we're just starting to see the implications of that."[37]

He does not talk much about Netscape these days, but the memory of Netscape, that swaggering exponent of the early Web, lives on. Its dazzling initial public offering of stock in August 1995—when the Internet seized the attention of the financial world—is a significant moment in digital lore as well as a telling point of reference. Netscape's IPO was recalled, for example, when LinkedIn, the social-networking platform popular among business professionals, scored a highly successful public debut in 2011. LinkedIn's shares soared 109 percent on the day they opened for trading, an introduction that was evocative of Netscape's head-turning, first-day success in 1995.[38] It was a "Netscape moment," said the *San Francisco Chronicle,* noting that the IPOs of Netscape and LinkedIn both "delivered nine-figure paydays to top executives and minted millionaires throughout the ranks," on paper, at least.[39]

The Netscape browser, which introduced the Web to millions of people, has its heir in Firefox, the open-source browser that was developed in a collaborative, nonprofit venture that Netscape set up. The project was called Mozilla. Several months before its acquisition by America Online in 1998, Netscape opened the source code of its Navigator Web browser—making it available online and effectively inviting anyone with the technical know-how to revise and improve the software. Netscape set up Mozilla to manage the project.[40] In 2003, America Online spun off the Mozilla project, and, the following year, Firefox 1.0 was introduced. It swiftly gained support among consumers and Web developers who had grown disenchanted with Internet Explorer, the victor in the 1990s "browser war" with Netscape.[41] The introduction of Firefox shook up a then-dormant browser market and signaled the emergence of other competitors, such as Google's Chrome browser and Apple's Safari. By 2014, Chrome had supplanted Internet Explorer as the most popular Web browser, commanding a market share of more than 40 percent. Explorer's market share had receded to 23 percent, a fraction of its dominance after vanquishing Netscape.[42]

To identify 1995 as a hinge moment of the recent past also is to say that time has come for a searching reappraisal of the 1990s, that time is ripe to confront and flatten the caricatures so often associated with the decade. The 1990s may still seem recent, but ample time has passed to allow the decade to be examined critically and with detachment. After all, as John Tosh noted in his well-regarded study *The Pursuit of History,* "it is the recent past on which people draw most for historical analogies and predictions, and their knowledge of it needs to be soundly based if they are to avoid serious error. The recent past has also proved a fertile breeding ground for crude myths—all the more powerful when their credibility is not contested by scholarly work."[43]

Crude myth has begun to define the American 1990s. In recent years, the conservative syndicated columnist Charles Krauthammer scoffed at the 1990s as a "holiday from history" and a "soporific Golden Age,"[44] a time when the United States largely ignored the gathering threat of Islamic terrorism only to pay a staggering price in 2001. The decade was, Krauthammer has said, "our retreat from seriousness, our Seinfeld decade of obsessive ordinariness." His critique is principally aimed at Bill Clinton, whom he has dismissed as "a president perfectly suited to the time—a time of domesticity, triviality and self-absorption."[45] Krauthammer's criticism of Clinton is not completely without merit, although recent scholarship has argued that Clinton recognized the growing terrorist threat and took steps to meet it, if not decisively.[46]

Admirers of Clinton, such as journalist Haynes Johnson, have likened the 1990s to "the best of times"—words in the title of Johnson's book published in 2001.[47] The "best of times" interpretation sees the American 1990s through a lens of a booming economy at home and unrivaled power abroad. But neither "holiday from history" nor "the best of times" is very accurate or nuanced. They are more like expedient labels than telling summaries. The American 1990s were a complex period when the United States grew hesitantly and fitfully into the role of the world's lone superpower, when a dazzling communication technology went from obscurity to near-ubiquity, and when a rising tide of democratization abroad reached, at least briefly, into once-inhospitable lands. For a heady moment in the first years of the decade, it seemed as if Western liberal democracy had triumphed everywhere, signaling an end point in mankind's long quest for rational and stable government.[48]

The 1990s were a searching time, rich in promise, in portent, and in disappointment. And squarely in the midstream of the decade was its most decisive year.

The Timeline of a
Watershed Year: 1995

January 1   The last original *Far Side,* a popular, single-panel cartoon by
             Gary Larson, appears in U.S. newspapers, closing a fifteen-
             year run.

January 2   Marion Barry is inaugurated mayor of Washington, D.C., an
             office he left in 1991 following an FBI undercover operation
             that captured him on videotape smoking crack cocaine. He
             served a six-month prison term. Barry won the district's may-
             oral election in November 1994.

January 4   For the first time in four decades, Congress convenes under
             Republican control. Newt Gingrich becomes speaker of the
             House.

January 5   The *New York Times,* in a report citing "several senior
             American and Israeli officials," says Iran "could be less than
             five years away from having an atomic bomb."

January 8   After 1,143 performances, the musical *Guys & Dolls* closes
             at the Martin Beck Theater in New York City.

January 9   Sheik Omar Abdel-Rahman and eleven other defendants
             go on trial in federal court in New York City. They are
             accused of conspiring to wage terrorist attacks across the
             city.

January 11   Oprah Winfrey, host of the country's most-watched
             daytime television talk show, breaks down during the
             taping of a program about drug abuse, saying she had
             smoked cocaine twenty years earlier. The program aired
             January 13.

January 12	A daughter of Malcolm X, Qubilah Shabazz, is arrested in Minneapolis and accused of attempting to hire a hitman to kill Louis Farrakhan, leader of the Nation of Islam.
January 16	A prosecutor in Union, S.C., says he would seek the death penalty for Susan Smith, accused in the car drowning of her sons, 3-year-old Michael and 14-month-old Alex. The boys died strapped in their car seats.
January 17	A magnitude 6.9 earthquake strikes Kobe, Japan, killing more than 6,400 people. It is Japan's worst earthquake in more than seventy years.
January 18	The French minister of culture, Jacques Toubon, announces the discovery of Stone Age paintings in a cave in southern France. The more than 300 images of animals and human hands are believed to have been made 20,000 years earlier.
January 22	Rose Fitzgerald Kennedy, mother of President John F. Kennedy and two U.S. senators, dies at Hyannis Port, Mass., at age 104.
January 24	The prosecution begins opening statements at the O.J. Simpson double-murder trial in Los Angeles. Deputy District Attorney Christopher Darden tells the jury: "I think it's fair to say that I have the toughest job in town today. Except for the job that you have. Your job may just be a little bit tougher." Darden adds, in something of an understatement: "It's going to be a long trial."
January 25	The defense begins opening statements in the Simpson trial. Lead defense lawyer Johnnie L. Cochran, Jr. tells jurors: "The evidence in this case, we believe, will show that O.J. Simpson is an innocent man wrongfully accused."
January 27	A quickly compiled book by O.J. Simpson, *I Want to Tell You,* arrives in stores. Proceeds from sales will help cover legal expenses incurred by Simpson in his high-profile trial in Los Angeles on charges of killing his former wife and her friend. Simpson says in the book that he is eager to testify in his own defense.
January 29	The high-powered San Francisco 49ers overwhelm the San Diego Chargers, 49–26, to become the first team to win five National Football League Super Bowl titles.
January 31	President Bill Clinton announces he will act unilaterally to provide Mexico with a $20 billion loan to support the beleaguered peso.
February 2	Prosecutors at the O.J. Simpson trial play for jurors a tape of an emergency 911 telephone call, in which Simpson is heard screaming, cursing, and threatening to harm his former wife, Nicole Brown Simpson. She placed the call from her home in October 1993.

February 3   Air Force Lt. Col. Eileen Collins becomes the first woman to pilot a NASA mission as space shuttle Discovery blasts off from Cape Canaveral, Fla.

February 6   Siddig Ibrahim Siddig Ali pleads guilty in federal court and implicates his former codefendants standing trial on charges of plotting elaborate terrorist attacks across New York City. Siddig Ali was accused of taking a central role in the conspiracy.

February 7   Ramzi Ahmed Yousef, suspected mastermind of the 1993 World Trade Center bombing and other terrorist plots, is arrested in Pakistan.

February 9   Former U.S. Senator J. William Fulbright, 89, an outspoken opponent of America's war in Vietnam, dies of a stroke in Washington, D.C.

February 10   Sweden's prime minister, Ingvar Carlsson, says the Russian submarines that were believed to have entered Swedish territorial waters from time to time since the 1980s were really minks.

February 12   Jurors in the O. J. Simpson double-murder trial are taken to the site in the Brentwood section of Los Angeles where Nicole Brown Simpson and Ronald L. Goldman were fatally stabbed in June 1994. They also visit Simpson's estate nearby.

February 13   House Speaker Newt Gingrich says he will not seek the Republican nomination for president in 1996.

February 15   FBI agents arrest Kevin Mitnick, a 31-year-old computer hacker and suspected cyberthief accused of stealing data files and credit card numbers from computer systems across the country. Mitnick would spend nearly five years in prison.

February 19   In an event signaling the start of the long run to the 1996 presidential election, nine Republican candidates who have entered or are likely to enter the race deliver remarks at a fund-raising dinner in New Hampshire. The event falls a year and a day before the state's first-in-the-nation presidential primary election.

February 21   Steve Fossett, a 50-year-old Chicago stockbroker, becomes the first person to fly solo in a balloon across the Pacific Ocean. His balloon lands in western Canada after a four-day flight from South Korea.

February 22   France accuses five Americans, including four diplomats, of espionage and reportedly asks them to leave the country.

February 23   The Dow Jones industrial average surges past the 4,000 mark, closing at 4,003.33, a record high.

February 26   Britain's oldest investment bank, Barings PLC, is forced into bankruptcy protection after a 28-year-old trader in its Singapore office, Nick Leeson, loses $1.38 billion speculating on Tokyo stock prices.

February 27   Publication date of a now-famous *Newsweek* commentary, "The Internet? Bah!" in which the author, Clifford Stoll, dismisses the emergent digital world as over-hyped and over-sold—"a wasteland of unfiltered data."

March 1   A relative newcomer, Sheryl Crow, wins "record of the year" honors at the annual Grammy Awards ceremony in Los Angeles for "All I Wanna Do." Tony Bennett's *MTV Unplugged* wins "best album" award.

March 2   The U.S. Senate narrowly turns down a constitutional amendment to require a balanced federal budget. The vote was 65–35, just shy of the two-thirds majority required for passage.

March 5   The *New York Times* reports that Clinton administration officials have shared intelligence evidence with U.N. Security Council members that Iraq "has been rebuilding factories that could produce chemical weapons."

March 7   New York becomes the thirty-eighth state to adopt capital punishment as Governor George E. Pataki signs a death penalty bill into law. Pataki calls the measure "the most effective of its kind in the nation."

March 8   Two U.S. diplomats are shot to death and another is wounded in the ambush of their van in Karachi, Pakistan.

March 9   Despite objections from Britain, President Clinton allows Gerry Adams, leader of Ireland's Sinn Féin party, to make a fund-raising visit to the United States and invites him to the White House for St. Patrick's Day.

March 14   Astronaut Norman E. Thagard becomes the first American launched into space aboard a Russian rocket as he and two crewmates blast off aboard a Soyuz spacecraft en route to the space station Mir.

March 16   Astronaut Norman Thagard is warmly welcomed by Russian cosmonauts as he arrives at the space station Mir.

March 19   After devoting months to becoming a major league baseball player, Michael Jordan returns to professional basketball and rejoins the Chicago Bulls. He scores nineteen points as the Bulls lose to Indiana in overtime.

March 20   A gas attack on Tokyo's subways kills twelve people. More than 5,500 others were sickened when poisonous sarin gas escaped from packages placed on five subway cars.

March 21   Thousands of Japanese police raid the offices of the religious cult Aum Shinrikyo in investigating the nerve-gas attacks on Tokyo subway system the day before. The cult's leader, Shoko Asahara, is arrested in May and accused of masterminding the attacks. In 2004, he is sentenced to death. Masato Yokoyama, the cult's leader, was sentenced to death in 1999.

March 22   The longest-ever stay in space—437 days—comes to an end as Valeri Polyakov, a Russian cosmonaut, returns to Earth.

March 23   In a front-page article, the *San Jose Mercury News* reports the development of Java, a computer language that brings animation to websites. The article says that Java's maker, Sun Microsystems of Mountain View, Calif., hopes the software "will turn the Web into a rocking new medium."

March 25   The first online use of the wiki by its inventor, Ward Cunningham.

March 27   *Forrest Gump* wins six Oscars, including the award for best picture, at the 67th Academy Awards. For the second successive year, Tom Hanks wins the best actor award, this time for his title role in *Gump*. Jessica Lange wins the best actress award for her performance in *Blue Sky*.

March 29   The U.S. House of Representatives rejects four measures that would have imposed term limits on lawmakers. One of the defeated proposals envisioned twelve-year limits for members of the House and Senate, to be applied retroactively.

March 30   Pope John Paul II issues an encyclical letter in which he condemns abortion and euthanasia as "crimes which no human law can claim to legitimize." He also vigorously states opposition to capital punishment.

March 31   A federal judge grants a preliminary injunction against owners of Major League baseball teams, breaking a deadlock in an eight-month strike that wiped out the 1994 World Series and delayed the start of the 1995 season. The players went on strike in August 1994.

April 1   More than 3,000 people pay tribute to Mexican-American singer Selena in Corpus Christi, Tex., where, the day before, she had been shot to death by the former president of her fan club.

April 2   A bomb blast destroys an apartment building in Gaza City, killing several people, among them a leading figure in the Islamic extremist group Hamas.

April 3   UCLA defeats Arkansas, 89–78, to win the NCAA men's basketball championship. The night before, Connecticut won the NCAA women's basketball title, downing Tennessee, 70–64.

April 4   A federal jury in Washington, D.C., convicts Francisco Martin Duran of attempting to assassinate President Clinton. Duran had fired an assault rifle at the White House in October 1994. He later is sentenced to forty years in prison.

April 5   The House of Representatives passes a major tax-reduction bill, an important component of the Republicans' agenda known as the "Contract with America."

April 6   Saying "If I offended anyone, I'm sorry," Republican Senator Alfonse D'Amato of New York apologizes for mocking Lance Ito, the judge presiding at the O.J. Simpson trial. D'Amato had appeared on a talk radio program and spoken in a fake Japanese accent.

April 10   Kansas Senator Bob Dole formally announces his candidacy for the Republican nomination for president. It is his third bid for the White House. Dole eventually becomes the Republican standard-bearer in the 1996 election.

April 12   Robert S. McNamara, a former U.S. defense secretary and an architect of the U.S. military effort in Vietnam, says in a memoir published this day that the war was "wrong, terribly wrong." He also writes that he had misgivings about the war as early as 1967. His *mea culpa* is widely criticized as coming many years too late.

April 14   Actor-singer Burl Ives dies at age 85 at his home in Washington State.

April 17   The final issue of the 111-year-old *Houston Post* is published. Houston becomes the largest U.S. city without rival daily newspapers.

April 18   President Clinton insists at a prime-time news conference that he remains relevant in Washington, despite Republican control of both houses of Congress. The comment marks a low point of his presidency.

April 19   A huge truck bomb explodes at the Alfred P. Murrah Federal Building in Oklahoma City, killing 168 people and injuring hundreds of others. It is the deadliest act of domestic terror in U.S. history, and suspicions immediately fall on Middle East terrorists.

April 21   Timothy McVeigh, an embittered Army veteran, is arrested by the FBI in the Oklahoma City bombing. McVeigh had spent the two days since the attack in jail in Perry, Okla., following his arrest on traffic and weapons charges.

April 23	Outspoken sportscaster Howard Cosell, 77, dies in New York.
April 24	The elusive Unabomber claims his final victim, Gilbert P. Murray, president of the California Forestry Association. Murray is killed by a package bomb at his headquarters in Sacramento. The package carried an Oakland postmark.
April 25	Actress Ginger Rogers, who won fame as the dance partner of Fred Astaire, dies in California. She was 83.
April 26	A minute of silence is observed across America to honor the victims of the Oklahoma City bombing, which occurred a week earlier.
April 30	President Clinton cuts off U.S. trade and investment with Iran and denounces the Tehran government as an "inspiration and paymaster to terrorists."
May 1	Federal prosecutors reach an agreement with Qubilah Shabazz, a daughter of Malcolm X, that effectively dismisses charges that she plotted to kill Louis Farrakhan, leader of the Nation of Islam. The deal came hours before jury selection was to begin in her trial in Minneapolis.
May 4	The father and sister of Ronald L. Goldman, who was slain with Nicole Brown Simpson in Los Angeles in 1994, file a wrongful death lawsuit against O. J. Simpson.
May 7	Jacques Chirac, mayor of Paris, wins the French presidency on his third try, defeating Lionel Jospin in a runoff election. Chirac's victory ends fourteen years of Socialist rule.
May 8	Fifty years after Nazi Germany's surrender in World War II, leaders representing Britain, France, Russia, the United States, and Germany gather in Berlin.
May 10	Terry Nichols, an Army buddy of Timothy McVeigh, is charged in the Oklahoma City bombing.
May 11	A United Nations conference extends in perpetuity the Nuclear Non-Proliferation Treaty, which underwent formal review twenty-five years after taking effect.
May 17	The U.S. Senate Ethics Committee, after a thirty-month investigation, accuses Republican Senator Bob Packwood of Oregon of sexual misconduct, tampering with evidence, and pressing lobbyists to find work for his estranged wife.
May 19	The historical fantasy *Braveheart* opens in Los Angeles. "It contains enough severed limbs and arrows piercing bodies to satisfy the blood-thirstiest filmgoer," writes a critic for the *New York Daily News*. In 1996, the film wins the Academy Award for best picture.

May 20   The federal government abruptly closes to vehicular traffic a
              two-block stretch of Pennsylvania Avenue near the White
              House. The move is described as an important security
              measure in the aftermath of the Oklahoma City bombing.

May 22   In a 5–4 vote, the Supreme Court rules that states cannot
              impose term limits on members of Congress without first
              amending the Constitution.

May 23   A 37-year-old man carrying an unloaded handgun scales a
              fence surrounding the White House and struggles with a
              Secret Service officer before being shot, wounded, and
              subdued. He is identified as Leland William Modjeski. "What
              caused him to go bananas, I don't know," the intruder's
              father tells the *Washington Post*. "But he did go bananas."

May 24   Heidi Fleiss, the 29-year-old "Hollywood Madam," is
              sentenced to three years in prison for running a call-girl ring
              in Los Angeles that catered to rich and famous men. Prostitu-
              tion "is very degrading and I am sure it does take its toll,"
              the sentencing judge tells Fleiss, who had been convicted on
              three pandering charges in December 1994.

May 26   Bill Gates writes an internal memorandum titled "The
              Internet Tidal Wave." In it, Gates tells senior staff at
              Microsoft Corporation: "I now assign the Internet the
              highest level of importance."

May 27   Actor Christopher Reeve is thrown from a horse during an
              equestrian competition in Virginia and left paralyzed.

May 31   Senate Majority Leader Bob Dole, who is seeking the
              Republican nomination for president, accuses the entertain-
              ment industry of crossing the line "not just of taste, but of
              human dignity and decency." He declares in a speech in Los
              Angeles that "the mainstreaming of deviancy must come to
              an end, but it will only stop when the leaders of the enter-
              tainment industry . . . shoulder their responsibility."

June 1   The U.S. Postal Service issues a 32-cent stamp honoring
              Marilyn Monroe on what would have been her sixty-ninth
              birthday.

June 2   Bosnian Serbs shoot down a U.S. Air Force F-16C fighter
              plane on a routine NATO monitoring mission over northern
              Bosnia. The pilot, Captain Scott F. O'Grady, ejects from the
              aircraft but his fate is not immediately known.

June 6   NASA's space-endurance record of eighty-four days is
              broken by astronaut Norman Thagard, a 51-year-old
              physician aboard the Russian space station, Mir.

June 7   The U.S. Senate votes, 91–8, to approve an antiterrorism bill
              that would stiffen penalties for terror-related crimes and

make it easier to deport foreign nationals suspected of terrorist activity. It is the predecessor to a similar measure—the Antiterrorism and Effective Death Penalty Act of 1996—that clears both houses of Congress in April 1996 and is signed into law by President Clinton.

June 8   Air Force Captain Scott O'Grady, whose fighter jet was shot down by Bosnian Serbs on June 2, is rescued by U.S. Marines in a helicopter raid.

June 10   Some 70,000 people gather in New York's Central Park for the premiere of Disney's animated film *Pocahontas,* which critics pan for taking excessive liberties with the historical record.

June 12   Air Force Captain Scott O'Grady, who was rescued six days after being shot down over Bosnia, is feted at lunch at the White House and then given a rousing welcome at the Pentagon.

June 13   Secret Service officers don elbow-length blue rubber gloves before searching the possessions of a delegation of forty gay and lesbian elected officials invited to the White House. News reports said the officers wore the gloves for protection—evidently fearing HIV, the virus that causes AIDS. A few days later, President Clinton writes to the gay and lesbian officials, apologizing for "the inappropriate and insensitive treatment" they had received.

June 15   In one of the most memorable moments of his prolonged double-murder trial, O. J. Simpson is asked to put on the bloody gloves prosecutors say the killer wore in slashing his victims, Nicole Brown Simpson and Ronald Goldman. Facing the jury, Simpson appears to struggle to pull the gloves over his fingers. "Too tight," he says. The demonstration is a stunning blunder by the prosecution and a turning point in the trial.

June 16   The XIX Winter Olympic Games, to take place in 2002, are awarded to Salt Lake City.

June 19   Harry Wu, a Chinese-American human rights activist, is detained trying to enter China. He spends sixty-six days in jail before being expelled to the United States.

June 21   Representatives of Netscape and Microsoft meet at Netscape's headquarters in Silicon Valley. According to Netscape's cofounder, Marc Andreessen, Microsoft proposed that the companies carve up the market for Web browsers—an offer Netscape said it turned down. Microsoft later said Andreessen erred in his description of the meeting and denied seeking to divvy up the browser market.

June 22	The movie *Apollo 13*, starring Tom Hanks, premiers in the United States.
June 23	Dr. Jonas Salk, who developed the first successful vaccine to combat the scourge of polio, dies in California at age 80.
June 24	The underdog New Jersey Devils win the National Hockey League's Stanley Cup championship by completing a four-game sweep of the Detroit Red Wings. It is their first title.
June 25	Warren E. Burger, former chief justice of the United States, dies in Washington, D.C., of congestive heart failure. He was 87.
June 26	The United Nations marks its fiftieth anniversary in ceremonies at its birthplace in San Francisco.
June 27	The space shuttle Atlantis blasts off on a mission to dock with the Russian space station Mir and bring home American astronaut Norman Thagard.
June 28	The U.S. House of Representatives approves a proposed constitutional amendment to ban desecration of the American flag. The measure is later defeated in the Senate.
July 1	After 904 performances, the musical *Kiss of the Spider Woman* closes at the Broadhurst Theatre in New York City.
July 2	Bill Gates is worth $12.9 billion, making him the world's richest private person, *Forbes* magazine says.
July 3	Publication date of *Time* magazine's exaggerated cover story about "cyberporn." Critical reaction to the article quickly develops online—a telling example of the Internet's emergent potential to debunk and discredit shoddy research.
July 4	The space shuttle Atlantis and the Russian space station Mir separate flawlessly after being docked in orbit for five days.
July 5	The 113-year-old typewriter manufacturer, Smith Corona Corporation, files for Chapter 11 bankruptcy protection from its creditors. The venerable maker of portable typewriters was unable to withstand or adapt to competition from personal computers.
July 6	The United Nations–designated "safe area" at Srebrenica in eastern Bosnia comes under attack by Bosnian Serb forces— the opening salvos of what ends in a massacre of 8,000 Muslim men and boys.
July 7	The space shuttle Atlantis lands at Cape Canaveral with astronaut Norman Thagard aboard. Thagard had spent three and a half months on Russia's space station, Mir.

July 8	A deadly heat wave builds in the midsection of the United States. Before it subsides ten days later, the heat will have claimed more than 800 lives, most of them in Illinois.
July 9	The Grateful Dead perform at Soldier Field in Chicago, at what would be their final concert. A month later, Jerry Garcia, the band's founder and frontman, dies of heart failure.
July 10	The defense opens its case at the O.J. Simpson double-murder trial in Los Angeles, calling Simpson's grown daughter, Arnelle, to testify.
July 11	The United States and Vietnam restore diplomatic relations, twenty years after the end of the Vietnam War.
July 13	Six union locals representing 2,500 journalists, printers, truck drivers, and other workers at the *Detroit Free Press* and *Detroit News* go on strike. The labor dispute would last nineteen months.
July 14	Temperatures top 100 degrees for a second successive day as a deadly heat wave intensifies in Chicago.
July 16	Amazon.com opens for business on the Internet.
July 18	Publication date of Barack Obama's memoir, *Dreams from My Father*.
July 22	A jury in Union, S.C., finds Susan Smith guilty of first-degree murder in the deliberate drowning of her two sons. She is later sentenced to life in prison.
July 25	Bosnian Serb leader Radovan Karadžić and his military commander, Ratko Mladić, are indicted for genocide by a U.N. war crimes tribunal at the Hague.
July 27	The Korean War Veterans Memorial is dedicated in Washington, D.C.
July 31	In an unexpected move, Walt Disney Company says it is acquiring Capital Cities–ABC Inc. for $19 billion. The deal includes the popular ESPN sports cable network.
August 1	In the second major television network deal in as many days, Westinghouse Electric Corporation announces that it is acquiring CBS for $5.4 billion.
August 4	Croatian forces launch "Operation Storm," an offensive to recapture the country's Krajina region, which Serbs had seized four years earlier. The Croat offensive drives 150,000 Croatian Serbs from their homes in another spasm of "ethnic cleansing" in the Balkans.
August 6	Bells ring and sirens wail as Hiroshima marks the moment fifty years earlier when it became the target of the world's first atomic bombing.

August 9   Netscape Communications Corporation goes public in a frenzied stock debut that attracts wide attention to the company and the Internet.

August 10   Norma McCorvey, the pseudonymous "Jane Roe" of the Supreme Court decision in 1973 that legalized abortion, says she has joined Operation Rescue, a militant antiabortion group.

August 13   Mickey Mantle, a Hall of Fame baseball star, dies of liver cancer at a Dallas hospital. He was 63.

August 14   Shannon Faulkner becomes the first woman in the cadet corps of The Citadel in South Carolina. She leaves school four days later, citing isolation from male cadets and the stresses of a long court battle to win admission to the military school.

August 15   The federal government says it will pay $3.1 million to white separatist Randy Weaver and his family to settle claims over the killing of Weaver's wife and teenage son at Ruby Ridge, Idaho, in 1992, during a siege by federal agents.

August 16   Microsoft introduces the first version of its Web browser, Internet Explorer.

August 17   President Clinton's former business partners, James B. McDougal and Susan H. McDougal, are indicted by a grand jury investigating the many-tentacled Whitewater scandal. Indicted with them is Arkansas Governor Jim Guy Tucker. All three later are convicted.

August 19   Three senior U.S. officials heading to talks in Sarajevo are killed when their armored vehicle slides off a muddy mountain road, rolls over several times, and bursts into flames.

August 20   In Firozabad, India, a passenger train slams into another train that had stalled after striking a cow. About 350 people are killed and more than 400 are injured.

August 21   ABC News settles a $10 billion libel suit and publicly apologizes to Philip Morris for having reported that the tobacco company added extra nicotine to its cigarettes.

August 22   At a trial in Chicago, Democratic Congressman Mel Reynolds of Illinois is convicted of sexual misconduct involving an underage campaign worker. Reynolds later is sentenced to five years in prison.

August 23   Famous *Life* magazine photographer Alfred Eisenstaedt, 96, dies while vacationing on Martha's Vineyard. His photograph of a sailor kissing a nurse in New York's Times Square was among the most memorable images of Americans celebrating the end of World War II.

August 24   Amid hoopla in the United States and abroad, Microsoft begins selling its Windows 95 personal computer software.

August 26   Evelyn Wood, the speed-reading guru whose course was popular in the late 1950s and 1960s, dies in Arizona. She was 86.

August 28   Bosnian Serb gunners lob five mortar rounds into a market in Sarajevo, one of which kills thirty-seven people, most of them civilians. The Serb attack triggers "Operation Deliberate Force"—retaliatory NATO airstrikes intended to prevent further shelling of Sarajevo.

September 1   More than 10,000 people gather in Cleveland, Ohio, to celebrate the opening of the Rock and Roll Hall of Fame.

September 4   The United Nations Fourth World Conference on Women opens in Beijing. More than 4,750 delegates attend, representing 189 governments. In a speech on the second day of the conference, First Lady Hillary Rodham Clinton declares: "It is a violation of human rights when babies are denied food, or drowned, or suffocated, or their spines broken, simply because they are born girls."

September 5   Jurors at the O.J. Simpson double-murder trial hear portions of a tape-recording in which Mark Fuhrman, a Los Angeles police detective, uttered a racist slur. Fuhrman previously testified that he had not uttered such a slur in at least ten years.

September 6   Cal Ripken of the Baltimore Orioles breaks Lou Gehrig's "iron man" record by playing in his 2,131st consecutive Major League baseball game.

September 7   Republican Bob Packwood of Oregon announces his resignation after twenty-seven years in the Senate, heading off a near-certain vote to expel him for sexual and official misconduct.

September 10   NBC's prime-time hospital drama *ER* wins eight Emmy Awards, and ABC's *NYPD Blue* wins the award for best dramatic series. NBC's *Frasier* wins five awards, including best comedy series for the second straight year.

September 11   The inaugural issue of the *Weekly Standard*, a conservative opinion journal, goes on sale. A few days earlier, the first issue of *George,* a glossy lifestyle magazine founded by John F. Kennedy Jr., had been unveiled.

September 13   *The Drew Carey Show* premiers on ABC television. The comedy program would run until 2004.

September 14   Bosnian Serbs agree to pull heavy guns away from Sarajevo. In response, NATO announces a halt to its aerial bombing campaign of Serb positions.

September 15   The Fourth World Conference on Women adjourns in Beijing.

September 16   On her 24th birthday, Shawntel Smith of Oklahoma is crowned "Miss America" at a pageant in Atlantic City, N.J.

September 19   After considerable internal debate, the *New York Times* and the *Washington Post* agree to the Unabomber's demands and jointly publish his 35,000-word manifesto, a rambling diatribe that appears as an eight-page insert in the *Post*.

September 22   Time Warner says it will acquire the 82 percent of Turner Broadcasting System stock it did not own in a $7.5 billion deal. It is the third major acquisition of a U.S. media company in two months.

September 26   The prosecution makes closing arguments in the murder trial of O.J. Simpson. The defense begins its closing arguments the following day.

September 27   The U.S. Treasury unveils a redesigned $100 bill that features a slightly off-center portrait of Benjamin Franklin.

September 28   Bob Denard, a 66-year-old French coup-master, leads a group of mercenaries in overthrowing Comoran President Mohammed Djohar in the Indian Ocean state. The French army intervenes in early October, under bilateral accords with the Comoros Islands, a former French colony, and captures the mercenaries.

October 1   Sheik Omar Abdel-Rahman, a blind Egyptian cleric, and nine defendants are convicted of plotting a terrorist campaign of bombings and assassinations. A federal jury in New York finds the defendants guilty on all but two of fifty charges.

October 2   Jurors in O.J. Simpson's double-murder trial in Los Angeles deliberate less than four hours before reaching unanimous verdicts. The trial judge, Lance Ito, says the verdicts will be read in court the following day.

October 3   O.J. Simpson is acquitted of charges that he fatally stabbed his former wife, Nicole Brown Simpson, and her friend, Ronald Goldman. Simpson afterward vows to devote his life to finding the killer or killers. "They are out there some-where," Simpson says in a statement read by his son, Jason.

October 4   Pope John Paul II arrives at Newark International Airport for a five-day visit to the United States. The 75-year-old pontiff is welcomed by President Clinton and Hillary Rodham Clinton, the governors of New York and New Jersey, and the hierar-chy of the Roman Catholic Church in the United States.

October 5   President Clinton announces that Bosnia's warring parties will meet for peace talks in the United States. They agree to a sixty-day ceasefire, which takes effect October 12.

October 6	Swiss astronomers Michel Mayor and Didier Queloz report the discovery of the first exoplanet, a massive object that revolves around 51 Pegasi, a star in the constellation Pegasus.
October 8	On the final day of his visit to the United States, Pope John Paul II celebrates mass in Baltimore, at Oriole Park at Camden Yards.
October 9	Saboteurs remove twenty-nine spikes from a remote stretch of railroad track in Arizona, derailing a Los Angeles–bound Amtrak train. One person was killed, and scores of others were injured.
October 11	Just hours before airtime, O. J. Simpson cancels a live interview with the NBC program *Dateline*. Simpson says his lawyers advised him that he "was being set up" and that the interview "was going to be tantamount to a grand jury hearing." NBC says its interviewers had planned to pose tough questions about Simpson's whereabouts at the time his former wife and her friend were slain in June 1994.
October 16	Hundreds of thousands of black men from across the country peaceably gather in Washington, D.C., for the "Million Man March," called by Louis Farrakhan, leader of the Nation of Islam.
October 17	President Clinton tells wealthy contributors at a fund-raising dinner in Houston that he raised taxes "too much" in his first budget in 1993. His offhand remark during a rambling talk stirs criticism from Republicans and Democrats alike. "Clinton makes life hardest on those who are for him," a *Washington Post* columnist observes.
October 18	The United States announces that peace talks on Bosnia would be convened at Wright-Patterson Air Force Base near Dayton, Ohio, about halfway around the world from the war-torn Balkans.
October 19	The Broadway revival of the classic musical *Hello, Dolly* opens at New York's Lunt-Fontanne Theatre, with Carol Channing in the lead role. Channing had starred as Dolly Levi in the show's long-running Broadway production in the 1960s.
October 20	A year after being appointed to head the alliance, NATO Secretary General Willy Claes resigns to face corruption charges in his native Belgium. The country's highest court three years later finds Claes guilty of corruption and he receives a three-year suspended jail sentence. The Spanish foreign minister, Javier Solana, succeeds Claes in NATO's top position.
October 22	The United Nations marks its fiftieth anniversary at a commemorative meeting in New York City. Leaders of most

countries of the world attend, and their speechmaking is spread over three days. To a writer for the *Washington Post*, the gathering is evocative of "the funeral of Edward VII in 1910—the last great meeting of royalty before the 20th century devoured most of them."

October 24 American archeologist and mountaineer Johan Reinhard announces the discovery of the 500-year-old body of a young Inca girl who was found frozen near the summit of Mt. Ampato in Peru.

October 25 The musical *Victor/Victoria* opens at the Marquis Theater in New York City in the first of 738 performances.

October 26 In the most inspired prank of the year, Montreal radio show host Pierre Brassard pretends to be the Canadian prime minister and reaches Queen Elizabeth II by telephone. They speak in English and French for seven minutes. The conversation is broadcast over Montreal's CKOI radio station.

October 28 The Atlanta Braves defeat the Cleveland Indians, 1–0, to win the World Series in six games.

October 30 Voters in Quebec narrowly reject a pro-independence referendum, the second defeat of a separatist measure in fifteen years.

October 31 Albert Belle, a Major League baseball star with a surly attitude, drives his Ford Explorer in pursuit of teenagers who had thrown eggs at his house in suburban Cleveland. Belle, the *Sporting News* Major League player of the year in 1995, says in a call to police: "You better get somebody over here, because if I find one of them, I'll kill them." He later was fined $100 for reckless operation of a motor vehicle.

November 1 U.S.-brokered negotiations aimed at ending the war in Bosnia open at Wright-Patterson Air Force Base on the outskirts of Dayton, Ohio. U.S. Secretary of State Warren Christopher convenes the talks, with the presidents of Bosnia, Croatia, and Serbia present.

November 4 Israel's prime minister, Yitzhak Rabin, is assassinated by a right-wing Israeli law student at a peace rally in Tel Aviv.

November 6 The owner of the Cleveland Browns, Art Modell, announces plans to move the storied professional football franchise to Baltimore.

November 8 Retired Army general Colin Powell announces he will not seek the presidency or other elected office in 1996, saying politics is "a calling that I do not yet hear."

November 9 O. J. Simpson says in a pair of telephone interviews with an Associated Press reporter that people have mostly supported rather than shunned him since his acquittal the month before on charges of killing his former wife and her friend. He says he recognizes that the "only thing that endures is character," and that wealth and fame are illusory. He also scoffs at reports that he has become a prisoner in his own home.

November 10   Ken Saro-Wiwa, a Nigerian writer and prominent human rights activist, is hanged with eight other dissidents in southern Nigeria. They were accused of complicity in four murders. Saro-Wiwa claimed that he and the others were framed because of their opposition to the oil industry practices in southern Nigeria.

November 13   The federal government prepares for a partial shutdown as President Clinton vetoes a stopgap budget bill in a fiscal standoff with Republicans in Congress.

November 14   A partial shutdown of the U.S. government begins, and about 800,000 federal workers are furloughed.

November 15   On the second day of the partial government shutdown, President Clinton and intern Monica Lewinsky begin their furtive sexual relationship at the White House. Their on-again, off-again affair would last until March 1997.

November 17   President Clinton and Monica Lewinsky meet for their second sexual encounter at the White House.

November 19   President Clinton and Republican leaders in Congress reach a deal to settle their budget dispute and end the partial government shutdown. Federal workers return to work the following day.

November 20   In a soul-baring, hour-long interview aired on BBC television, Princess Diana concedes to having been unfaithful to her husband, Prince Charles. But she says she does not want a divorce.

November 21   An agreement to end nearly four years of bloodletting in the Balkans is initialed by the leaders of Bosnia, Croatia, and Serbia. The agreement, brokered during three weeks of intensive negotiations at a U.S. Air Force base on the outskirts of Dayton, Ohio, calls for the deployment to Bosnia of 60,000 NATO peacekeeping troops—20,000 of them from the United States. The Dayton accords are formally signed in Paris in mid-December 1995.

November 22   Disney releases Pixar's *Toy Story*, the first feature-length computer-animated motion picture. *Toy Story* becomes a commercial success, grossing more than $360 million.

November 27   President Clinton goes on television to press his case for deploying 20,000 U.S. troops as part of a NATO peacekeeping force in Bosnia. "If we're not there," he says, "NATO will not be there. The peace will collapse, the war will reignite, the slaughter of innocents will begin again."

November 28   President Clinton signs a $6.5 billion highway bill that includes language repealing the federal speed limit of 55-miles-per-hour, which had been in place since 1974. The measure gives states the authority to set speed limits.

November 30   President Clinton becomes the first incumbent U.S. chief executive to visit Northern Ireland. He urges Catholics and Protestants to maintain their ceasefire and not to surrender to the impulses of "old habits and hard grudges." From behind a bulletproof screen, Clinton turns on Christmas lights in Belfast.

December 1   A federal appellate court removes District Judge Wayne Alley from hearing the case against Timothy McVeigh and Terry Nichols in the Oklahoma City bombing. The appellate court says that bomb damage to Alley's courtroom and chambers could give rise to doubts about his impartiality. The chief U.S. district judge in Denver, Richard Matsch, is appointed to replace Alley. Matsch later orders separate trials for McVeigh and Nichols, and he moves the proceedings to Denver.

December 2   In Germany, President Clinton tells American troops who will be in the vanguard of 60,000 NATO peacekeepers in Bosnia and Herzegovina that they are to strike "immediately, and with decisive force" if threatened. He also tells them "the stakes demand [the] American leadership that you will provide."

December 4   Publication date of Bob Metcalfe's prediction, in a column in *InfoWorld*, that the Internet "will soon go spectacularly supernova and in 1996 will collapse." Metcalfe, the founder of 3M Corporation, later vows to eat his Internet-collapse column if the prediction goes unfulfilled. It does, and he does, at an international conference in April 1997.

December 7   Declaring that Microsoft is now "hard core about the Internet," Bill Gates announces what in effect is a counterattack on Netscape and a bid to dominate the still-emerging Web-browser market.

December 8   Thirty years after the band was created and four months after the death of its founder and front man, Jerry Garcia, the remaining members of the Grateful Dead say the group is disbanding.

December 9   Kweisi Mfume, a five-term Democratic congressman from Maryland, is chosen executive director of the NAACP. Mfume fills a post vacant since the Rev. Benjamin Chavis was fired in 1993 following accusations of financial mismanagement and sexual harassment. Mfume serves nearly nine years.

December 11	The NBC *Today* show, featuring anchors Bryant Gumbel and Katie Couric, begins a sixteen-year weekly winning streak as television's most-watched morning news program. The streak lasts 852 weeks, ending in April 2012.
December 14	Microsoft and NBC announce a joint venture to establish MSNBC, an all-news cable channel intended to compete with CNN in covering breaking news.
December 15	The AltaVista online search engine is launched by Digital Equipment Corporation and quickly becomes one of the Internet's most popular tools. AltaVista uses several hundred "spiders" to index the World Wide Web.
December 16	President Clinton and Republicans in Congress blame each other as another budget impasse leads to another partial shutdown of the federal government.
December 18	Richard C. Holbrooke, a principal architect of the Dayton peace accords, says he will leave his State Department position early in 1996. "I am not walking away," Holbrooke says in an interview with the *Washington Post*. "I will leave with total support for this administration, and the policies which I was part of."
December 20	Buckingham Palace says that Queen Elizabeth has urged Prince Charles and Princess Diana to end their troubled marriage.
December 23	The Vatican announces that the pope's annual Christmas message will, for the first time, be posted on the Internet.
December 24	Smoke from a fire in the three-room primate house at the Philadelphia Zoo kills twenty-three rare gorillas, orangutans, gibbons, and lemurs.
December 25	Pope John Paul II, suffering flu-like symptoms, cuts short his traditional Christmas greetings, telling a crowd at the Vatican, "I cannot go on. Merry Christmas and God bless." He reappears twenty minutes later and apologizes.
December 27	Alaska Airlines becomes the first U.S. carrier to sell tickets on the Internet.
December 28	CompuServe, one of the leading online commercial computer services, complies with an order from a German prosecutor and suspends member access to two hundred sexually explicit Internet discussion groups.
December 31	President Clinton and Monica Lewinsky engage in the third sexual encounter of their erratic relationship. Later in the day, Clinton, his wife, and their daughter travel to South Carolina for a year-end retreat at Hilton Head.

Notes

PREFACE

1. See John Lancaster, "1979 and All That," *New Yorker,* August 5, 2013, 68. Lancaster observed: "There are years whose impact on human history is apparent to everyone at the time—1776, say, or 1945, or 2001—and then there are years whose significance seems to grow in retrospect, as it becomes clear that the consequences of certain events are still being felt decades later."

2. See, for example, Christian Caryl, *Strange Rebels: 1979 and the Birth of the 21st Century* (New York: Basic Books, 2013).

3. For examples of year-studies that assert such claims, at least in their titles, see Fred Kaplan, *1959: The Year Everything Changed* (Hoboken, N.J.: Wiley, 2009), and Rob Kirkpatrick, *1969: The Year Everything Changed* (New York: Skyhorse, 2011). Similarly, see Felipe Fernández-Armesto, *1492: The Year the World Began* (New York: HarperOne, 2009).

4. See David Maraniss, *Barack Obama: The Story* (New York: Simon and Schuster, 2012), 573. Maraniss noted that *Dreams from My Father* leapt "from the remainder bin to bestsellerdom" after Obama's keynote address in August 2004 at the Democratic National Convention. The speech made him "an overnight sensation," Maraniss wrote. *Dreams from My Father* was reviewed by the *New York Times,* which said Obama's story "bogs down in discussions of racial exploitation without really shedding any new light on the subject." Paul Watkins, "A Promise of Redemption: A Memoir by a Young Lawyer, the Son of a White American Mother and a Black Kenyan Father," *New York Times Sunday Book Review,* August 6, 1995, 17.

5. See, for example, Renee C. Romano, "Not Dead Yet: My Identity Crisis as a Historian of the Recent Past," in *Doing Recent History: On Privacy, Copyright, Video Games, Institutional Review Boards, Activist Scholarship, and*

History That Talks Back, ed. Claire Bond Potter and Renee C. Romano (Athens: University of Georgia Press, 2012), 28–29.

INTRODUCTION TO AN IMPROBABLE YEAR

1. Todd Copilevitz, "In 1995 Everyone Became Caught in the Same Web," *Dallas Morning News,* December 29, 1995.

2. J.M. Lawrence, "1995 Was Year of the Apology," *Boston Herald,* December 31, 1995, retrieved from Factiva database.

3. Thomas Ferrick, Jr., "1995 Marked by Turmoil Reminiscent of Another Era," *Philadelphia Inquirer,* December 31, 1995.

4. W. Michael Cox and Richard Alm, "The Good Old Days Are Now," *Reason* 27, no. 7 (December 1995): 24. Cox and Alm also observed: "No catalog of higher living standards would be complete without products that didn't even exist for past generations. . . . Microwave ovens, answering machines, food processors, home computers, exercise equipment, cable TV, Rollerblades, fax machines, and soft contact lenses are staples of the 1990s lifestyle. As important, many products, from computers to clothing[,] have been getting higher in quality even as they drop in price" (22).

5. Nick Leeson with Edward Whitley, *Rogue Trader: How I Brought Down Barings Bank and Shook the Financial World* (Boston: Little, Brown, 1996), 177.

6. Quoted in Fred Barbash, "A Pretender Tweaks the Throne," *Washington Post,* October 29, 1995. See also Ed Vulliamy, "Disc Jockey Dupes Queen into Chat on Phone-In," *Guardian* (London), October 28, 1995.

7. Afterward, a spokesman for the palace said testily: "We think it's annoying. We think it's irritating. We think it's a waste of the queen's time." Brassard, though, reveled in his hoax and said the queen "is very funny. . . . That kind of conversation is a good thing because we see the human side of the person." Quoted in Dirk Beveridge, "Buckingham Palace: Hoax Call to Queen Was Aided by Canadian Foul-Up," Associated Press, October 28, 1995, retrieved from LexisNexis database. Quebec voted narrowly to defeat the separatist referendum a few days later, putting an end to an internal threat to Canada's territorial integrity.

8. William J. Broad, "U.S. Craft Docks Flawlessly with Russian Space Station," *New York Times,* June 30, 1995. It was the first U.S.-Russian space linkup in twenty years.

9. The previous record was eighty-four days. See William J. Broad, "New Attack Planned on Ills of Space Travel," *New York Times,* July 11, 1995.

10. John Noble Wilford, "Lovesick Woodpeckers Poke Hole in a Shuttle's Schedule," *New York Times,* June 3, 1995. The birds were identified as yellow-shafted flickers, which can display "such behavior during courtship and to proclaim its territory," Wilford noted, adding that "the male flickers were undoubtedly trying to attract the attention of females by taking on something far more monumental than a dead [tree] limb."

11. Quoted in "Actor Hugh Grant Arrested for Alleged Sex Encounter with Prostitute," Associated Press, June 27, 1995, retrieved from LexisNexis database.

12. See "Hugh Grant Talks about His Arrest," CNN *Larry King Live*, July 12, 1995, transcript retrieved from LexisNexis database.

13. Quoted in W. Speers, "For Elizabeth Hurley, the Pain Just Won't Go Away," *Philadelphia Inquirer*, August 4, 1995. Hurley, who was interviewed on the ABC News television program *20/20*, also said, "There has never been a time in my life when I've felt less inclined to get married."

14. See George Rush, "No Longer Divine, Hugh & Liz Split," *New York Daily News*, May 23, 2000. It emerged years later that the British tabloid *News of the World* paid Divine Brown about $160,000 for an exclusive interview after her encounter with Grant. It also paid about $80,000 to fly Brown's family members to a resort in Nevada, to seclude them from rival journalists. See Katrin Bennhold, "Testimony at Hacking Trial Gives Peek into British Tabloids," *New York Times*, March 6, 2014.

15. John Crudele, "Profit and Loss: Why Stock Market Could Suffer in '95," *San Francisco Chronicle*, January 1, 1995.

16. Cited in Mike Clark, "Film's Finest Hours, From 'Babe' to 'Toy' Land," *USA Today*, December 27, 1995.

17. Janet Maslin, "Film Review: There's a New Toy in the House: Uh-oh," *New York Times*, November 22, 1995.

18. See Gregory P. Laughlin, "Extrasolar Planetary Systems," *American Scientist* 94, no. 5 (September–October 2006): 421. Laughlin also wrote: "To look at the illuminated face of the planet at all, you would need extremely dark sunglasses, or better yet, a welder's mask."

19. See Ray Jayawardhana, *Strange New Worlds: The Search for Alien Planets and Life beyond Our Solar System* (Princeton: Princeton University Press, 2011). Jayawardhana wrote: "On a number of occasions, starting as early as the mid-nineteenth century, astronomers thought they had hit the jackpot. Their announcements [about would-be extra-solar planets] often resulted in newspaper headlines, and fed into speculations of alien life, but did not survive closer scrutiny. In every case, the culprit turned out to be observational error" (46).

20. See Artie P. Hatzes and Guenther Wuchterl, "Giant Planet Seeks Nursery Place," *Nature* 436 (July 14, 2005): 182. For a discussion of the dominant theory of the time, see Alan P. Boss, "Proximity of Jupiter-Like Planets to Low-Mass Stars," *Science* (January 20, 1995): 360–62. Boss wrote: "Jupiter-like planets are thus likely to be found orbiting low-mass stars at distances not much different . . . than those in our solar system" (362).

21. As Jayawardhana noted in *Strange New Worlds*: "Planet formation models [then] did not allow for gas giants to form so close to their stars; the temperatures are too high for the material needed to form the planet cores to remain solid" (74).

22. Quoted in Jayawardhana, *Strange New Worlds,* 74. Mayor and Queloz reported their discovery—"the first example of an extrasolar planetary system associated with a solar-type star"—in "A Jupiter-Mass Companion to a Solar-Type Star," *Nature* 378 (November 23, 1995): 355–59.

23. Confirmation came from American astronomers Geoffrey Marcy and R. Paul Butler of San Francisco State University. Butler later said: "Mayor jump-started us. His discovery brought a level of excitement to the field." Quoted in

John Noble Wilford, "In a Golden Age of Discovery, Faraway Worlds Beckon," *New York Times,* February 9, 1997.

24. Michel Mayor and Pierre-Yves Frei, *New Worlds in the Cosmos: The Discovery of Exoplanets* (New York: Cambridge University Press, 2003), 18.

25. Michel Mayor, interview with author, June 6, 2011.

26. Michael Hanlon, "Heavens, It's Weird Out There," *Sunday Times* (London), December 11, 2011.

27. The prospect that intelligent life exists beyond the Earth may be extraordinarily small. As physicist Paul Davies has observed, "If life arose simply by the accumulation of many specific chemical accidents in one place, it is easy to imagine that only one in, say, a trillion trillion habitable planets would ever host such a dream run. Set against a number that big . . . it is irrelevant whether the Milky Way contains 40 billion habitable planets or just a handful. Forty billion hardly makes a dent in a trillion trillion." Davis, "Are We Alone in the Universe?" *New York Times,* November 19, 2013.

28. See Dennis Overbye, "NASA Planet-Hunting Star Idled by Broken Parts," *New York Times,* August 16, 2013. See also Lee Hotz, "Hundreds of Planets Found, Four Perhaps Suitable for Life," *Wall Street Journal,* February 27, 2014. Kepler also found a few circumbinary systems in which a planet revolves around two stars—not entirely unlike Tatooine, Luke Skywalker's home planet in the *Star Wars* movies. See Sindya N. Bhanoo, "Kepler Finds More Planets Orbiting Two Stars," *New York Times,* January 17, 2012.

29. Barbara Holland, *Endangered Pleasures: In Defense of Naps, Bacon, Martinis, Profanity, and Other Indulgences* (Boston: Little, Brown, 1995), ix.

30. Ibid., xi. Of cigarettes, Holland wrote: "They're no longer a legitimate pleasure, but they were a pleasure once. We may have been stupid to smoke, but we didn't smoke from sheer stupidity; we smoked because we liked it" (21). Holland died of lung cancer in 2010. See William Grimes, "Obituaries: Barbara Holland, Defender of Small Vices, Dies at 77," *New York Times,* September 14, 2010.

31. Russell Baker, "Hymns to Joy," *New York Times,* March 21, 1995. Baker also wrote: "I read her book during a recent vacation which provided a rare opportunity to read for the pure pleasure of reading. It's odd but true about the newspaper business that while it encourages a lot of reading, most of this reading is either not worth doing or not much fun."

32. See, for example, "Top 10 Commencement Speeches," *Time* magazine, accessed October 26, 2013, http://content.time.com/time/specials/packages/article/0,28804,1898670_1898671_1898650,00.html.

33. The full text of Baker's commencement speech is accessible at www.humanity.org/voices/commencements/russell-baker-connecticut-college-speech-1995?page=baker_at_connecticut&sectionName=voices.

34. See Brett Pulley, "Thousands in New York Prepare for Black Men's March," *New York Times,* October 14, 1995.

35. See Michael A. Fletcher and Hamil R. Harris, "United They'll Stand, March on Washington," *Washington Post,* September 10, 1995.

36. Angela Davis, an activist college professor and a former Black Panther, assailed the exclusion of women, saying: "No march, movement or agenda that defines manhood in the narrowest terms and seeks to make women lesser partners

in this quest for equality can be considered a positive step." Quoted in Rachel Jones, "Organizers Downplay Farrakhan's Role in the March," *Philadelphia Inquirer,* October 14, 1995. In addition, the *New York Times* reported that while "it is difficult to determine just how divided black women are about this long-planned assault on black male stagnation, there is an unmistakable buzz in black women's circles about the wisdom of the march. Expressions of exhilaration and frustration can be heard from book groups to church groups, from board rooms to bedrooms. And some of the buzz is downright angry." Michel Marriott, "Black Women Are Split Over All-Male March on Washington," *New York Times,* October 14, 1995. The *Times* article quoted Barbara Arnwine, executive director of the Lawyers' Committee for Civil Rights Under Law, as saying: "The role African-American women are given in this march is to tend the bake sale, raise the money or stay at home and take care of the children. I think that it is awful." In the end, the event brought what the *Washington Post* said was a "sprinkling of wives, mothers, daughters and sisters who mingled among [the participants] to show support and to share in a historical event." Marcia Slacum Greene and Tracy Thompson, "A Welcome for Women on the Mall; Most Heed Call to Stay Away from March, Meet Elsewhere," *Washington Post,* October 17, 1995.

37. A few days before the rally, the transcript was released of an interview Farrakhan had given in early October, in which he said: "Many of the Jews who owned the homes, the apartments in the black community, we considered them bloodsuckers because they took from our community and built their community but didn't offer anything back to our community." Quoted in Charles Bierbauer, "Its Goal More Widely Accepted Than Its Leader," CNN, October 17, 1995, accessed November 4, 2013, www.cnn.com/US/9510/megamarch /10–17/notebook/.

38. Ibid.

39. See Mario A. Brossard and Richard Morin, "Leader Popular among Marchers," *Washington Post,* October 17, 1995. Brossard and Morin reported that 87 percent of survey respondents viewed Farrakhan favorably, exceeding the popularity of other prominent African Americans, including Colin Powell and Jesse Jackson.

40. André P. Tramble, "Meeting the Challenge," in *Atonement: The Million Man March,* ed. Kim Martin Sadler (Cleveland: Pilgrim Press, 1996), 39.

41. Neil James Bullock, "No Ordinary Day," in Sadler, ed., *Atonement,* 27.

42. See "Minister Farrakhan Challenges Black Men," CNN, October 17, 1995, retrieved January 30, 2014, www-cgi.cnn.com/US/9510/megamarch/10–16 /transcript/.

43. Ibid.

44. See Joel Best, *Damned Lies and Statistics: Untangling Numbers from the Media, Politicians, and Activists* (Berkeley: University of California Press, 2001), 136.

45. See Sari Horwitz and Hamil R. Harris, "Farrakhan Threatens to Sue Park Police over March Count," *Washington Post,* October 18, 1995. The *Post* report quoted a march official named Abdul Alim Muhammad as saying that the Park Service count evoked "plantation days when we would pick 100 bales of cotton and they would give us credit for 40 bales."

46. For a discussion of the controversy, see Best, *Damned Lies and Statistics*, 132–37. As the dispute wore on, the Park Service director, Roger G. Kennedy, was quoted by the *New York Times* as saying: "Nobody really knows the number." Michael Janofsky, "Federal Parks Chief Calls 'Million Man' Count Low," *New York Times*, October 21, 1995.

47. Quoted in Leef Smith and Wendy Melillo, "If It's Crowd Size You Want, Park Service Says Count It Out," *Washington Post*, October 13, 1996.

48. See David Segal, "With Windows 95's Debut, Microsoft Scales Heights of Hype," *Washington Post*, August 24, 1995.

49. It was, *USA Today* observed, "the most talked-about product launch since New Coke's introduction in 1985." Dottie Enrico, "Microsoft's Marketing Coup," *USA Today*, July 31, 1995.

50. Segal, "With Windows 95's Debut, Microsoft Scales Heights of Hype."

51. Ibid.

52. Richard W. Stevenson, "Software Makes Strange Bedfellows in Britain," *New York Times*, August 24, 1995. Stevenson reported that, across the bottom of the *Times* of London front page that day, an advertisement read: "Windows 95. So Good Even The Times Is Complimentary."

53. See Lee Gomes, "And Gates Said . . . 'Let There Be Hype,'" *San Jose Mercury News*, August 24, 1995.

54. The Empire State Building was bathed in red, yellow, and green—three of Microsoft's four colors. The fourth was blue, but "technical problems" limited the display to three colors, the *New York Times* reported. Carey Goldberg, "Midnight Sales Frenzy Ushers in Windows 95," *New York Times*, August 24, 1995.

55. John Carlin, "Hard Sell for the Software 'Revolution,'" *Independent* (London), August 24, 1995.

56. "Software Hype and Hopes," *New York Times*, July 31, 1995.

57. See Dean Takahashi, "Apple Tries to Be Heard above the Din," *San Jose Mercury News*, August 24, 1995. The counter-campaign, Takahashi noted, "reflects the defensive posture of Apple, which still commands a cult-like following among its users, and how much it has fallen in the computer world. As recently as the early 1990s, the company claimed a market share of more than 10 percent in the computer market."

58. See Steve Lohr, "Windows of Opportunity for Microsoft," *New York Times*, July 31, 1995.

59. Goldberg, "Midnight Sales Frenzy Ushers in Windows 95."

60. Segal, "With Windows 95's Debut, Microsoft Scales Heights of Hype." Nearly one million copies of Windows 95 were sold in the five days following its release, according to *Computer Reseller News*, citing data compiled by PC Data. "Early Windows 95 Sales Sizzle," *Computer Reseller News*, September 6, 1995.

61. See Steve Lohr, "It's Been an Uphill Battle to Sell Windows 95," *New York Times*, January 18, 1996. Microsoft "has found that selling information technology as a mass-market, retail product remains an uphill struggle," Lohr wrote.

62. See Goldberg, "Midnight Sales Frenzy Ushers in Windows 95."

63. See Walter S. Mossberg, "The Top Products in Two Decades of Tech Reviews; Yes, the Newton," *Wall Street Journal*, December 18, 2013. He wrote:

"This was the Microsoft operating system that cemented the graphical user interface and the mouse as the way to operate a computer."

64. Lohr, "Windows of Opportunity for Microsoft."

65. See Times Mirror Center for the People & the Press, "Technology in the American Household: Americans Going Online . . . Explosive Growth, Uncertain Destinations" (Washington, D.C.: TMCPP, October 16, 1995), 10.

66. James K. Glassman, "Brave New Cyberworld," *Washington Post,* August 29, 1995. Glassman is perhaps best known as coauthor of *Dow 36,000* (New York: Crown Business, 1999).

67. Quoted in William Brandel, "The Internet Will Be Bigger Than Anyone Imagines," *Computerworld,* January 2, 1995, 34. "I don't think we know what has hit us," Negroponte was further quoted as saying.

68. Nicholas Negroponte, *Being Digital* (New York: Vintage, 1996), 229.

69. Ibid., 148. He also wrote: "The challenge for the next decade is . . . to make computers that know you, learn about your needs, and understand verbal and nonverbal languages" (92).

70. Ibid., 210. "Within the next five years," he wrote, "one of the largest areas of growth in consumer products is likely to be such wearable devices."

71. Ibid., 217.

72. Ibid., 94.

73. See Min-Jeong Lee and Jonathan Chen, "Now, Flexible Screens: Samsung, LG Work Toward Bendable Smartphones," *Wall Street Journal,* November 5, 2013.

74. Negroponte, *Being Digital,* 152.

75. Ibid., 173. See also Martin Peers and Shalini Ramachandran, "Bye-Bye for Blockbuster," *Wall Street Journal,* November 7, 2013. The article reported the expected closing of most remaining Blockbuster video-rental stores.

76. Negroponte, *Being Digital,* 84–85.

77. Gordon Borrell, "Ready, Fire, Aim," *Editor & Publisher,* February 4, 1995, 20TC–21TC.

78. The term "innovation blindness" has been in circulation since at least 2009. See, for example, Bret Swanson, "Innovation Yin and Yang," *Maximum Entropy* (blog), August 20, 2009, accessed February 8, 2014, www .bretswanson.com/index.php/2009/08/innovation-yin-and-yang/.

79. Quoted in Tony Case, "'Print Person' Pontificates," *Editor & Publisher,* February 11, 1995, 11. The *Editor & Publisher* article noted that Roberts's "views on electronic news transmission follow the widely held opinion of newspaper people that the Internet will never supplant their time-tested medium."

80. See Times Mirror Center for the People & the Press, "Technology in the American Household."

81. See Pew Research Center for the People & the Press, "In Changing News Landscape, Even Television Is Vulnerable" (Washington, D.C.: PRCPP, September 27, 2012), 14.

82. See Peter H. Lewis, "Big Newspaper to Help Locals on the Internet," *New York Times,* April 20, 1995. A ninth newspaper company joined soon after the launch.

83. Iver Peterson, "New Service Skims 150 Newspapers for Its Users," *New York Times,* June 30, 1997.

84. See I. Jeanne Dugan, "New-Media Meltdown at New Century," *Business Week,* March 12, 1998, accessed October 10, 2013, www.businessweek.com/1998/12/b3570103.htm.

85. *Business Week* magazine offered a telling epithet for the failed venture, describing New Century as embodying "everything that could go wrong when old-line newspapers converge with new media." Dugan, "New-Media Meltdown at New Century."

86. See, for example, Arthur Charity, *Doing Public Journalism* (New York: Guilford Press, 1995).

87. See, for example, Mike Hoyt, "Are You Now, Or Will You Ever Be, a Civic Journalist?" *Columbia Journalism Review,* September/October 1995, 28.

88. See Karen Haywood, "Business News," Associated Press, August 22, 1995, retrieved from LexisNexis database. The network also agreed to pay legal fees that the companies incurred during the dispute.

89. See "Apology Accepted" (advertisement), *New York Times,* August 25, 1995.

90. See, for example, Gary Levin, "Settling Smoke May Carry News Chill," *Variety,* August 28–September 3, 1995, 34.

91. See Lawrence K. Grossman, "CBS, 60 Minutes, and the Unseen Interview," *Columbia Journalism Review,* January/February 1996, 44. See also Daniel Rubin, "Exploring How an Expose Went Awry," *Philadelphia Inquirer,* October 31, 1999.

92. Quoted in Howard Kurtz, "'60 Minutes' Kills Piece on Tobacco Industry," *Washington Post,* November 10, 1995.

93. See Joe Calderone, "What '60 Minutes' Cut," *New York Daily News,* November 17, 1995. The *Daily News* published portions of the transcript of the *60 Minutes* interview in which Wigand also accused Brown & Williamson of abandoning plans to develop a safer cigarette.

94. Quoted in Grossman, "CBS, 60 Minutes, and the Unseen Interview," 47.

95. Robin Clark, "Much Ado about O.J.—and Lance and Johnnie and Marcia," *Philadelphia Inquirer,* December 31, 1995.

96. Howard Rosenberg, "The Simpson Verdicts: Valuable Lessons of TV in Courtroom," *Los Angeles Times,* October 5, 1995, accessed April 26, 2014, http://articles.latimes.com/1195-10-05/news/mn-53644_1_simpson-trial. Rosenberg deplored what he called the "Simpsonizing of TV news," writing that it "affirm[ed] that people going into the [TV news] business are dumber and dumber, the people directing them are dumber and dumber and, as a consequence, the public is dumber and dumber." Rosenberg, "The Simpson Verdicts: Television: Could Coverage Sink Lower?" *Los Angeles Times,* October 4, 1995.

97. Dave Barry, "All the Evidence Is In: 1995 Was Certifiable," *Washington Post,* December 31, 1995.

98. See William Glaberson, "Times Is Criticized for Using Simpson Account from Tabloid," *New York Times,* December 23, 1994. See also David Barstow, "King of Newspapers Quotes the Jester," *St. Petersburg Times* (Florida), December 23, 1994.

99. Quoted in David Shaw, "'The Godzilla of Tabloid Stories,'" *Los Angeles Times,* October 9, 1995.

100. Cited in Andrea Sachs, "Mud and the Mainstream," *Columbia Journalism Review,* May/June 1995, 34.

101. Ibid., 34.

102. "What's Hot, What's Not: People, Places and Products That Have Sizzled—Or Fizzled," *San Francisco Examiner,* December 31, 1995.

103. See Leslie Miller, "Tuning In to Brave New Sounds of the Internet," *USA Today,* November 1, 1995.

104. Quoted in ibid.

1. THE YEAR OF THE INTERNET

1. Evgeny Morozov, "The Death of the Cyberflâneur," *New York Times,* February 5, 2012.

2. Farhad Manjoo, "Jurassic Web: The Internet of 1996 Is Almost Unrecognizable Compared with What We Have Today," Slate.com, February 24, 2009, accessed June 23, 2013, www.slate.com/articles/technology/technology/2009/02/jurassic_web.html.

3. See John Battelle, *The Search: How Google and Its Rivals Rewrote the Rules of Business and Transformed Our Culture* (New York: Portfolio, 2005), 68. See also Steven Levy, *In the Plex: How Google Thinks, Works, and Shapes Our Lives* (New York: Simon and Schuster, 2011), 13. Levy noted that Page and Brin soon became fast friends at Stanford, "to the point where people thought of them as a set: LarryAndSergey."

4. Sam Vincent Meddis, "Net: New and Notable," *USA Today,* December 21, 1995.

5. Steven Levy, "The Year of the Internet," *Newsweek,* December 25, 1995/January 1, 1996, 28.

6. See, for example, David Bank, "Cerf Sees Net's Commercial Potential," *San Jose Mercury News,* January 11, 1995.

7. Vinton G. Cerf, "Computer Networking: Global Infrastructure for the 21st Century," Computer Research Association (North Dakota), accessed July 19, 2013, http://homes.cs.washington.edu/~lazowska/cra/networks.html.

8. See Jim Ritter, "Inventive Words Are the Talk of 1995," *Chicago Sun-Times,* December 29, 1995. The other word of the year selected by the American Dialect Society was "Newt," a reference to Newt Gingrich, who became speaker of the U.S. House of Representatives in January 1995.

9. A nationwide telephone survey conducted in mid-October 1995 for the Times Mirror Center for the People & the Press found that 55 percent of respondents were aware of the Internet, if vaguely. Forty-two percent of respondents said they had never heard of the Internet, or were not sure what the Internet was. Three percent of respondents gave incorrect answers. Data cited here were retrieved from the "Polling the Nations" database. Newspaper articles in 1995 were known to exhort readers "to quit spectating and check out the Net for yourself. . . . All you need is a willingness to learn—and the patience to put up with the inscrutable error messages and unexplained failures that are a

central fact of Net life." See, for example, "Nothing But Net: Quit Stalling, Read This, Get on the Internet," *Washington Post,* April 24, 1995.

10. The Internet Society's estimated range of users was cited in Peter H. Lewis, "Technology: On the Net," *New York Times,* May 29, 1995.

11. See Josh McHugh, "Mr. Craigslist, Master of the Nerdiverse," *Wired,* September 2004, accessed July 18, 2013, www.wired.com/wired/archive/12.09/craigslist.html.

12. See "Craig Newmark on Technology and Freedom," C-SPAN, June 2, 2009, video accessed October 19, 2013, www.c-spanvideo.org/program/CraigN.

13. See Adam Cohen, *The Perfect Store: Inside eBay* (Boston: Little, Brown, 2002), 20–21. "The site was not much to look at," Cohen wrote, adding, "The computer code Omidyar wrote let users do only three things: list items, view items, and place bids. The name he chose was as utilitarian as the site itself: AuctionWeb." The name "AuctionWeb" was retired in favor of eBay two years later.

14. "Pierre Omidyar," Forbes.com, accessed October 19, 2013, www.forbes.com/profile/pierre-omidyar/.

15. Linda J. Engelman, "Need a Date? Just Pick Up Your Modem," *San Jose Mercury News,* August 6, 1995. Engelman also wrote that "cyber-dating" was "a real alternative to singles bars and pathetic pickup lines."

16. Its first iteration was "Jerry's Guide to the World Wide Web." See Robert H. Reid, *Architects of the Web: 1,000 Days That Built the Future of Business* (New York: Wiley, 1997), 242.

17. Ibid., 41, 69.

18. Ibid., 103.

19. See Steve Lohr, "Tickling the Ivy and Tweaking the Javascript: Part Artist, Part Hacker and Full-Time Programmer," *New York Times,* September 9, 1996. See also David Flanagan, *JavaScript: The Definitive Guide,* 6th ed. (Sebastopol, Calif.: O'Reilly Media, 2011), 1–3.

20. See Times Mirror Center for the People & the Press, "Technology in the American Household: Americans Going Online . . . Explosive Growth, Uncertain Destinations" (Washington, D.C.: TMCPP, October 16, 1995), 10.

21. See ibid., 22.

22. In her book about America Online, Kara Swisher described the mid-1990s content offerings of the online service as "moribund." She wrote: "Like much of the online industry, AOL had come to depend on the major media brand names such as Time Warner, Disney, and others. Their parcels were heavy with regurgitated content from magazines and news services. The level of substance was low." Swisher, *AOL.com: How Steve Case Beat Bill Gates, Nailed the Netheads, and Made Millions in the War for the Web* (New York: Times Business, 1998), 116. The major commercial services by 1995 were offering browsers for navigating the Web. But doing so seemed a bit pointless, rather like traveling to Alaska from California by way of New York City, as Stephen Lynch wrote in a column, "Death Watch Begins for Online Services," *Orange County Register* (California), October 2, 1995. Lynch also noted: "Almost everything you can find on a commercial service can be found on the Web."

23. Levy, "The Year of the Internet," 21.

24. Ibid, 27.

25. See, for example, Rex Weiner, "Internet Upstages Techie TV," *Variety,* July 31–August 6, 1995, 1; Matt Roush, "Plugging in to the New Media," *Crain's Detroit Business,* August 7, 1995, 1; and Mary Brandel, "Ready or Not, Companies Are Getting Web'd for Commerce," *Computerworld,* April 29, 1996, 19.

26. Clifford Stoll, *Silicon Snake Oil: Second Thoughts on the Information Highway* (New York: Doubleday, 1995), 11.

27. Ibid., 36.

28. Ibid., 184–85.

29. Ibid., 190.

30. Ibid., 198.

31. Ibid., 157.

32. Quoted in Lory Zottola Dix, "An Interview with Cliff Stoll," *Computerworld,* August 14, 1995, 85. Stoll also said in the interview: "I'm concerned that for all of the on-line wonders, there is damned little content on-line. Very little of what I see on-line has any value, other than as juvenile entertainment for adults."

33. Clifford Stoll, "The Internet? Bah!" *Newsweek,* February 27, 1995, 41. "What the Internet hucksters won't tell you," Stoll wrote, "is that the Internet is an ocean of unedited data, without any pretense of completeness. Lacking editors, reviewers or critics, the Internet has become a wasteland of unfiltered data. You don't know what to ignore and what's worth reading."

34. Clifford Stoll, comments posted to Maggie Koerth-Baker, "Curmudgeonly Essay of 'Why the Internet Will Fail' from 1995," BoingBoing.net, February 26, 2010, accessed June 22, 2013, http://boingboing.net/2010/02/26/curmudgeony-essay-on.html#comment-229414366.

35. Bob Metcalfe, "Predicting the Internet's Catastrophic Collapse and Ghost Sites Galore in 1996," *InfoWorld,* December 4, 1995, 61.

36. Ibid.

37. Bob Metcalfe, "Will Netscape Eat Its Hat over Claims It Was Too Busy for Web Conference?" *InfoWorld,* January 8, 1996, 48.

38. Scott Kirsner, "The Legend of Bob Metcalfe," *Wired,* November 1998, accessed June 23, 2013, www.wired.com/wired/archive/6.11/metcalfe.html.

39. "Sage Who Warned of Net's Collapse Eats His Words," Reuters news agency, April 11, 1997, accessed February 3, 2014, www.ibiblio.org/pjones /ils310/msg00259.html. See also "Internet Sage Eats His Words," *Toronto Star,* May 8, 1997, and Sandy Reed, "Fulfilling His Promise Columnist Bob Metcalfe Dines on His Own Words," *InfoWorld,* April 28, 1997, 75.

40. Quoted in "Beyond the Ether," *Economist,* December 12, 2009, 23.

41. Reed, "Fulfilling His Promise."

42. See Lauren Kirchner, "Salon and Slate in the Way-Back Machine," *Columbia Journalism Review,* February 4, 2011, accessed June 23, 2013, www.cjr .org/the_news_frontier/salon_and_slate_in_the_way-bac.php?page=all. Kirchner noted that the Internet of the mid-1990s "was so wide open and undefined that the right language didn't even exist to talk about it yet."

43. "Site-Seeing on the World Wide Web," *New York Times,* January 3, 1995.

44. Laurie Flynn, "Browsers Make Navigating the World Wide Web a Snap," *New York Times,* January 29, 1995.

45. "Fidelity to Offer Services on World Wide Web," *New York Times,* February 15, 1995.

46. Steve Lohr, "His Goal: Keeping the Web Worldwide," *New York Times,* December 18, 1995. Lohr's article noted that "while the World Wide Web is a household name, its creator, Tim Berners-Lee, a 40-year-old Englishman, is certainly not."

47. Reid Kanaley, "Internet Bounding Beyond Expectations," *Philadelphia Inquirer,* December 27, 1995.

48. Reid Kanaley, "Caught in the World Wide Web: It's an Exploding Part of the Internet," *Philadelphia Inquirer,* February 27, 1995.

49. Levy, "The Year of the Internet," 27.

50. See Ken Cottrill, "Internet: Losing Its Backbone," *Guardian* (London), March 30, 1995.

51. Andrew L. Shapiro, "Street Corners in Cyberspace," *Nation,* July 3, 1995, 10.

52. Philip Elmer-DeWitt, "On a Screen Near You: Cyberporn," *Time,* July 3, 1995, 38.

53. "Cybersex: Policing Pornography on the Internet," ABC News *Nightline,* June 27, 1995, transcript retrieved from LexisNexis database.

54. Howard Kurtz of the *Washington Post,* in noting the "white-hot intensity" of the online debate about the *Time* cover story, wrote that "the on-line feedback loop is essentially a healthy development that helps put news organizations and consumers on a more equal footing." Kurtz, "A Flaming Outage: A 'Cyberporn' Critic Gets a Harsh Lesson in '90s Netiquette," *Washington Post,* July 16, 1995.

55. See Reid, *Architects of the Web,* 305.

56. See Peter H. Lewis, "Critics Troubled by Computer Study on Pornography," *New York Times,* July 3, 1995. Lewis's report quoted a sociology professor at Northern Illinois University as saying: "This [study] would never make it through a traditional peer review in even a third-line social science review."

57. See ibid.

58. Quoted in Elizabeth Corcoran, "Cybersensitivity? Did the Media Overreact to Pornography on the Internet?" *Washington Post,* June 28, 1995.

59. Jeff Cohen and Norman Solomon, "Time's Expose a Cyberdud," *Capital Times* (Madison, Wis.), July 24, 1995.

60. Philip Elmer-DeWitt, "Fire Storm on the Computer Nets," *Time,* July 24, 1995, 57.

61. Such characterizations prompted sneers from international observers. The German news agency Deutsche Presse-Agentur declared at year's end that "traditional American Puritanism [had] reared up and denounced the Internet as a new weapon for pornographers in their eternal quest to pervert the morals of America's children. Congress, in its moral superiority, stood poised . . . to make on-line pornography illegal, even though the U.S. government can hardly claim sovereignty over a global computer network." Dave McIntyre, "U.S. in 1995: The Verge of Change, or More of the Same?" Deutsche Presse-Agentur, December 26, 1995, retrieved from LexisNexis database.

62. Quoted in John Schwartz, "Sexually Explicit Story Sparks Debate over On-Line Rights," *Washington Post,* February 27, 1995. Exon later wrote that the Internet was "a great boon to mankind. But we should not ignore the dark roads of pornography, indecency and obscenity it makes possible." Jim Exon, "Letters to the Editor: My Bill Does Not 'Censor' the Internet," *Washington Post,* December 2, 1995.

63. Quoted in Paul Goodsell, "Exon 'Blue Book' Bolsters Case for Internet Porn Bill," *Omaha World Herald,* June 14, 1995. The *New York Times* pointed out in an editorial that everyone who inspected Exon's "blue book" "deplored the graphic spectacle, but since it already was illegal and subject to prosecution it had no bearing on the bill's ban on indecency." See "Censorship on the Internet," *New York Times,* June 22, 1995.

64. See Robert Cannon, "The Legislative History of Senator Exon's Communications Decency Act: Regulating Barbarians on the Information Superhighway," *Federal Communications Law Journal* 49, no. 1 (1996): 72. Exon's unfamiliarity with the Internet, Cannon wrote, begged "the question of how a senator with no technical knowledge of the medium can draft language which regulates it" (72–73).

65. Dan Glaister, "Tap of the Devil," *Guardian* (London), July 3, 1995.

66. See Mike Mills, "House, Senate Agree on Cable TV Rates; Negotiators Still Divided on Issue of Obscenity on the Internet," *Washington Post,* December 13, 1995. The Internet protest mainly addressed members of a congressional conference committee assigned to resolve differences between the telecommunications bills approved by the Senate and the House.

67. See Cannon, "The Legislative History of Senator Exon's Communications Decency Act," 92.

68. "Remarks by the President in Signing Ceremony for the Telecommunications Act Conference Report," February 8, 1996, accessed June 27, 2013, http://clinton4.nara.gov/WH/EOP/OP/telecom/release.html.

69. Rory J. O'Connor, "Law Stirs Protest on Internet," *Philadelphia Inquirer,* February 9, 1996.

70. See Peter H. Lewis, "Judges Turn Back Law to Regulate Internet Decency," *New York Times,* June 13, 1996.

71. "Excerpts from Ruling on Internet," *New York Times,* June 27, 1997.

72. John Schwartz and Joan Biskupic, "High Court Allows Ban on Assisted Suicide, Strikes Down Law Restricting Online Speech," *Washington Post,* June 27, 1997.

73. See Mike Cassidy, "Remembering the Thrilling Ride of Netscape," *San Jose Mercury News,* August 9, 2005. Cassidy wrote: "From the beginning, Netscape had all the elements to tell the story of the [Silicon] valley's Internet era: The young technologist. Explosive growth. A product that really could change the world."

74. See Jim Clark with Owen Edwards, *Netscape Time: The Making of the Billion-Dollar Startup That Took On Microsoft* (New York: St. Martin's, 1999), 183.

75. Quoted in Keenan Mayo and Peter Newcomb, "How the Web Was Won," *Vanity Fair,* July 2008, accessed July 18, 2013, www.vanityfair.com/culture/features/2008/07/internet200807.

76. Quoted in Kim S. Nash, "The Vision Guy," *Computerworld,* July 8, 1996, 1.

77. Rick Tetzeli, "What It's Really Like to Be Marc Andreessen," *Fortune,* December 9, 1996, retrieved from Ebsco Host database. Tetzeli also wrote that "Andreessen is incapable of what most people call cooking" and quoted him as saying, "I can do Campbell's Chunky Soup, SpaghettiOs, Pillsbury cinnamon rolls, and cereal."

78. Quoted in Jared Sandberg, "Netscape Has Technical Whiz in Andreessen," *Wall Street Journal,* August 11, 1995.

79. Quoted in Adam Lashinsky, "Remembering Netscape: The Birth of the Web," *Fortune,* July 25, 2005, accessed May 3, 2012, http://money.cnn.com /magazines/fortune/fortune_archive/2005/07/25/8266639/.

80. David A. Kaplan, "Nothing But Net," *Newsweek,* December 25, 1995 /January 1, 1996, 32.

81. Quoted in Chris Anderson, "The Man Who Makes the Future: *Wired* Icon Marc Andreessen," *Wired,* April 24, 2012, accessed June 30, 2012, www .wired.com/business/2012/04/ff_andreessen/all/1.

82. Quoted in "Marc Andreessen: Oral History," Smithsonian Institution (June 1995), accessed June 30, 2012, www.cwhonors.org/archives/histories /Andreessen.pdf.

83. About the inspiration for Mosaic, Andreessen recalled in 1999 that he and his colleagues "basically just thought that it didn't make sense that the Internet should be hard to use and require a degree in computer science.... That was a radical idea back in 1993, when virtually everyone on the net was a highly trained computer scientist or researcher." See "Shannon Henry's The Download—Live: Discussion With Netscape's Co-Founder Marc Andreessen," *Washington Post* online chat, September 16, 1999, accessed February 5, 2014, www.washingtonpost.com/wp-srv/business/talk/transcripts/henry/henry091699 .htm.

84. Andreessen was later quoted as saying: "Coming from Wisconsin, I thought Champaign was the big city. I was wrong. Champaign is cornfields and pig farms. If Champaign has a positive attribute, it's that it's so isolated and cut off that all you can do is work." Tetzeli, "What It's Really Like to Be Marc Andreessen."

85. See Reid, *Architects of the Web,* 36–37.

86. Quoted in Tetzeli, "What It's Really Like to Be Marc Andreessen." The choice of "Netscape" was an inspired one. Steve Silberman, a contributor to *Wired* magazine, wrote that there was "poetry and audacity in that name—an insistence that the Web wasn't merely a display, a tool, an application, an e-anything, but a *place*—a newly discovered, unmapped infinitude.... The word 'Netscape' announced that the frontier was open for exploration and habitation." Silberman, "Thanks, Mozilla," *Wired,* November 23, 1998, accessed December 23, 2013, archive.wired.com/culture/lifestyle/news/1998/11/16434.

87. Quoted in Tetzeli, "What It's Really Like to Be Marc Andreessen." The University of Illinois did try to kill Netscape in its early days," Andreessen said in 1999, calling those efforts "one of the all time big mistakes by any university." See "Shannon Henry's The Download—Live."

88. See Peter H. Lewis, "Will Netscape Be the Next Microsoft, or the Next Victim of Microsoft?" *New York Times,* October 16, 1995.

89. Elizabeth Corcoran, "Software's Surf King," *Washington Post,* July 23, 1995.

90. Quoted in Mayo and Newcomb, "How the Web Was Won."

91. See Bill Gates with Nathan Myhrvold and Peter Rinearson, *The Road Ahead* (New York: Viking, 1995), 95. Gates also wrote that "we stand at the brink of another revolution. This one will involve unprecedentedly inexpensive communication; all the computers will join together to communicate with and for us. Interconnected globally, they will form a network, which is being called the information highway. A direct precursor is the present Internet, which is a group of computers joined and exchanging information using current technology" (3–4).

92. See, among others, J. C. Herz, "What a Wonderful Web It Could Be," *Rolling Stone,* November 30, 1995, SS22.

93. Cited in Bob Metcalfe, "From the Ether: Without Case of Vapors, Netscape's Tools Will Give Blackbird Reason to Squawk," *InfoWorld,* September 18, 1995, 111. Metcalfe's column indirectly quoted Andreessen.

94. See Steve Lohr and John Markoff, "Microsoft's World: How Software's Giant Played Hardball Game," *New York Times,* October 8, 1998.

95. See Mayo and Newcomb, "How the Web Was Won."

96. Bill Gates, "The Internet Tidal Wave," confidential memorandum (May 26, 1995). Gates also wrote: "The Internet is a tidal wave. It changes the rules." The memorandum closed with a short list of related readings, including notes from a speech by Marc Andreessen. Gates misspelled the name "Andresson."

97. See Marc Andreessen, untitled internal memorandum [undated notes of Microsoft-Netscape meeting of June 21, 1995], document retrieved from www .justice.gov/atr/cases/ms_exhibits.htm.

98. Quoted in John R. Wilke, "Microsoft Subject of New Antitrust Probe," *Wall Street Journal,* April 24, 1998.

99. See ibid. Wilke's article quoted a Microsoft spokesman as saying: "Netscape's description of this meeting gets more distorted and more fictional every day." However, James Barksdale, Netscape's chief executive, described the meeting of June 21, 1995, as "something I had not ever seen happen in my more than thirty years of experience with major U.S. corporations." In direct testimony in the U.S. government's antitrust lawsuit against Microsoft, Barksdale said the Microsoft team "came to Netscape under the guise of attempting to set up some sort of cooperative agreement with Netscape. However, rather than proposing potential productive areas of cooperation, Microsoft apparently came to Netscape with a single focus: to convince Netscape not to compete with its . . . browser product, Internet Explorer. . . . Moreover, Microsoft made clear that if Netscape did not agree to its plan to divide the browser market, Microsoft would crush Netscape." Barksdale further said that he left the meeting "stunned that Microsoft had made such an explicit proposal." See "Direct Testimony of Jim Barksdale," *United States v. Microsoft Corporation,* October 13, 1998, document retrieved from www.justice.gov/atr/cases /f1900/1999.htm.

100. Laurence Zuckerman, "With Internet Cachet, Not Profit, a New Stock Is Wall St.'s Darling," *New York Times,* August 10, 1995.

101. Quoted in Lashinsky, "Remembering Netscape: The Birth of the Web."

102. See Zuckerman, "With Internet Cachet, Not Profit, a New Stock Is Wall St.'s Darling."

103. Zuckerman, "With Internet Cachet, Not Profit, a New Stock Is Wall St.'s Darling." Yet Netscape's IPO did not receive the largest headlines in the *San Jose Mercury News,* which covered Silicon Valley quite closely. News about the IPO was displayed on the front page of the *Mercury News,* but the lead story was about the death of Jerry Garcia, counterculture hero and leader of the Grateful Dead, who died August 9, 1995.

104. See Molly Baker, "Technology Investors Fall Head over Heels for Their New Love," *Wall Street Journal,* August 10, 1995.

105. Reid, *Architects of the Web,* 44.

106. Tim Berners-Lee described the first version of Internet Explorer as having "very little functionality. I could tell it was put together in a hurry, but it got Microsoft's toe in the water." Berners-Lee, *Weaving the Web: The Original Design and Ultimate Destiny of the World Wide Web* (New York: HarperSanFrancisco, 1999), 108.

107. See Reid, *Architects of the Web,* 46.

108. Quoted in Peter H. Lewis, "Microsoft Seeks Internet Market; Netscape Slides," *New York Times,* December 8, 1995.

109. See Dan Stets, "Microsoft May Bring a New Era for the Internet," *Philadelphia Inquirer,* December 8, 1995.

110. Bill Gates, "Some Thoughts on Netscape" (May 19, 1996), email memorandum retrieved from www.justice.gov/atr/cases/ms_exhibits.htm. Gates further wrote that Netscape was "moving at full speed. Every day companies are barraged with the message that they need to be doing more about the Internet. Today that means embracing Netscape products and trusting that Netscape will fill any holes that they have."

111. Quoted in Paul Andrews, "Netscape's General Smiles as the Smoke Clears," *Seattle Times,* December 14, 1997, accessed July 2, 2013, http://community.seattletimes.nwsource.com/archive/?date=19971214&slug=2578116.

112. Brad Chase, "FY 97 Planning Memo: Winning the Internet Platform Battle" (April 4, 1996), document retrieved from www.justice.gov/atr/cases/ms_exhibits.htm. Emphasis in the original.

113. See Reid, *Architects of the Web,* 61.

114. See Laurence Zuckerman, "Browser Moves by Microsoft Make Even Netscape Blink," *New York Times,* October 9, 1996.

115. Email correspondence from "Navisoft" [David Cole] to Steve Case and others (January 21, 1996), document retrieved from www.justice.gov/atr/cases/ms_exhibits.htm.

116. See Lawrence M. Fisher, "Netscape Reports Losses, and Its Shares Tumble," *New York Times,* January 6, 1998.

117. Quoted in Tom Abate, "Firefox Rises from Ashes of Abandoned Netscape," *San Francisco Chronicle,* January 28, 2008, accessed February 15, 2014,

www.sfgate.com/technology/article/Firefox-rises-from-ashes-of-abandoned-Netscape-3229083.php.

118. By the time the merger was completed, AOL stock had appreciated to a point where the deal was worth almost $10 billion. See David Streitfeld, "An Awkward Anniversary: One Year Later, AOL's Purchase of Netscape Raises Questions about Mergers," *Washington Post,* March 17, 2000.

119. See John Heilemann, "Suit 2.0," *New York,* July 3–10, 2006, 28.

120. See Steve Lohr, "Microsoft's AOL Deal Intensifies Patent Wars," *New York Times,* April 10, 2012.

121. See Dale Dougherty, "The Frantic Reign of Netscape," *Web Techniques,* February 1999, 88. Dougherty wrote: "The browser . . . was the key to the Netscape kingdom. Netscape's inability to convert the sizable number of browser users into customers is the real story behind its decline and fall."

122. See "Netscape Netcenter," *PC World,* June 22, 1998, accessed July 2, 2013, www.pcworld.com/article/23254/article.html.

123. Quoted in "Roundup: Writing Bytes," *New York Times,* October 31, 2013, accessed October 31, 2013, www.nytimes.com/2013/11/03/books/review/writing-bytes.html?emc=edit_tnt_20131031&tntemailo=y&_r=o&pagewanted=all.

124. Berners-Lee, *Weaving the Web,* 106. Journalist Haynes Johnson wrote in his book about the 1990s: "America's fascination with the wonders—and the wealth—being created by the Internet and its new dot-com world can be dated from an August day in 1995. That's when a Silicon Valley start-up company made what became a legendary initial public stock offering." Johnson, *The Best of Times: America in the Clinton Years* (New York: Harcourt, 2001), 20.

125. See Reid, *Architects of the Web,* 35. It was "one of the first programs," Tim Berners-Lee noted, "that allowed electronic commerce (e-commerce) to gain credibility." Berners-Lee, *Weaving the Web,* 97.

126. Walter S. Mossberg, "The Top Products in Two Decades of Tech Reviews; Yes, the Newton," *Wall Street Journal,* December 18, 2013.

127. Years later, Shel Kaphan, Amazon's first employee, said he was startled to realize that the day coincided with the fiftieth anniversary of the first atomic weapon test. Amazon's going live, Kaphan said, was "another kind of atomic explosion." Kaphan, interview with author (November 18, 2013).

128. See, for example, Patrick Seitz, "Amazon.com Whiz Jeff Bezos Keeps Kindling Hot Concepts," *Investor's Business Daily,* January 4, 2010.

129. Helen Jung, "Amazon's Bezos: Internet's Ultimate Cult Figure," *Seattle Times,* September 19, 1999, accessed July 4, 2013, http://community.seattletimes.nwsource.com/archive/?date=19990919&slug=2984093.

130. See "Amazon.com Breaks E-commerce Record," PR Newswire, October 14, 1997, retrieved from LexisNexis database. See also "Amazon.com Launches Online Auction Site," PR Newswire, March 30, 1999, retrieved from LexisNexis database. The mythic origins in a garage were mentioned in the first lengthy report about Amazon in the U.S. national media. An article in the *Wall Street Journal* said in May 1996: "Renting a house in the Seattle suburb of Bellevue, Mr. Bezos, like many a West-Coast entrepreneur before him, began working out of his garage." G. Bruce Knecht, "Reading the Market: How Wall

Street Whiz Found a Niche Selling Books on the Internet," *Wall Street Journal,* May 16, 1996.

131. Shel Kaphan said the converted garage in suburban Seattle "was just like an office." Kaphan, interview with author.

132. Jeff Bezos, "Electronic Book Selling," C-SPAN, March 18, 1999, video accessed July 5, 2013, www.c-spanvideo.org/program/121884–1.

133. See, for example, Ryan Nakashima, "Amazon Nears Debut of Original TV Shows," Associated Press, April 17, 2013, retrieved from LexisNexis database. See also Andrea Chang, "Bezos Known for His Unusual Forays," *Los Angeles Times,* August 6, 2013, and Peter Whoriskey, Jia Lynn Yang, and Cecilia Kang, "Chief Executive Is Noted for Patience," *Washington Post,* August 6, 2013.

134. See Jeff Bezos, "A Bookstore by Any Other Name," speech to the Commonwealth Club of California, July 27, 1998, accessed July 5, 2013, http://web.archive.org/web/20090622000804/http://www.commonwealthclub.org/archive/98/98–07bezos-speech.html.

135. Robert Spector, *Amazon.com: Get Big Fast* (New York: HarperBusiness, 2000), 69. See also Richard L. Brandt, *One Click: Jeff Bezos and the Rise of Amazon.com* (New York: Portfolio/Penguin, 2011), 81. Brandt wrote that Amazon's launch on July 16, 1995, "was just in time—just as masses of people started moving onto the Internet and before many competitors had created good commercial sites." Shel Kaphan said that had Amazon been launched "another year or two years later, it would have been rougher to get a toehold." Kaphan, interview with author.

136. See Times Mirror Center for the People & the Press, "Technology in the American Household," 51. Most online purchases at the time, according to the Times Mirror study, "were made with credit cards, but little concern was found regarding card number security. Forty-two percent said they were 'not at all' concerned, 40% were concerned 'a little' and 17% said they worried 'a lot' about the risk inherent in this procedure."

137. See Sangmoon Kim, "The Diffusion of the Internet: Trend and Causes," *Social Science Research* 40, no. 2 (2011): 603.

138. Bezos, "Electronic Book Selling." See also Spector, *Amazon.com: Get Big Fast,* 59. Spector noted that half of Amazon.com's early customers "phoned in their credit card numbers. . . . Some customers paid by check, while others chose to place their orders online. The latter group had to enter only the last five digits of their card number online, then call Amazon.com by phone with the remaining digits."

139. Quoted in John Cook, "Meet Amazon.com's First Employee: Shel Kaphan," *GeekWire,* June 14, 2011, accessed July 5, 2013, www.geekwire.com/2011/meet-shel-kaphan-amazoncom-employee-1/3/.

140. Kaphan, interview with author. He likened Amazon's launch to "some random guys trying to pull something out of their hats."

141. Cited in Brad Stone, *The Everything Store: Jeff Bezos and the Age of Amazon* (New York: Little, Brown, 2013), 39–40.

142. See Bezos, "Electronic Book Selling."

143. Bezos, "A Bookstore by Any Other Name." Amazon was hardly the first to make use of door desks. In the late 1960s, desks from doors were

installed in offices of the technology company Bolt Beranek and Newman, or BBN. See Katie Hafner, *Where Wizards Stay Up Late: The Origins of the Internet* (New York: Simon and Schuster, 1998), 94–95.

144. Bezos, "Electronic Book Selling."

145. Bezos, "A Bookstore by Any Other Name."

146. See John Cassidy, *Dot.con: The Greatest Story Ever Sold* (New York: HarperCollins, 2002), 140. See also Simon Avery, "From Early Web Visions, They Spun Gold," *Globe and Mail* (Toronto), August 1, 2005.

147. See Spector, *Amazon.com: Get Big Fast*, 70.

148. Jeffrey P. Bezos, "1997 Letter to Shareholders," accessed April 20, 2014, www.sec.gov/Archives/edgar/data/1018724/000119312511110797/dex991.htm.

149. In his book about Bezos and Amazon.com, Brandt described the claims as "a nice marketing gimmick of questionable veracity." Brandt, *One Click*, 70.

150. Spector, *Amazon.com: Get Big Fast*, 68. Spector quoted one of Amazon's first employees, Paul Barton-Davis, as saying: "We came up with a phrase 'almost-in-time' delivery. In other words, we don't have the books you want, but we can get them real soon."

151. Quoted in Cook, "Meet Amazon.com's First Employee," *GeekWire* (emphasis added).

152. See Stone, *The Everything Store*.

153. Kaphan, interview with author.

154. Spector, *Amazon.com: Get Big Fast*, 36.

155. Bezos, "A Bookstore by Any Other Name."

156. Kaphan, interview with author.

157. Bezos, "Electronic Book Selling."

158. In late 1999, the *Washington Post* anonymously quoted an Amazon customer-service representative as saying, "We're supposed to care deeply about customers, provided we can care deeply about them at an incredible rate of speed." Mark Leibovich, "At Amazon.com, Service Workers without a Smile," *Washington Post*, November 22, 1999.

159. Richard Howard, "How I 'Escaped' from Amazon.cult," *Seattle Weekly*, July 15, 1998, accessed July 5, 2013, www.seattleweekly.com/1998-07-15/news/how-i-escaped-from-amazon-cult/.

160. Ibid.

161. See Jonathan Chait and Stephen Glass, "Amazon.Con," *Slate*, January 5, 1997, accessed March 11, 2013, www.slate.com/articles/briefing/articles/1997/01/amazoncon.html.

162. See Jacqueline Doherty, "Amazon.bomb," *Barron's*, May 31, 1999, 28.

163. Knecht, "Reading the Market." A not-infrequent critic of Amazon in recent years has been Paulo Santos of Seeking Alpha, an online financial news site launched in 2004. See David Streitfeld, "Amazon's Prophet and Losses," *New York Times*, December 16, 2013.

164. John Cassidy, in his book *Dot.con*, asserted: "It was the media that transformed Amazon.com from an interesting small business story into a multibillion-dollar corporate thriller" (140). That characterization seems hyperbolic, but it does offer a sense of the benefits of favorable attention from America's largest business-oriented daily newspaper.

165. Knecht, "Reading the Market."

166. Stone, *Everything Store,* 176.

167. See David Streitfeld, "Amazon Delivers Some Pie in the Sky," *New York Times,* December 3, 2013, and Greg Bensinger, "Hurdles Surround Amazon's Goal of Using Drones," *Wall Street Journal,* December 3, 2013.

168. Bezos, not Amazon, owns the newspaper. About that purchase, Kaphan said: "It's clear that [Bezos] likes being in the limelight. What better place to put yourself in the limelight than being the owner of one of the most prestigious papers in the country, if not the world?" Kaphan, interview with author.

169. Jack Shafer, "Jeff Bezos Has Two Words for You: 'No Comment,'" Reuters, August 19, 2013, accessed October 19, 2013, http://blogs.reuters.com/jackshafer/2013/08/19/jeff-bezos-has-two-words-for-you-no-comment/.

170. Joshua Cooper Ramo, "The Fast-Moving Internet Economy Has a Jungle of Competitors . . . and Here's the King," *Time,* December 27, 1999, 51.

171. Ibid.

172. Steven Levy, "Jeff Bezos Owns the Web in More Ways Than You Think," *Wired,* November 13, 2011, accessed July 8, 2013, www.wired.com/magazine/2011/11/ff_bezos/.

173. Adam Lashinsky, "Jeff Bezos: The Ultimate Disrupter," *Fortune,* December 3, 2012, 100.

174. See Siva Vaidhyanathan, "Technology Review: The King of Internet Sales," *Washington Post,* January 8, 2012. Vaidhyanathan wrote: "A strong case can be made that Amazon, more than any other company or institution, made the Web safe for commerce. Or, at least, the security innovations that Amazon installed early in its existence gave people the confidence to enter credit card numbers and other sensitive information into Web sites."

175. The definition of the wiki was adapted from Brenda Chawner and Paul H. Lewis, "WikiWikiWebs: New Ways to Communicate in a Web Environment," *Information Technology and Libraries,* March 2006, 33.

176. Berners-Lee, *Weaving the Web,* 33.

177. Quoted in "Interviews: Ward Cunningham," *IEEE Annals of the History of Computing,* October–December 2011, 65.

178. Ward Cunningham, interview with author (March 13, 2013).

179. Ibid.

180. Ibid.

181. See Ryan Songel, "Veni, Vidi, Wiki," *Wired,* September 7, 2006, accessed July 19, 2013, www.wired.com/science/discoveries/news/2006/09/71733?currentPage=al.

182. Cunningham, interview with author.

183. The idealistic ethos of the Internet of the 1970s and 1980s, as Berners-Lee wrote in *Weaving the Web,* "was one of sharing for the common good" (197).

184. Ibid., 33.

185. See ibid., 57. Berners-Lee observed that as Web browsers were developed in the early 1990s, "no one working on them tried to include writing and editing functions. There seemed to be a perception that creating a browser had a strong potential for payback, since it would make information from around the world available to anyone who used it. Putting as much effort

into the collaborative side of the Web didn't seem to promise that millionfold multiplier."

186. Ibid., 57.

187. Quoted in "Interviews: Ward Cunningham," 66.

188. See Songel, "Veni, Vidi, Wiki."

189. "A Wiki for Your Thoughts," *Los Angeles Times,* June 17, 2005, accessed July 10, 2013, www.latimes.com/news/la-ed-wiki17jun17,0,924091.story.

190. See Joe Strupp, "'L.A. Times' Pulls Plug on 'wikitorial,'" *Editor & Publisher,* July 1, 2005, 16.

191. See Howard Kurtz, "Michael Kinsley, L.A. Times Part on 'Unfortunate Note,'" *Washington Post,* September 14, 2005.

192. Robert Niles, "Wikis Will Help Readers Direct the Community's Most Powerful Voice," *The Masthead,* Autumn 2005, 10. Niles also wrote: "What news publishers need is a tool that will allow any interested readers a seat at the table, with the ability to help direct what ought to be their community's most powerful voice. Something like, oh, say, a wiki" (11).

193. Quoted in Evan Hansen, "Wikipedia Founder Edits Own Bio," *Wired,* December 19, 2005, accessed July 10, 2013, www.wired.com/culture/lifestyle /news/2005/12/69880.

194. Cunningham, interview with author.

195. See Wendell Cochran, "A Watershed Event for Online Newspapers," *American Journalism Review,* June 1999, accessed May 3, 2012, www.ajr.org /article.asp?id=2006.

196. Jon Katz, "Guilty," *Wired,* September 1995, accessed July 11, 2013, www.wired.com/wired/archive/3.09/oj.html. Katz also noted: "For better or worse, great stories have always transformed the media that cover them and the institutions they cover." Todd Copilevitz, technology writer for the *Dallas Morning News,* said online coverage of the bombing ranked as his top "cyber-culture" moment of 1995. Second on Copilevitz's list was the emergence of Netscape; third was the telecommunications bill then making its way through Congress. See Copilevitz, "Top 10 Cyberculture Events," *Dallas Morning News,* December 29, 1995.

197. Sue Hale, interview with author (August 19, 2013).

198. Hale's recollections are from an oral history interview she gave in 2000. See Sue Hale, oral history interview (March 20, 2000), Oklahoma City National Memorial Center. Hale did not identify Williams in her oral history but supplied his name in an interview with the author. She also said she was not certain "how he got through to me. But he did." Hale, interview with author.

2. TERROR IN THE HEARTLAND, AND A WARY AMERICA

1. See Lou Michel and Dan Herbeck, *American Terrorist: Timothy McVeigh and the Oklahoma City Bombing* (New York: Regan Books, 2001), 229–30.

2. For details about the bomb and how McVeigh and Nichols prepared the explosives, see ibid., 215–20.

3. Ibid., 2. Michel and Herbeck wrote that McVeigh's perceived grievances against the federal government included "U.S. military actions against smaller

nations" and "no-knock search warrants" as well as "crooked politicians, over-zealous government agents, high taxes, political correctness, gun laws." McVeigh was also angered about the government siege in 1992 at the home of Randy Weaver in Ruby Ridge, Idaho. Weaver's wife was fatally shot in that standoff. The federal government paid Randy Weaver $100,000 to settle a wrongful-death lawsuit. His three daughters each were awarded $1 million.

4. "Sketches of Victims Killed in Bombing," Associated Press, April 28, 1995, retrieved from LexisNexis database.

5. "Terrorism's Innocent Victims," *USA Today,* May 12, 1995.

6. See "Those Who Were Killed: John Karl Van Ess III," Oklahoma City National Memorial & Museum, accessed February 5, 2014, www .oklahomacitynationalmemorial.org/secondary.php?section=1&ordering= 146&catid=24.

7. "Those Who Died," *Daily Oklahoman* (Oklahoma City, Okla.), April 29, 1995.

8. Aren Almon-Kok, oral history interview (March 19, 2000), Oklahoma City National Memorial Center.

9. Paul R. Pillar discussed the 1995 National Intelligence Estimate in a commentary in the *New York Times* in 2004, stating: "The estimate postulated that the bombing of the World Trade Center in 1993—in which the bombers' objective was to topple the twin towers and kill thousands—had probably crossed a threshold in terms of 'large-scale terrorist attacks' and that more of the same would be coming. The kinds of targets the estimate identified as being especially at risk were 'national symbols such as the White House and the Capitol and symbols of U.S. capitalism such as Wall Street.'" Pillar, "A Scapegoat Is Not a Solution," *New York Times,* June 4, 2004.

10. Ted Koppel, "America's Chronic Overreaction to Terrorism," *Wall Street Journal,* August 7, 2013. Koppel, a television journalist, wrote: "At home, the U.S. has constructed an antiterrorism enterprise so immense, so costly and so inexorably interwoven with the defense establishment, police and intelligence agencies, communications systems, and with social media, travel networks and their attendant security apparatus, that the idea of downsizing, let alone disbanding such a construct, is an exercise in futility."

11. Penny Owen, "Fresh Day in City Turns into New-Found Horror," *Daily Oklahoman,* April 20, 1995.

12. Porter's recollections are drawn from an oral history interview he gave to the Newseum, the museum of the news in Washington, D.C. See Charles Porter, oral history interview (April 22, 2003), Newseum.

13. A photograph very similar to Porter's was taken by Lester ("Bob") LaRue, then an employee of the Oklahoma Natural Gas Company. LaRue's photograph appeared on the cover of *Newsweek* the week after the bombing. The gas company claimed ownership of the photograph, given that LaRue took it with a company camera while on company time. LaRue disputed that view and lost his job. See "Work Week," *Wall Street Journal,* May 27, 1997.

14. Lindel Hutson, oral history interview (March 20, 2000), Oklahoma City National Memorial Center.

15. Ibid.

16. Quoted in Joe Strupp, "The Photo Felt Around the World," *Editor & Publisher,* May 13, 1995, 12.

17. Almon-Kok, oral history interview. Within hours of the bombing, Almon-Kok learned from a doctor that Baylee had been killed. Upon seeing Porter's photograph in the newspaper the next day, Almon-Kok said she felt "so crushed."

18. See Michel and Herbeck, *American Terrorist,* 231.

19. McVeigh had placed a hand-lettered sign in the windshield, asking that the car not be towed. Michel and Herbeck, *American Terrorist,* 231.

20. Michael Whiteley, "McVeigh in Long Line of 'Party Barge' Drivers," *Arkansas Democrat-Gazette,* June 20, 1995.

21. Michel and Herbeck, *American Terrorist,* 232.

22. Ibid., 237. They wrote that McVeigh thought he would be pulled over by police somewhere in Kansas, adding, "Cops in Oklahoma, he was sure, would be too busy dealing with the bombing."

23. Quoted in Melinda Henneberger, "The Trooper: A By-the-Book Officer, 'Suspicious by Nature,' Spots Trouble and Acts Fast," *New York Times,* April 23, 1995. Another acquaintance of Hanger was quoted as saying: "He even comes to church in his uniform."

24. Hanger's recollections and remarks about arresting McVeigh are drawn from his discussion in 2012 at the Oklahoma National Memorial and Museum. See Charles Hanger, "First Person Summer Series Features Charlie Hanger," Oklahoma National Memorial and Museum, August 24, 2012, video accessed June 4, 2013, www.youtube.com/watch?v=e35EDGXtIlE&feature=player_embedded#!

25. Michel and Herbeck, *American Terrorist,* 239–40.

26. Ibid., 226, 241.

27. Hanger, "First Person Summer Series Features Charlie Hanger."

28. See Richard A. Serrano, "Witness Describes Horror of Truck Debris Flying By," *Los Angeles Times,* May 15, 1997, accessed June 5, 2013, http://articles.latimes.com/1997-05-15/news/mn-59005_1_witness-stand.

29. See Weldon L. Kennedy, *On-Scene Commander: From Street Agent to Deputy Director of the FBI* (Washington, D.C.: Potomac Books, 2007), 208.

30. See Nolan Clay and Robby Trammell, "Quick Legwork, Luck Almost Didn't Catch Bomb Suspect," *Sunday Oklahoman,* April 23, 1995.

31. See "2 Suspects Arrested in Blast," *Saturday Oklahoman and Times,* April 22, 1995.

32. Jonathan Alter, a columnist for *Newsweek,* offered a sense of how jarring it was that the bombing suspects turned out to be white Americans. He wrote: "Who can deny that it would have been emotionally easier if foreigners had done it? Had 'They' been responsible, as so many suspected, the grief and anger could have been channeled against a fixed enemy, uniting the country as only an external threat can do. We might have ended up in war, but what a cathartic war it would have been! Or so it felt, in brief spasms of outrage, to more Americans than would care to admit it. And if we couldn't identify a country to bomb, at least we could have the comfort of knowing that the depravity of the crime—its subhuman quality—was the product of another

culture unfathomably different from our own." Alter, "The Media: Jumping to Conclusions," *Newsweek*, May 1, 1995, 55.

33. As another example, early news reports greatly exaggerated the violence and mayhem that Hurricane Katrina unleashed on New Orleans in 2005. See W. Joseph Campbell, *Getting It Wrong: Ten of the Greatest Misreported Stories in American Journalism* (Berkeley: University of California Press, 2010), 163–83.

34. Stephen Sloan, oral history interview (October 20, 1999), Oklahoma City National Memorial Center.

35. It was erroneously reported, for example, that a second bomb had been found inside the ruins of the Murrah Building and disarmed. See "Washington Officials Can Cite No Probable Cause," CNN, April 19, 1995, transcript retrieved from LexisNexis database.

36. See "Analyst—Oklahoma Bombing Has Look of Mid-East Terror," CNN, April 19, 1995, transcript retrieved from LexisNexis database. Sloan also said on the CNN program that the bombing likely was the work of "a well-organized group with a clandestine infrastructure and the logistics and capabilities to [survey] the area and engage in a very horrible operation."

37. Chung was fired about a month later as the CBS Evening News coanchor, an assignment she shared with Dan Rather. A front-page report in the *Philadelphia Inquirer* said about her dismissal: "Connie Chung had one real assignment as Dan Rather's co-anchor on CBS Evening News: Raise plummeting ratings and help the network resurrect itself as broadcasting's leading news outlet. She failed." Gail Shister and Stephen Seplow, "Chung's Exit Blamed on Falling Ratings; She Says She's the Fall Guy," *Philadelphia Inquirer*, May 23, 1995. At the time, Peter Jennings on ABC was the evening-news ratings leader. His program was watched in about 8.5 million homes. Tom Brokaw of NBC was next, in 7 million homes. The Rather-Chung duo was third, in 6.5 million homes.

38. "CBS News Special Report: Terror in the Heartland," CBS News, April 19, 1995, transcript retrieved from LexisNexis database.

39. "The Bombing in Oklahoma City," ABC News *Primetime Live*, April 19, 1995, transcript retrieved from LexisNexis database.

40. "FBI Beefs Up Security Nationwide after Explosion," CNN, April 19, 1995, transcript retrieved from LexisNexis database.

41. Laura E. Keeton et al., "In Broad Daylight, Terrorism Hits Home: U.S. Building Bombed," *Wall Street Journal*, April 20, 1995.

42. Owen, "Fresh Day in City Turns into New-Found Horror."

43. Indeed, the lead FBI agent on the Oklahoma City bombing case, Weldon L. Kennedy, wrote in a memoir in 2007: "It's not surprising that there would have been suspicion about Middle Easterners. The bombing took place only two years after the World Trade Center bombing, in which a Ryder rental truck had also been used." Kennedy, *On-Scene Commander*, 207.

44. See Steve Lackmeyer and David Zizzo, "City Struggles with Shock of Deadly Bombing; Scores Killed in Bomb Blast," *Daily Oklahoman*, April 20, 1995.

45. Sam Vincent Meddis, "Terror in Heartland: 12 Kids among 31 Dead in Oklahoma Bombing," *USA Today*, April 20, 1995.

46. See Steve Lackmeyer and David Zizzo, "Scores Dies in Downtown Explosion," *Daily Oklahoman,* April 20, 1995. See also Judy Gibbs, "At Least 33 Killed in Deadliest U.S. Bombing in 75 Years," Associated Press, April 20, 1995, retrieved from LexisNexis database. See also "Comparison of the Oklahoma City and World Trade Center Blasts," Associated Press, April 19, 1995, retrieved from LexisNexis database.

47. Hanger, "First Person Summer Series Features Charlie Hanger."

48. "Reliable Sources," CNN, April 23, 1995, transcript retrieved from LexisNexis database.

49. Wolf Blitzer, "Jordanian-American Bomb Suspect Discusses His Ordeal," CNN, April 23, 1995, transcript retrieved from LexisNexis database. Ahmad said he was well treated in Chicago and offered to stay the night there, to demonstrate he was not fleeing the country.

50. Blitzer, "Jordanian-American Bomb Suspect Discusses His Ordeal."

51. Quoted in Jeremy Bowen, "Investigating Islamophobia," documentary (2001), accessed October 20, 2013, www.youtube.com/watch?v=lGKzBrZhDS4.

52. Tim Weiner, "F.B.I. Hunts 2d Bombing Suspect and Seeks Links to Far Right," *New York Times,* April 23, 1995.

53. Keith Schneider, "Terror in Oklahoma: The Far Right; Bomb Echoes Extremists' Tactics," *New York Times,* April 26, 1995. Alter, the *Newsweek* columnist, also discussed suspicions about right-wing extremists: "The militia movement has mostly operated below the country's radar—this despite the fact that the numbers of violent right-wing extremists dwarf those of the much more publicized left-wing radicals of the past. . . . Right-wing groups are much harder to stereotype, which makes the need for vigilance against them all the stronger. They look like mainstream Americans (white, male, rural, blue collar), and their self-proclaimed patriotism masks their sometimes treasonous intent. If they are not us, they are close enough." Alter, "The Media: Jumping to Conclusions," 55.

54. Eric E. Sterling, president of the Criminal Justice Policy Foundation, quoted in Ed Timms, "McVeigh and the Militia: His Legacy Differs from Member to Member," *Dallas Morning News,* June 8, 2001. See also Jesse Walker, *The United States of Paranoia: A Conspiracy Theory* (New York: Harper, 2013), 279–80. Walker wrote: "There are conflicting accounts as to whether McVeigh attended a Michigan Militia meeting, but even the witness who believes he was there states that he attended as a guest, not a member" (280).

55. Victoria Loe Hicks invoked the diary metaphor in a detailed article in 1998, writing that McVeigh and Nichols "inadvertently kept a virtual diary of their plotting: the phone card they used to locate bomb components, reserve the bomb truck and communicate with each other." Hicks, "On the Trail of a Phantom: No Trace of John Doe Bomb Suspect," *Dallas Morning News,* June 7, 1998, article retrieved from Access World News Research Collection database.

56. Weldon Kennedy, the lead FBI agent on the Oklahoma City bombing case, stated in his memoir that agents "were able to reconstruct every move, contact, and telephone call" made by McVeigh, Nichols, and Fortier in the eighteen months before the bombing. Kennedy further wrote: "I can say with

total confidence that we identified all three conspirators in this case and arrested them." Kennedy, *On-Scene Commander*, 220.

57. For a book-length claim that the conspiracy likely went beyond McVeigh, Nichols, and Fortier, see Andrew Gumbel and Robert G. Charles, *Oklahoma City: What the Investigation Missed—and Why It Still Matters* (New York: William Morrow, 2012). The authors write: "The Oklahoma City bombing *was* a conspiracy, and McVeigh and Nichols were charged accordingly. The real question is: how far did the conspiracy go?" (12). It is a question, ultimately, that the authors did not fully answer.

58. See Fred Bayles, "Two Men Taken into Custody in Missouri," Associated Press, May 2, 1995, retrieved from LexisNexis database.

59. Peter Carlson, "In All the Speculation and Spin Surrounding the Oklahoma City Bombing, John Doe 2 Has Become a Legend," *Washington Post Magazine*, March 23, 1997, 14.

60. Peter Carlson wrote in the *Washington Post Magazine* that the front-on sketch of John Doe No. 2 was developed by a sketch artist using the FBI Facial Identification Catalogue—"a book of 960 photographs of faces, all of them front views." The mechanic, Kessinger, was asked "to point out the pictures that showed the correct nose and eyes and chin. The artist then used Kessinger's choices to create the sketches. In the case of John Doe 1, this method yielded a sketch that looked remarkably like McVeigh. In the case of John Doe 2, however, it produced a front-view sketch of a man never seen from the front, a bare-headed sketch of a man never seen without a hat." Carlson, "In All the Speculation and Spin Surrounding the Oklahoma City Bombing, John Doe 2 Has Become a Legend," 14.

61. See ibid.

62. Penny Owen, "McVeigh's Team Tries to Show Search Based on Wrong Men," *Daily Oklahoman*, May 24, 1997.

63. See Hicks, "On the Trail of a Phantom." Hicks's article quoted Dr. Elizabeth Loftus, an expert on human memory, as saying: "What we have here is unconscious transference, a mistaken recollection of a person seen in one situation with a person seen in another." See also David Ross et al., "Unconscious Transference and Mistaken Identity: When a Witness Misidentifies a Familiar But Innocent Person," *Journal of Applied Psychology* 79, no. 6 (December 1994): 918–30.

64. Todd Bunting told an interviewer in 1997: "I still get stares going down the street. They think, 'God, that guy looks familiar.'" He also said: "This whole thing has left me in limbo for the last two years." Quoted in Mona Breckenridge, "Former Soldier Still Haunted by Mistaken Label of 'John Doe No. 2,'" Associated Press, April 2, 1997, retrieved from LexisNexis database.

65. Sandra Sanchez, "Getting On with His Life: Man Who Wasn't 'John Doe No. 2' Seeks Anonymity," *USA Today*, July 12, 1995. See also Pierre Thomas and George Lardner Jr., "FBI Finds 'John Doe 2,' Drops Him as Suspect," *Washington Post*, June 15, 1995.

66. Quoted in Nolan Clay and Penny Owen, "Nichols' Defense Hopes to Shift Attention to John Doe 2," *Daily Oklahoman*, December 3, 1997.

67. After a trial in an Oklahoma state court seven years later, a jury convicted Nichols on 161 counts of first-degree murder in the bombing. He was sentenced, again, to life in prison.

68. See "Excerpts from Grand Jury Report," *Daily Oklahoman,* December 31, 1998. In her closing arguments at Terry Nichols's federal trial in 1997, prosecutor Beth Wilkinson said that "sightings of John Doe 2 were about as common and credible as sightings of Elvis." See Jo Thomas, "Closing Arguments Made In Oklahoma Bomb Case," *New York Times,* December 16, 1997.

69. "Excerpts from Grand Jury Report."

70. Quoted in "McVeigh Tells Newspaper There Never Was a John Doe No. 2," Associated Press, May 15, 2001, retrieved from LexisNexis database.

71. Quoted in Michel and Herbeck, *American Terrorist,* 286. The authors noted that McVeigh "never wavered from his story: he alone drove the truck bomb to Oklahoma City, parked it in front of the building, and lit the fuses. And he alone made the decision to bomb the building during daylight hours, when it was full of people. Yet Jones [his lawyer] seemed to think that McVeigh was sacrificing himself to protect others."

72. Stephen Jones and Peter Israel, *Others Unknown: The Oklahoma City Bombing Case and Conspiracy* (New York: Public Affairs, 1998), 90.

73. In their 2012 book, Gumbel and Charles noted this conundrum, writing: "One of the prickliest problems with the government's case was its failure to explain how McVeigh and Nichols could build a huge destructive device without advanced explosives training and be confident it would go off." Gumbel and Charles, *Oklahoma City,* 351.

74. Jones and Israel, *Others Unknown,* xii.

75. Ibid., 121.

76. Ibid., 143. The reference to "holding the bag" pertains to Yousef's escape from New York City following the first World Trade Center attack, which killed six people and injured hundreds. He was arrested in Pakistan in February 1995.

77. See Jones, *Others Unknown,* 142. Nichols was reported in 2005 to have denied involvement with Yousef, telling a California congressman, Dana Rohrabacher, that such claims were "baloney." See Jim Crogan, "The Rohrabacher Test," *LA Weekly,* July 7, 2005, accessed June 12, 2013, www.laweekly .com/2005–07–07/news/the-rohrabacher-test/.

78. James William Gibson, "An Explosion of Conspiracy Theories on the Oklahoma City Bombing," *Washington Post,* December 21, 1998. Mark Singer of the *New Yorker* called Jones's book "tendentious, self-serving, bloated with irrelevant details that bespeak its lack of substance." Singer, "Time to Kill: The Tents Are Up, the Crowds Are Ready—and Still Waiting," *New Yorker,* May 28, 2001, 60.

79. Vincent Bugliosi, in his hefty book debunking conspiracy theories in the assassination of President John F. Kennedy, noted that the "conspiracy argument in the Kennedy assassination requires the belief that for over forty years a great number of people have been able to keep silent about the plot behind the most important and investigated murder of the twentieth century. In other words, it requires a belief in the impossible." Bugliosi, *Reclaiming History: The Assassination of President John F. Kennedy* (New York: Norton, 2007), 1442.

80. Ibid., 1439 (emphasis in the original).

81. See Hicks, "On the Trail of a Phantom."

82. Time/CNN poll, June 6, 1997, data cited here retrieved from Polling the Nations database.

83. Gallup poll, April 19, 2000, data cited here retrieved from Polling the Nations database.

84. Gallup poll, June 8–10, 2001, data cited here retrieved from the Gallup organization's online "Gallup Brain" database.

85. For a discussion of one journalist's extended but unavailing search for John Doe No. 2, see Jo Thomas, "The Third Man: A Reporter Investigates the Oklahoma City Bombing," *Syracuse Law Review* 59 (2009): 459–69.

86. See "Precautions after Oklahoma City," *New York Times*, April 21, 1995. The *Times* editorial stated: "It is impossible to look at the grotesquely shattered remains of the Oklahoma City Federal Building without wondering whether such bombings will become a brutal commonplace of American life."

87. Data from the *Los Angeles Times* survey were retrieved from the Polling the Nations database. The question's wording was, "Would you be willing to give up some civil liberties if that were necessary to curb terrorism in this country, or not?" The question was among those asked in a telephone survey of 1,032 American adults on April 30, 1995.

88. See Lynn M. Kuzma, "Terrorism in the United States," *Public Opinion Quarterly* 64, no. 1 (2000): 103. Kuzma also wrote: "While Americans have consistently identified terrorism as a significant threat to U.S. security in the 1990s, there has been little evidence that most Americans have personalized this fear" (97).

89. Quoted in Ann Devroy and Steve Vogel, "Closing the Avenue: Barricades Seal Off a Symbol of Openness," *Washington Post*, May 21, 1995. But it was unfair and misleading to compare the Murrah Building with the White House, Robert L. Hershey, president of the D.C. Society of Professional Engineers, wrote several years later: "The Oklahoma City bomb was in a truck parked 10 feet from the federal building. The White House is 350 feet from Pennsylvania Avenue. Blast pressure decreases roughly with the square of the distance. This means that pressure on the White House would be far less than one-thousandth of the pressure to which the Murrah Building was exposed. The buildings also are not comparable. The White House was rebuilt for security in the '50s with heavy steel girders, 660 tons of steel reinforced concrete and walls roughly a foot thick. By contrast, most of the walls in the Oklahoma City building were quarter-inch glass. Because stress decreases with wall thickness, stresses at the White House would be a factor of several thousand less than at Oklahoma City if they were subjected to the same pressure. When the effects of distance and wall thickness are combined, the White House is safer from bomb blasts than the Oklahoma City building by a factor of several million." Hershey, "Reopen America's Street," *Washington Post*, March 9, 2003.

90. Quoted in Devroy and Vogel, "Closing the Avenue."

91. As noted in the *Washington Post*, the president's schedule "is kept more secret, his movements are less visible to the outside world. Bigger motorcades, wider and deeper 'perimeters' between the president and regular people, audiences forced to spend hours going through metal detectors before a presidential

event all signal the strengthening of the security cocoon around presidents." Devroy and Vogel, "Closing the Avenue."

92. "The Avenue: No Closed Case," *Washington Post,* December 13, 1995.

93. Quoted in Ron Shaffer, "Dr. Gridlock: How to Reopen Pennsylvania Ave.," *Washington Post,* May 30, 1996.

94. Rod Grams, "Dismantle Those Barricades," *Washington Post,* May 20, 1996.

95. Witold Rybcznski, "The Blast-Proof City," *Foreign Policy,* September 2, 2011, accessed June 11, 2013, www.foreignpolicy.com/articles/2011/09/02 /the_blast_proof_city.

96. "25 Moments: Capital Girds Against Terror," *Washington Post Magazine,* December 4, 2011, 18.

97. The security response to the Oklahoma City bombing reached far beyond downtown Washington. "The new realities of terrorism protection are working themselves into the fabric of the American cityscape," observed the architecture critic for the *Los Angeles Times* in 2011. "We are taking steps to permanently armor our major public spaces." Christopher Hawthorne, "Working Security— and People—into the Ellipse," *Washington Post,* August 21, 2011.

98. See John F. Harris, "Clinton Signs 'Mighty Blow' against Terrorism; Softened Measure Becomes Law," *Washington Post,* April 25, 1996. See also Terence Hunt, "Clinton Dedicates Anti-Terrorism Law to Victims' Families," Associated Press, April 24, 1996, retrieved from LexisNexis database.

99. Quoted in "Terrorism Bill Flaws," *Charleston Gazette* (West Virginia), April 26, 1996.

100. David Cole and James X. Dempsey, *Terrorism and the Constitution: Sacrificing Civil Liberties in the Name of National Security* (New York: New Press, 2006), 135.

101. Ibid., 136. They also noted: "Curtailing civil liberties does not necessarily promote national security" (241).

102. Ibid., 136.

103. See "William J. Clinton: Statement on Signing the Antiterrorism and Effective Death Penalty Act of 1996," April 24, 1996, the American Presidency Project, accessed June 11, 2013, www.presidency.ucsb.edu/ws/?pid =52713.

104. Quoted in Angie Cannon, "Law Aims to Hasten Executions by Limiting Federal Appeals," *Philadelphia Inquirer,* April 25, 1996.

105. See "Forbes Names Oklahoma City as Nation's Most Affordable," *Forbes,* October 28, 2010, accessed June 12, 2013, www.forbes.com/2010/10/28 /affordable-cities-cost-of-living-lifestyle-real-estate-salaries.html.

106. For a glowing tribute to the city and its successes, see Sam Anderson, "A Basketball Fairy Tale in Middle America," *New York Times Magazine,* November 8, 2012, accessed June 12, 2013, www.nytimes.com/2012/11/11 /magazine/the-oklahoma-city-thunders-fairy-tale-rise.html.

107. "So Much Has Changed Since Attacks on 9/11," *Daily Oklahoman,* August 7, 2011.

108. Sue Anne Pressly, "Dust and Tears Attend the Fall of a Tragic Symbol," *Washington Post,* May 24, 1995.

3. O.J., DNA, AND THE "TRIAL OF THE CENTURY"

1. For a discussion of "flashbulb events," see Jennifer M. Talarico and David C. Rubin, "Confidence, Not Consistency, Characterizes Flashbulb Memories," *Psychological Science* 14, no. 5 (September 2003): 455. Research about "flashbulb memories" dates to at least 1977. See Roger Brown and James Kulik, "Flashbulb Memories," *Cognition* 51, no. 1 (March 1977): 73–99.

2. N. R. Kleinfield, "The Moment: A Day (10 Minutes of It) the Country Stood Still," *New York Times,* October 4, 1995. Kleinfield's account likened the vigil to "an eerie moment of national communion" in which millions of people "in millions of places seemed to spend 10 spellbinding minutes doing exactly the same thing."

3. Nearly 80 percent of the respondents to a Gallup poll said they learned about the verdicts by watching television or listening on radio. The data were retrieved from the Gallup Organization's online "Gallup Brain" database. The question's wording was: "Did you personally watch or listen to the verdict announcement on television or radio today as it was being announced, or did you hear about it later?" The question was asked of 643 American adults on October 3, 1995.

4. John L. Mitchell and Jeff Leads, "Half of Americans Disagree with Verdict: Reaction: High-Voltage Joy, Angry Denouncements," *Los Angeles Times,* October 4, 1995.

5. Dan Levy, "A Nation Stops to Watch O.J.," *San Francisco Chronicle,* October 4, 1995.

6. Peter Kendall and Pamela Cytrynbaum, "Race Tints Shared Experience," *Chicago Tribune,* October 4, 1995.

7. Kleinfield, "The Moment: A Day (10 Minutes of It) the Country Stood Still."

8. "All Boston Stood Still at the Hour of Reckoning," *Boston Herald,* October 4, 1995.

9. Cited in John F. Harris, *The Survivor: Bill Clinton in the White House* (New York: Random House, 2005), 206. Harris noted: "As with other Americans, guessing the verdict became a macabre parlor game among the president's staff."

10. Levy, "A Nation Stops to Watch O.J."

11. Quoted in Paul Duggan, "Washington Comes to a Stop; Then Pent-Up Emotions Start Spilling Out," *Washington Post,* October 4, 1995. Democratic Senator Sam Nunn of Georgia had scheduled a news conference at the hour of the verdicts on October 3 to reveal whether he would seek reelection. Nunn postponed the event to the following week—and announced he would not seek reelection.

12. The exceptional character of the country's anticipation of the verdicts also was noted by Alan M. Dershowitz, one of the members of Simpson's legal team. In his book *Reasonable Doubts: The Criminal Justice System and the O.J. Simpson Case* (New York: Touchstone, 1996), he wrote that the reading of the Simpson verdicts was "different from the Kennedy assassination, the Japanese attack on Pearl Harbor or the death of Franklin D. Roosevelt. Those were unexpected events which came out of the blue like bolts of lightning on a

clear summer day" (11). The Simpson verdicts hardly qualified as "bolts of lightning."

13. Quoted in Robert Lipsyte, "Sports of the Times: O.J. Didn't Play," *New York Times*, August 2, 1969. It was also said that Simpson was a "wealthy celebrity who lived white, spoke white and married white." See William Safire, "After the Aftermath," *New York Times*, October 12, 1995.

14. See Joe Urschel, "Case That Captivated U.S.; Simpson Trial 'Monopolized' Our Attention," *USA Today*, September 29, 1995.

15. Gerald F. Uelmen, one of Simpson's lawyers, found at least thirty-two trials since 1901 that the news media had described as a "trial of the century." Among them were the cases of Leon Czolgosz, who assassinated President William McKinley in 1901; Bruno Hauptmann, who was convicted in 1935 of the kidnap-murder of Charles Lindbergh's infant son; and Julius and Ethel Rosenberg, who were convicted of espionage in 1951. "We average a new 'Trial of the Century' every three years," Uelmen said. Quoted in Elizabeth Wasserman, "O.J. Case Isn't the First, Won't Be the Last: Trials of the Century," *San Jose Mercury News*, May 22, 1995.

16. Peter Grier and Daniel B. Wood, "Why It's 'Not Guilty' in Trial of Century," *Christian Science Monitor*, October 4, 1995.

17. Dominick Dunne, "LA in the Age of O.J.," *Vanity Fair* 58 (February 1995): 48.

18. Shaun D. Mullen, "What Price Freedom?" *Philadelphia Daily News*, October 4, 1995.

19. Dave McIntyre, "U.S. in 1995: The Verge of Change, or More of the Same?" Deutsche Presse-Agentur, December 26, 1995, retrieved from Lexis Nexis database.

20. See Urschel, "Case That Captivated U.S."

21. The remark was attributed to author and lawyer Scott Turow. See Urschel, "Case That Captivated U.S."

22. Karen Heller, "Not Just a Spectacle, a Circus Outside the Courtroom," *Philadelphia Inquirer*, January 24, 1995.

23. David Shaw, "The Simpson Legacy: Obsession: Did the Media Overfeed a Starving Public?" *Los Angeles Times*, October 9, 1995, accessed May 29, 2013, http://articles.latimes.com/1995–10–09/news/ss-55103_1_simpson-case/3.

24. These salient characteristics were drawn from Peter Arenella, "The Perils of TV Legal Punditry," *University of Chicago Legal Forum* 25 (1998): 39. Arenella, an emeritus professor at the UCLA School of Law, was a legal analyst for ABC News during the Simpson trial.

25. See "The Power of DNA Evidence," *New York Times*, May 28, 1995.

26. See "O.J. Simpson Case by the Numbers," Associated Press, October 3, 1995, retrieved from LexisNexis database.

27. The jury's swift decision prompted some analysts to speculate that Simpson had been found guilty. See, for example, Harriet Chiang, "Swift Decision Called Bad Sign for Simpson," *San Francisco Chronicle*, October 3, 1995.

28. According to legal analyst and author Jeffrey Toobin, O.J. in speaking with police did not ask when Nicole Simpson had died, or how. See Toobin, *The Run of His Life: The People v. O.J. Simpson* (New York: Touchstone, 1997), 39.

29. See Seth Mydans, "Simpson Is Charged, Chased, Arrested," *New York Times,* June 18, 1994. Before slipping away, Simpson left behind three letters in sealed envelopes, one of which was addressed "to whom it may concern." That letter was opened by Robert Kardashian, a friend of Simpson, and read to journalists after Simpson had fled. The letter indicated that Simpson had contemplated suicide. "I think of my life, and feel I have done most of the right things," the letter said. "So why do I end up like this? I can't go on. No matter what the outcome, people will look and point. I can't take that. I can't subject my children to that." He also wrote: "Don't feel sorry for me. I have had a great life, great friends. Please think of the real O.J., and not this lost person." Quoted in Jim Newton and Shawn Hubler, "Simpson Held after Wild Chase; He's Charged with Murder of Ex-Wife," *Los Angeles Times,* June 18, 1994, accessed May 28, 2013, www.latimes.com/news/la-oj-anniv-arrest,0,922015.story.

30. See Mydans, "Simpson Is Charged, Chased, Arrested."

31. Newton and Hubler, "Simpson Held after Wild Chase."

32. David Dow, "What I Learned Covering the Trials of the Century," *Loyola of Los Angeles Law Review* 33, no. 2 (January 2000): 742.

33. See Susan Caba, "Trial Judgments: Consensus: Money Counts, Race Matters," *Philadelphia Inquirer,* October 8, 1995. See also Peter Arenella, "Foreword: O.J. Lessons," *Southern California Law Review* 69 (May 1996): 1233. Arenella further wrote that "using the Simpson trial to illustrate the defects of our trial system is somewhat misleading because his trial did not mimic how a typical trial proceeds" (1239).

34. Vincent Bugliosi, a former Los Angeles district attorney, scoffed at the praise embedded in the term "Dream Team," noting that Simpson's lawyers included no one who had "demonstrated any real competence in murder cases." Only the news media, Bugliosi said, could conjure "nonsense like 'Dream Team' to describe these lawyers." Bugliosi, *Outrage: The Five Reasons Why O.J. Simpson Got Away with Murder* (New York: Norton, 1996), 38, 40.

35. In questioning by police, Simpson acknowledged that, as the husband of one of the victims, he must be the lead suspect. He also gave vague explanations for the cut on his hand that left blood droplets inside and outside his home. The text of Simpson's statement appears as an appendix in Bugliosi, *Outrage,* 291–305.

36. "Transcript of Prosecution's Opening Statements," Associated Press, January 25, 1995, retrieved from LexisNexis database.

37. In his book about the Simpson case, Jeffrey Toobin noted that, except for Lee Bailey, "no one on the defense team ever took the idea [of Simpson's testifying] very seriously. . . . Cochran and Shapiro were more worried about losing the case, and their view prevailed." Simpson was not called to the witness stand. Toobin, *The Run of His Life,* 415.

38. Nell Henderson, "O.J. in L.A.: If You Must See the Sites, Here's How," *Washington Post,* September 3, 1995. Henderson also wrote: "The truth is, for all the hype, the so-called 'Trial of the Century' does trigger goose bumps in person. . . . Whether the testimony or arguments are moving, frightening, amusing or boring, just sitting in that courtroom produces a shiver that a viewer doesn't get from the tube."

39. See David Margolick, "Simpson Judge Delays Trial Opening and Will Allow Questioning of Detective on Bias," *New York Times,* January 24, 1995.

40. O. J. Simpson, *I Want to Tell You: My Response to Your Letters, Your Messages, Your Questions* (Boston: Little, Brown, 1995), 99.

41. Cited in Toobin, *The Run of His Life,* 254.

42. Simpson, *I Want to Tell You,* 129.

43. Ibid., 68.

44. Ibid., 98.

45. Quoted in Kenneth B. Noble, "Simpson Defense Grills 'Dreams' Witness," *New York Times,* February 3, 1995.

46. See Toobin, *The Run of His Life,* 273. Toobin also wrote: "There was a simple barometer of Simpson's reaction to testimony during his trial: The more it hurt, the more he talked. . . . Though ultimately unpersuasive to the jury, the domestic-violence evidence particularly set Simpson off" (272).

47. Quoted in Lawrence Schiller and James Willwerth, *American Tragedy: The Uncensored Story of the Simpson Defense* (New York: Random House, 1996), 373–74. Schiller and Willwerth also described how Simpson's defense team worked hard to establish "O.J.'s African-American identity" by redecorating his mansion before the jurors visited (371–72). A nude portrait of Paula Barbieri, a girlfriend of Simpson, was removed from Simpson's bedroom. Placed at the top of the stairs where jurors would not miss it was a framed copy of Norman Rockwell's 1963 painting of a black schoolchild escorted to school by federal marshals. "This has little to do with a search for the truth," Schiller and Willwerth wrote. "This is stagecraft" (372).

48. Darden later said he asked Simpson to put on the gloves as a preemptive move, figuring that the defense team was likely to do so. Darden also said Marcia Clark, the lead prosecutor, reluctantly agreed to the demonstration. See Christopher Darden with Jess Walter, *In Contempt* (New York: Regan Books, 1996), 323–24. Darden conceded that the demonstration had been a mistake, writing: "People ask me now would I do it again. No. Of course not. I should have taken into account shrinkage" of the gloves. "But, while I wouldn't do it again," he wrote, "I know those are his gloves" (326).

49. Quoted in Toobin, *The Run of His Life,* 367. Toobin noted that "O.J. slipped the gloves off in a flash, which would not have been possible if they were really too tight" (368).

50. This point was made by Peter Arenella in an interview with *USA Today.* "There he was professing his innocence," Arenella said. "Why in the world would the defense have to put him on as a witness?" Quoted in Gale Holland, "Small Gloves, Big Problem for O.J. Prosecution," *USA Today,* June 19, 1995. A few days after the disastrous demonstration, Darden claimed that Simpson had stopped taking anti-inflammatory medication for arthritis, which caused his hand to swell and made the evidence gloves harder to fit his hands. Simpson's lawyers denied Darden's accusation. See David Margolick, "Judge Ito to Open Files on 10 Dismissed Jurors," *New York Times,* June 24, 1995.

51. In his closing remarks in late September 1995, defense lawyer Johnnie Cochran described the gloves gambit as "perhaps the single most defining moment in this trial." See "Excerpts of Closing Arguments on Murder Charges

against O. J. Simpson," *New York Times,* September 28, 1995. It was astonishing, as many legal observers pointed out, for Darden to have asked Simpson to try on the evidence gloves without knowing for sure whether they would fit. Not even a first-year law student would likely commit such a blunder, Vincent Bugliosi observed. See Bugliosi, *Outrage,* 114. Gerald F. Uelmen, another lawyer on Simpson's legal team, later said of the botched demonstration: "From that point on, the prosecution was scrambling to undo the damage" done to its case. Uelmen, *Lessons from the Trial: The People v. O. J. Simpson* (Kansas City, Mo.: Andrews and McMeel, 1996), 166.

52. After the demonstration, Darden said, his colleagues in the district attorney's office "had nothing to say to me," adding that senior lawyers "convened a meeting to talk about the gloves. I wasn't invited or even told about the meeting. Marcia [Clark] didn't talk to me for a few days. For weeks after that, I was left out of major decisions involving the case." Darden, *In Contempt,* 326–27.

53. See "Jurors Hear Dramatic Appeals; Lawyers Present Two Faces of O.J.," *St. Louis Post-Dispatch,* September 28, 1995.

54. David Margolick, "Simpson Tells Why He Declined to Testify as Two Sides Rest Case," *New York Times,* September 23, 1995.

55. Ibid.

56. "'Did Not, Could Not, Would Not': Simpson Stuns Courtroom, Tells Ito He's Innocent," *Houston Chronicle,* September 23, 1995.

57. See Toobin, *The Run of His Life,* 429.

58. Dominick Dunne, a writer who covered the trial for *Vanity Fair,* noted that the "exhilaration that is part and parcel of an acquittal for a wrongly accused person was eerily missing" in the defense team's reaction to the verdicts. See Dunne, *Justice: Crimes, Trials, and Punishments* (New York: Crown, 2001), 229.

59. See Lorraine Adams, "Simpson Jurors Cite Weak Case, Not 'Race Card,'" *Washington Post,* October 5, 1995. The juror was forty-four-year-old Lionel Cryer, a former Black Panther. See also Schiller and Willwerth, *American Tragedy,* 679.

60. Quoted in Bugliosi, *Outrage,* 278.

61. President Clinton reacted to the verdicts with a single word: "Shit." See Harris, *The Survivor,* 206. Clinton, Harris wrote, "believed the evidence overwhelmingly proved Simpson guilty of the murders."

62. See, among others, Richard Grenier, "O. J. Simpson and the End of Trust," *Washington Times,* October 6, 1995, and Kenneth J. Garcia, "Jury United, But Nation Remains Divided," *San Francisco Chronicle,* October 4, 1995. Garcia wrote: "Rarely in America's history has the country's racial divide seemed wider or the cultural abyss deeper." See also "Two Nations, Divisible," *Economist,* October 7, 1995, 18.

63. Ronald Brownstein, "Simpson Defense's Focus on Racial Identity Further Divides a Nation," *Los Angeles Times,* October 9, 1995. He further wrote: "Most Americans of all races do not want their society divided into hostile enclaves, but their aspirations are defeated by racial posturing that encourages all Americans to dwell on their differences."

64. Garcia, "Jury United, But Nation Remains Divided."

65. Richard Cohen, "America's Racial Divide," *Washington Post,* October 4, 1995.

66. See Haya El Nasser, "Reaction Illustrates Racial Divide; Verdict Called a 'Message,'" *USA Today,* October 4, 1995.

67. See "Two Nations, Divisible," 18.

68. "Interview: Jeffrey Toobin," *Frontline,* April 22, 2005, accessed May 23, 2013, www.pbs.org/wgbh/pages/frontline/oj/interviews/toobin.html.

69. Data cited here were retrieved from the Gallup Organization's online "Gallup Brain" database.

70. In Los Angeles, a survey conducted by Loyola Marymount University just seven years after the Simpson trial found that respondents overwhelmingly believed that racial and ethnic groups in the city were getting along well, a reading confirmed in a similar survey in 2012. The 2002 survey reported that 74 percent of respondents said they felt racial and ethnic groups in Los Angeles were getting along "very well" or "somewhat well." Eighteen percent said the groups were getting along "very badly" or "somewhat badly." In 2012, 68 percent of respondents said the groups were getting along well, and 27 percent said the groups were getting poorly. However, a similar survey in 2007 indicated greater tensions among the city's racial and ethnic groups. Forty-seven percent said the groups were getting along well, and 51 percent said they were not. These data were reported in "20th Anniversary of the 1992 Los Angeles Riots Survey," Center for the Study of Los Angeles, Loyola Marymount University (2012), 4.

71. Data cited here were retrieved from the Gallup Organization's online "Gallup Brain" database. In 1958, only 4 percent of Americans said they approved of interracial marriage.

72. Data cited here were retrieved from the Gallup Organization's online "Gallup Brain" database.

73. Ibid.

74. Ibid.

75. See Robert D. Novak, "Farrakhan's Tour de Force," *Washington Post,* October 19, 1995.

76. See, for example, Dick Polman, "Supporters Launch New Wave of Powell-Mania Speculation," *Philadelphia Inquirer,* August 18, 1995.

77. Ibid.

78. Jonathan Yardley, a literary critic for the *Washington Post,* observed: "Powell himself is interesting, for obvious reasons. He is a black American, born in Harlem, who has not merely made it in white America but has conquered white America, not as an athlete or an entertainer but as, to all intents and purposes, a corporate executive. He has played the game by the white majority's rules but has not abandoned his black roots or compromised his identity as an African American." Yardley also noted, perceptively: "His promotional tour for his book will be a victory lap. One cannot expect the likes of Barbara Walters, Larry King, David Frost and Katie Couric—all past masters of genuflection—to do anything except fawn as he passes through the television shows on which they reign." Yardley, "Powell and the Political Trenches," *Washington Post,* September 11, 1995.

79. The memoir was the fastest-selling book its publisher, Random House, had had up to that time. See Elizabeth Kolbert, "A Rising Star Shines Brighter on His Book Tour," *New York Times*, September 24, 1995.

80. See ibid.

81. Frank Rich, "The Dole Dive," *New York Times*, October 7, 1995.

82. Ellen Goodman, "A Wedge or a Bridge?" *Baltimore Sun*, October 5, 1995, accessed May 21, 2013, http://articles.baltimoresun.com/1995–10–05 /news/1995278070_1_colin-powell-american-journey-simpson.

83. Carl Rowan, "A Year of Pain—and Some Plusses," *Chicago Sun-Times*, December 31, 1995. Rowan also wrote: "Didn't an adoring nation almost talk a black retired general, Colin Powell, into accepting a semi-draft into the presidency of the United States?"

84. See Philip J. Trounstine, "Powell for President: Would Race Matter?" *San Jose Mercury News*, November 5, 1995.

85. Harris, *The Survivor*, 207. Harris also wrote: "The interest in Powell was an implicit rebuke of the incumbent [Clinton]."

86. Colin L. Powell with Joseph E. Persico, *My American Journey* (New York: Random House, 1995), 609. He also wrote: "I would enter not to make a statement but to win. I understand the battlefield, and I know what winning takes" (609).

87. "Not in '96: Powell Rules Out Accepting Any Nomination for Vice President, Too," *San Jose Mercury News*, November 9, 1995. One of Powell's close friends, Richard Armitage, was quoted in the article as saying: "Over these past weeks, he was up and down, he agonized. He'd go out and meet with crowds and they'd fire him up. Then he'd get back home and wonder, 'Do I have the necessary fire in the stomach to be worthy of support of these people?' And he found he did not."

88. Ito put off announcing the verdicts to allow the prosecutors and defense lawyers ample time to reach the courtroom. Cochran, for example, was in San Francisco when the jury concluded its deliberations. In addition, the judge's decision served to lessen the prospect of civil disturbances had the verdicts gone against Simpson. For a brief discussion about the timing of the verdicts, see Dershowitz, *Reasonable Doubts*, 11–12. Dershowitz wrote: "Hours before the verdict was to be announced, President Bill Clinton was briefed on nationwide security measures in the event of possible rioting. The Los Angeles Police Department was on full alert" (12). See also Uelmen, *Lessons from the Trial*, 178.

89. Peter Arenella, interview with author (May 6, 2013).

90. See "The O.J. Verdict: Interview Peter Arenella," *Frontline*, April 1, 2005, accessed May 22, 2013, www.pbs.org/wgbh/pages/frontline/oj/interviews /arenella.html.

91. See Arenella, "The Perils of TV Legal Punditry," 50.

92. Ibid.

93. See Martin Gottlieb, "Racial Split at the End, as at the Start," *New York Times*, October 4, 1995.

94. Quoted in Caba, "Trial Judgments: Consensus: Money Counts, Race Matters."

95. Quoted in Vincent J. Schodolski, "Simpson Jurors: Police Lost Case," *Chicago Tribune,* October 5, 1995.

96. Quoted in Adams, "Simpson Jurors Cite Weak Case, Not 'Race Card.'"

97. Quoted in ibid.

98. See Todd S. Purdum, "Simpson Verdict Confronts a Public Seemingly Numbed," *New York Times,* February 6, 1997. Purdum's report quoted David J. Garrow, a biographer of the Rev. Dr. Martin L. King, Jr., as saying that he had detected "almost an evaporation of energetic black support for Simpson" since 1995.

99. Pam Bellack, "In New York, Many People Anticipated the Verdict," *New York Times,* February 5, 1997. Similarly muted reactions were noted elsewhere in the United States. In the San Francisco Bay Area, "there was neither the shock nor the jubilation that greeted the outcome of Simpson's criminal trial in 1995." Brandon Bailey, "Reaction to Simpson Verdict Split Along Racial Lines," *San Jose Mercury News,* February 5, 1997. A report in *USA Today* said: "Without cameras in the courtroom and a live audio feed, the unanimous verdict finding Simpson liable in two murders brought forth more muted reactions." Haya El Nasser, "More Muted Reaction Second Time Around," *USA Today,* February 5, 1997.

100. Steve Friess, "Stark Contrast to the '90s as Simpson Is Convicted of Armed Robbery and Kidnapping," *New York Times,* October 5, 2008. Friess also noted: "Public interest in the trial was minimal. Seats in the Las Vegas courtroom set aside for the public were vacant most of the time." The *Los Angeles Times* welcomed Simpson's conviction, saying in an editorial that the outcome represented "one of those unusual circumstances in which human law and karmic justice converge. . . . Without any doubt, Simpson belongs behind bars." See "The Juice and Justice," *Los Angeles Times,* December 6, 2008, accessed May 27, 2013, http://www.latimes.com/news/opinion/la-ed-simpson6–2008dec06,0,3478056.story.

101. This point was made by Tony Mauro in "Simpson Free: Prosecutors 'Ran from Their Evidence,'" *USA Today,* October 4, 1995.

102. Quoted in ibid. Had Simpson not been wealthy, Arenella said, his case would not have gone to trial. "It would have been pleaded out." Arenella, interview with author.

103. Simpson, *I Want to Tell You,* 91. "I truly realize now, for the first time," Simpson further stated, "that there are probably a great many people in jail who are innocent but who don't have the money to prove it in court."

104. Data cited here were retrieved from the Gallup Organization's online "Gallup Brain" database. The question's wording was: "In your opinion, if Simpson had not been rich, would he have been found guilty or not guilty?" The question was asked of 639 American adults on October 3, 1995.

105. Quoted in Caba, "Trial Judgments: Consensus: Money Counts, Race Matters."

106. Laurie L. Levenson, a professor at Loyola Law School in Los Angeles, has said, for example, that the Simpson case "made very little impact on legal doctrine." Levenson, "Cases of the Century," *Loyola of Los Angeles Law Review* 33, no. 2 (January 2000): 586.

107. Quoted in Linda Deutsch, "DNA Evidence Has Come a Long Way since O.J. Simpson Trial," Associated Press, August 21, 2002, retrieved from LexisNexis database.

108. Jerry E. Bishop, "How DNA Scientists Help Track Criminals and Clear the Innocent," *Wall Street Journal*, January 6, 1995.

109. Gina Kolata, "The Code: DNA and O.J. Simpson: Testing Science and Justice," *New York Times*, June 26, 1994.

110. See Rick Weiss, "Adversaries End DNA Evidence Fight," *Washington Post*, October 27, 1994. See also Jay D. Aronson, *Genetic Witness: Science, Law, and Controversy in the Making of DNA Profiling* (New Brunswick, N.J.: Rutgers University Press, 2007), 142. Aronson wrote that the at-times nasty "DNA Wars" featured a dispute "over which scientific community, or communities, had the expertise necessary to determine whether or not the practices and methodologies surrounding forensic DNA analysis were valid and reliable."

111. Jay Aronson described Lander as "one of the most vocal early opponents of DNA evidence." Aronson, *Genetic Witness*, 182. Lander, for example, wrote an often-cited article in 1989 that raised a variety of questions about DNA testing. See Eric S. Lander, "DNA Fingerprinting on Trial," *Nature* 339 (June 15, 1989): 501–5.

112. Eric S. Lander and Bruce Budowle, "DNA Fingerprinting Dispute Laid to Rest," *Nature* 371 (October 27, 1994): 735. They further wrote: "The technology itself represents perhaps the greatest advance in forensic science since the development of ordinary fingerprints in 1892." Jay Aronson noted that Lander and Budowle's article attracted criticism for "minimizing the importance of many issues that had not yet been resolved." For example, they failed to mention "that much of the DNA evidence in the Simpson investigation was produced through new . . . methods that had been subjected to limited scrutiny in court." Aronson, *Genetic Witness*, 185. See also Richard Lempert, "After the DNA Wars: Skirmishing with NRC II," *Jurimetrics* 37 (Summer 1997): 439–68.

113. Lander and Budowle, "DNA Fingerprinting Dispute Laid to Rest," 735.

114. Ibid., 738. That Simpson's defense team did not challenge the science of DNA testing was mildly surprising. For example, the *New York Times* noted: "Even in this bitterly contested murder trial, the principles and procedures of DNA testing have not . . . been seriously questioned." See "The Power of DNA Evidence." See also Aronson, *Genetic Witness*, 193. Aronson wrote: "Even the *New York Times*, which had published some of the most controversial accounts of the debates over DNA profiling in the late 1980s and early 1990s, was surprised about the lack of a fundamental technical challenge to DNA profiling" at the Simpson trial.

115. Barry Scheck, interview with Harry Kriesler, "Bringing Science to the Courtroom" (July 25, 2003), accessed April 1, 2012, http://globetrotter.berkeley.edu/people3/Scheck/scheck-con3.html.

116. Ibid.

117. For a discussion about the bungled DNA evidence collection, see Toobin, *The Run of His Life*, 338–43. See also Gina Kolata, "Simpson Trial Shows

Need for Proper Use of Forensic Evidence, Experts Say," *New York Times,* October 11, 1995. Kolata wrote: "Many experts say the Los Angeles Police Department's apparent mishandling of evidence in the Simpson trial may typify what happens in lower-profile cases nationally, but those defendants are generally too poor to mount a counterattack that scrutinizes the quality of the genetic evidence against them."

118. See Michael Lynch et al., *Truth Machine: The Contentious History of DNA Fingerprinting* (Chicago: University of Chicago, 2008), 237.

119. See "What Every Law Enforcement Officer Should Know about DNA," National Institute of Justice, September 1999, accessed May 29, 2013, www .nij.gov/pubs-sum/000614.htm.

120. Scheck, interview with Kriesler, "Bringing Science to the Courtroom." Textbooks have embraced Scheck's interpretation. "Arguably the most important outcome of the O.J. Simpson trial was the renewed emphasis placed on DNA evidence collection." John M. Butler, *Fundamentals of Forensic DNA Typing* (Boston: Academic Press, 2010), 85.

121. Such programs make for "good television but bad forensic science," Moses Schanfield, chair of George Washington University's Department of Forensic Sciences, said in an interview in 2004. Quoted in Ken Adelman, "CSI: DC," *Washingtonian,* October 2004, 37. For similar criticism, see Lynch et al., *Truth Machine,* x. "Experienced forensic scientists," they wrote, "are quick to point out that . . . fictional portrayals are notoriously inaccurate, and that the reality of forensic science is far less clear, certain, and glamorous than portrayed on television."

122. "Television without DNA would look a lot different, and prime time would need a makeover," Brandon L. Garrett, a law professor at the University of Virginia, noted in his essay "After Osama bin Laden's Death, Imagining a World without DNA Evidence," *Washington Post,* May 13, 2011. He also wrote: "In a world without DNA testing, these programs would have a hard time selling fiber comparison as a silver bullet."

123. David Martindale, "CSI Miami: Investigating CSI with the Creators," A&E television, accessed October 18, 2013, www.aetv.com/csi_miami/csi_ investigating_creators.jsp. On another occasion, Zuicker said: "I don't believe America was privy to forensics until the O.J. Simpson trial." Quoted in Charlie McCollum, "'CSI' Turns Up the Heat," *San Jose Mercury News,* September 23, 2002.

124. See, for example, Linda Deutsch, "Simpson Case Could Be Shaped by 13th Juror—the TV Camera," Associated Press, August 7, 1994, retrieved from LexisNexis database.

125. Simpson wrote that "cameras in the court all the time is a no-win situation for me. If I'm looking like I'm having a good day in court, if I'm too jovial, people say he's not serious or concerned enough. If I'm looking worried or upset, then it looks like I did it. You just can't win. I think the worst thing the court can do is let the TV camera in." Simpson, *I Want To Tell You,* 97.

126. See, among others, Arenella, "Foreword: O.J. Lessons," 1257. Arenella noted: "Watching the trial on television is not an adequate substitute for being in the courtroom every day. The TV juror might miss revealing non-verbal

behavior of the witnesses or the defendant that jurors can see from the jury box. Some witnesses appear more credible on TV than in the courtroom while others fare better in person than on the tube."

127. To that point, Dominick Dunne observed not long after the trial that Simpson was "not satisfied with a mere acquittal [but] wanted more from us. He wanted our adulation back. Adulation is what he craves. He is addicted to it." Dunne, *Justice,* 227.

128. Ibid., 225.

129. Cited in Whitaker, "Whites v. Blacks." Dunne observed that, while reading the statement, Jason Simpson "sat awkwardly, almost hiding his face . . . as if he were ashamed of the message he was reading." Dunne, *Justice,* 229.

130. Jeff Hall, interview with author (May 4, 2013).

131. Linda Deutsch, "Going, Going, Gone—Simpson's Dream Home Now Belongs to Bank," Associated Press, July 15, 1997, retrieved from LexisNexis database.

132. Linda Deutsch, "Simpson Shrugs Off Demolition of His Former Mansion," Associated Press, July 30, 1998, retrieved from LexisNexis database.

133. See Terry Baynes, "Ex-prosecutor: Cochran Manipulated Glove," *Washington Post,* September 9, 2012. Dershowitz also said that Darden should have taken his suspicions to the California bar association rather than raise them publicly, during a panel discussion.

4. PEACE AT DAYTON AND THE "HUBRIS BUBBLE"

1. See, for example, "Bosnia Peace Talks Reportedly Fail to Reach Agreement," Agence France Presse, November 21, 1995, retrieved from LexisNexis database. In addition, Warren Christopher, the U.S. secretary of state who participated in the endgame at Dayton, wrote in his memoir that he awakened on November 21, 1995, "prepared to announce" the failure of the talks. See Christopher, *Chances of a Lifetime: A Memoir* (New York: Scribner, 2001), 266.

2. See Peter Beinart, *The Icarus Syndrome: A History of American Hubris* (New York: Harper, 2010), 332, 360.

3. "Clinton's Words: 'The Promise of Peace,'" *New York Times,* November 22, 1995.

4. At the start of the war in April 1992, Bosnia's population of 4.3 million people was 44 percent Muslim, 31 percent ethnic Serb, 17 percent ethnic Croat, and 8 percent "Yugoslav" or other. See Elizabeth M. Cousens and Charles K. Carter, *Toward Peace in Bosnia: Implementing the Dayton Accords* (Boulder, Colo.: Lynne Rienner, 2001), 21. "Bosnia," the authors noted, "resembled the Yugoslav Federation uniquely among Yugoslav republics in its mix of nationalities, lack of an absolute ethnic majority, and intricate power-sharing formulas for managing ethnicity" (20–21).

5. See Cousens and Carter, *Toward Peace in Bosnia,* 19. See also Roger Cohen, "Balkan Leaders Face an Hour for Painful Choices," *New York Times,* November 1, 1995. Cohen, one of the leading chroniclers of the Bosnian war, wrote: "It was clear to almost everyone that the Bosnian independence [Izetbegović] sought in 1992 would provoke a violent reaction from the Serbian

minority of Bosnia, strongly backed by the Serbian-dominated Yugoslav Army. On April 4, 1992, two days before the fighting broke out, he declared: 'Citizens of Sarajevo, sleep peacefully, there will be no war.'"

6. Roger Cohen wrote of the Serbs: "They killed, raped, and plundered Muslims, and they 'cleansed' them by throwing them into concentration camps. Whatever the arguments on their side . . . the Serbs trampled them into the Bosnian mud with this vicious campaign that flouted all the principles on which Europe had been rebuilt since 1945." Cohen, *Hearts Grown Brutal: Sagas of Sarajevo* (New York: Random House, 1998), 194.

7. "Bosnia Serb Ethnic Cleansing," DCI Interagency Balkan Task Force, December 1994, from "End of the Cold War Collection," National Security Archive, Washington, D.C.

8. Cousens and Carter, *Toward Peace in Bosnia,* 21.

9. See David Rohde, *Endgame: The Betrayal and Fall of Srebrenica, Europe's Worst Massacre since World War II* (Boulder, Colo.: Westview Press, 1998), xi. See also Richard Holbrooke, *To End a War* (New York: Random House, 1998), 162. Holbrooke wrote that American negotiators at Dayton called the "Greater Serbia"–"Great Croatia" formulation "the 'Stalin-Hitler' scenario," recalling as it did the division of Poland between the Soviets and the Germans in 1939.

10. Data cited here were retrieved from the "Polling the Nations" database; the survey by the Times Mirror Center for the People & the Press was conducted January 13, 1993. When the question was asked again in June 1995, 47 percent of respondents identified the Serbs; 53 percent of respondents gave incorrect answers or said they did not know. These data were retrieved from the "Polling the Nations" database; the survey by the Times Mirror Center for the People & the Press was conducted June 14, 1995.

11. Fifty-six percent of respondents to a *Washington Post*/ABC News poll conducted in mid-November 1995 said they felt "America's vital interests" were not at stake in Bosnia; 35 percent said American vital interests were at stake there; and 9 percent offered no opinion. Data cited here were retrieved from the "Polling the Nations" database.

12. A *Time*/CNN poll conducted among 600 Americans in October 1995 reported that 34 percent of respondents felt the United States had a moral obligation to end the fighting in Bosnia; 59 percent of respondents said they did not feel that way. Data cited here were retrieved from the "Polling the Nations" database; the *Time*/CNN poll was conducted October 23, 1995.

13. Quoted in Anthony Lewis, "Abroad at Home: Anatomy of Disaster," *New York Times,* January 5, 1996.

14. Louise Branson and Dusko Dodger, *Milosevic: Portrait of a Tyrant* (New York: Free Press, 1999), 10.

15. See Marcus Tanner, "Gambler Stakes His All on War," *Independent* (London), August 6, 1995.

16. Holbrooke, *To End a War,* 162. See also Michael Dobbs, "New Talks on an Old Agenda: Bosnia's Future," *Washington Post,* November 1, 1995. Dobbs reported that a member of the British parliament had asked Tuđman in 1995 what postwar Bosnia might look like. The Croat president "promptly

took out his pen and drew a map of Bosnia with a squiggly line down the middle," Dobbs wrote. "On one side of the map, he wrote 'Croatia,' on the other side 'Serbia'"—an evocation of the "Greater Croatia"–"Greater Serbia" formulation.

17. See Paul Hockenos, *Homeland Calling: Exile Patriotism and the Balkan Wars* (Ithaca, N.Y.: Cornell University Press, 2003), 19. Carla Del Ponte, chief prosecutor at the international tribunal investigating war crimes in Bosnia, was quoted by Hockenos as saying of Tudman: "Were he not dead, he would have been one of The Hague tribunal indictees." See also Diane Orentlicher, "Who Will Judge the Court Itself?" *Washington Post*, July 8, 2001. Orentlicher wrote: "After Tudjman's death in December 1999, Del Ponte stated that Tudjman would have been indicted had he lived longer. I can't assess whether Tudjman deserved to be indicted, but I find it worrying that the prosecution was unable to complete its investigation more than four years after the most recent alleged crimes occurred."

18. See Cohen, "Balkan Leaders Face an Hour for Painful Choices."

19. NATO was supervising flight restrictions over Bosnia that the United Nations Security Council had imposed in 1992.

20. See Francis X. Clines, "Downed U.S. Pilot Rescued in Bosnia in Daring Raid," *New York Times*, June 9, 1995.

21. Quoted in Piero Valsecchi, "Pilot: 'Scared Little Bunny' While Eluding Serb Forces," Associated Press, June 10, 1995, retrieved from LexisNexis database.

22. Sergeant Scott Pfister, a crew chief of one of the helicopters, said of O'Grady: "He looked scared. . . . There were tears in his eyes. He definitely looked emotionally drained." Quoted in Daniel Williams, "I'm Ready to Get the Hell Out of Here," *Washington Post*, June 9, 1995.

23. Ibid.

24. Clinton stamped his feet with joy over the news of O'Grady's rescue. See Richard Sale, *Clinton's Secret Wars: The Evolution of a Commander in Chief* (New York: Thomas Dunne, 2009), 134.

25. Clines, "Downed U.S. Pilot Rescued in Bosnia in Daring Raid." News of Clinton's cigar-smoking celebration was derided by some observers. For example, a columnist for the *St. Paul Pioneer Press* in Minnesota wrote: "These days . . . national triumphs come in small packages. We can't stop the slaughter in Sarajevo. We can't agree what to do about it. We can't even stick to one policy for five minutes. But, dang it, we can rescue our boy! And, if we are president, we can gloat and smoke!" Nick Coleman, "Smoke Can't Hide Timid President," *St. Paul Pioneer Press*, June 11, 1995.

26. Quoted in Williams, "I'm Ready to Get the Hell Out of Here."

27. See Alison Mitchell, "After the Cigars, Clinton Still Faces Growing Criticism of Bosnia Policy," *New York Times*, June 9, 1995.

28. Peter Slevin, "Clinton Got Bold on Foreign Policy," *Philadelphia Inquirer*, September 29, 1996.

29. See Holbrooke, *To End a War*, 217.

30. Sale, *Clinton's Secret Wars*, 136.

31. See Warren Bass, "The Triage of Dayton," *Foreign Affairs* 77, no. 5 (September–October 1998): 98.

32. See, among others, Christopher, *Chances of a Lifetime*, 252. He wrote: "We had relied unrealistically and for longer than was justifiable on our European allies to resolve the problems in Bosnia."

33. The Serbs claimed to have been aware of the rescue mission but let it go ahead as a humanitarian gesture. See Clines, "Downed U.S. Pilot Rescued in Bosnia in Daring Raid."

34. Another factor propelling the Clinton administration to intervene was the realization that U.S. forces would be sent to Bosnia in keeping with a NATO commitment to extricate U.N. peacekeepers should conditions on the ground force their withdrawal. It became clear, Warren Bass wrote, that the only way to forestall such a scenario "was to push the parties" in Bosnia to a peace agreement. Thus the administration "became bold [in Bosnia] almost by accident." Bass, "The Triage of Dayton," 100, 101.

35. Bosnian Serbs had blocked resupply routes for the Dutch peacekeepers, who had received no diesel fuel or fresh food in weeks. See Rohde, *Endgame*, 5–6.

36. Quoted in Samantha Power, *"A Problem from Hell": America and the Age of Genocide* (New York: Basic Books, 2002), 401.

37. Ibid., 420.

38. See Rohde, *Endgame*, 229.

39. See ibid., 158–61.

40. Samantha Power wrote: "There was much the United States might have done" in response to the outrage at Srebrenica. But it did very little to prevent the enclave's fall or to punish the Serbs for their aggression. Power, *"A Problem from Hell,"* 406.

41. "Nothing else in the war had matched, or ever would match, Srebrenica," Holbrooke later wrote. Holbrooke, "Why Are We in Bosnia?" in *The Unquiet American: Richard Holbrooke in the World*, ed. Derek Chollet and Samantha Power (New York: Public Affairs, 2011), 219.

42. William Safire, "Essay: Time Has Come," *New York Times*, July 13, 1995.

43. Anthony Lewis, "Abroad at Home: Weakness as Policy," *New York Times*, July 14, 1995.

44. See Power, *"A Problem from Hell,"* 393.

45. See Thomas Lippman and Ann Devroy, "Clinton's Policy Evolution: June Decision Led to Diplomatic Gambles," *Washington Post*, September 11, 1995.

46. See Rohde, *Endgame*, 332–33.

47. See Holbrooke, *To End a War*, 199.

48. See Daniel Williams, "NATO Suspends Raids Indefinitely," *Washington Post*, September 21, 1995. See also Roger Cohen, "NATO Presses Bosnia Bombing, Promising to Make Sarajevo Safe," *New York Times*, August 31, 1995.

49. See Roger Cohen, "Taming the Bullies of Bosnia," *New York Times Magazine*, December 17, 1995, 62.

50. For a discussion of Holbrooke's character and how his independent streak may have kept him from becoming secretary of state, see James Traub, "Holbrooke's Campaign," *New York Times Magazine*, March 26, 2000, accessed August 18, 2013, www.nytimes.com/2000/03/26/magazine/holbrooke-s-campaign

.html?pagewanted=all&src=pm. Traub compared Holbrooke to former secretary of state Henry Kissinger, writing: "Holbrooke speaks often of Henry Kissinger, and there is something in the way Holbrooke bestrides the world that can put you in mind of him. Like Kissinger, Holbrooke wants to be on the inside of everything—every debate, every decision, every juicy secret and every desirable party. He is, like Kissinger, a social animal, equally sought-after as a guest and a host."

51. Quoted in Holbrooke, *To End a War*, 239.

52. Donald Kerrick, a member of the core U.S. negotiating team at Dayton, recalled Holbrooke as "very talented and very energetic. But sometimes crazy." Kerrick, a retired three-star Army general, also said: "I'm a big Dick Holbrooke fan. I think Dick Holbrooke was one of our generation's best diplomats and statesmen. . . . Of course, he was not without shortcomings." Kerrick, interview with author (August 12, 2013).

53. Roger Cohen, "The Unquiet American," *New York Times*, December 16, 2010.

54. According to journalist David Rohde, Ratko Mladić disingenuously said he "couldn't promise that Muslims wouldn't shoot at" an aircraft carrying Holbrooke and his negotiating team. See Rohde, *Endgame*, 336.

55. Holbrooke, *To End a War*, 269. Holbrooke dedicated his book to the memories of Frasure, Kruzel, and Drew. Holbrooke's wife, Kati Marton, was quoted by Roger Cohen of the *New York Times* as saying that Holbrooke "felt terrible over the deaths, and at some level responsible, and the only way to redeem this was for these people in the Balkans to come to terms and end the war." Cohen, "Taming the Bullies of Bosnia," 62.

56. Sale, *Clinton's Secret Wars*, 428.

57. Holbrooke wrote that whereas Christopher "was cautious and methodical, I tended to be intuitive and impatient." Holbrooke, *To End a War*, 239.

58. "Lexington: Mr. Christopher's Monument," *Economist*, November 25, 1995, 72.

59. Warren Christopher's visits to the Dayton talks "had a calming influence on everyone, especially in contrast to Holbrooke's relentless (and at times overbearing) intensity," Derek Chollet wrote. "Both in stature and style, the Secretary of State exuded control and steadiness." Chollet, *The Road to the Dayton Accords: A Study of American Statecraft* (New York: Palgrave MacMillan, 2005), 163. Kerrick recalled that Christopher "was able to add that gravitas that we needed" at Dayton. Kerrick, interview with author. See also Michael Dobbs, "Three Shaped Pact: Effort Began with Frasure, Picked up by Holbrooke, Closed with Christopher," *Washington Post*, November 22, 1995.

60. See Dirk Johnson, "Bemused Dayton Awaits Peace Talks," *New York Times*, October 29, 1995. See also Ran Raider, "Famous Miami Valley Inventors," Wright State University libraries, accessed July 27, 2013, http://guides.libraries.wright.edu/content.php?pid=51767&sid=716761.

61. Johnson, "Bemused Dayton Awaits Peace Talks," 24.

62. Holbrooke identified the other finalists as the U.S. naval station at Newport, R.I., and Langley Air Force Base in Norfolk, Va. See Holbrooke, *To End a War*, 204. The president's retreat at Camp David in Maryland was ruled out,

Holbrooke wrote, because it "was too close to Washington, too small, too 'presidential,' and too closely identified with the 1978 negotiations between Egypt and Israel."

63. Kerrick, interview with author.

64. See Roger Cohen, "Reporter's Notebook: A Limousine Carries Milosevic, and a Message," *New York Times*, November 2, 1995.

65. "We wanted them to see this physical symbol of American power," Holbrooke wrote in *To End a War*, 233. Kerrick said the Balkan leaders at Dayton "understood that the U.S. had a lot of military power. And we had shown we would use it, if need be." Kerrick, interview with author.

66. See Michael Dobbs, "Bosnia Talks Open with Warning to Leaders," *Washington Post*, November 2, 1995.

67. See Steve Love, "In the Heartland, Hope for Peace," *San Jose Mercury News*, November 1, 1995. The smoking ban in federal buildings reportedly was lifted at the talks, "to accommodate Eastern European habits." See Kathy Lally, "Warning Opens Bosnian Talks," *Baltimore Sun*, November 2, 1995, accessed August 5, 2013, http://articles.baltimoresun.com/1995–11–02/news/1995306124_1_christopher-herzegovina-bosnia/2.

68. Holbrooke said he found Dayton to be "a charming small Ohio city. . . . Unlike the population of, say, New York, Geneva, or Washington, which would scarcely notice another conference, Daytonians were proud to be part of history." Holbrooke, *To End a War*, 234.

69. Ibid.

70. See Roger Cohen, "U.S. Envoy in Bosnia Helps to Free Colleague (from an Ally)," *New York Times*, October 19, 1995. Kerrick recalled that Milošević pronounced the city's name "Day-tone." Kerrick, interview with author.

71. Holbrooke, *To End a War*, 185.

72. Cohen, "Reporter's Notebook: A Limousine Carries Milosevic."

73. See Elaine Sciolino, "3 Balkan Presidents Meet in Ohio to Try to End War," *New York Times*, November 2, 1995.

74. Kerrick, interview with author.

75. Remarks by Secretary of State Warren Christopher at Wright-Patterson Air Force Base, Associated Press, November 1, 1995, retrieved from LexisNexis database. See also Chollet, *The Road to the Dayton Accords*, 139.

76. See Holbrooke, *To End a War*, 204.

77. Sale, *Clinton's Secret Wars*, 158.

78. Holbrooke, *To End a War*, 232.

79. Chollet, *The Road to the Dayton Accords*, 133. Only Warren Christopher and the State Department's spokesman, Nicholas Burns, were authorized to speak for the record about the talks. Chollet also noted that, in many ways, "Dayton was not only radio silent to the public, but also to the rest of the American government." Officials in Washington, he wrote, "were not always aware of the precise substance of the discussions, especially given the complexity and speed with which things happened inside the compound" at Dayton (133).

80. See Holbrooke, *To End a War*, 199–200. Other conditions the United States insisted on were that each leader have "full power to sign agreements" and that "they stay as long as necessary" to close a deal.

81. Remarks by Secretary of State Warren Christopher at Wright-Patterson Air Force Base.

82. Ibid.

83. Kerrick, interview with author. Holbrooke later said he figured the chances of success at Dayton were 20–30 percent. See Traub, "Holbrooke's Campaign."

84. See Holbrooke, *To End a War*, 233.

85. Chollet, *The Road to the Dayton Accords*, 140.

86. See Richard C. Holbrooke, "Dayton Update: Tuesday, November 7, 1995, 11:50 p.m.," memorandum, "End of the Cold War Collection," National Security Archive, Washington, D.C. See also Chollet, *The Road to the Dayton Accords*, 148.

87. Quoted in Chollet, *The Road to the Dayton Accords*, 148.

88. Holbrooke wrote that the session "was a disaster. Putting the principal actors in front of maps brought out the worst in all of them." Holbrooke, *To End a War*, 255.

89. Quoted in Holbrooke, *To End a War*, 255. Kerrick recalled that the dynamics of the talks could shift suddenly and dramatically. "It changed constantly," he said. "It changed within meetings. You'd be sitting there one moment with what seemed to be consensus and it would just unravel before your eyes. And you would have to rebuild it all over again. It was very volatile, as were the characters." Kerrick, interview with author.

90. See Richard C. Holbrooke, "Dayton Update: Tuesday, November 8, 1995, 10:00 p.m.," memorandum, "End of the Cold War Collection," National Security Archive, Washington, D.C. See also Chollet, *The Road to the Dayton Accords*, 151.

91. Holbrooke, *To End a War*, 243.

92. Chollet, *The Road to the Dayton Accords*, 143. During NATO's aerial bombing in September 1995, Tomahawk missiles were fired at Serb military positions from U.S. warships in the Adriatic Sea. See Rohde, *Endgame*, 339.

93. Kerrick, interview with author.

94. See Peter Grier, "Quest Launched for Reporter's Freedom as He Paces behind Bars in Bosnian Serb Jail," *Christian Science Monitor*, November 21, 1995.

95. Holbrooke, *To End a War*, 242–43.

96. Ibid., 247.

97. Holbrooke, "Dayton Update: Tuesday, November 7, 1995."

98. Holbrooke later wrote that he violated the news blackout by taking a telephone call from Ted Koppel of the ABC News *Nightline* program who said Rohde had once worked for Koppel and urged Holbrooke to make the journalist's case "a high priority." Holbrooke, *To End a War*, 246.

99. See Michael Dobbs, "For Rohde, the Power of a Well-Placed Writer Paid Off," *Washington Post*, November 9, 1995. Dobbs wrote: "So far only one writer has managed to penetrate the tight security surrounding the Bosnia peace talks at Wright-Patterson Air Force Base just outside Dayton. It helps that author Kati Marton is married to chief U.S. negotiator Richard Holbrooke." At one point in Dayton during Rohde's ordeal, Holbrooke picked up the wool

fedora of Nikola Koljevic, the top Bosnian Serb official at the talks, and asked him: "Do you like this hat? Maybe I should hold it hostage." Quoted in Grier, "Quest Launched for Reporter's Freedom."

100. David Rohde, "Personal Diplomacy," *New York Times*, December 26, 2010. Rohde won a Pulitzer Prize in 1996 for his reporting about the Srebrenica massacre both before and after his arrest.

101. Derek Chollet described the Rohde case as "a time consuming diversion" at Dayton. Chollet, *The Road to the Dayton Accords*, 150. Twelve members of Rohde's family and two editors from the *Christian Science Monitor* traveled to Dayton to press for the journalist's release. See Rohde, *Endgame*, x.

102. Quoted in Chollet, *The Road to the Dayton Accords*, 155.

103. See Chollet's description of "napkin diplomacy" in *The Road to the Dayton Accords*, 165–66.

104. Ibid., 166.

105. Ibid., 166–67. See also Holbrooke, *To End a War*, 283, 285.

106. Quoted in Holbrooke, *To End a War*, 285. Holbrooke wrote that he had seen "no evidence that the alcohol affected" Milošević.

107. See Chollet, *The Road to the Dayton Accords*, 170.

108. Quoted in ibid., 170.

109. See Holbrooke, *To End a War*, 302.

110. See Elaine Sciolino, Roger Cohen, and Stephen Engelberg, "In U.S. Eyes, 'Good' Muslims and 'Bad' Serbs Did a Switch," *New York Times*, November 23, 1995.

111. Quoted in Holbrooke, *To End a War*, 289.

112. In 1992, the then–secretary of state, Lawrence Eagleburger, had said Milošević should be put on trial for "crimes against humanity" in Bosnia. See Don Oberdorfer, "Eagleburger Urges Trial of Serb Leaders," *Washington Post*, December 16, 1992.

113. Kerrick, interview with author.

114. See Chollet, *The Road to the Dayton Accords*, 167.

115. Quoted in Holbrooke, *To End a War*, 291. Holbrooke wrote that Milošević's remarks in announcing the concession on Sarajevo "were probably the most astonishing and unexpected of the conference." He further wrote: "We never fully understood why Milosevic decided to give Sarajevo to the Muslims. But in retrospect, the best explanation may be that he was fed up with the Bosnian Serbs and had decided to weaken their . . . base by giving away the Serb-controlled parts of Sarajevo" (293).

116. See ibid., 298.

117. Milošević would not go beyond the 51/49 territorial division, telling the Americans late in the talks, "I can do many things, but I cannot give you more than fifty-one percent." Quoted in Holbrooke, *To End a War*, 296. But Milošević made clear he would settle for real estate of almost any kind. Carl Bildt paraphrased Milošević as saying, "Give me something! Steppes, rocks, or swamps—anything will do." Bildt, *Peace Journey: The Struggle for Peace in Bosnia* (London: Weidenfeld and Nicolson, 1998), 155.

118. Chollet, *The Road to the Dayton Accords*, 173–74.

119. Ibid., 174.

120. Quoted in ibid., 174.

121. Ibid.

122. Christopher, *Chances of a Lifetime*, 265.

123. Chollet, *The Road to the Dayton Accords*, 175–77. See also Holbrooke, *To End a War*, 304–5.

124. See Chollet, *The Road to the Dayton Accords*, 177.

125. Christopher, *Chances of a Lifetime*, 266.

126. Ibid.

127. Holbrooke, *To End a War*, 305–6.

128. Quoted in ibid., 306. Kerrick recalled that Milošević told him: "General, please do not give up. This is too important." Kerrick said he replied, "We've done all we can. It's up to you to get in touch with these other leaders and say . . . 'we need to solve this.'" Kerrick, interview with author.

129. Kerrick, interview with author.

130. See Christopher, *Chances of a Lifetime*, 266.

131. Holbrooke, *To End a War*, 308.

132. Quoted in ibid., 308.

133. Chollet, *The Road to the Dayton Accords*, 179. Warren Christopher, in his memoir, offered a slightly different version of Izetbegović's comment, quoting him as saying, "It is not justice, but we need peace." Christopher, *Chances of a Lifetime*, 266.

134. Holbrooke, *To End a War*, 309.

135. "Clinton's Transcript on Peace Accord," United Press International, November 21, 1995, retrieved from LexisNexis database.

136. Izetbegović detested "Republika Srpska," likening it to a "Nazi name." See Holbrooke, *To End a War*, 130. Holbrooke conceded in *To End a War* that allowing the Bosnian Serbs to use that name was a defect of the Dayton accords (361).

137. Ibid., 309.

138. Ibid., 322.

139. Ibid., 318. "There was a lot of animosity behind the scenes" between the French and Americans, Mike McCurry recalled. He said some Clinton administration officials privately referred to Alain Juppé, the French prime minister, as "the skirt"—a play on Juppé's name. "Jupe" is the French word for skirt. McCurry, interview with author (September 1, 2013).

140. Craig R. Whitney, "Balkan Foes Sign Peace Pact, Dividing an Unpacified Bosnia," *New York Times*, December 15, 1995.

141. See William Drozdiak and John F. Harris, "Leaders Sign Pact to End Bosnia War," *Washington Post*, December 15, 1995.

142. See, for example, Bass, "The Triage of Dayton," 96. Bass wrote that the Dayton agreement brought Bosnia "ominously close to partition."

143. As many as 430,000 combatants were under arms in Bosnia at the end of the war. Most of them quit their units within a few years, in what was more a disintegration than a demobilization of armed forces in postwar Bosnia. See Tobias Pietz, "Overcoming the Failings of Dayton: Defense Reform in Bosnia-Herzegovina," in *Bosnian Security after Dayton: New Perspectives*, ed. Michael A. Innes (London: Routledge, 2006), 157.

144. Ted Galen Carpenter, "Holbrooke Horror: The U.S. Peace Plan for Bosnia," Cato Institute Foreign Policy Briefing No. 37, October 27, 1995, 1–2.

145. Ibid., 2.

146. Bass, "The Triage of Dayton," 104.

147. As Warren Christopher wrote in his memoir, the imperfect peace achieved at Dayton was preferable to a resumption of war. Christopher, *Chances of a Lifetime*, 267.

148. Stephen Sestanovich, *Maximalist: America in the World from Truman to Obama* (New York: Knopf, 2014), 262. Sestanovich also wrote: "The United States had mobilized and used military power where its allies had only dithered. It had brought a bloody ethnic war to a close through focused, purposeful diplomacy. It punctured the idea that there was nothing to be done about barbarism and disorder."

149. For example, a *New York Times*/CBS News poll conducted in December 1995 reported that 55 percent of Americans opposed sending U.S. troops to Bosnia as part of NATO's peacekeeping force. A *Time*/CNN poll conducted at the same time produced similar results: 55 percent of Americans opposed deploying U.S. troops to Bosnia. Data cited here were retrieved from the "Polling the Nations" database.

150. See Richard Holbrooke, "Foreword," in Chollet, *The Road to the Dayton Accords*, xii.

151. Holbrooke, *To End a War*, 217.

152. Holbrooke, "Foreword," xii. Holbrooke wrote that "the exact number" of body bags "was a closely guarded military secret."

153. "Clinton's Words on Mission to Bosnia: 'The Right Thing to Do,'" *New York Times*, November 28, 1995.

154. Ibid.

155. Ibid.

156. Ibid.

157. See "Excerpts from President Clinton's Victory Address at Arkansas Statehouse," *New York Times*, November 6, 1996.

158. See "In His Own Words: Clinton's Speech Accepting the Democratic Nomination for President," *New York Times*, August 30, 1996.

159. See "Text of Al Gore and President Clinton after Winning Re-election," Associated Press, November 6, 1996, retrieved from LexisNexis database.

160. Quoted in Barry Schweid, "Albright Says There Will Be Civilian Casualties," Associated Press, February 19, 1998, retrieved from LexisNexis database.

161. For a succinct discussion about the United States in a unipolar world, see Timothy J. Lynch and Robert S. Singh, *After Bush: The Case for Continuity in American Foreign Policy* (Cambridge, Engl.: Cambridge University Press, 2008), 52–53.

162. Holbrooke, *To End a War*, 216.

163. Ibid., 217. Holbrooke wrote that scars from the Somalia disaster, combined with memories of the quagmire of Vietnam, "had left what might be called a 'Vietmalia syndrome' in Washington."

164. Within two years, U.S. troop strength in Bosnia had been drawn down to about 8,500.

165. As it turned out, the "biggest challenge for U.S. army doctors in Bosnia . . . were sprained ankles and pulled muscles" that soldiers suffered while playing sports, as Gerald Knaus, a foreign policy analyst, later observed. Knaus, "The Rise and Fall of Liberal Imperialism," in *Can Intervention Work?* ed. Rory Stewart and Gerald Knaus (New York: Norton, 2011), 179.

166. Quoted in Stephen Kinzer, "Bosnian Serbs Pressed to Flee Area near Sarajevo," *New York Times*, February 21, 1996.

167. Holbrooke, *To End a War,* 336. To critics of the Dayton accords, the violence signaled that Bosnia never would become a functioning multiethnic state. See Gilles Peress and Kit R. Roane, "Savage Spite," *New York Times*, April 28, 1996. See also Roger Cohen, "After the Vultures: Holbrooke's Bosnia Peace Came Too Late," *Foreign Affairs* 77, no. 3 (May–June 1998): 109.

168. Holbrooke, "Foreword," xiii.

169. Michael Goldfarb, "Analysis: 15 Years since Bosnia Tired of War," *GlobalPost*, November 1, 2010, accessed January 14, 2012, www.globalpost .com/dispatch/worldview/101101/dayton-accord-lessons.

170. See Holbrooke, *To End a War,* 160. In mid-September 1995, Holbrooke said he encouraged Tuđman to press the Croat military offensive "as far as you can, but not to take Banja Luka." The city, Holbrooke wrote, "was unquestionably within the Serb portion of Bosnia." See also Rohde, *Endgame,* 340.

171. Bildt, *Peace Journey,* 155.

172. Bosnia, after all, was the most pressing and insistent foreign policy issue of Clinton's first years in office. See Chollet, *The Road to the Dayton Accords,* 201.

173. For example, Madeleine Albright, the U.S. ambassador to the United Nations at the time of the Dayton peace talks, wrote that the accords "showed that the limited use of force—even airpower alone—could make a decisive difference." Albright with Bill Woodward, *Madam Secretary: A Memoir* (New York: Miramax, 2003), 192.

174. Kerrick, interview with author. Clinton biographer John F. Harris observed that the president "emerged from the fall of 1995 as a vastly more self-confident and commanding leader." Harris, *The Survivor: Bill Clinton in the White House* (New York: Random House, 2005), 221.

175. "Dayton's greatest impact . . . was felt beyond the Balkans," Sestanovich noted in *Maximalist*: "The United States was reinvigorated as a global force" (262).

176. Knaus makes this point in "The Rise and Fall of Liberal Imperialism." He wrote that "the experience of Bosnia was to frame the debate on every [U.S.] intervention that followed" (127).

177. Sale, *Clinton's Secret Wars,* 429.

178. The weapons inspectors left Iraq shortly before the aerial attacks began.

179. See William M. Arkin, "Desert Fox Delivery: Precision Undermined Its Purpose," *Washington Post,* January 17, 1999.

180. See "Iraq Liberation Act of 1998," U.S. Government Printing Office, October 31, 1998, accessed August 19, 2013, http://www.gpo.gov/fdsys/pkg /PLAW-105publ338/html/PLAW-105publ338.htm.

181. In Kosovo, Sestanovich observed, "The United States had done exactly what it wanted, launching a military campaign against another member of the United Nations without the support of the Security Council. It then won a multilateral seal of approval when the fighting stopped. This was a stupendous result." Sestanovich, *Maximalist,* 269.

182. Beinart, *The Icarus Syndrome,* 288.

183. Ibid. See also Jacob Heilbrunn, "Man of the World," *New York Times Book Review,* January 1, 2012, 14. Heilbrunn observed that "the efficacy of air power in the Balkans led inexorably to the delusive belief that it would be a simple matter to wage war in Iraq."

184. Derek Chollet and James Goldgeier, *America between the Wars: From 11/9 to 9/11* (reprint, New York: Public Affairs, 2009), 321.

185. Beinart, *The Icarus Syndrome,* 288. This is not to say Clinton and Bush were eager to commit the U.S. military to conflicts abroad. As Fouad Ajami noted: "The leaders of the past two decades who sent American forces to Bosnia, to Kosovo, to Afghanistan, to Iraq, were not thirsting for foreign wars. These leaders located America, and its interests, in the world." Ajami, "Obama Is Lost in the Mideast Bazaar," *Wall Street Journal,* September 13, 2013.

186. Beinart, *The Icarus Syndrome,* 320.

187. Quoted in Peter Baker, *Days of Fire: Bush and Cheney in the White House* (New York: Doubleday, 2013), 191. Similarly, Henry Kissinger said he supported the U.S.-led war in Iraq because "Afghanistan wasn't enough." Quoted in Bob Woodward, *State of Denial: Bush at War, Part III* (New York: Simon and Schuster, 2006), 408.

188. See, for example, Oliver Stone and Peter Kuznick, "Oliver Stone: The Myth of American Exceptionalism," *USA Today,* October 25, 2013, accessed October 28, 2013, www.usatoday.com/story/opinion/2013/10/25/obama-putin-american-exceptionalism-column/3181829/.

189. In 2009, President Barack Obama signaled keen discomfort with the notion of American exceptionality, saying on his first trip to Europe as president: "I believe in American Exceptionalism, just as I suspect that the Brits believe in British Exceptionalism and the Greeks believe in Greek Exceptionalism." See "News Conference by President Obama," States News Service, April 4, 2009, retrieved from LexisNexis database.

190. Holbrooke, *To End a War,* 337.

191. For a discussion about Holbrooke's marginalization in the Obama administration, see Mark Leibovich, *This Town: Two Parties and a Funeral—Plus Plenty of Valet Parking!—in America's Gilded Capital* (New York: Blue Rider, 2013), 226–31.

192. See Robert D. McFadden, "Strong Voice in Diplomacy and Crisis," *New York Times,* December 14, 2010.

193. See, for example, Richard Holbrooke, "Lessons from Dayton for Iraq," *Washington Post,* April 23, 2008.

194. Holbrooke, "Lessons from Dayton for Iraq."

195. See Pietz, "Overcoming the Failings of Dayton," 157.

196. The Islamist volunteers gained a reputation for viciousness during the Bosnian war. They were accused of beheading Serb civilians and blowing up

homes with inhabitants trapped inside. See Scott Taylor, "Bin Laden's Balkan Connections," *Ottawa Citizen*, December 15, 2001.

5. CLINTON MEETS LEWINSKY

1. "William J. Clinton: The President's News Conference," The American Presidency Project, April 18, 1995, accessed October 21, 2013, www .presidency.ucsb.edu/ws/?pid=51237#axzz2iOgL87u3. John F. Harris, a biographer of Clinton, wrote that the president's team "cringed as the words [about his relevance] escaped his lips. Plaintively arguing for relevance was hardly the best way to establish it." Harris, *The Survivor: Bill Clinton in the White House* (New York: Random House, 2005), 178.

2. See "Relevance Is Not Enough, Mr. Clinton," *New York Times*, April 20, 1995. The *Times* noted that two of the three commercial television networks declined to broadcast the news conference live—decisions, it said, that "spoke volumes about [Clinton's] problems as the White House scrambles for a rallying cry." CBS, which did broadcast the news conference, scored a 6.5 rating in that time slot—less than half the ratings scored by programming on the other networks. NBC had a 14.7 rating for its *Frasier* program, and ABC scored a 15.8 rating for its *Home Improvement* show. Ratings cited in John F. Harris, "The Snooze Conference; Networks, Viewers Not Tuned In to Clinton," *Washington Post*, April 20, 1995.

3. Quoted in Terence Hunt, "Clinton's Role: Voice of the Nation's Grief and Anger," Associated Press, April 21, 1995, retrieved from LexisNexis database.

4. Quoted in Howard Kurtz and Dan Balz, "Clinton Assails Spread of Hate Through Media," *Washington Post*, April 25, 1995.

5. Quoted in Todd S. Purdum, "Shifting Debate to the Political Climate, Clinton Condemns 'Promoters of Paranoia,'" *New York Times*, April 25, 1995.

6. Quoted in Jo Mannies, "Ex-Senator 'Zings' Washington Scene," *St. Louis Post-Dispatch*, November 11, 1995.

7. Quoted in Michael Dobbs, "Bosnia Crystallizes U.S. Post-Cold War Role," *Washington Post*, December 3, 1995.

8. See Andrew Rosenthal, "Seeking to Avoid Carter Comparisons, President Refines Comments," *New York Times*, September 26, 1995. In seeking the next day to clarify his "funk" observations, Clinton said: "Malaise is a state of mind. Funk is something you can bounce out of."

9. Todd S. Purdum, "Clinton Angers Friend and Foe in Tax Remark," *New York Times*, October 19, 1995. Purdum's article quoted Clinton as saying at the fund-raising dinner: "Probably there are people in this room still mad at me at that budget because you think I raised your taxes too much. It might surprise you to know that I think I raised them too much, too." The remarks stunned Democratic lawmakers, and Clinton later sought to retreat from them by saying: "My mother once said I should never give a talk after 7 p.m. at night, especially if I'm tired, and she sure turned out to be right is all I can say." Quoted in Terence Hunt, "Clinton Retreats on Tax Comment, Raises Questions on Budget Plan," Associated Press, October 19, 1995, retrieved from LexisNexis database.

10. Jim Hoagland, "Standing up to China," *Washington Post*, July 13, 1995.

11. Helen Thomas, "Commentary," United Press International, November 8, 1995, retrieved from LexisNexis database.

12. E. J. Dionne Jr., ". . . And Clinton's Blunder," *Washington Post*, October 24, 1995.

13. See, for example, Doug Bandow, "Let's Have a Train Wreck!" *Washington Post*, November 15, 1995. "Instead of fearing a budget train wreck," Bandow wrote, "people should welcome it. It is time to ask the sort of questions rarely considered in Washington: Do we wish to remain a free society? Uncle Sam is too expansive and expensive. Yet over the years would-be revolutionaries in the nation's capital have found out how hard it is to kill even the smallest program, like federal tea-tasting. So shut down Washington. Then people will realize that they don't need the Department of Agriculture to eat food, the Environmental Protection Agency to drink water, the Department of Transportation to drive cars and the FDA to buy pharmaceuticals."

14. Mike McCurry, interview with author (September 1, 2013).

15. David Montgomery and Stephen Barr, "Watching, Waiting—and Worrying; Federal Workers Adrift in Uncertainty over What Happens Next," *Washington Post*, November 14, 1995.

16. See Clinton T. Brass, "Shutdown of the Federal Government: Causes, Processes, and Effects," Congressional Research Service, February 18, 2011, 7.

17. Ibid., 8.

18. David Montgomery, "The Ripple Effect: Empty Halls, Lost Money, Discontent," *Washington Post*, November 15, 1995. See also David Zimmerman, "Intimate, Exquisite View of Vermeer," *USA Today*, November 15, 1995.

19. See Steve Komarow, "Shutdown's Full Effect Has Not Been Felt Yet," *USA Today*, November 20, 1995.

20. Susan Levine, "Only Washington Would Try to Close the Grand Canyon; National Parks Are Turning Away Thousands," *Washington Post*, November 17, 1995.

21. See David Johnston, "U.S. Rejects Use of Guard Troops to Run Grand Canyon Park," *New York Times*, November 18, 1995.

22. "White House Was Ready to Federalize National Guard," *Salt Lake Tribune* (Utah), February 11, 1996, accessed September 14, 2013, http://tinyurl.com/q97ahjx.

23. Kenneth B. Noble, "Canyon Becomes Peaceful, Pleasing Nobody," *New York Times*, November 19, 1995. The *Times* report noted: "Normally, about 8,000 people a day visit [the] national treasure, and there is hardly an inch not flanked by a crush of gawking visitors." Symington reached agreement with the Interior Department to keep portions of the Grand Canyon open during the second government shutdown in 1995. See Jeremy Duda, "Arizona's Gov. Brewer Won't Keep Grand Canyon Open During Shutdown," *Arizona Capitol Times*, April 8, 2011, retrieved from LexisNexis database.

24. Quoted in John E. Yang, "Underlying Gingrich's Stance Is His Pique about President," *Washington Post*, November 16, 1995.

25. The cable news network CNN rated Gingrich's remarks the top political blunder of 1995. See William Schneider, "Gingrich Tops List of 1995's Top

Political Blunders," CNN *Inside Politics*, January 1, 1996, retrieved from Lex-isNexis database.

26. See Jeffrey Toobin, *A Vast Conspiracy: The Real Story of the Sex Scandal That Nearly Brought Down a President* (New York: Random House, 1999), 82. The Gingrich blunder, Toobin wrote, suddenly offered Clinton "a clear path to one of the most extraordinary political rebirths in American history." See also Alison Mitchell, "The Fall of Gingrich, an Irony in an Odd Year," *New York Times*, November 7, 1998. Mitchell wrote that Gingrich's gamble on the government shutdown in 1995 "assured Clinton's own reelection."

27. McCurry, interview with author. McCurry described Clinton "as emotionally drained as I ever saw him as president, during the trip" to attend Rabin's funeral. McCurry said "the emotional relationship that Clinton had with Rabin . . . was really important. . . . Here's a guy who was a heroic leader with enormous courage who paid a price of his own life for what he was trying to do to bring peace. That was a pretty compelling model to Clinton."

28. Quoted in Todd S. Purdum, "A Washington Potboiler Steals Budget's Thunder," *New York Times*, November 17, 1995.

29. See ibid.

30. Mary McGrory, a columnist for the *Washington Post*, wrote that, in his ill-considered remarks, "Gingrich went from being Julius Caesar to being a crybaby in one day." McGrory, "With Enemies Like These," *Washington Post*, January 7, 1996.

31. See Todd S. Purdum, "President and G.O.P. Agree to End Federal Shutdown and to Negotiate a Budget," *New York Times*, November 20, 1995. "What the President described as flexibility, the Republicans described as an irretrievable pledge" to balance the federal budget in seven years, Purdum wrote.

32. Quoted in ibid.

33. See Elizabeth Drew, *Showdown: The Struggle between the Gingrich Congress and the Clinton White House* (New York: Simon and Schuster, 1996), 376–77.

34. See Michael Wines, "Congress Votes to Return 760,000 to Federal Payroll and Resume Some Services," *New York Times*, January 6, 1996. Wines wrote: "Strong in numbers and steeped in their principles, Republicans in the House nevertheless looked as though they had seriously overreached after three full weeks of using a crippled Government to pressure Mr. Clinton into a budget deal. . . . And Mr. Clinton's stubborn refusal to cut a deal, seen all last year as evidence of political weakness, suddenly began to look like courage in the face of an enemy siege."

35. Richard Morin, "Public Sides with Clinton in Fiscal Fight," *Washington Post*, November 21, 1995.

36. Even the laudatory article in *Time* magazine noted that Gingrich's "venture is in a stormy mid-passage now. It may ultimately be forced back, or even sunk." See "Man of the Year: How One Man Changed the Way Washington Sees Reality," *Time*, December 25, 1995, 48.

37. See Susan Page and Bill Nichols, "Interns Help Pick up Slack at White House," *USA Today*, November 17, 1995.

38. Toobin, *A Vast Conspiracy*, 84. Jake Tapper, a television news reporter in Washington, once had a date with Lewinsky and offered a more charitable assessment of her, writing: "Monica was/is like a lot of young women inside the Beltway, only more so: young, ambitious, and . . . searching for that one friendly face in the crowd who will think she's worth talking to. A guy, a boss, a boyfriend, a mentor, a friend. For Monica, that person turned out to be Bill Clinton. Clinton apparently saw in her either a consummately gullible kid, or maybe, just maybe, he was taken by . . . an absence of jade, a willingness to look around the next corner, a sweetness that is rare in a city built on bitter and sour and salty." Tapper, "I Dated Monica Lewinsky," *Washington City Paper*, January 30, 1998, accessed October 21, 2013, www.washingtoncitypaper.com /articles/14334/i-dated-monica-lewinsky.

39. See *The Starr Report: The Official Report of the Independent Counsel's Investigation of the President* (Rocklin, Calif.: Forum, 1998), 78. See also Jeff Leen, "Lewinsky: Two Coasts, Two Lives, Many Images," *Washington Post*, January 24, 1998.

40. Lewinsky's biographer, Andrew Morton, wrote: "She was delighted to learn that she would have her own desk and computer . . . and that, because she had written an excellent essay [in applying for the internship], her duties were to be much more than simply answering the phone and copying documents; she would also from time to time deliver sorted mail to the West Wing" of the White House. See Morton, *Monica's Story* (New York: St. Martin's Press, 1999), 55.

41. Quoted in ibid., 58.

42. See Al Kamen, "Upstaged and Upset," *Washington Post*, August 11, 1995.

43. Morton, *Monica's Story*, 58.

44. Ibid., 59. The day after the party on the South Lawn, Lewinsky expected the Secret Service "to call her discreetly with the news that the President wanted to see her," Morton wrote, adding: "Every time the phone rang her nerves jangled." No call came from Clinton's intermediaries.

45. McCurry, interview with author.

46. *The Starr Report*, 79.

47. As the *New York Times* later reported, Clinton that day signed a proclamation designating "National Family Week, 1995." See Robert D. McFadden, John Kifner, and N.R. Kleinfield, "10 Days in the White House: Public Acts, Private Moments," *New York Times*, September 14, 1998. The proclamation encouraged "educators, community organizers, and religious leaders to celebrate the moral and spiritual strength to be drawn from family relationships." See "Proclamation 6852—National Family Week, 1995," U.S. Government Printing Office, November 15, 1995, accessed October 3, 2013, www.gpo.gov /fdsys/pkg/WCPD-1995-11-20/html/WCPD-1995-11-20-Pg2028.htm.

48. Quoted in "Final Monica Lewinsky Script," Barbara Walters interview with Monica Lewinsky, March 3, 1999, 9, script retrieved from Mary McGrory papers, Box 74, Manuscript Division, Library of Congress, Washington, D.C.

49. *The Starr Report*, 80.

50. See Monica S. Lewinsky, interview notes of the Office of Independent Counsel, July 30, 1998, 5, contained in "Appendices to the Referral to the

United States House of Representatives," submitted by the Office of the Independent Counsel.

51. Morton, *Monica's Story*, 63. To Lewinsky, showing the president the straps of her thong underwear was but a "small, subtle, flirtatious gesture." Quoted in "Final Monica Lewinsky Script," 9.

52. Jeffrey Toobin wrote that it was no surprise "Lewinsky had chosen the bathroom closest to the president's domain in the West Wing." See Toobin, *A Vast Conspiracy*, 85.

53. See Monica S. Lewinsky, interview notes of the Office of Independent Counsel, July 28, 1998, 2, contained in "Appendices to the Referral to the United States House of Representatives," submitted by the Office of the Independent Counsel.

54. Quoted in "Final Monica Lewinsky Script," 10. See also *The Starr Report*, 80.

55. Quoted in "Final Monica Lewinsky Script," 10.

56. Quoted in *The Starr Report*, 80–81.

57. Morton, *Monica's Story*, 64. Morton quoted Lewinsky as thinking to herself: "Oh my goodness, he's so gorgeous—and I can't believe I am here, standing here alone with the President of the United States."

58. Ibid., 64.

59. See Lewinsky, interview notes of the Office of Independent Counsel, July 30, 1998, 5.

60. Toobin, *A Vast Conspiracy*, 86. Harris noted in his biography about Clinton that "many people had assumed that there was little opportunity to carry on an adulterous affair in the confines of a modern White House, with all the staff and scrutiny that follow a president." See Harris, *The Survivor*, 224.

61. See Lewinsky, interview notes of the Office of Independent Counsel, July 30, 1998, 6. Lewinsky said she believed the caller was a congressman or a senator. In a televised interview with Barbara Walters in 1999, Lewinsky said she had told herself that she and Clinton "didn't have a sexual relationship because we didn't have intercourse." She also described oral sex as "messing around" and "fooling around." Quoted in "Final Monica Lewinsky Script," 20.

62. Quoted in *The Starr Report*, 81.

63. See Sandra Sugawara, "Clinton Cancellation Stuns Osaka Summit," *Washington Post*, November 17, 1995. See also McFadden, Kifner, and Kleinfield, "10 Days in the White House."

64. Bill Clinton, *My Life* (New York: Knopf, 2004), 811. In promoting the memoir, Clinton said on the CBS News program *60 Minutes* that he entered into the affair with Lewinsky "for the worst possible reason, just because I could." See "Former President Bill Clinton Discusses His Life in and out of the White House," *60 Minutes* (CBS News), June 20, 2004, transcript retrieved from LexisNexis database.

65. Lewinsky said her trysts with Clinton were marked by excitement "and maybe a little bit of danger," given the non-negligible prospect of being caught. Quoted in "Final Monica Lewinsky Script," 12.

66. *The Starr Report*, 79. Toiv became deputy White House press secretary in 1996. McCurry recalled that after the Clinton-Lewinsky scandal broke in

1998, Toiv sometimes was teased by White House staffers who told him, "Hey, you could've stopped it, then and there." McCurry, interview with author.

67. Quoted in Morton, *Monica's Story*, 65.

68. See Lewinsky, interview notes of the Office of Independent Counsel, July 30, 1998, 6.

69. Quoted in Morton, *Monica's Story*, 66.

70. *The Starr Report*, 83.

71. See Lewinsky, interview notes of the Office of Independent Counsel, July 30, 1998, 7.

72. Quoted in "Final Monica Lewinsky Script," 14.

73. Quoted in Morton, *Monica's Story*, 66.

74. Quoted in *The Starr Report*, 84.

75. Ibid., 84.

76. Lewinsky, interview notes of the Office of Independent Counsel, July 30, 1998, 7.

77. Ibid., 8.

78. Ibid.

79. Quoted in *The Starr Report*, 86.

80. Ibid., 86.

81. Morton, *Monica's Story*, 69.

82. Lewinsky, interview notes of the Office of Independent Counsel, July 30, 1998, 8.

83. See McFadden, Kifner, and Kleinfield, "10 Days in the White House."

84. Lewinsky, interview notes of the Office of Independent Counsel, July 30, 1998, 14.

85. Quoted in Monica S. Lewinsky grand jury testimony, U.S. District Court for the District of Columbia, August 6, 1998, 35, contained in "Appendices to the Referral to the United States House of Representatives," submitted by the Office of the Independent Counsel.

86. See "Deposition of Monica S. Lewinsky," Office of the Independent Counsel, Washington, D.C., August 26, 1998, 42, contained in "Appendices to the Referral to the United States House of Representatives," submitted by the Office of the Independent Counsel.

87. Quoted in Lewinsky grand jury testimony, 17. On another occasion, Lewinsky said Clinton had told her that she "had a lot of energy" and "lit up the room" when she entered. See "Final Monica Lewinsky Script," 15. Clinton in his memoir had little to say about Lewinsky's character beyond describing her as "an intelligent, interesting person." Clinton, *My Life*, 774.

88. Toobin wrote, ungenerously, that the "conversation with Lewinsky may have been the thing that cured the president of his infatuation, because the next time he summoned Lewinsky, two weeks later, it was to break off their relationship." Toobin, *A Vast Conspiracy*, 91. The break was not definitive, however.

89. McCurry recalled that Lewinsky was always "trying to ingratiate herself with the West Wing crowd. Little did she know she was going to hit the jackpot." McCurry, interview with author.

90. McCurry said Lieberman's "radar was always up and it was not for any other reason than she was very big on decorum. . . . She'd say to me, 'McCurry,

your shirt, your shirt. It needs to be—go get another shirt.' She had a kind of yenta quality to her." McCurry, interview with author.

91. Quoted in *The Starr Report*, 97. See also Richard A. Posner, *An Affair of State: The Investigation, Impeachment, and Trial of President Clinton* (Cambridge, Mass.: Harvard University Press, 2000), 18. Posner wrote: "The Secret Service agents who [guarded] the President were pretty certain that he was sexually involved with Lewinsky."

92. See *The Starr Report*, 97.

93. Quoted in Monica S. Lewinsky, interview notes of the Office of Independent Counsel, July 31, 1998, 6, contained in "Appendices to the Referral to the United States House of Representatives," submitted by the Office of the Independent Counsel. Leon Panetta, the White House chief of staff, recalled that "there was no finer first sergeant in the White House than Evelyn Lieberman," who, he said, was responsible "for telling staff members or interns or whoever if they were in the wrong place at the wrong time, if they weren't in the proper dress. She would discipline them. She would discipline members of the press as well if they were in the wrong place" at the White House. See "Whether Monica Lewinsky Could Have Spent Time with the President and the Issue of Impeachment," *Hardball with Chris Matthews* (CNBC), July 22, 1998, transcript retrieved from LexisNexis database.

94. *The Starr Report*, 68.

95. See ibid., 106–7.

96. Ibid., 99–100. According to biographer John Harris, Clinton inquired about who was responsible for moving Lewinsky out of the White House. Lieberman said she was. Clinton retreated, Harris wrote, "knowing the conversation was over. 'Oh, okay,' he said sheepishly." Harris, *The Survivor*, 227.

97. See "Immunity . . . Unsupported by Precedent," *Washington Post*, May 28, 1997.

98. Judge Wright's presence at the deposition was unusual, as Jeffrey Toobin noted in his book about the Clinton-Lewinsky scandal. She presided at the request of Clinton's lawyer, Bob Bennett, who argued that Wright's presence was essential to ensure the office of the presidency was protected from excessively intrusive questions during the deposition. See Toobin, *A Vast Conspiracy*, 212–13.

99. See Posner, *An Affair of State*, 24.

100. See *The Starr Report*, 38. The report said that Clinton "also stated that he had no specific memory of being alone with Ms. Lewinsky, that he remembered few details of any gifts they might have exchanged."

101. Lewinsky was suspected of obstructing justice in the Paula Jones case by submitting an affidavit denying a sexual relationship with Clinton. She was also suspected of suborning perjury by encouraging Linda Tripp to lie under oath if deposed in the Jones case. Starr's report to Congress in 1998 about the Clinton-Lewinsky scandal noted that Lewinsky "had spoken to the President and the President's close friend Vernon Jordan about being subpoenaed to testify in the Jones suit, and that Vernon Jordan and others were helping her find a job. The allegations with respect to Mr. Jordan and the job search were similar to ones already under review in the ongoing Whitewater investigation."

That is, Jordan had arranged lucrative consulting contracts for Webster L. Hubbell, a friend of the Clintons and a former associate U.S. attorney general, after Hubbell's conviction of fraud and tax evasion in the Whitewater scandal. He spent eighteen months in prison. Starr suspected that Hubbell was withholding important information about the Clintons' dealings in the Whitewater scandal and that the consulting contracts were to help ensure his silence. To Starr's investigators, Jordan's role in the Hubbell case and Lewinsky scandal seemed to fit with what they believed was a pattern by the Clinton White House of obstructing justice. See Posner, *An Affair of State,* 26. See also Don Van Natta, Jr. and Francis X. Clines, "Starr to Confront President 4 Years after Start of Inquiry," *New York Times,* August 17, 1998.

102. See "From 'Zippergate' to Crisis, TV Filled with Clinton Coverage," Associated Press, January 23, 1998, retrieved from LexisNexis database. The Associated Press report noted that the Habana Libre hotel, "once packed with journalists for the pope's visit to the Communist nation, was suddenly quiet."

103. "Only NBC, with its profitable Thursday night line-up of 'Seinfeld' and 'ER,' chose not to interrupt normal programming," Ethan Bronner noted in the *New York Times*. Bronner, "Reports of Sexual Scandal Have Everybody Talking," *New York Times,* January 23, 1998.

104. Quoted in ibid. Matt Drudge reported at his online site that senior editors of *Newsweek* magazine decided against publishing a report about Clinton's assignation with Lewinsky, saying it required additional research.

105. Clinton, *My Life,* 775. Clinton also wrote: "I knew I had made a terrible mistake [in entering into a relationship with Lewinsky], and I was determined not to compound it by allowing Starr to drive me from office" (775).

106. John Harris wrote: "The nervous gossip that swirled around the West Wing [of the White House] in 1996 about the president and Lewinsky was not an anomaly. An abundance of other rumors echoed." Harris, *The Survivor,* 227.

107. Quoted in "How the Web Was Won," *Vanity Fair* (July 2008), accessed September 21, 2013, www.vanityfair.com/culture/features/2008/07/internet200807.

108. See, for example, Ruth Marcus, "Allegations against Clinton Could Lead to Impeachment, Prosecution," *Washington Post,* January 22, 1998.

109. "Weekly Roundtable," *ABC This Week* (ABC News), January 25, 1998, retrieved from LexisNexis database.

110. Ibid.

111. Quoted in John F. Harris and Dan Balz, "Clinton More Forcefully Denies Having Had Affair or Urging Lies," *Washington Post,* January 27, 1998. Harris and Balz noted: "Some people listening to Clinton's statement, carried live on television networks, heard a note of contempt in his voice as he referred to 'that woman.' There was a moment's pause before he uttered the words 'Miss Lewinsky.'"

112. Quoted in *The Starr Report,* 202. Blumenthal so testified to the federal grand jury investigating the Clinton-Lewinsky matter.

113. Quoted in *The Starr Report,* 202.

114. See, for example, "How Clinton Fared in Polls During a Tumultuous Year," Associated Press, February 11, 1999, retrieved from LexisNexis database.

That the American public demonstrated sustained opposition to Clinton's impeachment or resignation was "quite remarkable," political scientist Arthur H. Miller wrote, given "the barrage of negative press and Republican charges against the president. . . . Critics of public opinion research often argue that public opinion is volatile and that attitudes are frequently uninformed and, hence, easily changeable. Public reaction to the Lewinsky matter not only proved these critics wrong, but also demonstrated the impotence of the mass media." Miller, "Sex, Politics, and Public Opinion: What Political Scientists Really Learned from the Clinton-Lewinsky Scandal," *PS: Political Science and Politics* 32, no. 4 (December 1999): 728.

115. Starr's investigation may have been plodding, but it was painstaking. His lawyers brought scores of witnesses before a federal grand jury investigating the Clinton-Lewinsky scandal. See Van Atta and Clines, "Starr to Confront President."

116. See Don Van Atta, Jr., "White House's All-Out Attack on Starr Is Paying Off, with His Help," *New York Times*, March 2, 1998. Van Atta noted that the strategy of attacking Starr "has squelched previous speculation of Mr. Clinton's resignation or impeachment." He further reported that "Mr. Clinton's partisans say they are amazed by the ease with which they have made Mr. Starr's tactics, and not the President's relationship with Ms. Lewinsky, the most scrutinized topic."

117. See *The Starr Report*, 334–39.

118. Clinton biographer David Maraniss wrote of Clinton's four-and-a half-minute speech: "As I listened to the president that night, the thought struck me that this uneasy little address, born of necessity, shaped for survival, delivered with stubborn persistence, argumentative to the last, brushing off history, clinging to hope, ringing with the urge to start over and move forward, hated by the elite, grudgingly accepted by the public, somehow reverberated with all the qualities of Bill Clinton's melodramatic political life." Maraniss, *The Clinton Enigma: A Four-and-a-Half Minute Speech Reveals This President's Entire Life* (New York: Simon and Schuster, 1998), 29.

119. As Clinton bitterly noted: "In Starr's report, the word 'sex' appeared more than five hundred times; Whitewater was mentioned twice." Clinton, *My Life*, 809.

120. See John M. Broder and Don Van Atta, Jr., "Starr Finds a Case for Impeachment in Perjury, Obstruction, Tampering," *New York Times*, September 12, 1998.

121. Andrew Johnson, the seventeenth U.S. president, was impeached in 1868 and acquitted by one vote at trial in the Senate. Johnson had been elected vice president in 1864 and succeeded to the presidency upon the assassination of Abraham Lincoln in 1865.

122. John F. Harris, "Clinton Vows to Finish out Term," *Washington Post*, December 20, 1998.

123. Neither impeachment count received a majority vote in the Senate. The perjury charge was rejected, 55–45; the vote on the obstruction count was 50–50. In an interview with CBS News in 2004, Clinton referred to the impeachment ordeal as "a badge of honor," saying: "I will always be proud that, when

they moved on impeachment, I didn't quit, I never thought of resigning, and I stood up to it and beat it back. To me, the whole battle was a badge of honor. I don't see it as a great stain, because it was illegitimate." See "Former President Bill Clinton Discusses His Life."

124. See R. W. Apple, "What Next? Don't Guess," *New York Times*, December 20, 1998.

125. Dan Balz, chief correspondent of the *Washington Post*, observed in 2013: "Today, there is almost no overlap between the voting behavior of the most conservative Democrats in the House and the most liberal Republicans. That's in part because there are few moderate-to-conservative Democrats and moderate-to-liberal Republicans left in the chamber." Balz, "Shutdown's Roots Lie in Deeply Embedded Divisions in American Politics," *Washington Post*, October 6, 2013.

126. See Dan Balz, "States of Polarization: In the New Era of Single-Party Control, Red and Blue Don't Mix," *Washington Post*, December 29, 2013. Balz wrote: "Political polarization has ushered in a new era in state government, where single-party control of the levers of power has produced competing Americas." See also "Lexington: What Does the Fox Say?" *Economist*, January 25, 2014, accessed January 25, 2014, www.economist.com/news/united-states/21595006-cable-news-less-blame-polarised-politics-people-think-what-does-fox-say.

127. See "Lexington: What Does Fox Say?"

128. See "Partisan Polarization Surges in Bush, Obama Years," Pew Research Center for the People & the Press, June 4, 2012, accessed September 29, 2013, www.people-press.org/2012/06/04/partisan-polarization-surges-in-bush-obama-years/.

129. Ibid.

130. Another likely factor explaining the rise of the partisan divide is the passing of Americans who lived through the Great Depression and World War II and who were inclined to swing their support to presidential candidates whose policies seemed most likely to produce prosperity and peace. Thus, Dwight Eisenhower, Lyndon Johnson, Richard Nixon, and Ronald Reagan rolled up landslide elections. Such consensus at the ballot box has been rare since 1984, however. Another prospective factor is fragmentation of popular culture, evident in the rise of pluralistic media choices. The news and entertainment content of the few television and radio networks on the air in the 1950s, 1960s, and 1970s was oriented toward attracting large audiences, making a sense of cultural unity easier to maintain. For a fuller discussion of such factors, see Michael Barone, "Washington Is Partisan—Get Used to It," *Wall Street Journal*, October 18, 2013.

131. See Steven M. Gillon, *The Pact: Bill Clinton, Newt Gingrich, and the Rivalry That Defined a Generation* (New York: Oxford University Press, 2008), 281. Gillon also observed: "Through his indiscretions, Clinton badly damaged his lifelong effort to blur the ideological differences between Democrats and Republicans. A centrist who preached reconciliation and moderation, Clinton left office having aroused the passions of conservatives and liberals" (277).

132. "Excerpts from the Judge's Ruling," *New York Times*, April 13, 1999.

133. Susan Webber Wright, "Memorandum Opinion and Order," Jones v. Clinton, April 12, 1999, accessed February 15, 2014, www.leagle.com/decision /1999115436FSupp2d1118_11007.xml/JONES%20v.%20CLINTON.

134. A disciplinary panel of the Arkansas Supreme Court recommended in May 2000 that Clinton be disbarred for the "serious misconduct" he demonstrated in testifying about Monica Lewinsky in the Paula Jones case. See Don Van Atta, Jr., "Panel Advises That Clinton Be Disbarred," New York Times, May 23, 2000.

135. Neil A. Lewis, "Exiting Job, Clinton Accepts Immunity Deal," New York Times, January 20, 2001.

136. Ray, a career prosecutor and an assistant to Starr, was appointed independent counsel in October 1999, after Starr resigned. In doing so, Starr acknowledged that the "intense politicization" of his tenure was a factor in his stepping down. "To reduce the unfortunate personalization of the process, in particular in the wake of the inherently divisive impeachment proceedings, the wiser course, I believe, is for another individual to head the investigation," Starr wrote. Quoted in Don Van Atta, Jr., "Starr's Successor Sworn In to Oversee Clinton Inquiry," New York Times, October 19, 1999.

137. See Lewis, "Exiting Job, Clinton Accepts Immunity Deal."

138. See "Statements of Clinton and Prosecutor and Excerpts from News Conference," New York Times, January 20, 2001.

139. The Starr Report, 318.

140. See Posner, An Affair of State, 80–81. Posner wrote (54) that it was undeniable Clinton "obstructed justice in violation of federal criminal law" by "perjuring himself repeatedly in his deposition in the Paula Jones case, in his testimony before the grand jury, and in his responses to the questions put to him by the House Judiciary Committee" as it considered the recommendations of the Starr report. Posner also wrote (55) that Clinton might have faced a prison sentence of thirty to thirty-seven months, had he been tried on the crimes arising from the sex-and-lies scandal.

141. See Posner, An Affair of State, 81.

142. Marc Fisher and David Montgomery, "Explicit Details Evoke Jokes and Revulsion; Public Reacts to Details with Anger, Amusement," Washington Post, September 12, 1998. A television beat writer for the Denver Post observed: "Once the outrageous and mind-boggling report was circulated, it was tough to top it with jokes" even by comedians on late-night TV. Joanne Ostrow, "Leno Show Focal Point for Nation," Denver Post, September 14, 1998. Some of their zingers were little short of inspired, though. David Letterman, for example, joked on the CBS Late Show that "Congress has three possibilities to consider. One, (Clinton) could be impeached; two he could be censured; three he could be neutered." Quoted in Lyle V. Harris, "President Sitting Duck, Even if Not a Lame One," Atlanta Journal and Constitution, September 19, 1998.

143. A week after the release of the Starr report, Clinton's approval rating stood at 62 percent. See Richard L. Berke, "Keep Clinton in Office, Most Say in Poll, But His Image Is Eroding," New York Times, September 16, 1998. However, Berke also reported that 66 percent of respondents said they did not share

Clinton's moral values. Even so, more than six in ten respondents said Clinton should complete his term in office.

144. See Marjorie Connelly, "House Faulted for Releasing All of Report," *New York Times*, September 18, 1998. Connelly's report said that two-thirds of respondents to a national public opinion poll the *Times* conducted with CBS News said it was "'inappropriate' for the Starr report to have included graphic sexual details" of Clinton's relationship with Lewinsky. In addition, 59 percent of respondents to the poll said the inclusion of such detail was done to embarrass the president.

145. Among those to have made this point was Clinton biographer David Maraniss. "Clinton's transgressions do not approach the importance of Watergate," Maraniss wrote in a mini-biography built around Clinton's four-and-a-half-minute speech in August 1998 in which he acknowledged an "inappropriate relationship" with Lewinsky. Maraniss, *The Clinton Enigma*, 63. In contrast, syndicated political columnist David Broder of the *Washington Post* described Clinton's behavior as "truly Nixonian. And it is worse in one way. Nixon's actions, however neurotic and criminal, were motivated by and connected to the exercise of presidential power. He knew the place he occupied, and he was determined not to give it up to those he regarded as 'enemies.' Clinton acted—and still, even in his supposed mea culpa, acts—as if he does not recognize what it means to be president of the United States. This office he sought all his life, for what? To hit on an intern about the age of his own daughter, an act for which any business executive or military officer would be fired immediately?" Broder, "Truly Nixonian," *Washington Post*, August 19, 1998.

146. For a detailed account about the unmasking of Nixon's misconduct in Watergate, see Stanley I. Kutler, *The Wars of Watergate: The Last Crisis of Richard Nixon* (New York: Knopf, 1990), 534–38.

147. Abbe David Lowell, chief counsel to Democrats in the House of Representatives during the impeachment of Clinton, told the House Judiciary Committee that it was useful "to be on the lookout for Watergate similarities, because that sad chapter of American history really does describe that which are truly impeachable offenses. . . . The more you look at Watergate, the more you will see just how different these [impeachment] proceedings are." See "Washington Dateline," Associated Press, December 10, 1998, retrieved from Lexis Nexis database.

148. Journalist Michael Isikoff offered in his book, *Uncovering Clinton*, an intriguing theory about Clinton, Nixon, and their differences. "Nixon and Clinton," he wrote, "had one thing in common: They both hated their enemies. But in another respect, they were fundamentally different. Nixon, deep down, suspected his enemies might be right—that they were better than he." Clinton, on the other hand, "believes, deep down, that his enemies are scum." Isikoff, *Uncovering Clinton: A Reporter's Story* (New York: Crown, 1999), 358.

149. See Thomas L. Friedman, "Character Suicide," *New York Times*, January 27, 1998. "I am sure that those who argue that the country cares a lot more about Dow Jones than Paula Jones are right," Friedman wrote.

150. Adam Clymer, "Page by Page, a Chronicle of Misdeeds," *New York Times*, September 8, 1995.

151. "Statement from Senate Ethics Committee," *New York Times,* September 7, 1995.

152. See *The Packwood Report: The Senate Ethics Counsel on Senator Robert Packwood* (New York: Times Books, 1995), 125.

153. See Trip Gabriel, "The Trials of Bob Packwood," *New York Times Magazine,* August 29, 1993, 32–33.

154. "Senator Packwood Resignation," C-SPAN Video Library, September 7, 1995, accessed September 30, 2013, www.c-spanvideo.org/program/67036–1.

155. "Excerpts from Packwood's Statement of Resignation," *New York Times,* September 8, 1995.

156. Kevin Merida, "As Packwood's 27-Year Career Ends, a Tortuous Saga for the Senate Draws to a Close," *Washington Post,* September 8, 1995.

157. Ibid.

158. "Senator Packwood Resignation."

159. See Katharine Q. Seelye, "Packwood Says He Is Quitting as Ethics Panel Gives Evidence," *New York Times,* September 8, 1995.

160. Kim I. Eisler, "Show Me the Money," *Washingtonian* (January 1998): 78.

CONCLUSION

1. Rick Hampson, "1994: Shock and Aftershock," Associated Press, December 30, 1994, retrieved from LexisNexis database.

2. Quoted in "Person of the Week: Cartoonist Gary Larson to Retire," *ABC World News Tonight,* December 16, 1994, transcript retrieved from Lexis Nexis database.

3. Quoted in Frank Ahrens, "So Long, Kid: An Obituary for a Boy, His Tiger and Our Innocence," *Washington Post,* November 19, 1995.

4. David Hinckley, "Shedding '96 Tears for 'Calvin and Hobbes,'" *New York Daily News,* December 26, 1995. Hinckley wrote: "The departure of 'Calvin and Hobbes' pokes a hole in our day and nothing in sight is going to close it soon."

5. Frank Ahrens of the *Washington Post* pointed out in a lengthy farewell to *Calvin and Hobbes* that Watterson was "notoriously cranky" and steadfastly refused to license his cartoon characters, "which is why there are no 'Calvin and Hobbes' greeting cards, no 'Calvin and Hobbes' refrigerator magnets, and most astonishing of all, no Hobbes stuffed tigers." Ahrens, "So Long, Kid."

6. Watterson did not participate in the documentary. See Andrew O'Hehir, "'Dear Mr. Watterson': Remembering the Last Great Newspaper Comic," Salon.com, November 13, 2013, accessed November 13, 2013, www.salon.com/2013/11/13/dear_mr_watterson_remembering_the_last_great_newspaper_comic/.

7. Dan Zak, "Back in 1995," *Washington Post,* October 5, 2013. See also Robert J. Terry, "12 Ways Federal Workers Bided Their Time during the Last Shutdown," *Washington Business Journal,* October 1, 2013, accessed October 2, 2013, www.wtop.com/41/3469776/12-ways-federal-workers-bided-their-time-during-the-last-shutdown.

8. Rupert Cornwell, "America's Power Failure," *Independent* (London), October 2, 2013.

9. See Amy Chozick, "Clinton Scandal of '90s Resurfaces with Papers," *New York Times*, February 11, 2014.

10. Untitled memorandum (September 9, 1998), Diane Blair papers, University of Arkansas, accessed February 9, 2014, http://freebeacon.com/politics/the-hillary-papers/.

11. Monica Lewinsky, "Shame and Survival," *Vanity Fair*, May 2014, 145.

12. Ibid., 124. Lewinsky also wrote that, as the scandal unfolded in 1998, "I sorely wished for some sign of understanding from the feminist camp. Some good, old-fashioned, girl-on-girl support was much in need. None came."

13. As David Remnick observed in the *New Yorker*: "Monica is the woman of secrets who no longer has any. Her eyes are not windows but mirrors, and what we see in them is awful. Yet we go on staring." Remnick, "Comment: Our Woman of Secrets," *New Yorker*, February 8, 1999, accessed February 16, 2014, www.newyorker.com/archive/1999/02/08/1999_02_08_023_TNY_LIBRY_000017472.

14. Lewinsky, "Shame and Survival," 123–24.

15. Quoted in "O.J.'s Game Day," *New York Post*, February 12, 2013.

16. Dominick Dunne, who covered the trial for *Vanity Fair* and deplored Simpson's acquittal, noted that Simpson in court was "beautifully dressed as always." Dunne, *Justice: Crimes, Trials, and Punishments* (New York: Crown, 2001), 186.

17. John M. Glionna, "Faded Star Takes the Stand," *Los Angeles Times*, May 16, 2013.

18. The county judge who presided at the hearing, Linda Marie Bell, said in ruling against Simpson: "Given the overwhelming amount of evidence, neither the errors in this case, nor the errors collectively, cause this court to question the validity of Mr. Simpson's conviction." Quoted in John M. Glionna, "Judge Denies O.J. Simpson a New Trial," *Los Angeles Times*, November 27, 2013.

19. Andrea Peyser, "The Glove Fits—This Head Case Becomes New O.J.," *New York Post*, July 6, 2011.

20. Marcia Clark, "Worse Than O.J.!" *Daily Beast*, July 5, 2011, accessed November 3, 2013, www.thedailybeast.com/articles/2011/07/05/casey-anthony-trial-marcia-clark-says-the-verdict-was-worse-than-the-o-j-simpson-case.html.

21. Alan M. Dershowitz, "Casey Anthony: The System Worked," *Wall Street Journal*, July 7, 2011.

22. See "Top Ten O.J. Simpson Excuses," *Late Show with David Letterman*, September 26, 2013, accessed February 13, 2014, www.cbs.com/shows/late_show/top_ten/138545/.

23. McVeigh's biographers, writing before his execution, stated that "he refuses to consider his actions through any lens but the single-minded one that casts him as a patriot. He clings to the position that his act was needed to right a faltering America." Lou Michel and Dan Herbeck, *American Terrorist: Timothy McVeigh and the Oklahoma City Bombing* (New York: Regan Books, 2001), 382.

24. See Will Englund and Michael Birnbaum, "In Attacks, Norwegians See Echo of Oklahoma City," *Wall Street Journal*, July 24, 2011.

25. See Niclas Rolander, Katarina Gustafsson, and Charles Duxbury, "Trial of Norway Killer Spurs Debate," *Wall Street Journal*, April 21–22, 2012. Breivik confessed to detonating a bomb in the government district in Oslo before taking a ferry to an island nearby, where he opened fire on youths at a summer camp.

26. "Syria's Srebrenica," *Wall Street Journal*, May 29, 2012.

27. Michael Dobbs, "Houla: Shadows of Srebrenica," *Washington Post*, June 3, 2012.

28. See, for example, Philippe Leroux-Martin, "Bosnia's Lessons for Syria," *New York Times*, January 22, 2014, and Richard Cohen, "From Sarajevo to Homs," *Washington Post*, April 2, 2012.

29. Roger Boyes, "Images Emerging from Syria Are a Stark Reminder of Bosnia," *The Australian*, January 23, 2014.

30. Philip Kennicott, a Pulitzer Prize–winning critic for the *Washington Post*, addressed the conundrum of the limited impact of powerful images, noting: "The one consistent fact about the horrifying images that have come out of Syria . . . is that in many cases, we don't know who made them and what they depict. All we see are decontextualized cruelty and misery. Cynicism creeps in, and there is a natural tendency to push the images away as a kind of insoluble puzzle." Kennicott, "Why Syria's Images of Suffering Haven't Moved Us," *Washington Post*, September 15, 2013.

31. Bob Metcalfe, "Predicting the Internet's Catastrophic Collapse and Ghost Sites Galore in 1996," *InfoWorld*, December 4, 1995, 61.

32. Johna Till Johnson, "Is the Internet Doomed to Fail?" *Network World*, April 1, 2009, 15.

33. David A. Kaplan, "Nothing But Net," *Newsweek*, December 25, 1995/January 1, 1996, 32.

34. Chris Anderson, "The Man Who Makes the Future: Wired Icon Marc Andreessen," *Wired*, April 24, 2012, accessed January 25, 2014, www.wired.com/business/2012/04/ff_andreessen/.

35. Marc Andreessen, "Why Software Is Eating the World," *Wall Street Journal*, August 20, 2011, retrieved from ProQuest Central database.

36. See "Disrupting the Disrupters," *Economist*, September 3, 2011, SS27. The observation that "software is eating the world," was, the *Economist* said, "Andreessen-speak, for the phenomenon in which industry after industry, from media to financial services to health care, is being chewed up by the rise of the [I]nternet and the spread of smartphones, tablet computers and other fancy electronic devices."

37. Quoted in Douglas MacMillan, "Andreessen: It's Not a Tech Bubble," *Wall Street Journal*, January 4–5, 2014.

38. See Stu Woo, Lynn Cowan, and Pui-Wing Tam, "LinkedIn IPO Surges, Feeding Web Boom," *Wall Street Journal*, May 20, 2011.

39. See, for example, James Temple, "Free Advice for the Newly Rich (on Paper)," *San Francisco Chronicle*, May 22, 2011, accessed July 1, 2013, www.sfgate.com/business/article/Free-advice-for-the-newly-rich-on-paper-2370336.php.

40. For a discussion about the Netscape-Mozilla-Firefox connection, see Tom Abate, "Firefox Rises from Ashes of Abandoned Netscape," *San Francisco*

Chronicle, January 28, 2008, accessed February 15, 2014, www.sfgate.com/technology/article/Firefox-rises-from-ashes-of-abandoned-Netscape-3229083.php.

41. See ibid.

42. See "StatCounter Global Stats: Top 5 Desktop, Tablet and Console Browsers from Jan 2013 to Jan 2014," StatCounter, accessed February 16, 2014, http://gs.statcounter.com/. The Firefox share in January 2014 was almost 19 percent.

43. John Tosh, *The Pursuit of History*, 5th ed. (New York: Routledge, 2013), 52. Tosh further noted: "Academic neglect of contemporary history . . . has dangerous consequences" (52).

44. See, for example, Charles Krauthammer, "Bill Clinton Is Fighting to Have Some Historical Relevance," *Washington Post*, February 2, 2008.

45. Charles Krauthammer, "Clinton Writ Small," *Washington Post*, June 25, 2004.

46. See, for example, Stephen Sestanovich, *Maximalist: America in the World from Truman to Obama* (New York: Knopf, 2014), 265–66. See also Steve Ricchetti, "Don't Put the Blame on Clinton," *Washington Post*, February 22, 2003.

47. See Haynes Johnson, *The Best of Times: America in the Clinton Years* (New York: Harcourt, 2001).

48. That essentially was the thesis of Francis Fukuyama, author of *The End of History and the Last Man* (New York: Free Press, 1992). Fukuyama wrote that "liberal democracy remains the only coherent political aspiration that spans different regions and cultures around the globe" (xiii).

Select Bibliography

Albright, Madeleine, with Bill Woodward. *Madam Secretary: A Memoir*. New York: Miramax, 2003.

Arenella, Peter. "The Perils of TV Legal Punditry." *University of Chicago Legal Forum* 25 (1998): 25–52.

Aronson, Jay D. *Genetic Witness: Science, Law, and Controversy in the Making of DNA Profiling*. New Brunswick, N.J.: Rutgers University Press, 2007.

Auletta, Ken. *World War 3.0: Microsoft and Its Enemies*. New York: Random House, 2001.

Baker, Peter. *Days of Fire: Bush and Cheney in the White House*. New York: Doubleday, 2013.

Bass, Warren. "The Triage of Dayton." *Foreign Affairs* 77, no. 5 (September–October 1998): 95–108.

Beinart, Peter. *The Icarus Syndrome: A History of American Hubris*. New York: Harper, 2010.

Berners-Lee, Tim. *Weaving the Web: The Original Design and Ultimate Destiny of the World Wide Web*. New York: HarperSanFrancisco, 1999.

Best, Joel. *Damned Lies and Statistics: Untangling Numbers from the Media, Politicians, and Activists*. Berkeley: University of California Press, 2001.

Bildt, Carl. *Peace Journey: The Struggle for Peace in Bosnia*. London: Weidenfeld and Nicolson, 1998.

Bonia, Adam, Nolan McCarty, Keith T. Poole, and Howard Rosenthal. "Why Hasn't Democracy Slowed Rising Inequality?" *Journal of Economic Perspectives* 27, no. 3 (Summer 2013): 103–24.

Boss, Alan P. "Proximity of Jupiter-Like Planets to Low-Mass Stars." *Science* 267 (January 20, 1995): 360–62.

Brandt, Richard L. *One Click: Jeff Bezos and the Rise of Amazon.com*. New York: Portfolio/Penguin, 2011.

Bugliosi, Vincent. *Outrage: The Five Reasons Why O.J. Simpson Got Away with Murder.* New York: W. W. Norton.

Cannon, Robert. "The Legislative History of Senator Exon's Communications Decency Act: Regulating Barbarians on the Information Superhighway." *Federal Communications Law Journal* 49, no.1 (1996): 51–94.

Cassidy, John. *Dot.con: The Greatest Story Ever Sold.* New York: HarperCollins, 2002.

Charity, Arthur. *Doing Public Journalism.* New York: Guilford Press, 1995.

Chollet, Derek. *The Road to the Dayton Accords: A Study of American Statecraft.* New York: Palgrave Macmillan, 2005.

Chollet, Derek, and Samantha Power, eds. *The Unquiet American: Richard Holbrooke in the World.* New York: Public Affairs, 2011.

Christopher, Warren. *Chances of a Lifetime: A Memoir.* New York: Scribner, 2001.

Clark, Jim, with Owen Edwards. *Netscape Time: The Making of the Billion-Dollar Startup That Took On Microsoft.* New York: St. Martin's Press, 1999.

Clinton, Bill. *My Life.* New York: Knopf, 2004.

Cohen, Adam. *The Perfect Store: Inside eBay.* Boston: Little, Brown, 2002.

Cohen, Roger. "After the Vultures: Holbrooke's Bosnia Peace Came Too Late." *Foreign Affairs* 77, no. 3 (May–June 1998): 106–11.

———. *Hearts Grown Brutal: Sagas of Sarajevo.* New York: Random House, 1998.

Cole, David, and James X. Dempsey. *Terrorism and the Constitution: Sacrificing Civil Liberties in the Name of National Security.* New York: New Press, 2006.

Cox, W. Michael, and Richard Alm. "The Good Old Days Are Now." *Reason* 27, no. 7 (December 1995): 20–27.

Daalder, Ivo H. *Getting to Dayton: The Making of America's Bosnia Policy.* Washington, D.C.: Brookings Institution, 2000.

Darden, Christopher, with Jess Walter. *In Contempt.* New York: Regan Books, 1996.

Dershowitz, Alan M. *Reasonable Doubts: The Criminal Justice System and the O.J. Simpson Case.* New York: Touchstone, 1996.

Dow, David. "What I Learned Covering the Trials of the Century." *Loyola of Los Angeles Law Review* 33, no. 2 (January 2000): 737–42.

Drew, Elizabeth. *Showdown: The Struggle between the Gingrich Congress and the Clinton White House.* New York: Simon and Schuster, 1996.

Dunne, Dominick. *Justice: Crimes, Trials, and Punishments.* New York: Crown, 2001.

Fukuyama, Francis. *The End of History and the Last Man.* New York: Free Press, 1992.

Gates, Bill, with Nathan Myhrvold and Peter Rinearson. *The Road Ahead.* New York: Viking, 1995.

Gillon, Steven M. *The Pact: Bill Clinton, Newt Gingrich, and the Rivalry That Defined a Generation.* New York: Oxford University Press, 2008.

Gumbel, Andrew, and Roger G. Charles. *Oklahoma City: What the Investigation Missed—and Why It Still Matters.* New York: William Morrow, 2012.

Hafner, Katie. *Where Wizards Stay Up Late: The Origins of the Internet.* New York: Simon and Schuster, 1998.

Harris, John F. *The Survivor: Bill Clinton in the White House.* New York: Random House, 2005.

Hockenos, Paul. *Homeland Calling: Exile Patriotism and the Balkan Wars.* Ithaca, N.Y.: Cornell University Press, 2003.

Holbrooke, Richard. *To End a War.* New York: Random House, 1998.

Holland, Barbara. *Endangered Pleasures: In Defense of Naps, Bacon, Martinis, Profanity, and Other Indulgences.* Boston: Little, Brown, 1995.

Isikoff, Michael. *Uncovering Clinton: A Reporter's Story.* New York: Crown, 1999.

Jayawardhana, Ray. *Strange New Worlds: The Search for Alien Planets and Life beyond Our Solar System.* Princeton: Princeton University Press, 2011.

Johnson, Haynes. *The Best of Times: America in the Clinton Years.* New York: Harcourt, 2001.

Jones, Stephen, and Peter Israel. *Others Unknown: The Oklahoma City Bombing Case and Conspiracy.* New York: Public Affairs, 1998.

Kennedy, Weldon L. *On-Scene Commander: From Street Agent to Deputy Director of the FBI.* Washington, D.C.: Potomac Books, 2007.

Kim, Sangmoon. "The Diffusion of the Internet: Trend and Causes." *Social Science Research* 40, no. 2 (2011): 602–13.

Kurlansky, Mark. *1968: The Year That Rocked the World.* New York: Ballantine, 2004.

Kuzma, Lynn M. "Terrorism in the United States." *Public Opinion Quarterly* 64, no. 1 (2000): 90–105.

Lander, Eric S. "DNA Fingerprinting on Trial." *Nature* 339 (June 15, 1989): 501–5.

Lander, Eric S., and Bruce Budowle. "DNA Fingerprinting Dispute Laid to Rest." *Nature* 371 (October 27, 1994): 735–38.

Laughlin, Gregory P. "Extrasolar Planetary Systems." *American Scientist* 94, no. 5 (September–October 2006): 420–29.

Leeson, Nick, with Edward Whitley. *Rogue Trader: How I Brought Down Barings Bank and Shook the Financial World.* Boston: Little, Brown, 1996.

Leibovich, Mark. *This Town: Two Parties and a Funeral—Plus Plenty of Valet Parking!—in America's Gilded Capital.* New York: Blue Rider Press, 2013.

Leuf, Bo, and Ward Cunningham. *The Wiki Way: Quick Collaboration on the Web.* Boston: Addison-Wesley, 2001.

Levenson, Laurie L. "Cases of the Century." *Loyola of Los Angeles Law Review* 33, no. 2 (January 2000): 585–612.

Levy, Steven. *In the Plex: How Google Thinks, Works, and Shapes Our Lives.* New York: Simon and Schuster, 2011.

Lynch, Michael, Simon A. Cole, Ruth McNally, and Kathleen Jordan. *Truth Machine: The Contentious History of DNA Fingerprinting.* Chicago: University of Chicago, 2008.

Lynch, Timothy J., and Robert S. Singh. *After Bush: The Case for Continuity in American Foreign Policy.* Cambridge, Mass.: Cambridge University Press, 2008.

Maraniss, David. *Barack Obama: The Story*. New York: Simon and Schuster, 2012.

———. *The Clinton Enigma: A Four-and-a-Half Minute Speech Reveals This President's Entire Life*. New York: Simon and Schuster, 1998.

Marcus, James. *Amazonia*. New York: New Press, 2004.

Mayor, Michel, and Pierre-Yves Frei. *New Worlds in the Cosmos: The Discovery of Exoplanets*. New York: Cambridge University Press, 2003.

Mayor, Michel, and Didier Queloz, "A Jupiter-Mass Companion to a Solar-Type Star." *Nature* 378 (November 23, 1995): 355–59.

Metcalfe, Bob. *Internet Collapses and Other InfoWorld Punditry*. Foster City, Calif.: IDG Books, 2000.

Michel, Lou, and Dan Herbeck. *American Terrorist: Timothy McVeigh and the Oklahoma City Bombing*. New York: Regan Books, 2001.

Miller, Arthur H. "Sex, Politics, and Public Opinion: What Political Scientists Really Learned from the Clinton-Lewinsky Scandal." *PS: Political Science and Politics* 32, no. 4 (December 1999): 721–29.

Negroponte, Nicholas. *Being Digital*. New York: Knopf, 1995.

Newman, Nathan. *Net Loss: Internet Prophets, Private Profits, and the Costs to Community*. University Park: Pennsylvania State University Press, 2002.

The Packwood Report: The Senate Ethics Counsel on Senator Robert Packwood. New York: Times Books, 1995.

Pietz, Tobias. "Overcoming the Failings of Dayton: Defense Reform in Bosnia-Herzegovina." In *Bosnian Security after Dayton: New Perspectives*, edited by Michael A. Innes, 155–72. London: Routledge, 2006.

Posner, Richard A. *An Affair of State: The Investigation, Impeachment, and Trial of President Clinton*. Cambridge, Mass.: Harvard University Press, 2000.

Potter, Claire Bond, and Renee C. Romano, eds. *Doing Recent History: On Privacy, Copyright, Video Games, Institutional Review Boards, Activist Scholarship, and History That Talks Back*. Athens: University of Georgia Press, 2012.

Powell, Colin L., with Joseph E. Persico. *My American Journey*. New York: Random House, 1995.

Power, Samantha. *"A Problem from Hell": America and the Age of Genocide*. New York: Basic Books, 2002.

Reid, Robert H. *Architects of the Web: 1,000 Days That Built the Future of Business*. New York: Wiley, 1997.

Rohde, David. *Endgame: The Betrayal and Fall of Srebrenica, Europe's Worst Massacre since World War II*. Boulder, Colo.: Westview Press, 1998.

Ross, David F., Stephen J. Ceci, David Dunning, and Michael P. Toglia. "Unconscious Transference and Mistaken Identity: When a Witness Misidentifies a Familiar But Innocent Person." *Journal of Applied Psychology* 79, no. 6 (December 1994): 918–30.

Ross, Shelley. *Fall from Grace: Sex, Scandal, and Corruption in American Politics from 1702 to the Present*. New York: Ballantine, 1988.

Sadler, Kim Martin, ed. *Atonement: The Million Man March*. Cleveland: Pilgrim Press, 1996.

Sale, Richard. *Clinton's Secret Wars: The Evolution of a Commander in Chief.* New York: Thomas Dunne, 2009.

Schiller, Lawrence, and James Willwerth. *American Tragedy: The Uncensored Story of the Simpson Defense.* New York: Random House, 1996.

Schuetz, Janice, and Lin S. Lilley. *The O.J. Simpson Trials: Rhetoric, Media, and the Law.* Carbondale: Southern Illinois University Press, 1999.

Sestanovich, Stephen. *Maximalist: America in the World from Truman to Obama.* New York: Knopf, 2014.

Simpson, O.J. *I Want to Tell You: My Response to Your Letters, Your Messages, Your Questions.* Boston: Little, Brown, 1995.

Spector, Robert. *Amazon.com: Get Big Fast.* New York: HarperBusiness, 2000.

The Starr Report: The Official Report of the Independent Counsel's Investigation of the President. Rocklin, Calif.: Forum, 1998.

Stewart, Rory, and Gerald Knaus, eds. *Can Intervention Work?* New York: Norton, 2011.

Stoll, Clifford. *Silicon Snake Oil: Second Thoughts on the Information Highway.* New York: Doubleday, 1995.

Stone, Brad. *The Everything Store: Jeff Bezos and the Age of Amazon.* New York: Little, Brown, 2013.

Swisher, Kara. *AOL.com: How Steve Case Beat Bill Gates, Nailed the Netheads, and Made Millions in the War for the Web.* New York: Times Business, 1998.

Talarico, Jennifer M., and David C. Rubin. "Confidence, Not Consistency, Characterizes Flashbulb Memories." *Psychological Science* 14, no. 5 (September 2003): 455–61.

Thaler, Paul. *The Spectacle: Media and the Making of the O.J. Simpson Story.* Westport, Conn.: Praeger, 1997.

Thomas, Jo. "The Third Man: A Reporter Investigates the Oklahoma City Bombing." *Syracuse Law Review* 59 (2009): 459–69.

Toobin, Jeffrey. *The Run of His Life: The People v. O.J. Simpson.* New York: Touchstone, 1997.

———. *A Vast Conspiracy: The Real Story of the Sex Scandal That Nearly Brought Down a President.* New York: Random House, 1999.

Tosh, John. *The Pursuit of History,* 5th ed. New York: Routledge, 2013.

Uelmen, Gerald F. *Lessons from the Trial: The People v. O.J. Simpson.* Kansas City, Mo.: Andrews and McMeel, 1996.

Walker, Jesse. *The United States of Paranoia: A Conspiracy Theory.* New York: Harper, 2013.

Index

(2013), 153–54; interventionist ethos of, 124–25; 100 dollar bill, redesigning of, 176; papal visit to, 176, 177; partisan divide in, 146, 243nn125–26, 243n130; psychology of fear in, 55; race relations as perceived in, 88–94, 90 *fig. 15*, 92 *fig. 16*, 217n70; wealth and justice in, 96
United States Bureau of Alcohol, Tobacco, and Firearms, 53
United States Congress, 11, 18, 20; antiterrorism legislation passed in, 75–76; budget impasses in, 131–35, 134 *fig. 19*, 179, 181, 235n13, 236nn31, 34; Clinton impeachment vote in, 145, 242–43n123; flag desecration legislation in, 172; Republican control of, 130, 163; Starr report to, 145, 148, 240–41n101, 242n119; telecommunications bill in, 203n196; term-limit amendment proposed, 167, 170. *See also specific branch*
United States House of Representatives, 130, 134 *fig. 19*, 145, 191n8; Judiciary Committee, 245n147
United States Interior Department, 133, 235n23
United States Justice Department, 174
United States Marine Corps, 64, 171
United States Navy station (Newport, RI), 226n62
United States Postal Service, 170
United States Secret Service, 170, 171
United States Senate, 31, 145, 149–51, 166, 169, 170, 172, 242n123
United States State Department, 80, 181
United States Supreme Court, 32, 142, 146, 170, 174
United States Treasury Department, 73
University of Arkansas, 167
University of Connecticut, 167
University of Illinois at Urbana-Champaign, 34–35, 196nn83, 87
University of Oklahoma, 63
University of Pennsylvania, 74
University of Tennessee, 168
USA Patriot Act (2001), 76
USA Today, 50, 64, 188n49, 215n50

Vaidhyanathan, Siva, 202n174
Vanderbilt University, 30
Van Ess, John K., III, 53
Vanity Fair magazine, 100, 154–55, 216n58, 247nn12, 16

Vatican, 181
Victor/Victoria (musical), 178
video-rental business, 14–15, 189n75
"Vietmalia" syndrome, 125, 126, 231n163
Vietnam-US relations, reestablishment of, 173
Vietnam War, 123, 125

Waco (TX), Branch Davidian standoff in (1993), 52–53
Wales, Jimmy, 49–50
Walker, Jesse, 207n54
Wallace, Mike, 17–18
Wall Street Journal, 13, 17, 18, 37, 45–46, 64, 156–57, 159, 189n75, 199–200n130
Walt Disney Company. *See* Disney Corporation
Walters, Barbara, 238n61
Washington (DC), 1, 73–75, 163, 170, 173, 210n89, 210–11n91
Washington Free Beacon (conservative website), 154
Washingtonian magazine, 151
Washington Post: Amazon.com coverage, 201n158; Bezos's purchase of, 46, 202n168; Bosnian War poll conducted by, 223n11; on *Calvin and Hobbes* retirement, 246n5; on Clinton-Lewinsky vs. Watergate scandals, 245n145; on Clinton presidency, 131, 145, 148; DC heightened security precautions opposed by, 72 *fig. 11*, 73, 74–75, 210–11n91; on Gingrich, 236n30; government shutdown, coverage of, 132, 153–54; Holbrooke interview with, 181; Internet coverage of, 194n54; Million Man March, coverage of, 10, 187nn36, 45; O.J. Simpson trial, coverage of, 89; Oklahoma City bombing, coverage of, 67; Packwood sex scandal, coverage of, 150; on political polarization, 243n125; on Powell, 217n78; Syrian civil war, coverage of, 248n30; tobacco industry advertising in, 17; Unabomber manifesto published by, 176
Washington Post Magazine, 208n60
Watergate scandal, 70, 135, 143, 149
Watson, Thomas, Jr., 46
Watterson, Bill, 152, 153, 246nn5–6
Weaver, Randy, 174, 204n3
Weaving the Web (Berners-Lee), 202n183
Web logs (blogs), 29
Weekly Standard (conservative opinion journal), 175